CELLULAR Ca^{2+} REGULATION

ADVANCES IN EXPERIMENTAL MEDICINE AND BIOLOGY

Recent Volumes in this Series

CELLULAR Ca^{2+} REGULATION

Edited by

Douglas R. Pfeiffer

Hormel Institute
University of Minnesota
Austin, Minnesota

Jeanie B. McMillin

Department of Medicine
University of Alabama
Birmingham, Alabama

and

Steve Little

Beckman Instruments
Palo Alto, California

PLENUM PRESS • NEW YORK AND LONDON

Library of Congress Cataloging in Publication Data

Cellular Ca²⁺ regulation / edited by Douglas R. Pfeiffer, Jeanie B. McMillin, and
Steve Little.
  p.   cm.
(Advances in experimental medicine and biology, v. 232)
"Proceedings of a satellite symposium of the 30th International Congress of Phys-
iological Sciences, held July 11–12, 1986, in Seattle, Washington" — T.p. verso.
Includes bibliographies and index.
ISBN 0-306-42904-7
1. Calcium — Metabolism — Regulation — Congresses. 2. Cellular control mechanisms
— Congresses. I. Pfeiffer, Douglas R. II. McMillin, Jeanie B. III. Little, Steve. IV.
Series.
QP535.C2C45   1988   88-9400
612′.3924 — dc19   CIP

Proceedings of a satellite symposium of the 30th International Congress of
Physiological Sciences, held July 11–12, 1986, in Seattle, Washington

© 1988 Plenum Press, New York
A Division of Plenum Publishing Corporation
233 Spring Street, New York, N.Y. 10013

Printed in the United States of America

PREFACE

This book arose from a meeting held at the University of Washington, Seattle, in July of 1986. The meeting was a satellite symposium of the XXXth International Congress of Physiological Sciences which occurred in Vancouver, Canada, at that time.

Adjustments in the cytoplasmic Ca^{2+} concentration of cells occur in response to a variety of external signals. These fluctuations are a central component of one mechanism by which cells adapt their activities to changes in the external environment and to the requirements of whole body homeostatic mechanisms. It is now clear that redistribution of Ca^{2+} within intracellular compartments, as well as changes in the rates of Ca^{2+} influx and extrusion at the whole cell level, occur during signal-dependent changes in the cytoplasmic Ca^{2+} concentration. In summarizing current research in this area, this volume considers first the properties of individual cation transporting activities located in various cell membranes. It then moves to the cellular level, where the consequence of individual transporting activities acting in concert is examined. Emphasis is also placed on pathological conditions which result in loss of cell Ca^{2+} regulation as a part of the disease process. We hope that this approach will help the reader to integrate developments in this large and rapidly changing field.

For production of this book, special thanks are due Julie Knutson and Kimberly Broekemeier from The Hormel Institute for the various organizational skills and efforts which they provided. We also thank Dr. Gary Fiskum who was involved in organizing the symposium and Molecular Probes, Inc., The Mitchell Energy Corporation, Marion Laboratories, Inc., Pfizer, and The Hormel Institute for the financial support which they provided.

Douglas R. Pfeiffer, Ph.D.
Jeanie B. McMillin, Ph.D.
Steve Little, Ph.D.

CONTENTS

PATHOPHYSIOLOGICAL ASPECTS OF Ca^{2+} TRANSPORT

THE IN VIVO ROLE OF CELLULAR Ca^{2+} PUMPS IN METABOLIC REGULATION

MECHANISMS OF MITOCHONDRIAL CALCIUM TRANSPORT

Thomas E. Gunter, Douglas E. Wingrove, Srabani Banerjee,
and Karlene K. Gunter

Department of Biophysics, University of Rochester
School of Medicine and Dentistry, Rochester, New York 14642

ABSTRACT

Mitochondria are known to possess a rapid calcium uptake mechanism or
uniport and both sodium-dependent and sodium-independent efflux mechanisms.
Whether sodium-independent calcium efflux is mediated and whether sodium-
dependent calcium efflux can be found in liver mitochondria have been
questioned. Kinetics results relevant to the answers of these questions
are discussed below.

A slow, mediated, sodium-independent calcium efflux mechanism is
identified which shows second order kinetics. This mechanism, which shows
"nonessential activation" kinetics, has a V_{max} around 1.2 nmol calcium per
mg protein per min and a half maximal velocity around 8.4 nmol calcium per
mg protein.

A slow, sodium-dependent calcium efflux mechanism is identified, which
is first order in calcium and second order in sodium. This mechanism has a
V_{max} around 2.6 nmol of calcium per mg protein per min. The sodium
dependence is half saturated at an external sodium concentration of 9.4 mM,
and the calcium dependence is half saturated at an internal calcium concentration of 8.1 nmol calcium per mg protein. The cooperativity of the
sodium dependence effectively permits a terreactant system to be fit by a
bireactant model in which [Na] only appears as the square of [Na]. This
liver system shows simultaneous, as opposed to ping-pong, kinetics. It is
also found to be sensitive to inhibition by tetraphenylphosphonium, magnesium, and ruthenium red.

A model is proposed in which mitochondrial calcium transport could
function to "shape the pulses" of cytosolic calcium. Simultaneously,
mitochondria may mediate a "calcium memory" coupled perhaps to activation
of cytosolic events through calmodulin or perhaps to activation of electron
transport through the activation of specific dehydrogenases by intramitochondrial calcium.

INTRODUCTION

Mitochondria transport calcium using separate mechanisms for influx
and for efflux (1-3). Calcium influx is mediated by a uniport mechanism

which is capable of reaching a very high maximum velocity (higher than 500 nmol/mg per min for liver mitochondria) (4-7). Two distinguishable mechanisms of calcium efflux are known; one is sodium dependent and the other sodium independent (2,3,5-7). The physiological reasons for the complexity of the mitochondrial calcium transport system are not clearly understood. However, several points, probably relevant to understanding this complexity, have been established: 1) Mitochondria in vitro can regulate the calcium concentration of the medium by setting up a steady-state level of calcium cycling inward over the uniport and outward over the efflux mechanism (2,8). 2) This steady-state cycling permits a higher precision of control than would transport over a single mechanism (6,9,10). 3) The medium calcium concentration at which mitochondrial calcium cycling can occur is dependent on the concentration of agents such as magnesium (11) and spermine (12). Regulation can be observed down to levels around 200 nM at concentrations of magnesium and spermine similar to those found in the cytosol of most cells (12). This level of 200 nM is at (13) or only slightly higher (14,15) than those levels of cytosolic calcium thought to be found in "resting" cells. 4) Increasing matrix calcium can activate electron transport and phosphorylation by activating three calcium-sensitive dehydrogenases coupled to the electron transport chain (16,17). This may be an important component of the expression of the message of specific hormones.

The primary mechanism of calcium efflux from the mitochondria of heart, skeletal muscle, and other "excitable" tissue is sodium dependent (18). The primary mechanism of calcium efflux from the mitochondria of liver and kidney ("non-excitable" tissue) has generally been thought to be sodium-independent (19) although some sodium-dependent efflux from liver mitochondria has been reported (20-22).

Mitochondrial calcium efflux might be mediated either by a calcium/cation exchange, a calcium-anion co-transporter, or by an active mechanism (2). Support for each of these types of mechanism and counter-evidence for some have appeared in the literature (10,19,23-33). Sponta-neous de-energization of mitochondria, which have sequestered calcium, can also occur under some conditions (34-37). Under these conditions, calcium is lost either by reversal of the uniport mechanism (28,38) or by a transformation of the mitochondrial membrane which renders it permeable to small ions and molecules including calcium (37-39). It has been suggested that sodium-independent mitochondrial calcium release might not involve a specific pore or carrier but could be carried out instead by a fraction of the mitochondria in a suspension undergoing a reversible de-energization and transformation of membrane permeability (40). A host of agents have been identified which, in the presence of calcium, can induce this permea-bility transformation (37-41). Some of them may be found endogenously in mitochondria.

An important question then is whether all sodium-independent calcium efflux could be accounted for by a de-energization-coupled process or whether efflux under some conditions must be described as a mediated mecha-nism such as an exchanger, a co-transporter, or an active mechanism. One way of answering this question would be to choose conditions under which no membrane permeability transformation can be detected and carry out a study of the kinetics of calcium efflux. This is the approach taken in the work described below (42,43). A kinetic approach of this type is valid for describing both active and passive mechanisms. The properties of the sodium and potassium exchanging ATPase of the plasma membrane, an active mechanism, have been analyzed by a kinetic approach [see Glynn and Karlish (44)].

2

Coll et al. have measured the relationship between intramitochondrial free calcium and total calcium by a titration procedure, concluding that free calcium is proportional to total intramitochondrial calcium in the range of calcium loads up to 55 nmol/mg protein (45). This suggests that calcium is bound by a large number of low affinity sites and that high affinity intramitochondrial calcium binding is negligible. These observations are very important for studies of efflux kinetics. Kinetics studies involve plotting the data against functions of the calcium activity or at least the free calcium concentration. Since this variable has been found to be proportional to total intramitochondrial calcium, total calcium values can be substituted in these plots for free calcium. Measurement of total mitochondrial calcium is much more accurate than measurement of intramitochondrial free calcium. Consequently, kinetics studies using total internal calcium may show subtleties unobservable if measurements of intramitochondrial free calcium are used instead.

MATERIALS AND METHODS

Preparations of Mitochondria

Mitochondria were prepared either by the mannitol-sucrose procedure used previously (27) or by a procedure using sucrose media (42).

Depletion of Endogenous Calcium

Since the levels of exchangable endogenous calcium, following the preparation, were usually higher than the 2 to 3 nmol calcium per mg protein necessary for most of the kinetics studies, depletion of endogenous calcium was necessary. The calcium depletion was carried out either by a room temperature (22°C) incubation (15-20 min) in the absence of respiratory substrate as in past work in other labs (45,46), or by a newly devised and gentle procedure which does not involve mitochondrial de-energization (42). In this new procedure the mitochondria from one rat liver were suspended for 10-12 min with constant stirring at 22°C in 75 ml of 124 mM KCl, 10 mM NaCl, 8 mM K Hepes (pH 7.2), 100 μM KPi, 1 mM K EGTA, 4 mM K succinate, and 100 μM $MgCl_2$. In some experiments magnesium and inorganic phosphate were deleted and sodium was increased to 30 mM. This treatment was followed by stirring at 4°C for 5 min and by three centrifugations at 17,500 x g (12,000 rpm in a Beckman J-20 rotor) for 9 min with resuspension in 0.3 M sucrose plus 6 mM Hepes. This procedure yielded mitochondria with a typical exchangable, endogenous calcium of 2-3 nmol/mg protein (42).

Measurement of Calcium Efflux

Calcium efflux was measured either using [45]Ca and radioisotope techniques as described earlier (27) or using dual wavelength spectroscopy with the dye arsenazo III at the wavelength pair 675-685 nm as described before (42,47). In a typical experiment, after mitochondria were allowed to take up calcium and after a steady-state calcium distribution was reached, 2 nmol ruthenium red per mg protein was added to initiate efflux. For some experiments this was followed by addition of sodium chloride to induce sodium-dependent calcium efflux. Exchangable, endogenous calcium was measured by addition of CCCP (10 μM) and, in some cases, A23187 (0.13 nM) and allowing calcium to efflux to completion. EGTA was then added and the difference in the arsenazo III absorbance level after efflux of calcium without and with EGTA was taken as the exchangable, endogenous calcium level (42). Endogenous inorganic phosphate was measured as in earlier work (48).

Avoidance of Membrane Permeability Transformation During Efflux

The membrane permeability transformation may be potentiated by activation of lysophospholipid production through calcium activation of phospholipase A_2 (39). This could account for the observed increase in the probability of mitochondria undergoing the transformation as calcium load is increased. The membranes of transformed mitochondria are permeable to potassium, magnesium, calcium, and other small ions and molecules. The onset of the transformation in a subpopulation of mitochondria would be expected to result in a significant increase in efflux as calcium load is increased. Such a study is shown in Fig. 1. No real evidence of saturation of efflux is observed as calcium load is increased (solid triangles) where the calcium depletion procedure involved de-energization. Instead, the efflux velocity "runs away" with increasing calcium load. A clear-cut saturation region is seen, on the other hand, followed by "velocity runaway" at higher calcium levels (open squares) where calcium depletion did not involve de-energization. Using this same preparation and adding 20-40 μM ATP, which is known to delay or eliminate the permeability transformation, leads to a remarkably flat saturation region up to around 150 nmol total calcium per mg protein before any sign of the transformation is observed (open circles). These latter conditions in which no sign of the permeability transformation is seen were chosen as standard conditions for the kinetic studies (42).

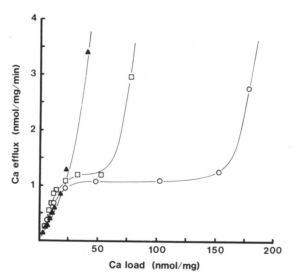

Fig. 1. Calcium efflux vs total calcium load. The desired calcium load was added to 2.5 ml of medium (see Methods) containing 67 μM arsenazo III (but not sodium) which had equilibrated at 23°C. The change in absorbance was used to determine the amount of calcium added. Mitochondria were added (1 mg/ml) and allowed to sequester calcium until steady state was reached (2-3 min). Ruthenium red (2 μM) was added to initiate calcium efflux. Mitochondria were depleted of calcium by the method involving de-energization (▲), or by the method where succinate is present and no de-energization occurs (□,O). One set of mitochondria (O) was also supplemented with 40 μM ATP (42). (Reprinted with permission from J. Biol. Chem., Copyright 1986, Soc. of Biol. Chemists.)

RESULTS

The sodium-independent efflux mechanism has been suggested to be a calcium/proton exchanger (19,23,24) or a calcium-phosphate symport (31). Therefore, it is important to determine whether or not the pH dependence or phosphate dependence of this calcium efflux must be investigated, at length, in a kinetics study. The pH dependence of sodium-independent calcium efflux is shown in Fig. 2 (open squares) and shows no significant dependence on medium pH (27).

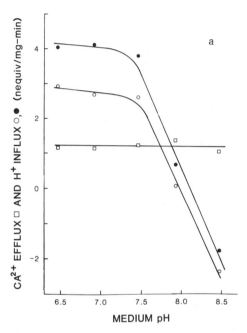

Fig. 2. Calcium efflux vs medium pH. Calcium efflux (□) and proton efflux (O,●) following ruthenium red addition were determined from the slopes of electrode traces as described (26). Solid circles indicate proton flux corrected for flux of AcO⁻ and inorganic phosphate also as described (26). (Reprinted with permission from Biochemistry, Copyright 1981, Am. Chem. Soc.)

Eadie-Hofstee plots of sodium-independent calcium efflux data are shown in Fig. 3 at three concentrations of inorganic phosphate from a low level of endogenous phosphate to one millimolar added phosphate (42). While efflux increases slightly with increasing phosphate in the low phosphate region, there is no significant variation of sodium-independent calcium efflux with phosphate concentration in the more physiological end of the range studied (above 100 µM). Further studies of the pH and inorganic phosphate dependencies of calcium efflux then appear to be unnecessary for evaluation of efflux kinetics. The remainder of the kinetics data was taken at pH 7.2 and 100 µM added inorganic phosphate, unless otherwise stated.

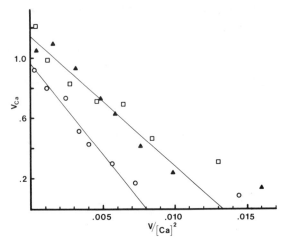

Fig. 3. Eadie-Hofstee plots of sodium-independent calcium efflux at three concentrations of inorganic phosphate. Conditions were similar to those of Fig. 1. Phosphate concentrations were: endogenous phosphate only (20 μM) (O), 0.1 mM added phosphate (▲), and 1 mM added phosphate (□) (42). (Reprinted with permission from J. Biol. Chem., Copyright 1986, Soc. Biol. Chem.)

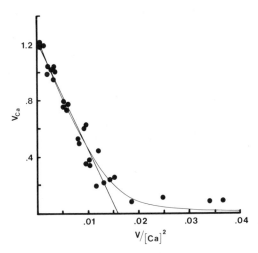

Fig. 4. Eadie-Hoffstee plots of sodium-independent efflux. Velocity of efflux is in nmol calcium/mg per min. Total calcium load in nmol/mg. Notice that the abscissa is velocity divided by the square of calcium load, indicating second order kinetics. The straight line is given by Eq. 1 where V_m = 1.22 nmol/mg per min, K_m = 8.75 nmol/calcium per mg protein, and a = 0.9 nmol/mg. The curved line is given by Eq. 1 using the parameters in the text (42). (Reprinted with permission from J. Biol. Chem., Copyright 1986, Soc. Biol. Chem.)

Six independent sets of sodium-independent efflux data were obtained. Statistical analysis of the Hill plots of these data (42) yields an average Hill coefficient of 1.9 ± 0.2. This mechanism is clearly second order. Typical results are shown in a second order Eadie-Hofstee plot in Fig. 4. The fit to a second order Hill equation is very good over most of the calcium concentration range covered. However, a significant deviation occurs at the lowest calcium concentration point. This was consistently found in all preparations. A linear term may be added to the numerator of the second order Hill equation to account for this deviation from the fit at low calcium concentration. This produces the curved line shown in Fig. 4. The kinetic models of both a nonessential activation mechanism, with one transport site and one activation site, and an Adair-Pauling mechanism with two identical transport sites, would also require a related linear term in the denominator as:

$$V = \frac{V_{max} \, ([Ca]^2 + a[Ca])}{K_m^2 + [Ca]^2 + 2a[Ca])} \qquad (1)$$

Since the addition of this linear term to the denominator does not significantly affect the curve fit to the data, the data fit both of these kinetics models equally well. The values of the parameters indicated in Eq. 1 for the average of six independent sets of data are: $V_{max} = 1.2 \pm 0.1$ nmol/mg per min, $K_m = 8.4 \pm 0.6$ nmol/mg and $a = 0.9 \pm 0.2$ nmol/mg (x ± SE) (42).

Preliminary data using strontium as a calcium analog can provide further insight into the nature of this sodium-independent efflux mechanism. Calcium efflux over this sodium-independent mechanism is slowed by the presence of strontium, as would be expected if the ions compete for binding to the transport site(s). However, strontium efflux kinetics appear to be first order. The simplest explanation of these observations is that the two sites associated with sodium-independent calcium efflux are not identical. Strontium binding to one site, unlike binding of calcium, does not increase the probability of binding of a like ion to the other site. Since strontium is transported by the mechanism, albeit at a much lower velocity than calcium, this suggests that the mechanism is probably nonessential activation as opposed to Adair-Pauling.

Hill coefficients obtained from Hill plots of sodium-dependent efflux data yielded values of 1.0 ± 0.1 for the calcium dependence and 2.0 ± 0.2 for the sodium dependence, respectively (43). First and second order Eadie-Hofstee plots of these data are shown in Figs. 5a and 5b (43). These data can be fit quite well by the product of a Michaelis-Menten equation for the calcium dependence times a second order Hill equation for the sodium dependence. The form for the resultant expression is shown in Eq. 2.

$$V = V_{max} \left[\frac{[Ca]}{K_{Ca} + [Ca]} \right] \left[\frac{[Na]^2}{K_{Na}^2 + [Na]^2} \right] \qquad (2)$$

Values of parameters obtained as a best fit to the data shown in Figs. 5a and 5b (indicated by the fit lines shown in the figure) are:

$$V_{max} = 2.6 \pm 0.5 \text{ nmol/mg per min}$$
$$K_{Ca} = 8.1 \pm 1.4 \text{ nmol/mg}$$
$$K_{Na} = 9.4 \pm 0.6 \text{ mM}$$

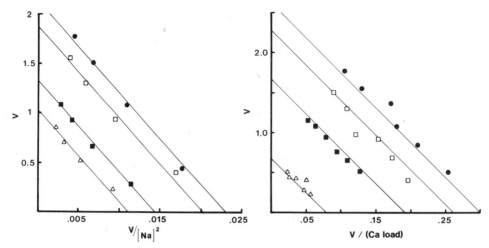

Fig. 5. Eadie-Hofstee plots of sodium-dependent calcium efflux.
Velocity and calcium load are defined as in Fig. 4.
Sodium concentrations are in mM. Experimental conditions
are similar to those of Fig. 1 except that after the
sodium-independent efflux rate is determined, varying
amounts of sodium are added to the suspension to initiate
sodium-dependent efflux. The difference in rates
measured after and before sodium addition give the
sodium-dependent efflux velocity. Sodium concentrations
of 5 (△), 10 (■), 15 (□), and 20 (●) mM are used in Fig.
5a. Calcium loads (added plus endogenous) of 4 (△), 6
(■), 12 (□), and 17 (●) nmol/mg protein are used in Fig.
5b (43). (Reprinted with permission from J. Biol. Chem.,
Copyright 1986, Soc. Biol. Chem.)

These results fit a random order, terreactant model for which the
cooperativity of the sodium dependence allows the model to be reduced to an
effective bireactant model. The binding of the first sodium increases the
probability of binding of the second sodium sufficiently so that the sodium
dependence only appears as the square of sodium concentration.

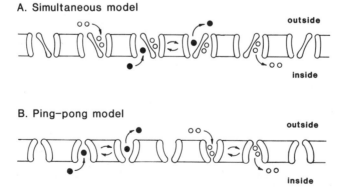

A. Simultaneous model

B. Ping-pong model

Fig. 6. Cartoon showing representation of two types of exchangers. Above is a representation of a "simultaneous"
exchanger. Below is a representation of a "ping-pong"
exchanger.

The sodium-dependent calcium efflux mechanism of heart mitochondria is usually described as a sodium-calcium exchanger which exchanges 2 sodium ions for 1 calcium ion. While much less work has been performed studying the sodium-dependent efflux mechanism of liver mitochondria it is usually thought of as a similar mechanism. This is consistent with the kinetic results shown in Fig. 5. Exchangers can be of two types. For the "ping-pong" exchanger, an ion (or ions) of the first type is (are) bound on one side of the membrane, transported to the other side of the membrane and released before binding of one or more ions of the second type, occurs. The cycle is completed by binding of one or more ions of the second type, transported to the original side of the membrane and released. For the "simultaneous" exchanger, ions of both types must be bound at one stage of the cycle before transport and release occurs (see Fig. 6).

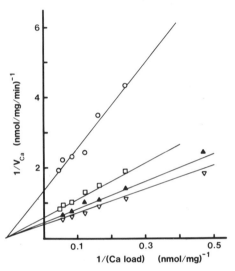

Fig. 7. Lineweaver-Burk plot of calcium dependence of sodium-dependent efflux data. Data is the same as that plotted in Fig. 5a. The slope of the lines fit to each set of data (each sodium concentration) gives the value of V_{max}/K_m (apparent) for that sodium concentration (43). (Reprinted with permission from J. Biol. Chem., Copyright 1986, Soc. Biol. Chem.)

One characteristic of ping-pong exchangers is that the ratio of apparent V_{max}/K_m for transport of one type of ion (for example, calcium) does not change as a function of the concentration of the second type of ion (sodium). While there has been no prior development of these concepts for mitochondrial calcium efflux, a ping-pong model has been used in conjunction with descriptions of the sodium-calcium exchanger from heart mitochondria (49). The sodium-dependent calcium efflux mechanism of liver mitochondria clearly shows "simultaneous" kinetics. In a Lineweaver-Burk plot, the slope of a line fit to a set of data represents the ratio of apparent V_{max}/K_m. For a ping-pong exchanger these lines should be parallel. The lines fit to data taken at different sodium concentrations shown in Fig. 7 converge to a locus on the negative abscissa, clearly violating the requirement for a ping-pong exchanger. There is precedent for a mitochondrial exchanger showing simultaneous kinetics. The adenine nucleotide exchanger has been shown to function as a simultaneous exchanger (50).

The sodium-dependent calcium efflux mechanism of liver shows sensitivity to a wide range of inhibitors. Even though this mechanism is often described as "ruthenium red-insensitive," it is sensitive to inhibition by high concentrations of ruthenium red with 50 percent inhibition (K_I) around 12 nmol ruthenium red per mg protein (43). The sodium-dependent mechanism is also sensitive to inhibition by magnesium in the suspending medium (K_I between 1 and 1.5 mM) (43). The sodium-independent mechanism shows no sensitivity to inhibition by either ruthenium red or external magnesium. Both the sodium-dependent and sodium-independent calcium efflux mechanisms show sensitivity to inhibition by the lipophilic cation tetraphenylphosphonium (TPP). The sodium-dependent mechanism is extremely sensitive to inhibition by TPP, however, with a K_I around 0.2 μM while that of the sodium-independent mechanism is around 10 μM (43). As can be seen in Fig. 8, both of these mechanisms are also sensitive to a greater or lesser extent to inhibition by the related lipophilic cations triphenylmethylphosphonium and tetraphenylarsenium. The sodium-dependent mechanism consistently shows much more sensitivity to inhibition by each type of lipophilic cation. Preliminary data also indicate that the sodium-dependent mechanism is quite sensitive to inhibition by spermine.

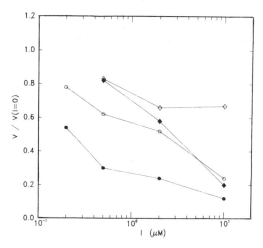

Fig. 8. Inhibition of efflux by compounds related to TPP. I represents the concentration of inhibitor. The symbols are as follows: sodium-independent efflux in the presence of triphenylmethylphosphonium (TPMP) (◇) or tetraphenylarsenium (TPA) (O) and sodium-dependent efflux in the presence of TPMP (◆) or TPA (●). Calcium load was 8 nmol/mg protein and sodium concentration was 15 mM.

DISCUSSION

It is clear from the results shown in Fig. 1 that under conditions in which effects of the membrane permeability transformation cannot be observed, a sodium-independent calcium efflux mechanism having the clearly observable kinetic properties of a mediated mechanism can be identified. The observed low maximum velocity of this mechanism has been anticipated (27,28,40,41).

The results presented above support the conclusion of Coll et al. (45) that intramitochondrial free calcium is proportional to total intramitochondrial calcium. Since the current results are based on kinetics plots using total intramitochondrial calcium, violation of the assumption that these two variables are proportional would result in curvature in the kinetics plots. Good fits could not be obtained to both a first order (sodium-dependent) mechanism and second order (sodium-independent) mechanism if the assumption was not valid. Furthermore, if as much as 1 nmol/mg of high affinity calcium binding site having an affinity of 1 μM were present in the mitochondrial matrix space, this would cause observable curvature in the linear portion of the Eadie-Hofstee plots shown in Figs. 4 and 5a. Since such curvature is not observed, this supports the conclusions of Coll et al. (45).

The liver mitochondrial calcium efflux mechanisms have several notable characteristics. The maximum velocity for each of these mechanisms is quite low. Even the sum of their V_{max}'s is over 100 times less that of the V_{max} of the uptake mechanism (uniport). This observation alone would be enough to suggest that any possible steady-state setup by these three mechanisms would regulate calcium at an external concentration well below the K_m of the uniport. Therefore the high V_{max} of the uniport must have a physiological significance related to unusual as opposed to typical calcium concentrations in the cytosol.

The sodium-independent efflux mechanism has a sigmoidal dependence of velocity on concentration. At very low intramitochondrial calcium concentration, say below 2 to 3 nmol calcium/mg protein, the efflux through this mechanism is extremely slow, below 0.1 nmol calcium/mg per min. Because of the second-order nature of velocity on concentration, the velocity increases rapidly above this concentration reaching 80 percent of its saturation value by 16 nmol calcium per mg protein. Also because of its second order nature, the saturation dependence is extremely flat.

The sodium-dependent efflux mechanism shows simultaneous kinetics. It also seems extremely sensitive to a wide range of inhibitors. In addition to magnesium, ruthenium red and tetraphenylphosphonium, and its analogs as reported here, it has also been reported to be sensitive to inhibition by diltiazem (51) and other calcium channel blockers, trifluoperazine (52), an inhibitor of calmodulin coupled reactions, and to amiloride and amiloride derivatives (51,53). This mechanism, in general, seems much more sensitive to inhibition than the sodium-independent mechanism. This suggests that its function may be more subject to either positive or negative control under in vivo conditions. Because of the cytosolic sodium concentration, and the sensitivity of this mechanism to inhibition by magnesium, spermine, etc., it should normally operate well below its V_{max} and generally be much slower than the sodium-independent mechanism.

Mitochondria are known to regulate medium calcium through a cycling process in vitro (8). In this process calcium is sequestered by "downhill" transport through the passive uniport mechanism and is then transported back up the energy gradient by the very slow efflux mechanisms. If the kinetics of uptake and efflux are similar in vitro and in vivo, then the mitochondrial calcium transport system clearly is capable, under some conditions, of regulating calcium in the cytosol. Nevertheless, the combination of a potentially rapid uptake mechanism and a very slow system for efflux seems strange if the primary function of the system is to regulate calcium at low concentrations in the cytosol. These characteristics suggest instead a system designed to rapidly sequester calcium, when its concentration is temporarily high, and then to slowly release it back into the cytosol.

Furthermore, it is not clear that mitochondria can actually regulate cytosolic calcium concentrations under "resting" conditions which are believed to be rather low (100-150 nM) (14,15). It seems more likely that the mitochondrial calcium transport system is poised to "intervene" at a level just slightly above the calcium concentration characterizing the "resting" conditions of the cytosol.

If so, the mitochondrial calcium transport system would function as a "calcium pulse shaper," blunting the sharp peak of a calcium pulse by rapid calcium uptake and extending the duration of the pulse for many minutes. Because efflux is slow, the cytosolic calcium level during this extension period would return to a low value but still might be 2 or 3 times higher than the resting level. Furthermore, since efflux would be expected to be dominated by the sodium-independent efflux mechanism which has a flat saturation dependence, this period of pulse extension could produce a quasi-steady-state of cytosolic calcium. Under these conditions the net flux into the cytosol from the mitochondria would be low and almost time-independent and would approximately equal the loss from the cytosol due to outward pumping by the plasma membrane and uptake by the endoplasmic reticulum. Such an extension of the pulse could have two functions.

First, in the cytosol it would produce a low level, long-term memory of the pulse. Since calmodulin binds calcium in this concentration range, it is possible that even this small increase in cytosolic calcium above the resting level could produce an "activation level" distinguishable from the resting level, which could be important with regard to say, carrying out the message of a hormone.

Second, Denton and McCormack (16) and Hansford (17) have shown that increased intramitochondrial calcium activates three dehydrogenases, pyruvate dehydrogenase, α-ketoglutarate dehydrogenase, and isocitrate dehydrogenase. This in turn increases the rate of electron transport and subsequently the rate of phosphorylation of ADP. Mitochondrial calcium uptake following a calcium pulse then would be expected to produce a "memory" of the pulse reflected in a sizable increase in intramitochondrial calcium. In both these cases, then, the kinetic characteristics of the mitochondrial calcium transport system determined in vitro might be expected to produce a calcium memory or a timing device whose duration reflected the intensity and duration of the pulse itself but which could be many times longer than the original pulse.

ACKNOWLEDGEMENTS

This work was supported by NIH Grants GM 35550, 5T32 GM 07356, and United States Public Health Service Grant RR 05403.

REFERENCES

1. Sordahl, L.A., Arch. Biochem. Biophys. 167:104-115 (1975).
2. Puskin, J.S., Gunter, T.E., Gunter, K.K., and Russell, P.R., Biochemistry 15:3834-3842 (1976).
3. Crompton, M., Capano, M., and Carafoli, E., Eur. J. Biochem. 69:453-462 (1976).
4. Bygrave, F.L., Reed, K.C., and Spencer, T., Nature, New Biology 230:89-91 (1971).
5. Bygrave, F.L., Biol. Rev. Cambridge Phils. Soc. 53:43-79 (1978).
6. Nicholls, D.G., and Crompton, M., FEBS Lett. 111:261-268 (1980).
7. Nicholls, D., and Åkerman, K.E.O., Biochim. Biophys. Acta 683:57-88 (1982).

8. Nicholls, D.G., Biochem. J. 176:463-474 (1978).
9. Carafoli, E., FEBS Lett. 104:1-5 (1979).
10. Rosier, R.N., Tucker, D.A., Meerdink, S., Jain, I., and Gunter, T.E., Arch. Biochem. Biophys. 210:549-564 (1981).
11. Becker, G.L., Biochim. Biophys. Acta 591:234-239 (1980).
12. Nicchitta, C.V., and Williamson, J.R., J. Biol. Chem. 259:12978-12983 (1984).
13. Fiskum, G., Cell Calcium 6:26-38 (1985).
14. Metcalf, J.C., Hesketh, T.R., and Smith, G.A., Cell Calcium 6:183-195 (1985).
15. McNeil, P.L., and Taylor, D.L., Cell Calcium 6:83-93 (1985).
16. Denton, R.M., and McCormack, J.G., Am. J. Physiol. 249:E543-E554 (1985).
17. Hansford, R.G., Rev. Physiol. Biochem. Pharmacol. 102:1-72 (1985).
18. Crompton, M., Kunzi, M., and Carafoli, E., Eur. J. Biochem. 79:549-559 (1977).
19. Fiskum, G., and Lehninger, A.L., J. Biol. Chem. 254:6236-6239 (1979).
20. Haworth, R.A., Hunter, D.R., and Berkoff, H.A., FEBS Lett. 110:216-218 (1980).
21. Nedergaard, J., and Cannon, B., Acta Chem. Scand. B34:149-151 (1980).
22. Goldstone, T.P., and Crompton, M., Biochem. J. 204:369-371 (1982).
23. Åkerman, K.E.O., Arch. Biochem. Biophys. 189:256-262 (1978).
24. Fiskum, G., and Cockrell, R.S., FEBS Lett. 92:125-128 (1978).
25. Cockrell, R.S., Arch. Biochem. Biophys. 243:70-79 (1985).
26. Vercesi, A., and Lehninger, A.L., Biochem. Biophys. Res. Commun. 118:147-153 (1984).
27. Gunter, T.E., Chace, J.H., Puskin, J.S., and Gunter, K.K., Biochemistry 22:6341-6351 (1983).
28. Bernardi, P., and Azzone, G.F., Eur. J. Biochem. 102:555-562 (1979).
29. Bernardi, P., Biochim. Biophys. Acta 766:277-282 (1984).
30. Moyle, J., and Mitchell, P., FEBS Lett. 73:131-136 (1977).
31. Moyle, J., and Mitchell, P., FEBS Lett. 77:136-140 (1977).
32. Moyle, J., adn Mitchell, P., FEBS Lett. 84:135-140 (1977).
33. Moody, A.J., West, I.C., Mitchell, R., and Mitchell, P., Eur. J. Biochem. 157:243-249 (1986).
34. Pfeiffer, D.R., Schmid, P.C., Beatrice, M.C., and Schmid, H.H.O., J. Biol. Chem. 254:11485-11494 (1979).
35. Nicholls, D.G., and Brand, M.D., Biochem. J. 188:113-118 (1980).
36. Jurkowitz, M.S., Geisbuhler, T., Jung, D.W., and Brierly, G.P., Arch. Biochem. Biophys. 223:120-128 (1983).
37. Beatrice, M.C., Palmer, J.W., and Pfeiffer, D.R., J. Biol. Chem. 255:8663-8671 (1980).
38. Beatrice, M.C., Stiers, D.L., and Pfeiffer, D.R., J. Biol. Chem. 257:7161-7171 (1982).
39. Beatrice, M.C., Stiers, D.L., and Pfeiffer, D.R., J. Biol. Chem. 259:1279-1287 (1984).
40. Pfeiffer, D.R., Palmer, J.W., Beatrice, M.C., and Stiers, D.L., in: "The Biochemistry of Metabolic Processes," D.F.L. Lenon, F.W. Stratman, and R.N. Zahlten, eds., Elsevier/North Holland, Inc., New York, pp. 67-80 (1983).
41. Broekemeier, K.M., Schmid, P.C., Schmid, H.H.O., and Pfeiffer, D.R., J. Biol. Chem. 260:105-113 (1985).
42. Wingrove, D.E., and Gunter, T.E., J. Biol. Chem. (in press).
43. Wingrove, D.E., and Gunter, T.E., J. Biol. Chem. (in press).
44. Glynn, I.M., and Karlish, S.J.D., Ann. Rev. Physiol. 37:13-55 (1975).
45. Coll, K.E., Joseph, S.K., Corkey, B.E., and Williamson, J.R., J. Biol. Chem. 257:8696-8704 (1982).
46. Crompton, M., Kessar, P., and Al-Nasser, I., Biochem. J. 216:332-342 (1983).
47. Scarpa, A., Brinly, F.J., Tiffert, T., and Dabyak, G.R., Ann. NY Acad. Sci. 307:86-112 (1978).

48. Wingrove, D.E., Amatruda, J.M., and Gunter, T.E., J. Biol. Chem. 259:9390-9394 (1984).
49. Hayat, L.H., and Crompton, M., Biochem. J. 202:509-518 (1982).
50. Barbour, R.L., and Chan, S.H.P., J. Biol. Chem. 256:1940-1948 (1981).
51. Sordahl, L.A., La Belle, E.F., and Rex, K.A., Am. J. Physiol. 246:C172-C176 (1984).
52. Harris, E.J., and Heffron, J.F.A., Arch. Biochem. Biophys. 218:531-539 (1982).
53. Jurkowitz, M.S., Altschuld, R.A., Brierley, G.P., and Cragoe, E.J., FEBS Lett. 162:262-265 (1983).

PERMEABILITY PATHWAYS OF Ca^{2+} EFFLUX FROM MITOCHONDRIA:

H^+ SPECIFICITY AND REVERSIBILITY OF THE PERMEABILITY DEFECT

Douglas R. Pfeiffer, Kimberly M. Broekemeier,
Urule Igbavboa, Martin Reers, and William W. Riley, Jr.

The Hormel Institute, University of Minnesota
801 16th Avenue NE, Austin, Minnesota 55912

INTRODUCTION

During the 1970's it was established that the inner membrane of isolated mitochondria from adrenal cortex, heart, and liver can display an unusually high permeability to small molecules and ions following the imposition of certain metabolic conditions (1-10). Generally, what is required to produce the permeable inner membrane state is energy-dependent Ca^{2+} accumulation preceding or following the administration of another agent which is often referred to as a "Ca^{2+}-releasing agent" (11-14). Substances possessing "Ca^{2+}-releasing agent" activity normally lack detergent properties and are diverse with respect to their chemical properties and biological activities. The "Ca^{2+}-releasing agents" investigated by our group include N-ethylmaleimide (5,6,11,13,15), t-butylhydroperoxide (14-16), oxalacetate, (11), inorganic phosphate (11,13), rhein (16), and hypolipidemic drugs such as WY-14643 and clofibric acid (17).

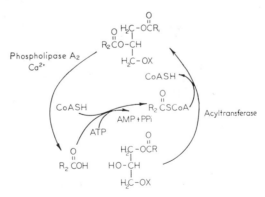

Fig. 1. The reactions of cyclic phospholipid deacylation and reacylation in liver mitochondria. R_1 and R_2 refer to long-chain acyl groups esterified to the sn-1 and sn-2 positions of glycerol, respectively. X refers to the base moiety (ethanolamine, choline, etc.) of the phospholipid head group structure. Literature showing the existence of the indicated enzyme activities within the inner membrane-matrix fraction of liver mitochondria is reviewed in ref. 17.

We have proposed that Ca^{2+} plus "Ca^{2+}-releasing agents" bring about the permeable inner membrane state by perturbing the phospholipid deacylation-reacylation cycle shown in Fig. 1 (6,18,19). According to the hypothesis, this cycle is ongoing within mitochondria and can establish and regulate the steady state level of lysophospholipids, notably lysophosphatidylethanolamine, and polyunsaturated free fatty acids associated with the inner membrane. Ca^{2+} plus "Ca^{2+}-releasing agents" are seen as acting on cycle enzymes to increase the levels of these phospholipid degradation products; Ca^{2+} by increasing the activity of phospholipase A_2, and "Ca^{2+}-releasing agents" by inhibiting lysophospholipid reacylation activity. Increased levels of the lipid degradation products, in turn, are thought to produce increased membrane permeability.

Rather than acting directly on matrix space acyl-Coenzyme A (CoA) synthetases or acyl-CoA:lysophospholipid acyltransferases, several "Ca^{2+}-releasing agents" are thought to act indirectly by causing a shift in the matrix space GSH/GSSG distribution towards increased GSSG (16). For these "Ca^{2+}-releasing agents," it is GSSG which is thought to be the actual inhibitor of lysophospholipid reacylation activity, and it is the several mechanisms of promoting intramitochondrial GSSG accumulation which then can account for the chemically and biochemically diverse "Ca^{2+}-releasing agents" having a common metabolic effect (16).

The hypotheses and supporting findings summarized above have arisen from studies with isolated mitochondria and it is not clear if the permeability transformation could or does occur in vivo. It is easy to visualize phospholipase A_2-dependent elimination of the inner membrane permeability barrier as a central component of mechanisms leading to mitochondrial destruction in pathological conditions. Indeed, a role for loss of the inner mitochondrial membrane permeability barrier by this mechanism is suspected in the etiology of ischemic and toxin-induced cell injury (e.g. 20,21), in Reye's syndrome (e.g. 22-25), in malignant hyperthermia (e.g. 26,27), and in other disease states. At present, there is less reason to believe that the permeability transformation is a component of physiological processes. The nonselectivity of the permeability defect, the large potential capacity of "leaky" mitochondria to waste metabolic energy, and the destruction of the organelle which ultimately pertains, argue against physiological relevance. However, the characteristics of the permeability transformation which argue against physiological relevance may be more apparent than real. This is because the selectivity of the permeability defect at early times following the transformation has not been investigated, because energy wasting by mitochondria permeabilized by the phospholipase A_2-dependent mechanism has not been clearly shown, and because destruction of the organelle need not occur were the permeability transformation reversible as is predicted by the hypothesis.

We report here on preliminary studies designed to probe these unknown properties of the permeability transformation and of permeablized mitochondria. The results indicate H^+ selectivity and reversibility of the permeability defect as well as inhibition of succinate oxidation within the permeabilized organelles.

METHODS

Rat liver mitochondria were prepared by our normal procedures (19) in media containing EGTA and BSA for the homogenization step only. Incubations were conducted at $25^{\circ}C$, 1.0 mg mitochondrial protein/ml, in media containing succinate (Na^+), 10 mM; rotenone, 0.5 nmol/mg protein; Hepes (Na^+), 5 mM, pH 7.4; and sufficient mannitol-sucrose (3:1 mole ratio) to adjust the osmolarity to 300 mOsM. Further additions to the medium are described in the figure legends.

The lysophosphatidylethanolamine content of mitochondria was determined by derivatizing with fluorescamine, isolating the fluorescent adduct
by thin-layer chromatography, and subsequent fluorescence quantitation as
described before (28). Our procedures for determining mitochondrial swelling and cation release have also been described (17). Briefly, swelling
was determined by changes in apparent absorbance at 540 nm using an Aminco
DW2a spectrophotometer, whereas the release of cations was determined by
atomic absorption measurements on supernatants following the rapid sedimentation of mitochondria in a microcentrifuge. Oxygen consumption was
monitored with a Gilson oxygraph utilizing a Clark-type oxygen electrode.

RESULTS AND DISCUSSION

While it is clear from existing literature that the enzymes required
to create the deacylation-reacylation cycle (Fig. 1) are present within the
inner membrane plus matrix of liver mitochondria (see 17 and refs. therein)
the kinetic competence of these enzymes to produce activity of the cycle
has not been shown. Fig. 2 supports activity of the cycle as we propose.

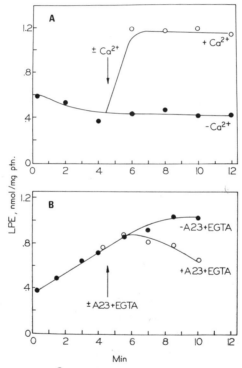

Fig. 2. The effect of Ca^{2+} accumulation and release on the content of
lysophosphatidylethanolamine (LPE) in mitochondria. Incubations in
the succinate-containing medium were as described in Methods except
that the protein concentration was 0.8 mg/ml, the temperature was
$35^{\circ}C$, and $MgCl_2$ was present at 1.0 mM. Periodically, samples were
taken for the determination of lysophosphatidylethanolamine by the
fluorescamine method (28). Panel A, when indicated, $CaCl_2$ was
added at 50 nmol/mg protein. $\bigcirc$, Ca^{2+} added. $\bullet$, Ca^{2+} not added.
Panel B, when indicated, ionophore A23187 and EGTA were added at
0.5 nmol/mg protein and 0.5 mM, respectively. $CaCl_2$, 50 nmol/mg
protein, was present from the beginning of the incubation. $\bigcirc$,
A23187 and EGTA added. $\bullet$, A23187 and EGTA not added.

Freshly prepared rat liver mitochondria contain less than 1 nmol/mg protein of lysophosphatidylethanolamine. The content of this lipid is unchanged or decreases slightly during incubation under energized conditions (Fig. 2A). If the deacylation-reacylation cycle regulates the level of this hydrolysis product as proposed, the actual level of lysophosphatidylethanolamine should be a steady state level established by the opposing hydrolysis and reacylation reactions. Ca^{2+} accumulation, with resulting activation of phospholipase A_2, would be expected to increase the steady state level. In Fig. 2, panel A, it is seen that Ca^{2+} accumulation, at 50 nmol/mg protein is accompanied by a prompt increase in the level of lysophosphatidylethanolamine which subsequently remains constant. This finding is consistent with the establishment of a higher steady state level.

When Ca^{2+} is present from the beginning of the incubation (Fig. 2, panel B), an elevated steady state level of lysophosphatidylethanolamine is also established, although the approach to this state is slower than when Ca^{2+} is added after preincubation. More importantly, Fig. 2, panel B, shows that Ca^{2+} removal with ionophore A23187 plus EGTA results in decreasing levels of lysophosphatidylethanolamine during further incubation. This result is also consistent with operation of the cycle as we propose because removal of intramitochondrial Ca^{2+} should eliminate further phospholipase A_2 activity and allow subsequent reacylation activity to reduce the content of lysophosphatidylethanolamine.

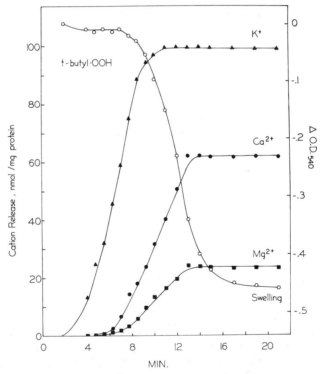

Fig. 3. Time courses for cation loss and swelling in mitochondria treated with Ca^{2+} plus t-butylhydroperoxide. Incubations were conducted as described in Methods. Swelling (O), K^+ release (▲), Ca^{2+} release (●), and Mg^{2+} release (■) were determined on the same sample using a separate incubation for each time point so that the time courses can be accurately compared (see ref. 15 for discussion of this procedure). $CaCl_2$ (70 nmol/mg protein) was added at 2 min. whereas t-butylhydroperoxide (150 μM) was added at 4 min.

To obtain information on the H$^+$ specificity, reversibility, and energy wasting characteristics of the permeability defect, we have investigated changes in oxygen consumption accompanying the development of the permeable state. To orient the reader on the time course of the permeability change, Fig. 3 is included to show the development of K$^+$ release, Ca^{2+} release, Mg^{2+} release, and swelling following the addition of t-butylhydroperoxide to Ca^{2+}-loaded mitochondria. As can be seen in the figure, there is a lag time of several minutes following addition of peroxide, before these indicators of permeability state begin to change, and thereafter changes in the various parameters proceed at different rates. The significance of the order in which the parameters change and the rate variations between them have been considered before (15). For the present purposes, the points of interest are the 2-3 minute lag period before the permeability-dependent parameters begin to change (K$^+$ release is believed to be carrier mediated under these conditions) and the fact that at least 10 minutes are required to complete the transformation after it has been initiated by peroxide addition.

The above time factors are to be considered when interpreting Fig. 4, which shows changes in respiratory activity in similar experiments. As seen in Fig. 4, trace A, the permeability change produces only a modest increase in the rate of succinate oxidation, even after extended incubation when the transformation would be complete. This is an unexpected finding, since the fully permeable mitochondria are completely deenergized, should be highly permeable to H$^+$, and so should respire at a rapid rate.

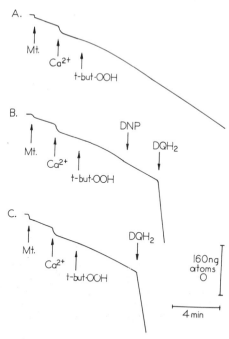

Fig. 4. The effects of Ca^{2+} plus t-butylhydroperoxide on the respiratory properties of rat liver mitochondria. Incubations were conducted and oxygen consumption was determined as described in Methods. Additions where indicated were Mt (mitochondrial protein, 1.0 mg/ml), Ca^{2+} (CaCl$_2$, 50 nmol/mg protein), t-but·OOH (t-butylhydroperoxide, 100 μM), DNP (2,4-dinitrophenol, 100 μM), and DQH$_2$ (durohydroquinone, 0.5 mM).

Fig. 4, traces B and C, explain the absence of rapid respiration seen in trace A. The failure to observe expected rates of succinate oxidation is not due to a persistent H^+-permeability barrier that limits rates of H^+ back diffusion into the matrix space and therefore respiratory activity, since the addition of uncoupler does not further increase the rate of oxygen consumption. High rates of respiration are seen following the addition of durohydroquinone, however, and furthermore, the respiratory effect of this substrate is seen when uncoupler is absent (Fig. 4, trace C). Durohydroquinone is a high-activity respiratory substrate which feeds electrons into the respiratory chain at or near the level of coenzyme Q (29,30). Therefore, these data indicate that the oxidation of succinate becomes inhibited between the substrate and coenzyme Q, approximately in parallel with the development of the permeable membrane state. The data indicate further that within the lag time between the addition of t-butyl-hydroperoxide and the onset of swelling, the H^+ conductance of the inner membrane has increased sufficiently to produce rates of respiration (in the presence of durohydroquinone) typical of those seen in the presence of uncoupler, even when uncoupler is absent. Thus, H^+ conductance has increased markedly before swelling or Mg^{2+} release become significant, indicating that the permeability defect allows H^+ to cross the membrane with substantial specificity.

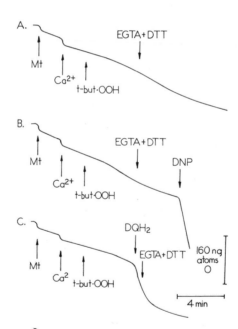

Fig. 5. Reversal of Ca^{2+} plus t-butylhydroperoxide effects on the respiratory properties of rat liver mitochondria. Incubations were conducted and oxygen consumption was determined as described in Methods. Additions where indicated were as described in the legend to Fig. 4. In addition, EGTA and dithiothreitol were both used at 1.0 mM.

As emphasized above, reversibility of the permeability transformation must also be observed before serious consideration can be given to the possible physiological roles of the phenomenon. Ready reversibility with respect to increased H^+ permeability, and the inhibition of succinate oxidation, is shown by the data in Fig. 5. The addition of EGTA, together with dithiothreitol, following the Ca^{2+} plus t-butylhydroperoxide-induced permeability increase causes a return to state 4 respiration rates from the modestly elevated rates which otherwise persist (Fig. 5, trace A). In addition, during the period when state 4 respiration rates are recovered, the mitochondria regain the capacity to respire normally in the presence of uncoupler (Fig. 5, trace B). Thus, during this time, the inhibition of succinate oxidase activity is also reversed. Finally, Fig. 5, trace C, shows that the uncoupler-independent high rate of durohydroquinone oxidation, seen following incubation with Ca^{2+} plus t-butylhydroperoxide, is also rapidly returned to state 4 rates by EGTA plus dithiothreitol. Referring to Fig. 1, both EGTA and dithiothreitol should act to reduce the mitochondrial content of lysophospholipids and free fatty acids; EGTA by inhibiting phospholipase A_2 and dithiothreitol by reducing glutathione disulfide and thereby reactivating reacylation activity. Thus, not only are permeability-sensitive functional activities of the mitochondria restored, but the conditions required make sense with respect to the proposed metabolic basis of permeability control.

These are not the first data which indicate reversibility of some or all of the phenomena associated with the membrane permeability change. Bovine adrenal cortex mitochondria made permeant to pyridine nucleotides by Ca^{2+} uptake at high Ca^{2+} concentrations recover their normal permeability barrier upon Ca^{2+} chelation (2,4). Heart mitochondria, which have been made permeable by incubation with Ca^{2+} under deenergized conditions, recover the capacity for coupled functions and regain a permeability barrier to sucrose and other low molecular weight solutes upon Ca^{2+} chelation and/or incubation in the presence of Mg^{2+} plus ADP (3). Furthermore, restoration of the heart mitochondrial permeability barrier is Ca^{2+} concentration-dependent with reduction to approximately 16 µM Ca^{2+} required for a half maximal effect (8,31). More recently, Al-Nasser and Crompton demonstrated restoration of an impermeable membrane and coupled functions in liver mitochondria following the transformation induced by Ca^{2+} and the "Ca^{2+}-releasing agent" inorganic phosphate (32). Reduction of the extramitochondrial Ca^{2+} concentration was again the method employed, with Ca^{2+} concentration dependence being observed. These workers have demonstrated that permeabilizing and resealing can be used to trap Ca^{2+} indicator molecules within the matrix space for subsequent continuous monitoring of matrix Ca^{2+} concentration (33,34).

Based on the findings presented and cited above, it seems clear that the permeability transformation, were it to occur in vivo, would be promptly reversed under normal conditions. This is because cytoplasmic Ca^{2+} concentrations of higher than 1 µM would not be expected to persist or even to exist, and this concentration range is low enough to promote reversal (32). During the time when mitochondria were in the permeable state, wasteful oxidative activity, dependent on the tricarboxylic acid cycle, would be limited by the inhibition of succinate oxidase shown herein. However, effects of the permeability transformation on ATPase activity and on the oxidation of other substrates remain to be determined. Finally, the mixing of cytoplasmic and matrix space solutes might be limited by the apparent H^+ selective character of the permeability defect. These preliminary findings suggest to us that the possibility that the mitochondrial permeability transformation is a component of physiological processes should not be dismissed out of hand.

REFERENCES

1. D. R. Pfeiffer and T. T. Tchen, 1973, The role of Ca^{2+} in control of malic enzyme activity in bovine adrenal cortex mitochondria, Biochem. Biophys. Res. Commun., 50:807.

2. D. R. Pfeiffer and T. T. Tchen, 1975, The activation of adrenal cortex mitochondrial malic enzyme by Ca^{2+} and Mg^{2+}, Biochemistry, 14:89.

3. D. R. Hunter, R. A. Haworth, and J. H. Southard, 1976, Relationship between configuration, function and permeability in calcium-treated mitochondria, J. Biol. Chem., 251:5069.

4. D. R. Pfeiffer, T. H. Kuo, and T. T. Tchen, 1976, Some effects of Ca^{2+}, Mg^{2+} and Mn^{2+} on the ultrastructural, light-scattering properties and malic enzyme activity of adrenal cortex mitochondria, Arch. Biochem. Biophys., 176:556.

5. D. R. Pfeiffer, R. F. Kauffman, and H. A. Lardy, 1978, Effects of N-ethylmaleimide on the limited uptake of Ca^{2+}, Mn^{2+} and Sr^{2+} by rat liver mitochondria, J. Biol. Chem., 253:4165.

6. D. R. Pfeiffer, P. C. Schmid, M. C. Beatrice, and H. H. O. Schmid, 1979, Intramitochondrial phospholipase activity and the effects of Ca^{2+} plus N-ethylmaleimide on mitochondrial function, J. Biol. Chem., 254:11485.

7. D. R. Hunter and R. A. Haworth, 1979, The Ca^{2+}-induced membrane transition in mitochondria; I. the protective mechanisms, Arch. Biochem. Biophys., 195:453.

8. R. A. Haworth and D. R. Hunter, 1979, The Ca^{2+}-induced membrane transition in mitochondria; II. nature of the trigger site, Arch. Biochem. Biophys., 195:460.

9. D. R. Hunter and R. A. Haworth, 1979, The Ca^{2+}-induced membrane transition in mitochondria; III. transitional Ca^{2+} release, Arch. Biochem. Biophys., 195:468.

10. E. J. Harris, M. Al-Shaikhaly, and H. Baum, 1979, Stimulation of mitochondrial calcium ion efflux by thiol-specific reagents and by thyroxine. The relationship to adenosine diphosphate retention and to mitochondrial permeability, Biochem. J., 182:455.

11. M. C. Beatrice, J. W. Palmer, and D. R. Pfeiffer, 1980, The relationship between mitochondrial membrane permeability, membrane potential, and the retention of Ca^{2+} by mitochondria, J. Biol. Chem., 255:8663.

12. E. J. Harris and H. Baum, 1980, Production of thiol groups and retention of calcium ions by cardiac mitochondria, Biochem. J., 186:725.

13. J. W. Palmer and D. R. Pfeiffer, 1981, The control of Ca^{2+} release from heart mitochondria, J. Biol. Chem., 256:6742.

14. M. C. Beatrice, D. L. Stiers, and D. R. Pfeiffer, 1982, Increased permeability of mitochondria during Ca^{2+} release induced by t-butylhydroperoxide or oxalacetate. The effect of ruthenium red, J. Biol. Chem., 257:7161.

15. W. W. Riley, Jr. and D. R. Pfeiffer, 1985, Relationships between Ca^{2+} release, Ca^{2+} cycling, and Ca^{2+}-mediated permeability changes in mitochondria, J. Biol. Chem., 260:12416.

16. M. C. Beatrice, D. L. Stiers, and D. R. Pfeiffer, 1984, The role of glutathione in the retention of Ca^{2+} by liver mitochondria, J. Biol. Chem., 259:1279.

17. W. W. Riley, Jr. and D. R. Pfeiffer, 1986, The effect of Ca^{2+} and acyl-Coenzyme A:lysophospholipid acyltransferase inhibitors on permeability properties of the liver mitochondrial inner membrane, J. Biol. Chem., 261:14018.

18. D. R. Pfeiffer, J. W. Palmer, M. C. Beatrice, and D. L. Stiers, 1983, The mechanism and regulation of Ca^{2+} efflux from mitochondria, in: "The Biochemistry of Metabolic Processes," D. F. L. Lenon et al., eds., Elsevier North-Holland, Inc., New York, pp. 67-80.

19. K. M. Broekemeier, P. C. Schmid, H. H. O. Schmid, and D. R. Pfeiffer, 1985, Effects of phospholipase A_2 inhibitors on ruthenium red-induced Ca^{2+} release from mitochondria, J. Biol. Chem., 260:105.

20. T. Okayasu, M. T. Curtis, and J. L. Farber, 1985, Structural alterations of the inner mitochondrial membrane in ischemic liver cell injury, Arch. Biochem. Biophys., 236:638.

21. P. E. Starke, J. B. Hoek, and J. L. Farber, 1986, Calcium-dependent and calcium-independent mechanisms of irreversible cell injury in cultured hepatocytes, J. Biol. Chem., 261:3006.

22. J. R. Aprille, 1977, Reye's syndrome: patient serum alters mitochondrial function and morphology in vitro, Science, 197:908.

23. T. Y. Segalman and C. P. Lee, 1982, Reye's syndrome: plasma-induced alterations in mitochondrial structure and function, Arch. Biochem. Biophys., 214:522.

24. K.-Sa You, 1983, Salicylate and mitochondrial injury in Reye's syndrome, 1983, Science, 221:163.

25. M. E. Martens, C. H. Chang, and C. P. Lee, 1986, Reye's syndrome: mitochondrial swelling and Ca^{2+} release induced by Reye's plasma, allantoin, and salicylates, Arch. Biochem. Biophys., 244:773.

26. K. S. Cheah and A. M. Cheah, 1981, Skeletal muscle mitochondrial phospholipase A_2 and the interaction of mitochondrial and sarcoplasmic reticulum in porcine malignant hyperthermia, Biochim. Biophys. Acta, 638:40.

27. K. S. Cheah, 1984, Skeletal-muscle mitochondria and phospholipase A_2 in malignant hyperthermia, Biochem. Soc. Trans., 12:358.

28. P. C. Schmid, D. R. Pfeiffer, and H. H. O. Schmid, 1981, Quantitation of lysophosphatidylethanolamine in the nanomole range, J. Lipid Res., 22:882.

29. A. Boveris, R. Oshino, M. Erecińska, and B. Chance, 1971, Reduction of mitochondrial components by durohydroquinone, Biochim. Biophys. Acta, 245:1.

30. J. F. Hare and F. L. Crane, 1971, A durohydroquinone oxidation site in the mitochondrial transport chain, Bioenergetics, 2:317.

31. R. A. Haworth and D. R. Hunter, 1987, Allosteric inhibition of the Ca^{2+}-activated hydrophilic channel of the mitochondrial inner membrane by nucleotides, J. Membr. Biol., 54:231.

32. I. Al-Nasser and M. Crompton, 1986, The reversible Ca^{2+}-induced permeabilization of rat liver mitochondria, Biochem. J., 239:19.

33. I. Al-Nasser and M. Crompton, 1986, The entrapment of the Ca^{2+} indicator arsenazo III in the matrix space of rat liver mitochondria by permeabilization and resealing, Biochem. J., 239:31.

34. L. H. Hayat and M. Crompton, 1987, The effects of Mg^{2+} and adenine nucleotides on the sensitivity of the heart mitochondrial Na^+-Ca^+ carrier to extramitochondrial Ca^{2+}, Biochem. J., 244:533.

THE ROLE OF CALCIUM AND PHOSPHOLIPASE A$_2$ IN GLUCAGON-INDUCED ENHANCEMENT OF MITOCHONDRIAL CALCIUM RETENTION.

Jan B. Hoek, Naotaro Harada, Gisela Moehren, Michelle Tomsho and Chris D. Stubbs

Department of Pathology and Cell Biology, Thomas Jefferson University, Philadelphia, Pa, 19107

INTRODUCTION

Glucagon affects metabolic activities in different compartments of the liver cell, including the mitochondria. These effects of glucagon are often preserved during isolation of the mitochondria (see 1 for review). The mitochondrial actions of glucagon may not be directly mediated by a rise in the level of cAMP; instead, mitochondrial calcium uptake may be involved in transferring the hormonal signal to the mitochondrial matrix. Glucagon induces a mobilization of calcium from non-mitochondrial stores in hepatocytes, presumably by activation of the phosphoinositide-specific phospholipase C (2,3). This leads to a transient increase in cytosolic free calcium levels, disturbing the balance between matrix and cytosolic calcium concentrations maintained by the calcium transport systems present in the inner membrane. There is evidence that mitochondrial calcium content is increased after glucagon treatment (4).

Mitochondrial calcium handling is also affected by short-term glucagon treatment of the liver. Na$^+$-dependent Ca^{2+} efflux is activated (5) and Ca^{2+} uptake is increased, the latter presumably secondary to changes in the proton-motive force (6). It is not clear that these factors contribute to the control of cytosolic calcium levels in the intact cell, but they may play a role in the regulation of intramitochondrial Ca^{2+} concentrations.

Glucagon treatment also enhances the capacity of the mitochondria to retain a high load of calcium without a loss of respiratory control or a leak of endogenous ions. This phenomenon may be only indirectly related to the abovementioned changes in calcium transport activities. There is evidence that the accumulation of calcium in mitochondria, in combination with other triggers, such as sulfhydryl reagents, hydroperoxides, oxaloacetate or menadione, causes activation of an endogenous phospholipase A$_2$ and an increase in lysophospholipids and free fatty acids in the mitochondrial membrane (7,8). A modification of these responses by glucagon treatment may reflect a decreased activity of mitochondrial phospholipase A$_2$ or a diminished sensitivity of the inner membrane to phospholipase attack. In either case, these effects of glucagon may be related to short-term changes in the regulation of membrane composition. In earlier studies, we have provided evidence in support of membrane structural modifications after glucagon treatment (9); other authors (10) have argued that glucagon treatment could be associated with a decrease in mitochondrial phospholipase A$_2$ activity. In this study, we have investigated whether an increased calcium retention capacity could reflect a change in the Ca^{2+}- induced activation of phospholipase A_2 or a difference in the accumulation of lysophospholipids after calcium-loading.

It is not known whether the elevation of the cytosolic calcium level is an essential step in the glucagon-induced potentiation of mitochondrial calcium retention or how a hormone-induced increase in cytosolic calcium concentration is translated into an increased capacity to retain calcium. We have therefore also studied the role of cytosolic free calcium concentration as an intracellular signal employed to elicit these and other mitochondrial responses to glucagon in intact hepatocytes.

INTRACELLULAR SIGNALS FOR GLUCAGON-INDUCED CALCIUM RETENTION

Much of the evidence in favor of a role for calcium in the mitochondrial actions of glucagon comes from the recognition that glucagon, in addition to activating adenylate cyclase, also causes a mobilization of calcium from intracellular stores, presumably by the activation of phosphoinositide-specific phospholipase C, with the formation of $Ins(1,4,5)P_3$ (2,3). The experiment in Fig. 1 illustrates the glucagon-induced calcium mobilization in intact hepatocytes. Pretreatment of the cells with the phorbol ester 12-O-tetradecanoyl 4-phorbol 13-acetate (TPA) completely inhibits the glucagon-induced calcium mobilization (see also ref. 3). A comparable inhibitory effect of TPA on the activation of phospholipase C by other agonists (phenylephrine, low concentrations of vasopressin, ethanol) has

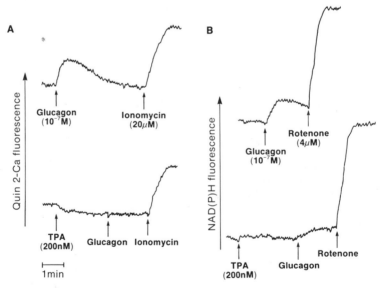

Fig. 1   Inhibition of glucagon-induced calcium mobilization and NAD(P) reduction by TPA in hepatocytes.   In A, changes in cytosolic free calcium levels were measured in quin2-loaded hepatocytes as described earlier (12). In B, unloaded cells were incubated under the same conditions and NAD(P)H fluorescence was measured at a wavelength pair 350-465 nm.

been reported (11,12). This inhibition is probably due to a protein kinase C-mediated phosphorylation of one or more components of the signal trans-duction complex in the membrane, e.g., a receptor or G-protein. In contrast to the glucagon-induced calcium mobilization, cAMP production is only slightly affected by the pretreatment with phorbol esters and phosphorylase activation by glucagon was unimpaired under conditions where TPA severely inhibited α_1-adrenergic activation (data not shown). Thus, phorbol ester pretreatment can be used to assess the role of calcium mobilization in the action of glucagon on intracellular events. The data in Fig. 1b illustrate this effect.

One of the metabolic events induced by glucagon treatment in intact hepatocytes is the rapid reduction of NAD(P), presumably in large part by an activation of mitochondrial dehydrogenases. The work of McCormack (4) has indicated that calcium may play a crucial role in the activation of mitochondrial dehydrogenases. These authors proposed that the mitochondrial calcium, taken up in response to the elevation of cytosolic free calcium levels, activates calcium-sensitive enzymes. Thus, calcium would be the signal by which glucagon activates NAD(P) reduction in the mitochondrial matrix space. The data in Fig. 1b support this idea in that preincubation of the hepatocytes with TPA largely inhibited the glucagon-induced NAD(P) reduction. TPA treatment also inhibited glucagon-induced reduction of NAD(P) in the presence of several other substrates, including alanine, glutamine and glucose, as well as with endogenous substrate only (data not shown). The fact that different substrate conditions gave an essentially similar response to glucagon suggests that a common process is affected by glucagon; this could well be one or more of the citric acid cycle enzymes which respond to an elevation of mitochondrial calcium levels, including pyruvate dehydrogenase phosphatase, alpha-ketoglutarate dehydrogenase or NAD-isocitrate dehydrogenase, as suggested by McCormack (4).

In the experiments of Fig. 2, the same approach was used to assess the role of an increased cytosolic calcium level in the glucagon-induced potentiation of mitochondrial calcium retention. Isolated hepatocytes were incubated for different periods up to 30 min, in the presence or absence of glucagon (10^{-7}M) and TPA (200 nM). Calcium retention was measured after permeabilization of the cells with digitonin. Succinate was added as a source of energy. Ca^{2+} (0.2 mM) and Mg^{2+} (1mM) were also present. Under these conditions, the mitochondria of untreated permeabilized cells took up calcium to a level of approximately 40 nmol/mg cell protein, but released it after a few minutes. By contrast, the cells treated with glucagon for 20 or 30 min retained their calcium load for an extended period, similar to effects observed with isolated mitochondria. Unexpectedly, pretreatment of the cells with TPA mimicked this effect, even without the addition of glucagon and, rather than being inhibited by TPA, the effect of glucagon on calcium retention was enhanced. Since TPA treatment has no effect on the cytosolic calcium level and prevents the calcium response to glucagon, these data indicate that the potentiation of mitochondrial calcium retention is not solely determined by changes in the concentration of calcium in the cytosol. It is possible that TPA affects the responsiveness of mitochondria to the calcium level in the cytosol. There is evidence that the mitochondrial capacity to retain calcium is a function of the adenine nucleotide content, although it is not clear by what mechanism these parameters are related (13). However, we have been unable to detect an effect of TPA on mitochondrial adenine nucleotide levels (Unpublished observations). Experiments are currently underway to further define the conditions under which these effects of TPA on mitochondrial activity are observed.

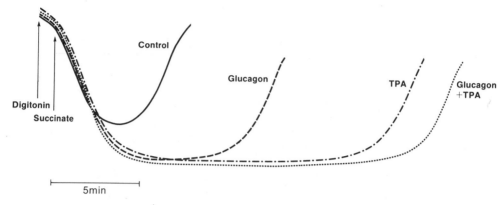

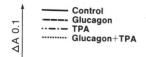

Fig. 2. Enhancement of calcium retention in permeabilized hepatocytes after pretreatment with glucagon or phorbol ester. Cells were preincubated for 20 min in Krebs-Ringer bicarbonate buffer before addition of glucagon (10^{-7} M) or TPA (200 nM). After 30 min, the cell suspension was washed with ice-cold washing medium containing NaCl (145 mM), KCl (5 mM), $MgCl_2$ (1 mM), potassium phosphate (1 mM), Hepes buffer, pH 7.4 (10 mM) and $CaCl_2$ (0.2 mM) and placed on ice until calcium retention could be measured. The treated cell suspensions were washed with the same medium containing Arsenazo III (20 uM) and incubated in the cuvet of a DW2a dual wavelength spectrophotometer at 37°C. The calcium content of the medium was measured at a wavelength pair of 675-685 nm. Cells were permeabilized with digitonin (40 ug/ml) and mitochondrial calcium uptake was initiated by the addition of succinate (10 mM). The calcium concentration of the medium was selected to cause the untreated cells to release calcium in 2-3 minutes.

THE USE OF NBD-LABELED PHOSPHOLIPIDS TO MEASURE MITOCHONDRIAL PHOSPHOLIPASE A2 ACTIVITY

For the measurement of phospholipase A2 activity in intact mitochondria, we employed an artificial phospholipid substrate containing a fluorescent 4-nitrobenzo-2-oxa-1,3-diazole (NBD) group attached to the 2-acyl chain. These fluorescent NBD-phospholipids have been used extensively by Pagano and coworkers (14) in intact cell systems, to follow the metabolic fate of different phospholipid substrates. The NBD-labeled phospholipids offer advantages in that they are effectively incorporated into membranes and are excellent substrates for phospholipase A_2 in a reaction that is readily detectable after a simple extraction step.

NBD-phospholipids are incorporated into membranes predominantly by a process of monomer transfer (14); their incorporation into a biological membrane is therefore not dependent upon the availability of a phospholipid transfer protein. Incorporation is especially effective and rapid when the 2-acyl chain containing the NBD-group is relatively short; in our experiments we have employed NBD-labeled phospholipids with a six-carbon chain in the 2-position, NBD-hexanoyl-phosphatidylethanolamine (NBD-PE) and NBD-hexanoyl-phosphatidylcholine (NBD-PC). These phospholipids can also be incorporated effectively into the membranes of isolated mitochondria. After incubation for 10 min on ice, with NBD-PC and NBD-PE (added in the form of mixed micelles of NBD-PE and dioleylphosphatidyl choline (1:1)) at 2-3 % of the total mitochondrial phospholipids, more than 95 % of the NBD-PC and about 60 % of the NBD-PE added was recovered in the mitochondrial membrane. When these NBD-labeled mitochondria were then treated with different concentrations of digitonin to remove the outer membrane, about 35 % of the NBD-PC and 50 % of the NBD-PE incorporated was recovered in the inner membrane. Thus, the NBD-phospholipids readily cross the mitochondrial outer membrane, even during incubation on ice.

During the first few minutes after its incorporation into mitochondria, essentially all the NBD-PC could be removed from the membrane by a two minutes incubation with BSA which tightly binds the phospholipid. With longer incubation times, however, an increasing fraction of the total NBD-phospholipid incorporated became inaccessible to the BSA. This presumably represents the slow transmembrane movement of the NBD-phospholipids. Similar results were obtained with mitochondria treated with digitonin to remove the outer membrane (mitoplasts), indicating that the NBD-phospholipids also could move across the mitochondrial inner membrane to the matrix face. An equilibrium distribution was obtained after about 30 min on ice, when only about 50 % of the NBD-PC and 45 % of NBD-PE incorporated could be removed by a 2 min BSA treatment. Sonication of the mitochondria made all the NBD-PC accessible again to the BSA. These experiments suggest that during the preincubation the NBD-phospholipids gain access to all faces of the mitochondrial membranes and therefore could be expected to react with both intra- and extramitochondrial phospholipid metabolizing enzymes.

NBD phospholipids are effective substrates for a number of different phospholipase A activities present in the mitochondrial preparation. These activities can be estimated by the formation of NBD-hexanoic acid which is released into the water phase and is not reincorporated into membrane lipids. Representative experiments are shown in Table 1. Ca^{2+}-dependent and -independent formation of NBD-hexanoic acid was detected in NBD-PE labeled mitochondria in the presence of an uncoupler. Most of the Ca^{2+}-independent activity was lost when mitochondria were treated with digitonin to remove the outer membrane and contaminating cell constituents. The Ca^{2+}-dependent activity measured in the presence of an uncoupler was not affected by this treatment, indicating its association with the mitochondrial inner membrane. The Ca^{2+}-dependent activity could be enhanced three to four-fold by the addition of the divalent cation ionophore A23187. Part of this ionophore-induced activity was lost when mitochondria were treated with digitonin. This activity may be due to a latent phospholipase A_2 in vesicles of non-mitochondrial origin. It is further evidence that the NBD-PE can gain access to intravesicular phospholipase A_2 activities by moving across different membranes. The rate of Ca^{2+}-dependent NBD-PE hydrolysis measured in sonicated mitochondria or mitoplasts was substantially higher than that obtained in the intact organelles and was not further enhanced by A23187. (not shown) However, this activity did not appear to be lost by digitonin treatment. In three separate experiments using sonicated mitoplasts labeled with 6.3 nmol NBD-PE/mg protein, NBD-hexanoate was formed at a rate of 32.3±4.2 pmol/min/mg at 30 °C in the presence of 5 mM Ca^{2+}, and at 4.2±1.4 pmol/min/mg in the presence of 1 mM EGTA. Dibucaine (2 mM) inhibited the Ca^{2+}-dependent activity by over 90 %. Thus, the NBD-PE was a substrate for both calcium-dependent and -independent activities in the inner as well as
the outer membrane.

Table 1. NBD-PE hydrolysis in mitochondria.

PREPARATION	ADDITIONS	NBD-HEXANOATE FORMATION		Ca^{2+}-
		EGTA	CaCl$_2$	Dependent
Exp I		(pmol/min/mg)		
Intact Mitochondria	CCCP(2μM)	29.0	35.6	6.6
	CCCP+A23187(5μM)	29.0	52.4	23.4
Intact Mitoplasts	CCCP	4.2	10.8	6.6
	CCCP+A23187	5.8	17.9	12.1
Exp II				
Sonicated Mitochondria		17.1	38.2	21.1
Sonicated Mitoplasts		4.5	28.9	27.4

All preparations were labeled with 6-3 nmol NBD-PE/mg protein and incubated for 20 min at 30° with 0.1 mM EGTA or 5 mM CaCl$_2$. Mitoplasts were prepared by treating mitochondria with digitonin (96 μg/mg) on ice for 10 min, followed by washing. NBD-hexanmate was assayed fluorometrically in the water layer after extraction with chloroform-methanol. Results are averaged from duplicate incubations.

The experiment of Fig 3 shows that NBD-PE is hydrolyzed by mitochondrial phospholipases at about the same rate as natural PE. In intact mitochondria labeled with NBD-PE (2% of total phospholipids), the formation of NBD-hexanoic acid was compared with that of lyso-phosphatidylethanolamine (lyso-PE), measured by the method of Schmid et al (15). Calcium permeability barriers were overcome by the addition of A23187 and CCCP. The rate of Ca^{2+}-dependent formation of lyso-PE was not significantly different from that of NBD-hexanoic acid, expressed as a fraction of the parent phospholipid in the membrane. Using the hydrolysis of NBD-PE in intact mitochondria as a tool to measure phospholipase A2 activation, we asked the following questions:

a. Does calcium accumulation result in an activation of phospholipase A$_2$ in intact mitochondria?
b. Do agents that cause a loss of calcium retention activate mitochondrial phospholipase A$_2$?
c. Is the enhanced calcium retention found in mitochondria from glucagon-treated rats associated with a lower level of mitochondrial phospholipase A$_2$ activation?

The experiments in Table 2 and 3 demonstrate that the answer to all of these questions is negative. Similar to the situation in sonicated mitochondria, phospholipase A$_2$ activity in intact uncoupled mitochondria was enhanced significantly by 5 mM Ca^{2+} (Table 1), but not by 0.1 mM Ca^{2+}

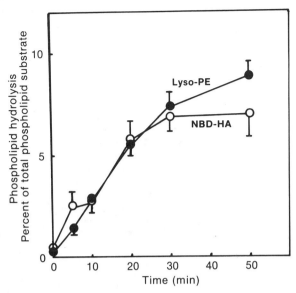

Fig.3 Comparison of calcium-dependent NBD-hexanoate formation and lyso-PE formation in intact mitochondria. Parallel incubations were carried out with unlabeled mitochondria and with NBD-PE labeled mitochondria (4 nmol/mg) for the determination of lyso-PE and NBD-hexanoate, respectively. Incubations contained 5mM Ca^{2+}, 1uM CCCP and 5 uM A23187. Corrections for Ca^{2+}-independent activities were made from parallel incubations without Ca^{2+}, but with 1mM EGTA.

Table 2.   Effect of mitochondrial Ca loading on NBD-PE hydrolysis.

Additions	NBD-Hexanoate	
	+EGTA	+CaCl$_2$
	(pmol/min/mg)	
Succinate (8mM)/Rotenone (5μM)	39.2 $\pm$ 5.0	38.3 $\pm$ 5.8
Succinate/Rotenone & Ruthenium Red (4μM)	33.5 $\pm$ 5.2	32.6 $\pm$ 5.4
CCCP (2μM)	28.4 $\pm$ 2.3[a]	29.5 $\pm$ 3.0[a]
CCCP & Ruthenium Red	27.1 $\pm$ 3.0[a]	27.5 $\pm$ 3.7[a]

Intact mitochondria (2 mg/ml) were labeled with 5.0-6.3 nmol NBD-PE per mg protein and incubated for 20 min at 30°C, with EGTA (1 mM) or CaCl$_2$ (0.1 mM, 50 nmol/mg) and other additions as indicated. Results are mean $\pm$ SEM for 7 individual experiments.[a]P<0.05 compared to incubation with succinate and rotenone.

(Table 2). NBD-PE hydrolysis was also activated when mitochondria were energized by the addition of succinate (Table 2), even in the absence of added calcium. Under these conditions, mitochondria retain significant amounts of calcium (4-6 nmol/mg protein in these experiments), which may have been present in the mitochondria in the intact cell or accumulated during the isolation procedure. Further accumulation of calcium in the mitochondrial matrix (up to 50 nmol/mg protein) did not give rise to an enhancement of the phospholipase activity as detected by NBD-hexanoic acid formation (Table 2). At higher calcium levels, energization of the mitochondria could not be maintained under these conditions. Ruthenium red, an inhibitor of mitochondrial calcium uptake, slightly diminished the formation of NBD-hexanoic acid in the energized mitochondria, presumably by promoting the efflux of intramitochondrial calcium. The effect was variable, however, and did not reach statistical significance.

These data indicate that none of the phospholipase A_2 activities detected by NBD-PE hydrolysis in intact mitochondria responds to the accumulation of calcium in amounts that can markedly affect their capacity to retain this (and other) ions. It should be noted, however, that the rate of calcium-dependent NBD-PE hydrolysis in intact mitochondria (Table 2) is substantially lower than that obtained in sonicated mitochondria and mitoplasts (Table 1). This suggests the possibility that the matrix phospholipase A_2 activity is not in a maximally active state, but can be activated by breaking the mitochondrial inner membrane.

Table 3. Effect of menadione on NBD-PE hydrolysis in Ca^{2+}-loaded mitochondria from control and glucagon-treated rats.

	Additions	NBD-Hexanoate formation (% of added NBD-PE)
Control	None	0.39 + 0.05%
	Menadione (40μM)	0.37 + 0.02%
Glucagon-treated	None	0.39 + 0.06%
	Menadione (40μM)	0.38 + 0.09%

Mitochondria were labeled with 4.9-6.3 nmol NBD-PE/mg and loaded with 70 nmol Ca^{2+}/mg in the presence of succinate (8 mM). Incubations were for 10 min at 30°C in the presence or absence of 40μM menadione.

If intramitochondrial phospholipase A_2 is inactive in intact mitochondria, it is conceivable that the addition of agents such as menadione, butylhydroperoxide, phosphate or N-ethylmaleimide, which induce the loss of calcium retention (7,8), act by potentiating this activity. In the experiment of Table 3 this hypothesis was tested using menadione. Mitochondria were loaded with Ca^{2+} (70 nmol/mg) and treated with 40 μM menadione. This treatment caused a complete loss of intramitochondrial Ca^{2+} and Mg^{2+} within 10 min, while control mitochondria retained their calcium load for at least 20 min in this experiment. However, the menadione treatment had no detectable effect on phospholipase A_2 activity in these mitochondria, as measured by the release of NBD-hexanoic acid from NBD-PE incorporated in the mitochondrial membrane. Similar results were obtained when mitochondria from glucagon-treated rats were used. Menadione treatment had no significant effect on the rate of NBD-hexanoate release. The apparent phospholipase A_2 activity was not significantly different between mitochondria from control and glucagon-treated rats, even though the latter preparation was capable of retaining a standard calcium load about twice as long as the control mitochondria. These findings indicate that glucagon treatment does not exert its effect on mitochondrial calcium retention by affecting phospholipase A_2 activity in the matrix.

LYSOPHOSPHOLIPID ACCUMULATION IN MITOCHONDRIAL MEMBRANES AFTER CALCIUM LOADING

The results with NBD-labeled phospholipids shown above do not exclude the possibility that the matrix phospholipase A_2 in intact mitochondria is reactive only with endogenous phospholipids, but not with phospholipid analogues introduced during the preincubation. Moreover, the activation of phospholipase A_2 in the mitochondrial matrix may not be the trigger which induces permeabilization of the mitochondrial inner membrane. It has been proposed that the accumulation of a critical amount of lyso-PE increases

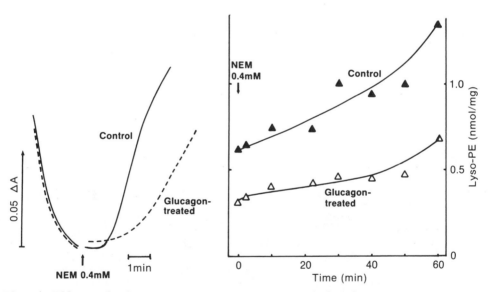

Fig. 4 Effect of glucagon pretreatment on NEM-induced calcium release and lysoPE accumulation. Liver mitochondria isolated from rats pretreated for 20 min with glucagon or from control rats treated with vehicle only, were incubated in a mannitol-sucrose-Hepes (MSH) medium in the presence of succinate (10 mM), rotenone (2 ug/ml) and $CaCl_2$ (60 nmol/mg). After calcium uptake was completed, NEM (0.2 mM) was added. In the left-hand panel, the medium contained 20 uM Arsenazo III and calcium release was followed in the Aminco DW2a dual wavelength spectrophotometer at a wavelength pair of 675-685. In the right-hand panel, no Arsenazo III was added and samples were taken at different times to be extracted with chloroform-methanol for the determination of lysoPE as described in (15).

the membrane permeability to protons, thereby short-circuiting the proton-motive capacity of the inner membrane (7). We therefore determined the effect of glucagon treatment on the calcium-induced accumulation of lyso-PE in intact mitochondria, under conditions where loss of calcium retention occurs. In Fig. 4a, NEM was used to trigger calcium loss in preparations from control and glucagon-treated rats; Ca^{2+} uptake and release were detected with the indicator Arsenazo III. Lyso-PE levels were measured during the time over which calcium loss occurs. As shown in Fig. 4b, Ca^{2+} loading was associated with a slow increase in the lyso-PE formation, similar to the data reported by Schmid et al.(15). However, significant changes in the level of lyso-PE were observed only after the release of calcium had occurred. At that time, the mitochondria had completely lost their respiratory control and presumably were depleted of matrix cofactors.

The accumulation of lysophospholipids in the mitochondria from glucagon-treated animals followed a similar pattern, with a major increase in lysophospholipid content occurring only after about 60 min; loss of calcium retention was observed much earlier, at a time when lysophospholipid levels were not significantly affected yet. Interestingly, the mitochondria from glucagon-treated animals had a significantly lower content of lyso-PE, even before the accumulation of Ca^{2+}; in a series of seven experiments, the lyso-PE level in freshly isolated mitochondria from glucagon-treated and control rats was 0.41 ± 0.04 and 0.61 ± 0.04 nmol/mg protein, respectively. It was not affected by Ca^{2+} uptake, however, and at the time of Ca^{2+} release, the mitochondria from glucagon-treated animals had a much lower content of lysoPE than the control mitochondria before the Ca^{2+} loss. Essentially similar findings were obtained when the release of Ca^{2+} was triggered by other agents, such as phosphate, menadione or oxaloacetate. These results indicate that the calcium release was not caused by the accumulation of lyso-PE in the membrane. The lysophospholipid formation associated with loss of Ca^{2+} retention appeared to be the consequence rather than the cause of permeabilization of the mitochondrial membrane.

DISCUSSION

The data presented in this paper are not in agreement with a major role of phospholipase A_2 activation in the loss of Ca^{2+} retention and therefore do not support a model whereby glucagon treatment affects the calcium retention time due to a decreased activity of mitochondrial phospholipase A_2. It is conceivable that the lack of detectable phospholipase A_2 activity in intact mitochondria is due to a lack of reactivity of the NBD-phospholipid probes that we used in these experiments with the intramitochondrial phospholipase A_2. However, in sonicated mitochondria the activity was readily detectable and was of the same order of magnitude as that reported by other authors who measured this activity by very different methods (16). It is difficult to obtain a good estimate of the activity of this enzyme in intact mitochondria, since radioactively labeled substrates do not readily penetrate through the mitochondrial membranes to be accessible from the matrix. Moreover, reaction products of phospholipase (lysophospholipids, free fatty acids) may be reincorporated into newly synthesized phospholipids by reacylation. In both respects, the NBD-phospholipids offer distinct advantages. They appear to cross the mitochondrial membranes, even at low temperatures. The NBD-hexanoate released is readily water soluble and is not reincorporated into other phospholipids. Recovery experiments indicate that approximately 90 % of the fluorescent fatty acid released was recovered in the water phase after a Bligh and Dyer extraction. Our conclusion that the mitochondrial phospholipase A_2 was largely in an inhibited state in the matrix, even after loading the mitochondria with Ca^{2+} could be related to the presence of an inhibitor of the enzyme in intact mitochondria; for instance, Pfeiffer (Personal Communication) has observed that low concentrations of lysocardiolipin are strongly inhibitory for isolated mitochondrial phospholipase A_2.

It is conceivable that a very low activity of the matrix phospholipase A_2 could not be detected against the background of calcium-independent activity and extramitochondrial NBD-phospholipid hydrolysis. However, the analysis of changes in the lyso-PE level during calcium loading and release indicates that this parameter did not correlate with the conditions under which release of calcium from the mitochondria could be induced. Most relevant for the focus of this paper, the mitochondria from glucagon-treated rats lost control of their calcium load even when the lyso-PE levels were significantly lower than that in control mitochondria at the start of the incubation.

The reason for the lower level of lyso-PE in the mitochondria from glucagon-treated animals is not clear, but the observation is in agreement with data reported by others (17). It is possible that a higher ATP/ADP or acylCoA/CoA ratio in these mitochondria shifts the equilibrium of the acylation reaction to maintain a lower level of the lysophospholipids. These observations further raise the question of whether the level of lyso-PE in the membrane plays a more indirect potentiating role in changing the mitochondrial response to calcium loading. Lysophospholipids can exert a significant influence upon the formation of non-bilayer structures, which can destabilize the mitochondrial inner membrane. Calcium is known to promote the formation of non-bilayer structures in cardiolipin-containing membranes; dibucaine and ruthenium red inhibit this process and a variety of membrane disturbing agents can promote it (18). Although there is no evidence that such non-bilayer structures are generated in mitochondrial membranes during calcium loading (19), the presence of localized, transient non-bilayer structures (lipidic particles) could be difficult to detect.

ACKNOWEDGEMENT

This study was supported by US Public Health Service grants AM 38461, AA07106 and AA07215.

REFERENCES

1.   Halestrap, A.P. (1986) in Hormonal Regulation of Gluconeogenesis (Kraus-Friedmann, N., ed.), 3:31-48, CRC Press, Cleveland.

2.   Sistare, F.D., Picking, R.A. and Haynes, R.C. (1985) J. Biol. Chem. 260:12744-12747.

3.   Staddon, J.M. and Hansford, R.G. (1986) Biochem. J. 238:737-743.

4.   McCormack, J.G. (1985) Biochem. J. 231:597-608.

5.   Goldstone, T.P., Duddridge, R.J. and Crompton, M. (1983) Biochem. J. 210:463-472.

6.   Wingrove, D.E., Amatruda, J.M. and Gunter, T.E. (1984) J. Biol. Chem. 259:9390-9394.

7.   Pfeiffer, D.R., Palmer, J.W., Beatrice, M.C. and Stiers, D.L. (1983) in: The Biochemistry of Metabolic Processes (Lenon, D.F.L, Stratman,

F.W. and Zahlten, R.N., eds.) 67-80, Elsevier-North Holland, Inc., New York.

8. Broekemeier, K.M., Schmid, P.C., Schmid, H.H.O. and Pfeiffer, D.R. (1985) J. Biol. Chem. 260:105-113.

9. Hoek, J.B., Moehren, G. and Waring, A.J. (1983) in: Isolation, Characterization and Use of Hepatocytes (Harris, R.A. and Cornell, N.W., eds.), pp.245-250, Elsevier Science Publishing Co., Amsterdam

10. Sies, E.A., Fahimi, F.M. and Wieland, O.H. (1981) Hoppe-Seyler's, Z. Physiol. Chem. 362:1643-1651.

11. Cooper, R.H., Coll, K.E. and Williamson, J.R. (1985) J. Biol. Chem. 260:3281-3288.

12. Hoek, J.B., Thomas, A.P., Rubin, R. and Rubin, E. (1987) J. Biol. Chem. 262:682-691.

13. Kimura, S. and Rasmussen, H. (1977) J. Biol. Chem. 252:1217-1225.

14. Pagano, R.E. and Sleigh, R.G. (1985) Science 229:1051-1057.

15. Schmid, P.C., Pfeiffer, D.R. and Schmid, H.H.O. (1981) J. Lipid Res. 22:882:886.

16. Nachbaum, J., Colbeau, A. and Vignais, P.M. (1972) Biochim. Biophys. Acta 274:426-446.

17. Armston, A.E. and Halestrap, A.P. (1984) Bioscience Reports 4:903-908.

18. Verkley, A.J. (1984) Biochim. Biophys. Acta 779:43-63.

19. DeKrujff, B., Nayer, R. and Cullis, P.R. (1982) Biochim. Biophys. Acta, 684:47-52.

SODIUM/PROTON ANTIPORTERS IN THE MITOCHONDRIAL INNER MEMBRANE

Keith D. Garlid

Department of Pharmacology and Therapeutics
Medical College of Ohio
C. S. 10008
Toledo, Ohio 43699

INTRODUCTION

The existence of membrane proteins designed for Na^+/H^+ exchange has been established in both eukaryotic and prokaryotic systems (1), and the plethora of recent reviews (see, for example, refs. 1-3 and references therein) testifies to the perceived importance of plasma membrane Na^+/H^+ antiporters to the physiology of the cell. A consensus is now developing that the plasmalemma of most cells contains an electroneutral Na^+/H^+ antiporter which is inhibited by amiloride and lithium ions, and whose primary physiological role is cellular pH homeostasis. These operating characteristics have been found to be similar in a variety of cell types (2), and the conclusion has been drawn that these properties are representative of all plasma membrane Na^+/H^+ antiporters (3). This implies that plasma membranes contain only one type of Na^+/H^+ antiporter, that Na^+ is the only physiological substrate for such antiporters, and that K^+, in particular, is not a substrate for plasmalemmal Na^+/H^+ antiporters. How reliable are these conclusions?

This question is stimulated by the strong evidence favoring the coexistence of <u>two</u> Na^+/H^+ antiporters within the inner membrane of mitochondria, the only eukaryotic membrane system which has been thoroughly studied in this regard (4). One of these porters transports K^+ as well as Na^+, unlike the renal Na^+/H^+ antiporter. In this respect, it resembles a Na^+/H^+ antiporter from cardiac sarcolemma (5) which has also been found to transport K^+ as well as Na^+ (S. Kakar, A. Askari and K. Garlid, unpublished data). In contrast, the other mitochondrial porter is Na^+-selective, like the renal Na^+/H^+ antiporter (6) which it also resembles in other respects. It is tempting to suggest that nature, having chosen two modes of Na^+/H^+ antiport in mitochondria, did not need to invent a third and a fourth for the plasmalemma. From this perspective alone, it is important to study and characterize these mitochondrial Na^+/H^+ antiporters.

This is not to say that such studies are only important with respect to the cell's communication with its environment. They are also vitally important for the mitochondrion's communication with the cytosol and, therefore, essential for the cell's survival. In particular, consider the Mg^{2+}-dependent Na^+/H^+ antiporter, which catalyzes both Na^+/H^+ and K^+/H^+ exchange across the inner membrane of mitochondria. Its physiological function is to regulate the mitochondrial potassium transport cycle and thereby, through the asymmetric carrier-braking action of matrix magnesium ions, control matrix volume (7). Because of the central role played by K^+, we have been calling this the K^+/H^+ antiporter. The second Na^+/H^+ antiporter is Mg^{2+}-independent, does not transport K^+ and is apparently involved primarily in the mitigation of the effects of calcium on matrix enzymes (8, 9), an effect which may be mediated by a sodium/calcium exchange protein (10).

Neither of these Na^+/H^+ antiporters provides pH homeostasis to mitochondria, in contradistinction to their role in the plasma membrane (2). This follows from the simple fact that the Pi/H^+ symporter is present in great excess in all mitochondria whose primary function is to make ATP and export it to the cytosol. Thus, the Pi/H^+ symporter dominates electroneutral proton traffic under steady state conditions (11).

This paper will review the experimental evidence for the claim (4) that the inner membrane of mitochondria contains two distinct Na^+/H^+ antiporters. The operating characteristics of these two antiporters will be shown to differ sharply, suggesting a new basis for the classification of alkali cation/proton anti-porters in eukaryotic membranes.

EXPERIMENTAL PROCEDURES

Mitochondrial Preparations

Rat liver mitochondria, isolated by differential centri-fugation as previously described (12), were resuspended to 50 mg of protein/ml in 0.25 M sucrose and stored on ice. Mg^{2+}-depleted mitochondria, in which respiration in TEA^+ salts and addition of A23187 and EDTA result in the loss of K^+ and Mg^{2+} from the matrix and their substitution by TEA^+ cation, were prepared essentially as previously described (4).

Light Scattering Studies

Uptake of salts and water into the mitochondrial matrix results in matrix swelling and a consequent decrease in the light scattered by a mitochondrial suspension (12-14). The variable β normalizes reciprocal absorbance (A^{-1}) for mitochondrial conc-entration, $P(mg/ml)$:

$$\beta = \frac{P}{P_S} (A^{-1} - a) \tag{1}$$

where P_S (equals 1 mg/ml) is introduced to make β a scaled, dimensionless quantity and a is a machine constant equal to 0.25 with our apparatus (12). Absorbance is measured at 520 nm and sampled at 100 or 600 msec intervals with a Brinkmann PC700 probe colorimeter connected to a Cyborg 91A analog/digital converter. The signal is passed to an Apple IIe computer for conversion to inverse absorbance, real time plotting and storage. Under given experimental conditions, light scattering traces are highly reproducible, even when carried out on different days by different workers using different rat liver mitochondrial preparations. For example, the traces in Fig. 1 have been repeated at least 50 times during the last four years. Estimates of initial rates, which are proportional to the rate of KOAc transport and which are obtained from linear regressions of the data curves, have been the same (± 10%).

RESULTS AND DISCUSSION

Na^+/H^+ and K^+/H^+ Exchange in Normal Mitochondria

In a nutshell, isolated mitochondria incubated under "normal" conditions readily exhibit Na^+/H^+ exchange activity and fail to exhibit K^+/H^+ exchange activity. Following are three examples which illustrate this sharp dichotomy between behavior toward Na^+ and behavior toward K^+:

[1] Mitochondria isolated in sucrose medium have undergone several centrifugations and resuspensions in a K^+- and Na^+-free medium. Nevertheless, these mitochondria retain high amounts of K^+ and maintain a high K^+ gradient: Matrix $[K^+]$ is on the order of 180 mM, while medium $[K^+]$ is 100-200 uM. Furthermore, the matrix pH of these mitochondria is very alkaline, about 8.5, as a consequence of the passive loss of weak organic acids and phosphoric acid on their respective substrate porters (12). Despite their enormous gradient for K^+ efflux via K^+/H^+ antiport, mitochondria retain endogenous K^+ for long periods, even in the absence of respiration (15, 16). This finding indicates that freshly isolated mitochondria lack K^+/H^+ antiport activity.

[2] When 100 mM NaOAc is added to sucrose medium containing non-respiring mitochondria, there is uptake of NaOAc and water into the matrix until equilibrium is achieved. When these mitochondria are washed, involving centrifugations and resuspensions in K^+- and Na^+-free sucrose, the NaOAc is readily removed from the matrix. Through all of these steps, during which a high two-way traffic of Na^+ has taken place across the membrane and despite being carried out in K^+-free media, more than 95% of endogenous K^+ is retained in the matrix. This experiment, confirming results from a similar protocol by Gamble and Hackenbrock (17), indicates that Na^+/H^+ antiport can readily take place without perturbing mitochondrial K^+.

[3] When mitochondria are suspended in acetate salts, swelling rates are determined by the rates of cation/proton antiport (18, 19), because the inner membrane is highly permeable to acetic acid and water. By this criterion, the inner membranes of fresh mitochondria exhibit Na^+/H^+ but not K^+/H^+ exchange, as first demonstrated by Mitchell and Moyle (18).

Unmasking K^+/H^+ Antiport in Mitochondria

The preceding experiments show that Na^+ and K^+ are handled differently by mitochondria. Indeed, to many workers, these and similar results appeared to require that K^+ was not handled at all! As I have pointed out, however, the existence of a K^+/H^+ antiporter is a physiological necessity in view of the osmotic constraints imposed on mitochondria as they respire in the high-K[+] environment of the cytosol (7). Furthermore, the same physiological constraints impose a requirement for sensitive regulation of K[+]/H[+] antiport, in order to assure zero net fluxes of K[+] salts and water. These considerations led me to propose that the failure of isolated mitochondria to exhibit K[+]/H[+] antiport is due, not to the <u>absence</u> of a K[+]/H[+] antiporter in the membrane, but rather to its <u>regulation</u> (7).

Our ability to unmask K[+]/H[+] antiport by procedures which lower matrix [Mg^{2+}] is illustrated in Fig. 1, in which addition of the divalent cation ionophore A23187 (20) is shown to cause a large stimulation of KOAc transport. We have demonstrated, in both influx and efflux studies, that the K[+] transport pathway is electroneutral and has all the characteristics of K[+]/H[+] antiport (16, 19). The discovery that Mg^{2+} ions inhibit K[+]/H[+] antiport by interacting with an allosteric site asymmetrically placed on the matrix side of the antiporter protein led to the Mg^{2+} carrier-brake hypothesis. This is the proposed mechanism by which Mg^{2+} provides sensitive and dynamic regulation of K[+]/H[+] antiport, thereby providing volume homeostasis for mitochondria in vivo (7).

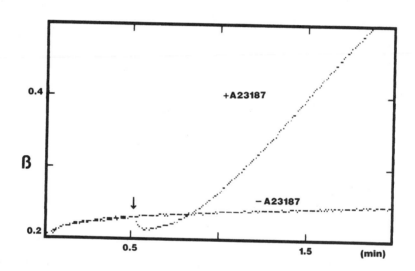

Fig. 1. <u>Potassium transport on the mitochondrial Mg^{2+}-dependent Na[+]/H[+] antiporter</u>. Mitochondria were suspended at 0.1 mg/ml in 55 mM KOAc, buffered at pH 7.8, 25°. 0.1 mM EDTA was also included in the medium. Without A23187, there is little or no change in light scattering, indicating an absence of K[+]/H[+] antiport. Upon addition of A23187 (5 nmol/mg), there is an initial contraction, as indicated by the downward shift of the trace, followed by matrix swelling, as indicated by the upward shift of the trace. The contraction is due to A23187-induced loss of Mg^{2+} in exchange for H[+], resulting in intense matrix acidification and loss of HOAc. Removal of matrix Mg^{2+} releases the antiporter from inhibition, resulting in electroneutral uptake of KOAc along with osmotically obligated water.

pH Profiles of K^+/H^+ and Na^+/H^+ Antiport

The pH and Mg^{2+} dependencies of mitochondrial Na^+/H^+ antiport are illustrated in Fig. 2. The plots in Fig. 2A were obtained in normal (Mg^{2+}-containing) mitochondria and further demonstrate their ability to discriminate between Na^+ and K^+. HOAc transport is very rapid, but it does contribute somewhat to estimates of initial rates. This is controlled by the curves in TEAOAc, which is not transported. The broad pH maximum for NaOAc transport is also observed in heart mitochondria (22).

Fig. 2B contains pH profiles for transport of the same acetate salts in Mg^{2+}-depleted mitochondria. It is evident, as has already been demonstrated by the experiments shown in Fig. 1, that a new pathway for K^+ transport is opened up by Mg^{2+} depletion. It also appears that a new pathway for Na^+/H^+ antiport has been unmasked by Mg^{2+} depletion. This conclusion is strengthened by the observation (4) that the difference in rates for the two cations (Na^+ minus K^+, see Fig. 2C) is nearly identical with the NaOAc curve obtained in normal mitochondria (Fig. 2A).

A plausible interpretation for the results described so far is that two independent pathways are available for Na^+/H^+ antiport in mitochondria, one of which is Mg^{2+}-dependent and transports K^+ as well as Na^+ and the other of which is Mg^{2+}-independent and does not transport K^+ (4). Unfortunately, these experiments are not capable of excluding the possibility that these processes are manifestations of a single carrier; i.e., that Na^+ is able to utilize the antiporter when it is in a conformation which can transport K^+ only slowly or not at all.

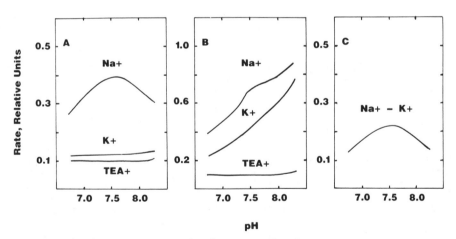

Fig. 2. **pH profiles for K^+/H^+ and Na^+/H^+ exchange in mitochondria**. Light scattering assays (21) were carried out in 55 mM acetate salts as described in Fig. 1. pH was adjusted over the range 6.5 to 8.5. <u>Fig. 2A</u>: Swelling rates in normal (Mg^{2+}-containing) mitochondria suspended in NaOAc, KOAc and TEAOAc media. <u>Fig. 2B</u>: Swelling rates in Mg^{2+}-depleted mitochondria suspended in media identical to that used in Fig. 2A. <u>Fig. 2C</u>: Difference between swelling rates observed in NaOAc and KOAc media in Mg^{2+}-depleted mitochondria.

Differential Inhibitors of the Mg^{2+}-independent and Mg^{2+}-dependent Na^+/H^+ antiporters

As pointed out in a review by Brierley and Jung (23), research on mitochondrial cation transport had been severely hampered by the lack of inhibitors of these processes. This was particularly true in regard to the issue at hand; namely, whether mitochondria possess one or two Na^+/H^+ antiporters. Beginning with the discovery in 1982 that quinine inhibits the Mg^{2+}-dependent Na^+/H^+ antiporter (4), we have now uncovered a small battery of inhibitors whose use permits a decisive resolution of this issue.

Quinine and other amphiphilic amines. We have carried out dose-response studies with quinine and quinacrine (19) as well as other amphiphilic amines (24). The Mg^{2+}-dependent Na^+/H^+ antiporter is inhibited by phenothiazines, antidepressants, antihistaminics, antiarrhythmics and local anesthetics. Jung, et al. (25) have recently confirmed that quinine and quinacrine inhibit K+ transport in beef heart mitochondria in a manner consistent with inhibition of K^+/H antiport.

The evidence from inhibitor studies strongly supports the hypothesis of two independent Na^+/H^+ antiporters and can be summarized as follows: [1] None of the amphiphilic amines studied to date inhibit Na^+/H^+ antiport in normal (Mg^{2+}-containing) mitochondria. [2] A high dose of quinine (500 μM) converts the pH profile of Mg^{2+}-depleted mitochondria, as in Fig. 2B, to that of normal mitochondria, as in Fig. 2A. That is, K^+/H antiport is completely inhibited while Na^+/H^+ antiport is only inhibited to the level observed in normal (Mg^{2+}-containing) mitochondria (4). [3] Dose-response curves for quinine inhibition of K^+/H^+ and Na^+/H^+ antiport, carried out in Mg^{2+}-depleted mitochondria, again reveal partial (50-60%) inhibition of NaOAc transport and complete inhibition of KOAc. Nevertheless, the I_{50} (40 uM) and the Hill slope (1.0) are identical in the two salts.

N,N'-dicyclohexylcarbodiimide (DCCD). In 1984, we showed that the Mg^{2+}-dependent Na^+/H^+ antiporter in mitochondria is irreversibly inhibited by DCCD (26). This discovery has enabled us to label the Mg^{2+}-dependent Na^+/H^+ antiporter with $[^{14}C]$-DCCD and to identify antiport activity with an 82 kDa protein following SDS polyacrylamide gel electrophoresis and fluorography. This is the first Na^+/H^+ antiporter to be so identified, and this carrier has now been characterized to this extent in mitochondria from liver (26), heart (27) and brown adipose tissue (27). From the kinetics of DCCD binding to the 82 kDa protein, we have estimated that rat liver mitochondria contain 7-8 pmol of Mg^{2+}-dependent Na^+/H^+ antiporter per mg mitochondrial protein (28).

The evidence from DCCD studies also seems to require that the inner membrane possesses two independent Na^+/H^+ antiporters: [1] Pretreatment with DCCD had no effect on Na^+/H^+ antiport in normal (Mg^{2+}-containing) mitochondria (26). [2] Pretreatment with DCCD under reactive conditions (26, 28) converts the pH profiles observed in Mg^{2+}-depleted mitochondria, as in Fig. 2B, to those of normal mitochondria, as in Fig. 2A. That is, K^+/H^+ antiport is completely inhibited while Na^+/H^+ antiport is only inhibited to a level consistent with Na^+/H^+ antiport in normal (Mg^{2+}-containing) mitochondria.

Igarashi and Aronson (29) have recently reported that the
renal Na^+/H^+ antiporter is also inhibited by DCCD. The inhibition is pseudo-first-order and protection is conferred by
reversible inhibitors, exactly as in mitochondria (28). These
authors have also attempted to identify the transporter, using an
approach identical to that of Martin, et al. (26, 28). While the
results are somewhat less straightforward than those obtained in
mitochondria, the authors tentatively conclude that the renal
Na^+/H^+ antiporter is a 100 kDa protein (29).

Lithium. Li^+, like Na^+, is transported in normal (Mg^{2+}-
containing) mitochondria, but at a slower rate and with a pH
profile different from that of Na^+. We observe essentially the
same pH profile for Li^+/H^+ and Na^+/H^+ antiport in rat liver
mitochondria as has been reported by Brierley, et al. (22) in
beef heart mitochondria.

If protons and cations compete for a common transport site
on the Mg^{2+}-independent Na^+/H^+ antiporter, the location of the pH
maxima for transported cations provides information on their
relative affinities for this site. This can be seen in the
following way: In acetate medium, matrix pH closely follows
medium pH due to rapid equilibration of acetic acid. Na^+ loading
from the medium is therefore favored at high pH, while H^+ loading
from the matrix is favored at low pH. This balance between
opposing pH dependencies accounts for the biphasic pH dependence
of NaOAc transport (see Fig. 2A). The pH optimum is shifted
downward from the pKa of the site, the magnitude of the shift
depending on the K_m of the site for the given cation (K. Garlid,
in preparation).

The essential fact about Li^+/H^+ antiport is that its pH
optimum is strongly down-shifted. While this fact was previously

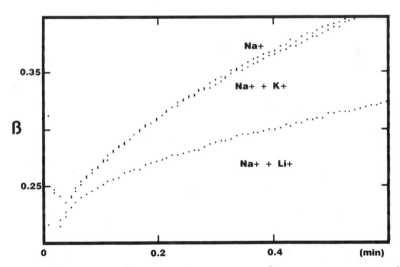

Fig. 3. **Effects of K^+ and Li^+ on the Mg^{2+}-independent Na^+/H^+**
antiporter. Mitochondria were suspended at 0.1 mg/ml in 55
mM acetate medium, pH 7.2, 25°C. In the curve marked "Na^+",
Na^+ was the sole cation (55 mM). In the curves marked "Na^+
+ K^+" and "Na^+ + Li^+", 10% of the Na^+ was substituted by the
indicated cation.

43

known (22), its significance was not recognized. The implication is that the affinity of the Na^+/H^+ antiporter for Li^+ must be much higher than that for Na^+ and, therefore, that Li^+ should inhibit Na^+ transport via this antiporter.

The data in Fig. 3 confirm this expectation and comprise the first evidence for Li^+ ion inhibition of Na^+/H^+ antiport in mitochondria. Substitution of 10% of the Na^+ by Li^+, keeping all other components constant, results in 70% inhibition of NaOAc transport. When the same experiment was carried out with 10% K^+, no inhibition was observed. In preliminary kinetic studies, we find that Li^+ is a competitive inhibitor of the Mg^{2+}-independent Na^+/H^+ antiporter, with a K_m of 1 mM (S. Nath and K. Garlid, in preparation).

Like Na^+ and K^+, Li^+ is also transported by the Mg^{2+}-dependent Na^+/H^+ antiporter, and this component of Li^+/H^+ antiport is fully inhibitable by quinine and DCCD. The transport of KOAc in Mg^{2+}-depleted mitochondria is <u>not</u> inhibited by substitution of 10% of the K^+ by Li^+, indicating that the Mg^{2+}-dependent Na^+/H^+ antiporter does not discriminate sharply between different alkali cations.

In summary, the results of inhibitor studies appear to require the existence of two Na^+/H^+ antiporters in mitochondria (4): The Mg^{2+}-dependent Na^+/H^+ antiporter transports K+ as well as Na^+, it is inhibited by amphiphilic amines and DCCD, and it is not inhibited by Li^+. The Mg^{2+}-independent Na^+/H^+ antiporter does not transport K+, it is not inhibited by amphiphilic amines or DCCD, and it is inhibited by Li^+.

Cation Specificities of the Mg^{2+}-dependent and Mg^{2+}-independent Na^+/H^+ antiporters.

Cs^+, Rb^+ and K^+ are not transported by the Mg^{2+}-independent Na^+/H^+ antiporter at detectable rates under any conditions of assay; i.e., whether the Mg^{2+}-dependent Na^+/H^+ antiporter is inhibited by quinine, by DCCD or by endogenous matrix Mg^{2+}. We conclude that these cations are not substrates for the Mg^{2+}-independent Na^+/H^+ antiporter. Furthermore, K^+ does not inhibit the Mg^{2+}-independent Na^+/H^+ antiporter (see Fig. 3).

In contrast, all alkali cations are substrates of the Mg^{2+}-dependent Na^+/H^+ antiporter. At 55 mM, they are transported at similar rates by this carrier, and no cross-inhibition can be detected using the light scattering assay. Organic cations, such as TEA^+, and divalent cations, such as Mg^{2+}, are not transported by either antiporter.

SUMMARY AND CONCLUSIONS

The two mitochondrial Na^+/H^+ antiporters differ in several important respects, and the most physiologically significant of these may be their differences in regulation. The Mg^{2+}-dependent Na^+/H^+ antiporter controls mitochondrial volume in a dangerous, high-K^+ environment. To play this vital role, this porter must always lie poised far from K^+/H^+ equilibrium; i.e., it must be under dynamic regulation, as proposed in the Mg^{2+} carrier-brake hypothesis (7). Being regulated, it is not necessary for this antiporter to be cation-selective, since all electroneutral cation movements will be followed by redistributions of anions and water. On the other hand, there is no indication at present that the Mg^{2+}-independent Na^+/H^+ antiporter is regulated. This transporter is therefore required to exhibit high discrimination against K^+ in order to prevent the collapse of matrix volume dueto uncontrolled loss of K^+ salts and water (4).

Do the properties of the mitochondrial Na^+/H^+ antiporters help us in any way to understand the plasmalemmal Na^+/H^+ anti-porters? I believe they do, if we allow that there are a limited number of ways in which nature constructs such porters. The difference in cation selectivities very likely reflects a fundamental structural difference between the two mitochondrial antiporters, and this difference appears to be mirrored in two types of plasmalemmal Na^+/H^+ antiporters. Thus, the Mg^{2+}-independent Na^+/H^+ antiporter resembles the renal tubular Na^+/H^+ antiporter in its discrimination against K^+ and its competitive inhibition by Li^+. On the other hand, the Mg^{2+}-dependent Na^+/H^+ antiporter resembles a cardiac sarcolemmal Na^+/H^+ antiporter which transports all alkali cations, including Na^+ and K^+, and which is inhibited by DCCD and amphiphilic amines (S. Kakar, A. Askari and K. Garlid, in preparation).

The existence of the latter class of antiporter in plasma-lemma may seem unlikely at first glance, since it would tend to catalyze Na^+/K^+ exchange and dissipate the effects of the Na^+,K^+-ATPase. Nevertheless, a sound design principle would be followed if the cell, like mitochondria, were to regulate volume by governing a passive back-flow process rather than an active transport process.

In conclusion, it seems premature to conclude that plasma membranes contain only one type of Na^+/H^+ antiporter. Nor does it seem likely that there is an unlimited variety of such transporters. I propose as a working hypothesis that antiporters from both mitochondria and plasmalemma may be separated into two classes: Na^+-selective and non-Na^+-selective. Within each class there may exist significant differences in regulation of Na^+/H^+ antiport (for example, see Grinstein and Rothstein (2)), and these differences may reflect interactions of the antiporters with different regulatory subunits. This hypothesis appears to provide the diversity needed to account for the known properties of the family of Na^+/H^+ antiporters, and it is also consistent with the idea that each antiporter must be regulated according to the needs of the membrane system containing it.

ACKNOWLEDGEMENTS

This research was supported by Grants GM 31086 and HL 36573 from the National Institutes of Health.

ABBREVIATIONS

DCCD, N,N'-dicyclohexylcarbodiimide; TEA^+, tetraethyl-ammonium ion.

REFERENCES

1. Krulwich, T. A. (1983) Biochim. Biophys. Acta 726, 245-264
2. Grinstein, S., and Rothstein, A. (1986) J. Membr. Biol. 90, 1-12
3. Aronson, P. S. (1985) Annu. Rev. Physiol. 47, 545-5604.
4. Nakashima, R. A., and Garlid, K. D. (1982) J. Biol. Chem. 257, 9252-9254
5. Seiler, S. M., Cragoe, E. J., Jr., and Jones, L. R. (1985) J. Biol. Chem. 260, 4869-4876
6. Aronson, P. S. and Igarashi, P. (1986) In: Current Topics in Membranes and Transport, Vol. 26 (Aronson, P. S. and Boron, W. F., eds.) pp. 57-75, Academic Press, Orlando
7. Garlid, K. D. (1980) J. Biol. Chem. 255, 11273-11279
8. Denton, R. M., and McCormack, J. G. (1985) Am. J. Physiol. 249, E543-E554
9. Hansford, R. G. (1987) Biochem. J. 241, 145-151
10. Crompton, M., and Heid, I. (1978) Eur. J. Biochem. 91, 599-608
11. Garlid, K. D. (1979) Biochem. Biophys. Res. Commun. 87, 842-847
12. Beavis, A. D., Brannan, R. D., and Garlid, K. D. (1985) J. Biol. Chem. 260, 13424-13433
13. Chappell, J. B. and Perry, S. V. (1954) Nature 173, 1094-1095
14. Tedeschi, H. and Harris, D. L. (1955) Arch. Biochem. Biophys. 58, 52-67
15. Gamble, J. L., Jr. and Garlid, K. D. (1970) Biochim. Biophys. Acta 211, 223-232
16. Garlid, K. D. (1978) Biochem. Biophys. Res. Commun. 83, 1450-1455
17. Gamble, J. L., Jr. and Hackenbrock, C. R. (1969) Federation Proc. 28, 283a
18. Mitchell, P. and Moyle, J. (1969) Eur. J. Biochem. 9, 149-155
19. Garlid, K. D., DiResta, D. J., Beavis, A. D., and Martin, W. H. (1986) J. Biol. Chem. 261, 1529-1535
20. Pfeiffer, D.R. and Lardy, H. A. (1976) Biochemistry 15, 935-943
21. Garlid, K. D., and Beavis, A. D. (1985) J. Biol. Chem. 260, 13434-13441
22. Brierley, G. P., Jurkowitz, M., and Jung, D. W. (1978) Arch. Biochem. Biophys. 190, 181-192
23. Brierley, G. P., and Jung, D. W. (1980) Pharmac. Ther. 8, 193-216
24. Martin, W. H. (1984) Ph. D. thesis, Medical College of Ohio, Toledo
25. Jung, D. W., Farooqui, T., Utz, E. and Brierley, G. P. (1984) J. Bioen. Biomemb. 16, 379-390
26. Martin, W. H., Beavis, A. D. and Garlid, K. D. (1984) J. Biol. Chem. 259, 2062-2065
27. DiResta, D. J., Kutshke, K. P., Hottois, M. D., and Garlid, K. D. (1986) Amer. J. Physiol. 251, R787-R793
28. Martin, W. H., DiResta, D. J., and Garlid, K. D. (1986) J. Biol. Chem. 261, 12300-12305

46

MONOVALENT CATION ANTIPORT REACTIONS IN ISOLATED MITOCHONDRIA

Gerald P. Brierley and Dennis W. Jung

Department of Physiological Chemistry, The Ohio State
University Medical Center, Columbus, Ohio 43210

INTRODUCTION

One of the postulates of Mitchell's chemiosmotic coupling
hypothesis (55-57) is that the mitochondrion contains transport
components that permit the movement of anions and cations across the
inner membrane. The presence of such transport reactions is now
well-established, as is the concept that these ion fluxes are secondary
to the generation of an electrochemical H^+ gradient (protonmotive
force) by the respiratory chain. There are clear indications that the
inner membrane contains at least three different antiporters that
transport monovalent cations. These are the Na^+/H^+, the
Na^+/Ca^{2+}, and the K^+/H^+ antiporters. The first two of these
components appear to be present in an active form in unmodified
mitochondria, whereas the K^+/H^+ antiporter is latent and must be
activated by specific alterations to the mitochondrion. The Na^+/H^+
and Na^+/Ca^{2+} antiporters do not appear to transport K^+, whereas the
so called K^+/H^+ component will accept Na^+, K^+ and Li^+ as
substrates. This review summarizes the evidence for the presence of each
of these transport components, their properties, and the status of
current work on their characterization, particularly with respect to
several areas of controversy.

Na^+/H^+ ANTIPORT

The presence of a Na^+/H^+ antiport in the coupling membrane of
the mitochondria was first suggested by Mitchell and Moyle (58), who
noted that the pH gradient generated by addition of a pulse of oxygen to
anaerobic mitochondria was dissipated more rapidly in the presence than
in the absence of Na^+. Like dinitrophenol, Na^+ appeared to increase
the H^+ conductivity of the membrane. The rapid Na^+-dependent H^+
movement observed varied with the initial external pH (increasing at
lower pH values) and showed a large dependence on temperature.

Mitchell and Moyle (59) also ascribed the observed passive swelling
of mitochondria in Na^+ acetate and Na^+ phosphate to the activity of
the Na^+/H^+ antiporter. Swelling in Na^+ acetate appears to result
from the fact that acetate salts contain equilibrium amounts of free
acetic acid and that the free acid readily crosses the mitochondrial

membrane. Ionization of the free acid in the matrix compartment generates acetate ion and H^+, which in turn exchanges for Na^+ on the Na^+/H^+ antiporter. The resulting net accumulation of Na^+ and acetate as an ion pair produces osmotic swelling (see 6-8 or 59 for reviews). Passive swelling of unmodified heart mitochondria in Na^+ acetate shows a pH optimum at pH 7.2-7.3 (10). Swelling in Li^+ acetate is much less rapid and does not show the characteristic pH profile seen in Na^+ acetate. Virtually no swelling can be detected in K^+, Rb^+, or Cs^+ acetates (10). The reaction in heart mitochondria is insensitive to either Mg^{2+} or to EDTA (10, but see 2 and 24). Some of the discrepancies in the literature with respect to the properties of the Na^+/H^+ antiporter appear to result from a degree of unmasking of the latent K^+/H^+ antiport (to be discussed below) and the fact that this latter component can also transport Na^+.

The activity of the Na^+/H^+ antiport can also be followed as a Na^+-induced ejection of H^+ from intact heart mitochondria (17). In this protocol the increase in H^+ was followed with a glass electrode using non-respiring mitochondria treated with mersalyl to prevent pH shifts on the phosphate transporter. This H^+ release showed a Km for Na^+ in the absence of Ca^{2+} of about 5 mM and a high V_{max} (110 nmol $H^+ \cdot mg^{-1} \cdot min^{-1}$). Crompton and Heid (17) also generated pH gradients across the mitochondrial membrane by alkali pulses and measured the distribution of Na^+. This data (17) fit well for an electroneutral, 1:1 exchange between Na^+ and H^+ at equilibrium. The exchange of Na^+/H^+ was inhibited competitively by Ca^{2+} with an apparent K_i of 0.24 mM (17).

The presence of the Na^+/H^+ antiport probably accounts for the observation that mitochondria swollen in Na^+ acetate release Na^+, but retain K^+, when contracted osmotically in sucrose (27). There are also indications that Na^+/H^+ antiport can protect Ca^{2+}-loaded heart mitochondria from the deleterious effects of pulses of acid (43). Addition of the exogenous K^+/H^+ antiporter nigericin is necessary to obtain a similar degree of protection in a K^+ medium (see also 71).

The Na^+/H^+ antiporter appears to be widely distributed throughout both the animal and plant kingdoms, but is apparently not ubiquitous. A survey of mitochondria prepared from various mammalian tissues found Na^+/H^+ antiport (as assayed by Na^+ acetate swelling) in all but lung mitochondria (20). Potato mitochondria also fail to swell passively in Na^+ acetate (38) and can be presumed to lack a Na^+/H^+ antiporter. Other mitochondria from plant sources, such as turnip mitochondria, swell in both K^+ and Na^+ acetates (60) and it is therefore not possible to conclude whether the Na^+/H^+ is present or if the swelling can all be ascribed to an activated K^+/H^+ component.

A relationship between Na^+/H^+ antiport and matrix K^+ is suggested by the observation (10) that K^+ depletion decreases the rate of passive swelling in Na^+ acetate. In addition, the rate of swelling in Na^+ acetate decreases rapidly as a function of time when heart mitochondria are stored in sucrose, but not when stored in KCl (10).

Progress in elucidating the properties of the Na^+/H^+ antiport in mitochondria has been hampered by the lack of effective inhibitors of the reaction (9). Crompton and Heid (17) found that La^{3+} blocks the reaction at high levels (25-30 $nmol \cdot mg^{-1}$) and that Ca^{2+} is a

competitive inhibitor. A less effective inhibition by Mn^{2+} has also
been noted (10). The Na^+/H^+ antiport is not affected by diltiazem or
clonazepam, reagents that affect Na^+/Ca^{2+} antiport at very low levels
(51). The Na^+/H^+ antiport also appears to be insensitive to quinine,
since passive swelling of unmodified liver or heart mitochondria is not
inhibited by this reagent (61). This property may prove specific enough
to be used to distinguish Na^+ movements on this antiporter from other
potential pathways.

Ion and H^+ movements indicative of Na^+/H^+ antiport can also be
seen in submitochondrial particles (SMP) in which the
respiration-dependent H^+ gradient has the opposite orientation from
that of intact mitochondria. SMP have been shown to acumulate monovalent
cations, with the rate of Na^+ uptake favored over that of K^+ by about
6-fold (15,24). The reaction closely resembles that promoted by the
exogenous cation/H^+ exchanger nigericin. The rate of spontaneous Na^+
uptake was nearly 70 $nmol \cdot mg^{-1} \cdot min^{-1}$ with an apparent Km of 1 mM
(24). The uptake of K^+ was slower with a similar K_m. Rosen and
Futai (72) used quinacrine fluorescence to demonstrate the presence of an
ATP-dependent ΔpH (acid interior) in SMP from rat liver and showed that
addition of Na^+ or Li^+ caused a shift in steady-state ΔpH that was
consistent with cation/H^+ antiport. Similar effects were reported by
Brierley et al (11) for respiring, Mg^{2+}-depleted SMP from heart
mitochondria. Both groups found a Km for Na^+ near 26 mM for the
cation-dependent pH change, whereas that for Li^+ was nearer 1 mM.

There is a large apparent discrepancy between the Km for Na^+ of
the Na^+/H^+ antiporter as measured in intact mitochondria (17) and
that for the corresponding reaction in SMP as measured for Na^+ uptake
(24) and for H^+-extrusion (72). These Km values are 5, 1, and 26 mM,
respectively. It is quite possible that the antiporter is not symetrical
in its exchange of Na^+ and H^+, so correspondence between the values
for SMP and mitochondria may not be necessary. However, the indications
are that Na^+/H^+ is electroneutral (17), so the lack of correspondence
between the Km for Na^+ uptake and that for Na^+-dependent H^+ release
in SMP presents a problem that needs to be resolved experimentally.

An analysis of H^+ efflux from SMP at anaerobiosis (67) concluded
that H^+ was lost by two parallel first order processes, H^+ diffusion
and H^+/cation antiport. The cation exchange component was the faster
reaction and was greater with Na^+ than K^+. A later analysis (66),
however, concluded that both the fast and the slow components of H^+
loss from SMP consist, at least in part, of charge uncompensated H^+
flow and that both can be considered as expression of the H^+-conducting
pathway of the F_0F_1-ATPase. It seems likely that virtually all
examples of cation/H^+ antiport in SMP result from contributions of a
variety of cation-conducting pathways.

Some progress in the isolation and reconstitution of the
mitochondrial Na^+/H^+ antiporter has been reported (25). Extraction
of beef heart SMP with Triton X-100 produced fractions capable of
stimulating Na^+ flux in liposomes. Whereas this approach seems quite
promising, the criteria for establishing the relationship of
transport-active fractions to the native antiporter do not yet appear to
be adequate. A more complete characterization of the properties of the
Na^+/H^+ antiporter (and more specific inhibitors) are clearly needed,
as is the characterization of possible alternative pathways for cation
conduction.

The uptake and release of Ca^{2+} by mitochondria has been the subject of intense interest for many years (see 12,22,32,65,73,76 for recent interviews). It is now well-established that mitochondria take up Ca^{2+} by a ruthenium red-sensitive uniport that is balanced kinetically by a Ca^{2+} efflux mechanism. Current evidence suggests that a Na^+/Ca^{2+} antiporter, acting in concert with with the Na^+/H^+ antiporter, provides this Ca^{2+}-efflux pathway in heart, brain and many other types of mitochondria. In this model the inward exchange of Na^+ for interior Ca^{2+} (out) is followed by a Na^+ (out) for H^+ (in) exchange that is driven by the ΔpH component of protonmotive force. In liver mitochondria the involvement of Na^+ is not as clear and many authors ascribe Ca^{2+} efflux to a $Ca^{2+}/2H^+$ antiport (see reviews cited above). Recent work by McCormack (54), however, indicates that the presence of Na^+ during isolation of liver mitochondria results in lower matrix Ca^{2+} levels and suggests that Na^+/Ca^{2+} antiport may also play a major role in Ca^{2+} homeostasis in liver mitochondria. There are indications that the Na^+/Ca^{2+} antiport may not have the same properties in liver as in heart mitochondria (46).

Evidence for the presence of a Na^+/Ca^+ antiport in heart mitochondria came first from the studies of Crompton et al (18) who found a Na^+-dependent release of accumulated Ca^{2+} that was insensitive to ruthenium red. The release was activated half-maximally by 8 mM Na^+, a value well within the physiological range of Na^+ in cardiac myocytes. Li^+ was less effective than Na^+ (K_m of 15 mM; lower V_{max}), but K^+ was ineffective. These studies were extended (19) to show that the reaction was sensitive to La^{3+} (at higher levels than those required to block the Ca^{2+} uniport) and that Ca^{2+} and Sr^{2+} induced a loss of $^{45}Ca^{2+}$ with identical inhibitor profile. The Ca^{2+}-induced efflux of Ca^{2+} was inhibited by Na^+ and showed an K_m for Ca^{2+} of 13 μM. The data are consistent with the presence of a cation antiporter able to exchange internal Ca^{2+} against external Na^+, Li^+, Ca^{2+} or Sr^{2+}.

The Na^+-dependent efflux of Ca^{2+} is stimulated by respiration and inhibited by uncouplers, whereas Ca^{2+}-dependent Ca^{2+} loss shows neither of these properties (18,19). Such responses would be consistent with an electrogenic exchange on the antiporter (such as three Na^+ for one Ca^{2+}) that would result in acceleration of the exchange by the membrane potential ($\Delta\psi$). The velocity of Na^+-induced Ca^{2+} efflux shows a sigmoid dependence on Na^+ concentration (20) and the slope of the Hill plots has been found to be near 3 under many conditions. However, the slope of such plots varies considerably with the type of heart mitochondria preparation and with incubation conditions (18,20,33,77). Brand (5), using a thermodynamic analysis, concluded that the antiporter promotes an electroneutral $Ca^{2+}/2Na^+$ exchange in rat heart mitochondria.

Crompton et al (20) and Crompton and Heid (17) raised the possibility that the Na^+/H^+ and Na^+/Ca^{2+} antiporters act in concert to extrude Ca^{2+} at the expense of ΔpH. They postulated a Na^+-dependent Ca^{2+} efflux followed by Na^+/H^+ antiport to remove the matrix Na^+. The high rate of Na^+/H^+ exchange relative to Na^+/Ca^{2+} (17) would allow Na^+/H^+ to reach equilibrium and the flux to be integrated into a cycle. The resulting cycling of Ca^{2+}, Na^+ and H^+ would explain the acceleration of the reaction by respiration, since metabolic ΔpH would be required for efficient Na^+

extrusion. An alternative interpretation, that Na^+ merely activates a Ca^{2+}/H^+ antiport has not been eliminated. However, the distribution of Ca^{2+}, H^+ and Na^+ is in line with Ca^{2+}/Na^+ exchange (17) and nigericin in a K^+ medium does not replace Na^+ in such exchanges (64). This would be expected if Na^+ activated a Ca^{2+}/H^+ exchange by removing internal acidity via Na^+/H^+ antiport.

The Na^+-dependent efflux of Ca^{2+} is markedly activated by K^+ with a K_m of 17-19 mM (21). As noted above, K^+ cannot replace Na^+ as a substrate for the antiport reaction, but it appears to promote the interaction of Na^+ and Sr^{2+} with substrate-binding sites (35). External Ca^{2+} inhibits Na^+-dependent Ca^{2+} efflux (about 70% decrease in V_{max}) by cooperative binding to sites that are half-saturated by 0.7 to 0.8 μM free Ca^{2+} (35). Binding to this site is not affected by K^+. These and other observations suggest that the Na^+/Ca^{2+} antiport may contain regulatory sites that permit the exchanger to respond to physiological changes in extramitochondrial Ca^{2+} (35). A recent study by Lukacs and Fonyo (46) indicates that Ba^{2+} is a potent inhibitor of Na^+-dependent Ca^{2+} release from heart mitochondria and that Ba^{2+} interacts with such an external regulatory Ca^{2+}-binding site.

A number of different reagents have been shown to inhibit Na^+/Ca^{2+} antiport in heart mitochondria (see Table I). Among the most effective are diltiazem, a benzothiazepine, and several other so-called Ca^{2+} antagonists (75). These include prenylamine, fendiline, nifedipine and verapamil with I_{50} values of 12,13,66 and 150 μM, respectively. Benzodiazepines, such as clonazepam, and diazepam, also inhibit Na^+-dependent Ca^{2+} release at low levels (51-53). Higher levels of these drugs have little or no effect on Ca^{2+}-uniport, Na^+/H^+ antiport and other mitochondrial reactions. They also do not effect the Na^+/Ca^{2+} reaction found in the sarcolemma of heart cells (51). It appears that these reagents can be considered specific for the mitochondrial Na^+/Ca^{2+} antiporter. The extent of inhibition of this reaction by verapamil has been reported to depend on the method of preparation of heart mitochondria and the composition of the suspending medium (77). The Na^+-dependent Ca^{2+} release in heart mitochondria, like many other Na^+ transport reactions, is inhibited by amiloride and its analogues (44), but rather high concentrations are necessary. Local anesthetics, such as butacaine, also inhibit Na^+/Ca^{2+} antiport (34).

Trifluoperazine inhibits Na^+/Ca^{2+} antiport more strongly in mitoplasts than in intact mitochondria (36) and the inhibition depends on the presence of external Ca^{2+}. These authors suggest that binding sites for the drug and for Ca^{2+} are very closely interactive, if not identical. The Na^+/Ca^{2+} antiporter is very sensitive to La^{3+} and this property has been used to devise an inhibitor-stop for the reaction (19). The Na^+-dependent release of Ca^{2+} from heart mitochondria is inhibited by Mg^{2+} at concentrations normally encountered in vivo (46; see also 14). An I_{50} of 0.5 mM Mg^{2+} was found for a sucrose medium and 1.3 mM in KCl (46). Spermine has been shown to regulate Ca^{2+} cycling in liver mitochondria (63) and this polyamine shows an I_{50} of 360 μM as an inhibitor of Na^+-induced Ca^{2+} release from beef heart mitochondria (Jung and Brierley, unpublished). The inhibition of Ca^{2+} efflux by Mg^{2+} and spermine suggests that the Na^+-dependent reaction will be much slower in vivo than that measured under optimal conditions with isolated mitochondria.

Table I   Inhibitors of Mitochondrial Na^+/Ca^{2+} Antiport

Inhibitor	I_{50} (μM)	Reference
Clonazepam	5	Matlib and Schwartz (52)
Diltiazem	7	Vaghy et al (75)
Trifluoroperazine	20	Harris and Heffron (34)
Verapamil	37	Wolkowicz et al (77)
Benzamil	90	Jurkowitz et al (44)
Dibucaine	120	Harris and Heffron (34)
Spermine	350	Jung and Brierley (unpub.)
Ba^{2+}	0.9	Lukacs and Fonyo (46)
La^{3+}	< 0.1	Crompton et al (19)
Mg^{2+}	1.3 mM	Lukacs and Fonyo (46)

Heffron and Harris (37) found that the Na^+/Ca^{2+} antiport of heart and skeletal muscle mitochondria showed only a slight dependence on temperature in the range from 17° to 34° (E_a of about 3 kcal/mole). In contrast, Harding and Fry (33) using digitonin permeabilized cells, found considerable temperature sensitivity for Na^+-dependent Ca^{2+} efflux and also noted that the K_m for Na^+ and the slope of the Hill plots changed as a function of temperature. Unpublished studies from our laboratory support the contention (33) that mitochondrial Na^+/Ca^{2+} antiport shows a high dependence on temperature. The Na^+ dependent release of Ca^{2+} shows a break in the Arhennius plot at 24°C with an E_a of 11 Kcal/mol in the higher temperature range and 29 Kcal/mol in the lower.

Crompton and Heid (17) concluded that Na^+/H^+ and Na^+/Ca^{2+} antiport took place on separate components because of the high apparent K_i for Ca^{2+} (240 μM) as an inhibitor of Na^+/H^+ exchange as compared to the K_m for Ca^{2+}/Ca^{2+} exchange (13 μM). The well-defined inhibitor profile of Na^+/Ca^{2+} antiport (Table I) along with the lack of effect of most of these reagents on Na^+/H^+ antiport, makes the presence of two separate transporters a virtual certainty. It appears that some microbial symport and antiport reactions may share a common Na^+-specific subunit (78, for example) and such a possibility should be kept in mind for these Na^+-dependent transporters of the mitochondrion (however, see 45).

K^+/H^+ ANTIPORT

Respiring mitochondria maintain a membrane potential ($\Delta\psi$) of about 200 mV (interior negative) and can be expected to take up cations electrophoretically whenever a pathway is available across the inner membrane (56). The mitochondrion appears to be able to carry out its activity in the high-K^+ environment of the cell principally because it maintains a low electrophoretic permeability to K^+ (see 6-8,39). However, it would seem unlikely that the membrane could exclude K^+ completely under all circumstances and there are numerous indications that latent uniport pathways are available in the membrane under appropriate conditions (see reviews just cited). As Garlid (30) has pointed out, even a modest K^+ traffic across the coupling membrane would require the presence of an extrusion pathway capable of balancing K^+ uniport, in order to maintain mitochondrial volume homeostasis in vivo. It is therefore somewhat paradoxical that clear-cut evidence for the presence of a K^+/H^+ antiport in the mitochondrion has been slow in emerging.

Mitchell and Moyle (58) showed that K$^+$ promotes a limited decay of ΔpH in anaerobic mitochondria following an oxygen pulse. The reaction was enhanced by a low external pH. K$^+$ also was found to support a low rate of passive swelling in acetate (59). These authors took such results as indications of the presence of a "sluggish K$^+$/H$^+$ antiport". A number of lines of evidence led to the later suggestion (7,13,41) that mitochondria contain both a K$^+$ uniport and a K$^+$/H$^+$ antiport, but that these components are normally regulated in such a way as to minimize futile K$^+$ cycling. Along the same lines, Garlid (30) concluded that a regulatory mechanism for either cation uniport, cation/H$^+$ antiport, or both pathways was a physiological necessity.

Garlid (28,30) reported a spontaneous, electroneutral efflux of K$^+$ from liver mitochondria swollen in hypotonic sucrose. This swelling-induced K$^+$ loss took place at 0°, did not require respiration, and was accompanied by an inward H$^+$ movement (measured by acetate distribution) and anion loss (30). These and other studies (29), led to the concept of the "Mg^{2+} carrier brake" in which it is proposed that matrix Mg^{2+} ions bind reversibly to the K$^+$/H$^+$ antiporter, preventing K$^+$ efflux. When the free Mg^{2+} is decreased by dilution (as in osmotic swelling) or by complexing with anions, the antiport is released from inhibition and extrudes matrix K$^+$ in exchange for external H$^+$ (30).

This concept is supported by several recent studies (1,3,11,23,26,31,42,74) in which matrix Mg^{2+} and Ca^{2+} are depleted using the divalent cation ionophore A23187 (70). The divalent cation-depleted mitochondria extrude K$^+$ in a respiration dependent, uncoupler-sensitive reaction that has the properties expected of a K$^+$/H$^+$ antiport (3,23,74). The extrusion of K$^+$ is related to the rate and extent of divalent cation depletion by A23187. The mitochondria retain a high membrane potential and do not swell during K$^+$ efflux (74). A number of lines of evidence suggest that the observed K$^+$ extrusion is not due to the weak K$^+$-ionophore capacity of A23187 itself (see 68,69). Bernardi and Azzone (3) showed that ΔpH decreases during K$^+$ extrusion and the ΔpH returns to nearly the initial value when the loss of K$^+$ is complete. This provides experimental verification that H$^+$ enters the matrix as K$^+$ is lost. Addition of valinomycin during or after K$^+$ extrusion results in a immediate shift from K$^+$ efflux to K$^+$ uptake, as the increased electrophoretic permeability allows K$^+$ to respond to Δψ (28-30). This observation can be taken as evidence that the observed K$^+$ efflux occurs against an electrochemical gradient and must be electroneutral. Nakashima and Garlid (61) showed that respiration-dependent K$^+$ efflux from liver mitochondria is inhibited by quinine and proposed that quinine acts to inhibit K$^+$/H$^+$ antiport.

The extrusion of K$^+$ from divalent cation-depleted mitochondria is greatly increased by alkaline pH and by hypertonic conditions (3) and, under each of these conditions, the K$^+$ extrusion becomes much less sensitive to uncouplers. These authors also found a strong relationship between K$^+$/H$^+$ antiport activity and Δψ. Bernardi and Azzone (3) propose that the rate of the antiporter is accelerated by a particular conformation that can be controlled by Δψ and also affected by Mg^{2+}-depletion, by elevated pH and membrane stretching.

Nakashima et al (62) established that the activation of respiration-dependent K$^+$ efflux is related to the removal of endogenous Mg^{2+}, but not Ca^{2+}. Removal of all endogenous Ca^{2+} with the ionophore ionomycin had no effect on K$^+$ efflux, whereas K$^+$/H$^+$

antiport was strongly activated by Mg^{2+} removal. Loss of 50% of endogenous K^+ did not occur until nearly 90% of the endogenous Mg^{2+} was removed by A23187, however.

Divalent cation-depleted mitochondria also show passive osmotic swelling in K^+ salts that is consistent with the entry of K^+ by K^+/H^+ antiport (1,11,26,61). The swelling of these mitochondria in K^+ acetate shows a strong activation as pH is increased (61) and the pH profile for this reaction is quite different from that of unmodified mitochondria swelling in Na^+ acetate. It was proposed that H^+ interacting with the Mg^{2+}-binding site of the antiporter could also block K^+/H^+ antiport and that increasing pH removed this inhibition (49). Nakashima and Garlid, (61) concluded from their studies of the passive swelling of divalent cation-depleted mitochondria in Na^+ and K^+ acetate that mitochondria contain both a Na^+/H^+ antiport, highly specific for Na^+ and insensitive to quinine or Mg^{2+}, and a K^+/H^+ antiport that handles both K^+ and Na^+, is regulated by Mg^{2+} and inhibited by quinine. Garlid and coworkers have used the passive swelling assay to establish an inhibitor profile for the putative K^+/H^+ antiport (48). The I_{50} for quinine was found to be 60 μM at pH 7.4 and 30μM at pH 7.8, whereas that for quinacrine was only 6 μM (31). Propranolol, dibucaine, quinidine, trifluoperazine, chlorpromazine, cyclobenzaprine and imipramine were found to be effective inhibitors (I_{50} on the order of 100 μM or less) and lidocaine, diazepam and benzocaine were ineffective as inhibitors (47).

Martin et al (49,50) used the swelling assay to establish that dicyclohexylcarbodiimide (DCCD) irreversibly inhibits K^+/H^+ antiport. DCCD does not interact with the antiporter in the presence of Mg^{2+} or at low pH. The inhibition of K^+/H^+ by H^+ is presumed to result from protonation of the Mg^{2+}-binding site, so it would appear that occupancy of this site by either H^+ or Mg^{2+} prevents the reaction with DCCD. A similar protection is provided by the reversible inhibitor, quinine (49). These authors have used these properties to differentially label an 82,000-dalton protein with [14C]-DCCD and they equate this component to the K^+/H^+ antiporter.

Depletion of mitochondrial divalent cations with A23187 also induces a passive $^{42}K^+/K^+$ exchange in heart mitochondria (42,11). The exchange is relatively non-specific. Matrix K^+ labeled with $^{42}K+$, exchanges against external K^+, Na^+, or Li^+, but not choline or tetramethylammonium ion. This exchange has properties that correspond to those of the respiration-dependent extrusion of K^+ and it is presumed that the exchange reaction reflects the activity of the K^+/H^+ antiporter operating in the absence of a metabolic ΔpH (11,42).

From the foregoing discussion it seems clear that studies of the respiration-dependent K^+ extrusion, the passive exchange of K^+ with other cations and $^{42}K+$, and passive swelling reactions are all consistent with the presence of a latent K^+/H^+ antiporter, unmasked by removal of Mg^{2+}, activated by decreased levels of matrix H^+ and by hypotonic conditions, and inhibited by Mg^{2+}, quinine, and other organic amines. All but a few of these studies also suggest that the latent antiporter exchanges Na^+ and Li^+, as well as K^+ and H^+, but does not transport choline$^+$ or TEA$^+$ (however, see 1,2,4).

Brierley, et al (11) expressed reservations as to whether all of the K^+ flux in Mg^{2+}-depleted mitochondria measured at elevated pH could be ascribed to K^+/H^+ antiport activity. In response, Garlid et al

(31) have concluded that Mg^{2+}-depletion unmasks a K^+/H^+ antiporter, opens an intrinsic anion uniporter, and does not induce a high K^+ uniport conductance. They argue that uniport pathways for K^+ and H^+ may exist, but they do not contribute significantly to the swelling reactions observed (31). In our opinion, a reasonably strong case can now be made for the presence of a K^+/H^+ antiporter in Mg^{2+}-depleted mitochondria. However, even if this premise is accepted, the question remains as to whether such a component can be mobilized to extrude cations under conditions faced by mitochondria in situ.

A recent report by Jung and Brierley (40) speaks to this issue. In this study matrix Mg^{2+} was depleted in increments and related to K^+/H^+ antiport activity as measured by passive swelling in K^+ acetate and other salts. K^+/H^+ antiport was not expressed until the total Mg^{2+} was decreased from 36 to about 8 $nmol \cdot mg^{-1}$ protein, a value in good agreement with previous estimates (3,62,74). Since it is the matrix free Mg^{2+} which is proposed as the carrier brake (30), estimates of this component were made by two different methods (40). It was found necessary to decrease free Mg^{2+} from an initial value of over 700 μM to the range from 50 to 150 μM in order to activate K^+/H^+ antiport. Corkey et al (16) have recently reported a value of 350 μM for matrix free Mg^{2+} in liver mitochondria and found no significant gradient of free Mg^{2+} between the matrix and cytosol compartments. They concluded that a high ligand binding capacity for Mg^{2+} in both compartments, combined with relatively low affinity, result in a constant free Mg^{2+} when total cell Mg^{2+} remains constant. In view of these results it it appears unlikely that matrix free Mg^{2+} would change sufficiently under conditions found in situ to fullfil the role of the "carrier brake" envisioned by Garlid (30). On the other hand, the increase in K^+/H^+ antiport in heart mitochondria correlated very well with the removal of bound Mg^{2+} from the inner membrane (40). The relationship of this Mg^{2+} component to K^+/H^+ antiport would seem to offer an explanation for a large number of in vitro observations summarized above. However, since these high affinity sites would be occupied in vivo, any role for such a component in the regulation of K^+ flux in vivo would also appear to be unlikely.

Such considerations leave the nature of the endogenous regulatory component of the K^+/H^+ antiport in doubt. It may be that the antiport is regulated by other mechanisms, such as $\Delta\psi$ (3). Alternatively, it may be that K^+/H^+ antiport is not activated under physiological conditions and that the conclusion that mitochondria require such a K^+-extrusion mechanism should be re-examined.

ACKNOWLEDGEMENTS

Studies from this laboratory were supported in part by United States Public Health Services Grant HL09364.

REFERENCES

1. Azzone, G.F., Bortolotto, F. and Zanotti, A. (1978) FEBS Lett. 96, 135-140.
2. Azzone, G.F., Zanotti, A. and Colonna, R. (1978) FEBS Lett. 96, 141-147.
3. Bernardi, P. and Azzone, G.F. (1983) Biochim. Biophys. Acta 724, 212-223.
4. Bernardi, P., Pozzan, T. and Azzone, G.F. (1982) J. Bioenerg. and Biomembr. 14, 387-403.

5. Brand, M. (1985) Biochem. J. 229, 161-166.
6. Brierley, G.P. (1976) Mol. Cell. Biochem. 10, 41-62.
7. Brierley, G.P. (1978) In: The Molecular Biology of Cell Membranes, Fleischer, S., Hatefi, Y., MacLennan, D.H. and Tzagaloff, A. (eds.) Plenum Pub. Co., pp. 295-308.
8. Brierley, G.P. (1983) In: Pathobiology of Cell Membranes, Vol. 3, Trump, B.F. and Arstila, A.V. (eds.) Academic Press, N.Y. p 23-61.
9. Brierley, G.P. and Jung, D.W. (1980) Pharmac. Ther. 8, 193-216.
10. Brierley, G.P., Jurkowitz, M. and Jung, D.W. (1978) Arch. Biochem. Biophys. 190, 203-214.
11. Brierley, G.P., Jurkowitz, M.S., Farooqui, T. and Jung, D.W. (1984) J. Biol. Chem. 259, 14672-14678.
12. Carafoli, E. (1982) In: Carafoli, E. (ed.) Membrane Transport of Calcium. Academic Press, London, p 109-139.
13. Chavez, E., Jung, D.W. and Brierley, G.P. (1977) Arch. Biochem. Biophys. 183; 460-470.
14. Clark, A.F. and Roman, I.J. (1980) J. Biol. Chem. 255, 6556-6558.
15. Cockrell, R.S. (1973) J. Biol. Chem. 248, 6828-6833.
16. Corkey, B.E., Duszynski, J., Rich, T.L., Matschinsky, B. and Williamson, J.R. (1986) J. Biol. Chem. 261, 2567-2574.
17. Crompton, M. and Heid, I. (1978) Eur. J. Biochem. 91, 599-608.
18. Crompton, M., Capano, M. and Carafoli, E. (1976) Eur. J. Biochem. 69, 453-462.
19. Crompton, M., Kunzi, M. and Carafoli, E. (1977) Eur. J. Biochem. 79, 549-558.
20. Crompton, M., Moser, R., Lundi, H. and Carafoli, E. (1978) Eur. J. Biochem. 82, 25-31.
21. Crompton, M., Heid, I. and Carafoli, E. (1980) FEBS Lett. 115, 257-259.
22. Denton, R.M. and McCormack, J.G. (1985) Am. J. Physiol. 249, E543-E554.
23. Dordick, R.S., Brierley, G.P. and Garlid, K.D. (1980) J. Biol. Chem. 255, 10299-10305.
24. Douglas, M.G. and Cockrell, R.S. (1974) J. Biol. Chem. 249, 5464-5471.
25. Dubinsky, W., Kandrach, A. and Racker, E. (1979) In: Lee, C.P., Schatz, S. and Ernster, L. (Eds) Membrane Bioenergetics, Addison-Wesley Pub. Co., Reading, Mass. p 267-280.
26. Duszynski, J. and Wojtczak, L. (1977) Biochem. Biophys. Res. Comm. 74, 417-424.
27. Gamble, J.L., Jr and Hackenbrock, C.R. (1969) Fed. Proc. 28, 283a.
28. Garlid, K.D. (1978) Biochem. Biophys. Res. Commun. 83, 1450-1455.
29. Garlid, K.D. (1979) Biochem. Biophys. Res. Commun. 87, 842-847.
30. Garlid, K.D. (1980) J. Biol. Chem. 255, 11273-11279.
31. Garlid, K.D., DiResta, D.J., Beavis, A.D. and Martin, W.H. (1986) J. Biol. Chem. 261, 1529-1535.
32. Hansford, R.G. (1985) Rev. Physiol. Biochem. Pharmacol. 102, 1-72.
33. Harding, D. and Fry, C. (1985) Biochim. Biophys. Acta. 847, 136-139.
34. Harris, E.J. and Heffron, J.J.A. (1982) Arch. Biochem. Biophys. 218, 531-539.
35. Hayat, L.H. and Crompton, M. (1982) Biochem. J. 202, 509-518.
36. Hayat, L.H. and Crompton, M. (1985) FEBS Lett. 182, 281-286.
37. Heffron, J.J.A. and Harris, E.J.(1981) Trans. Biochem. Soc. 9, 82-83.
38. Jung, D.W. and Brierley, G.P. (1979) Plant Physiol. 64, 948-953.
39. Jung, D.W. and Brierley, G.P. (1984) J. Biol. Chem. 259, 6904-6911.
40. Jung, D.W. and Brierley, G.P. (1986) J. Biol. Chem. 261, 6408-6415.
41. Jung, D.W., Chavez, E. and Brierley, G.P. (1977) Arch. Biochem. Biophys. 183, 452-459.

42. Jung, D.W., Shi, G-Y, and Brierley, G.P. (1981) Arch. Biochem. Biophys. 209, 356-361.
43. Jurkowitz, M.S. and Brierley, G.P. (1982) J. Bioenerg. Biomembr. 14, 435-449.
44. Jurkowitz, M.S., Altschuld, R.A., Brierley, G.P. and Cragoe, E.J., Jr. (1983) FEBS Lett. 162, 262-265.
45. Krulwich, T.A. (1986) J. Membrane Biol. 89, 113-125.
46. Lukacs, S.L. and Fonyo, A. (1986) Biochim. Biophys. Acta 858, 125-134.
47. Martin, W.H. (1983) Ph.D. dissertation, Medical College of Ohio, Toledo.
48. Martin, W.H. and Garlid, K.D. (1983) Fed. Proc. 42, 1278 abs.
49. Martin, W.H., Beavis, A.D. and Garlid, K.D. (1984) J. Biol. Chem. 259, 2062-2065.
50. Martin, W.H., DiResta, D.J. and Garlid, K.D. (1986) J. Biol. Chem. 261, 12300-12305.
51. Matlib, M.A. (1986) Biophys. J. 49, 206a.
52. Matlib, M.A. and Schwartz, A. (1983) Life Sci. 32, 2837-2842.
53. Matlib, M.A., Lee, S-W., Depover, A. and Schwartz, A. (1983) Eur. J. Pharmacol. 89, 327-328.
54. McCormack, J.B. (1985) Biochem. J. 231, 597-608.
55. Mitchell, P. (1966) Glynn research, Bodmin, Cornwall.
56. Mitchell, P. (1968) Glynn Research, Bodmin, Cornwall.
57. Mitchell, P. (1970) Symp. Soc. Gen. Microbiol. 20, 121-166.
58. Mitchell, P. and Moyle, J. (1967) Biochem. J. 105, 1147-1162.
59. Mitchell, P. and Moyle, J. (1969) Eur. J. Biochem. 9, 149-155.
60. Moore, A.L. and Wilson, S.B. (1977) J. Exp. Bot. 28, 607-618.
61. Nakashima, R.A. and Garlid, K.D. (1982) J. Biol. Chem. 257, 9252-9254.
62. Nakashima, R.A., Dordick, R.S. and Garlid, K.D. (1982) J. Biol. Chem. 257, 12540-12545.
63. Nicchitta, C.V. and Williamson, J.R. (1984) J. Biol. Chem. 259, 12978-12983.
64. Nicholls, D.G. (1978) Biochem. J. 170, 511-522.
65. Nicholls, D.G. and Ackerman, K. (1982) Biochim. Biophys. Acta 683, 57-88.
66. Pansani, A., Guerrieri, F. and Papa, S. (1978) Eur. J. Biochem. 92, 545-551.
67. Papa, S. Guerrieri, F., Simone, S., Lorusso, M. and Larosa, D. (1973) Biochim. Biophys. Acta 292, 20-38.
68. Pfeiffer, D.R. and Lardy, H.R. (1976) Biochemistry 15, 935-943.
69. Pyant, K.S. and Brierley, G.P. (1982) Experientia 38, 1202-1204.
70. Reed, P.W. and Lardy, H.A. (1972) J. Biol. Chem. 247, 6970-6977.
71. Roman, I., Gomaj, P., Nowicka, C. and Angielski, S. (1979) Eur. J. Biochem. 102, 615-623.
72. Rosen, B.P. and Futai, M. (1980) FEBS Lett. 117, 39-43.
73. Saris, N.E. and Akerman, K.E.O. (1980) Cur. Topics Bioenergetics 10, 103-179.
74. Shi, G-Y., Jung, D.W., Garlid, K.D. and Brierley, G.P. (1980) J. Biol. Chem. 255, 10306-10311.
75. Vaghy, P.L., Johnson, J.D., Matlib, M.A., Wang, T. and Schwartz, A. (1982) J. Biol. Chem. 257, 6000-6002.
76. Williamson, J.R., Cooper, R.H. and Hoek, J.B. (1981) Biochim. Biophys. Acta 639, 243-295.
77. Wolkowicz, P., Michael, L.H., Lewis, R.M. and McMillan-Wood, J. (1983) Am. J. Physiol. 244, H644-H651.
78. Zilberstein, D., Ophir, I.J., Padan, E. and Schuldiner, S. (1982) J. Biol. Chem. 257, 3692-3696.

THE HEPATIC MICROSOMAL Ca^{2+} SEQUESTERING SYSTEM

Naomi Kraus-Friedmann, C. Ricky Fleschner[+],
Piotr Zimniak[++] and Pamela Moore[+++]

Dept. of Physiology and Cell Biology
University of Texas Medical School
P.O. Box 20708, Houston, TX   77225   U.S.A.

The hepatic microsomal Ca^{2+} sequestering system is analogous to that of sarcoplasmic reticulum and fulfills a similar role to it; namely, regulation of cytoplasmic Ca^{2+} concentration. It does so by taking up Ca^{2+} in an ATP dependent manner and releases it by either the reversal of the uptake process and/or by a different, unknown mechanism.

Of these two processes the reactions involved in the uptake of Ca^{2+} are the better understood. This chapter focuses mainly on studies which were carried out in our laboratory on the Ca^{2+} uptake process.

The first description of Ca^{2+} uptake by vesicles prepared from the hepatic microsomal fraction by Moore et al. (1) described the ATP requirement and pH dependence of the system and the need for oxalate to support the accumulation of Ca^{2+}. The K_m for ATP was 1.8 mM, and the apparent K_m for Ca^{2+} was 23 μM. The smooth endoplasmic reticulum was found to be more enriched in the enzyme than was the rough endoplasmic reticulum. The enzyme could be inhibited by chloromecuribenzoate and mersalyl. Subsequent studies in other laboratories confirmed these initial observations (2-6).

In some of the earlier studies in our laboratory the method outlined by Moore et al. (1) was employed to study Ca^{2+} uptake (5,6). Thus $^{45}Ca^{2+}$, the millipore technique and long incubation periods were used. The high Mg^{2+} concentration present in the incubation mixture made the detection of Ca^{2+}-ATPase activity difficult in those studies. More recently, the assay conditions were changed enabling us to further characterize of the enzyme (7,8).

[+]Present address: Department of Biochemistry, Kirksville College of Osteopathic Medicine, Kirksville, MO 63501.

[++]Present address: Department of Internal Medicine, Division of Gastroenterology, University of Texas Medical School at Houston.

[+++]Present address: Laboratory Animal Research Center, Rockerfeller University, New York, NY 10021.

A typical uptake curve using the millipore technique is presented in Fig. 1. It shows that Sr^{2+} is taken up in a similar fashion to Ca^{2+}. Both Ca^{2+} and Sr^{2+} uptake are ATP-dependent and the accumulated ions can be released from the vesicular space by an ionophore. An examination of the rates of the uptake reveals a considerably slower rate from that observed in the sarcoplasmic reticulum derived vesicles. This large difference in rate can be explained by the differences in the protein composition of the membrane fractions. The major protein in the sarcoplasmic reticulum is the Ca^{2+}-ATPase, which represents about 60-80% of the total protein (9). In contrast, the endoplasmic reticulum fulfills a wide variety of functions and the pumping of the Ca^{2+} is only one of them. It is estimated that the Ca^{2+} ATPase represents about 1% or less of the total proteins present.

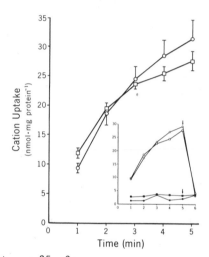

Fig. 1. $^{45}Ca^{2+}$ and $^{85}Sr^{2+}$ uptake by rat liver microsomal fraction.

$^{45}Ca^{2+}$ uptake and $^{85}Sr^{2+}$ uptake were measured as described in Experimental Procedure. Addition to be basic incubation medium was 5 mM $MgCl_2$. The data plotted represent the means ± SEM of four experiments. $^{45}Ca^{2+}$ uptake (□); $^{85}Sr^{2+}$ uptake (O). The data of the insert represent the results of a typical expertiment. $^{45}Ca^{2+}$ uptake (□,▨); $^{85}Sr^{2+}$ uptake (O, ◕); ATP omitted (▨, ●). At the time point indicated by the arrows, 1 μM A23187 was added. (From Ref. 8).

The ATPase activity of the enzyme is higher than the measured rate of uptake (Table 1). The reasons for this are probably the leakiness of the vesicles and maybe the lack of certain coupling factors. Even so, the rate of the ATPase activity, because of the above mentioned reasons, is much less than the observed rates in the sarcoplasmic reticulum (10).

Examination of the data in Table 1 reveals two important characteristics of the microsomal system: 1) The preparation possesses a Mg^{2+} dependent enzyme which breaks down ATP. As to be discussed in more detail below, this enzyme activity is not a transport ATPase. 2) There is a Ca^{2+} dependent ATPase present, the activity of which is strongly inhibited by Mg^{2+}. Thus, only in the presence of low Mg^{2+} concentration is the activity of the Ca^{2+}-ATPase detectable. In the presence of 5 mM Mg^{2+}, a concentration commonly employed in Ca^{2+} uptake studies, the Ca^{2+} ATPase activity is not measurable. This point is going to be discussed later.

Table 1. Ca^{2+} and Mg^{2+} dependent ATP utilization of the microsomal fraction

Additions	ATPase activity, nmoles Pi liberated/mg protein	
	$-Ca^{2+}$	$+Ca^{2+}$
none	877 ± 88	1442 ± 150
0.1 mM Mg^{2+}	1134 ± 109	1528 ± 252
5.0 mM Mg^{2+}	1886 ± 300	1822 ± 109

The activities of both the Ca^{2+} and the Mg^{2+}-ATPases are associated with phosphoprotein formation (Fig. 2). The Ca^{2+}-dependent phosphoprotein has a Mr of approximately 125,000. This value is close to the reported Mr from other laboratories for the phosphoenzyme intermediate of the microsomal Ca^{2+}-ATPase (4,11). The Ca^{2+} dependent phosphoprotein is labile in hydroxylamine and NaOH; thus, it is likely to be an acyl phosphate and phosphorylated intermediate of the Ca^{2+} -ATPase.

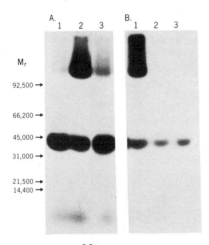

Fig. 2. Autoradiogram of ^{32}P-labelled hepatic microsomal proteins

Phosphorylation, SDS/polyacrylamide-gel electrophoresis and autoradiography were performed as described in the Experimental section. Additions to the basic incubation medium were as follows. (a): Lane 1, 2 mM EGTA, 0.1 mM-$MgCl_2$; lane 2, 2 mM-EGTA, 0.1 mM-$MgCl_2$; 2.05 mM-$CaCl_2$; lane 3, 2 mM-EGTA, 1.1 mM-$MgCl_2$; (b): lanes 1-3, 2 mM-EGTA, 0.1 mM-$MgCl_2$, 2.05 mM-$CaCl_2$. In (a) the resultant free Ca^{2+}, free Mg^{2+} and MgATP concentrations were (respectively): lane 1, 18 nM, 0.6 mM, 0.16 μM; lane 2, 75 μM, 0.6 mM, 0.15 μM; lane 3, 18 nM, 1.6 mM, 18 nM. (b) Phosphoprotein stability: phosphoprotein samples were examined for this as described in the text. Lane 1, control; lane 2, 0.8 M-hydroxylamine; lane 3, 0.5 M-NaOH. (From Ref. 7)

In contrast, the Mg^{2+}-dependent phosphoprotein is stable in hydroxylamine and NaOH; thus, it is likely to be a phosphoester. Such a phosphoprotein could result from the activity of either a Mg^{2+}-dependent phosphatase or kinase. The formation of the Mg^{2+}-dependent phospho-enzyme was shown to be inhibited by the presence of Ca^{2+} in the incubation mixture (7,8,12). This observation is important for the evaluation of the absolute values of the Ca^{2+} ATPase activity. The activity of this enzyme is estimated routinely by the subtraction of the so-called basal, Mg^{2+}-dependent activity from the activity obtained in the presence of Ca^{2+}. Because Ca^{2+} suppresses the Mg^{2+}-dependent phosphorylation and ATP breakdown, it is evident that the value of the basal activity is a variable depending on the Ca^{2+} concentration. Thus, the Ca^{2+} ATPase activity obtained is always somewhat underestimated.

The fact that Ca^{2+} suppresses the Mg^{2+}-dependent phosphoenzyme formation is also relevant to the observation that under conditions of maximal Ca^{2+} uptake, namely in the presence of 5 mM Mg^{2+}, Ca^{2+}-ATPase activity is not detectable. It is likely, in light of the above, that the Ca^{2+}-ATPase activity is masked by the decrease in the Mg^{2+}-dependent phosphoenzyme formation. This might, at least partially, explain the paradoxical finding that under optimal conditions for Ca^{2+} uptake no Ca^{2+}-ATPase activity is detectable.

Dissociation between Ca^{2+}-ATPase activity and Ca^{2+} uptake was also evident in other experimental conditions. Many different substrates generate inorganic phosphate in a Ca^{2+}-dependent manner (Table 2). However, the activation of the Ca^{2+} ATPase is coupled to the stimulation of Ca^{2+} uptake only with ATP. While ADP seemingly does substitute for ATP to some extent, closer examination reveals that ADP stimulation of Ca^{2+} uptake is due to the regeneration of ATP, probably through the activity of an adenylate kinase. This conclusion is based on the observation that the stimulatory effect of ADP is abolished in the presence of AP_5A, an inhibitor of adenylase kinase, or in the presence of hexokinase and glucose, a condition leading to ATP depletion.

Table 2. Nucleotide specificity of Ca^{2+} transport and Ca^{2+}-ATPase activity

Substrate	Ca^{2+} transport		Ca^{2+} ATPase
	Rate	Accumulation	
ATP	100	100	100
ADP	55	100	53
ADP+HK+glucose	0	0	-
ADP+Ap_5A	10	-	-
AMP	0	0	17
GTP	5	4	87
CTP	0	0	81
ITP	0	0	74
UTP	0	0	50
pNPP	0	0	131

Abbreviations:
    HK- hexokinase
    AP_5A-P^1, P^5-di(adenosine 5')pentaphosphate
    pNPP- p-nitrophenylphosphate.

An additional parameter which affects Ca^{2+}-uptake and Ca^{2+}-ATPase activity differently is the pH. While Ca^{2+} uptake is very pH sensitive with a pH optimum of 6.8, the Ca^{2+} ATPase activity is far less sensitive to pH (unpublished data). Thus, Ca^{2+} ATPase and Ca^{2+} uptake activities were shown to differ in three parameters: a) pH sensitivity; b) nucleotide specificity; and, c) requirements for Mg^{2+}.

A similar dissociation of Ca^{2+} transport and Ca^{2+} ATPase activity was observed in the liver plasma membrane by Lin (13,14), and by Minami and Penniston (this volume) in the corpus luteum plasma membrane. These authors suggested that the dissociation is due to the presence in those membranes of both Ca^{2+}-pumping ATPase and a Ca^{2+}-dependent nucleoside triphosphatase which is different from the Ca^{2+} pumping enzyme. It is possible that a similar situation exists in the hepatic microsomal fraction. Alternatively, it might be that the enzyme has different binding sites for the different nucleotides; thus, binding of ATP would result in both ATP splitting and activation of transport, while binding of the other nucleotides or pNPP would activate only the Ca^{2+}-ATPase.

Another possibility is the presence or need for coupling factor(s) to activate uptake. Such coupling factors have been described in the sarcoplasmic reticulum (15,16). Thus, the conditions described might affect the association of the coupling factor with the Ca^{2+}-ATPase. It is clear that the observations indicating a dissociation of Ca^{2+} uptake and Ca^{2+}-ATPase activity under certain experimental conditions necessitate further studies before conclusions can be drawn about the reasons for it.

As mentioned before, the hepatic microsomal Ca^{2+}-ATPase resembles the sarcoplasmic reticulum Ca^{2+}-ATPase in molecular weight and in the formation of a phosphorylated intermediate. The sarcoplasmic reticulum enzyme contains two ATP binding sites, a high affinity binding site with a K_m of 1-5 μM, and a low affinity site. The former is considered to be the catalytic site which, in the presence of Ca^{2+}, is phosphorylated by ATP. The low affinity binding site for ATP might regulate the interaction of the monomers of the enzyme. Alternatively, the enzyme might possess a single ATP binding site which has two configurations. It was demonstrated that the compound fluorescein isothiocyanate (FITC) binds specifically to the ATP binding site by combining with an essential lysine residue present at the binding site (17,18). It was therefore of interest to explore the possibility that the microsomal enzyme also has a lysine containing ATP-binding site by employing FITC.

The microsomal fraction was labelled with FITC using the method described in Refs. 16 and 17. An essential feature of the method is the fact that the labelling has to be done at alkaline pH (pH 8.8-9). Because the optimal pH for Ca^{2+}-uptake and enzyme activity is acidic (pH 6.8) the use of basic pH for the labeling leads to some loss of activity by itself. This loss was estimated by using appropriate controls.

Preincubation of the microsomal fraction with 50 μM FITC resulted in an almost complete inhibition of Ca^{2+} transport (12). The inhibitory effect of FITC could be prevented to a large extent by including 5 mM ATP in the incubation medium. This finding supports the notion that FITC interacts with the ATP binding sites.

Similarly to the uptake, preincubation with FITC inhibited the Ca^{2+} ATPase activity and also the formation of the phosphorylated intermediate of the enzyme. Thus, one can conclude from these data that, like the sarcoplasmic reticulum Ca^{2+} ATPase, the ATP-binding site of the hepatic enzyme also contains an essential lysine residue.

In contrast to the Ca^{2+}-ATPase activity, the basal Mg^{2+} dependent ATP breakdown was not inhibited by preincubation with FITC. This is in line with the conclusion reached earlier that this activity represents either a Mg^{2+}-dependent phosphatase or kinase. Thus, the ATP binding site of that enzyme is not identical with that of the ion transporting ATPases.

Another similarity between the hepatic microsomal fraction and the sarcoplasmic reticulum relates to calmodulin. It has been demonstrated that the sarcoplasmic reticulum contains calmodulin (19,20). Also, two specific calmodulin antagonists, calmidazolium and compound 48/80, were shown to inhibit Ca^{2+} uptake in sarcoplasmic reticulum derived vesicles. However, in this system the Ca^{2+}-ATPase activity was not affected by the drugs. These drugs also inhibited the calmodulin-dependent phosphoryl-ation of three proteins, with molecular weights of 80,000, 60,000 and 20,000 Daltons. Based on their studies, the authors suggested that the calmodulin dependent phosphorylation has a functional role in coupling ATP hydrolysis to Ca^{2+} uptake, perhaps through the regulation of Ca^{2+} release (21).

Calmodulin-dependent phosphorylation and stimulation of Ca^{2+} uptake was also reported to occur in the cardiac sarcoplasmic reticulum (22,23,24). The protein phosphorylated was identified in most of the studies as a 22,000 Dalton protein called phospholamban. As mentioned before, a similar molecular weight protein was shown by Famulski and Carafoli (4) to be phosphorylated in the hepatic microsomal fraction though in our laboratory we could not confirm this observation. Because of the above observations obtained in the sarcoplasmic reticulum it was of interest to us to clarify whether calmodulin is a component of the hepatic microsomal fraction. In order to do so the microsomal fraction was applied to a fluphenazine-sepharose calmodulin affinity column. The fractions specifically binding to the column in a Ca^{2+}-dependent manner were eluted and analyzed by sodium dodecyl sulphate/polyacrylamide gel electrophoresis. This method revealed the presence of tightly bound calmodulin in the microsomal fraction. Similar results were obtained by the method of Western-blot analysis (Fig. 3). Calmodulin also stimulated Ca^{2+} uptake when added to partially calmodulin depleted microsomes. Similarly, the calmodulin antagonist trifluoperazine inhibited Ca^{2+}-uptake. Calmodulin also stimulated Ca^{2+}-ATPase activity (25).

These results confirmed the previous observation on the calmodulin sensitivity of the hepatic microsomal fraction (4,26). In contrast, Dawson and Fulton were unable to detect calmodulin-sensitivity in this fraction (27).

In summary, according to the present results obtained on the interaction of calmodulin with the microsomal fraction, one can state that it was proven unequivocally that calmodulin is a component of the microsomal fraction. The majority of the data point to a role for calmodulin in the Ca^{2+} sequestering process. Whether calmodulin acts by affecting uptake or release of Ca^{2+} or by somehow coupling the uptake and Ca^{2+} ATPase activities is not clear. Whether calmodulin is involved in the hormonally stimulated release of Ca^{2+} from the endoplasmic reticulum is not yet known.

The hormonal effects on Ca^{2+} release from the endoplasmic reticulum are currently a focus of scientific activity. Initially, studies from our laboratory demonstrated the hormone sensitivity of the system (5,6). Addition of glucagon or cyclic-AMP to perfused rat livers resulted in increased Ca^{2+} uptake by the subsequently isolated microsomal fraction. The hormonal treatment increased the Vmax of Ca^{2+} uptake but had no influence on the affinity of the enzyme for Ca^{2+}.

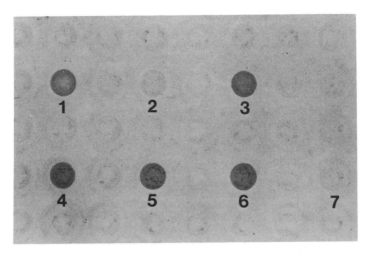

Fig. 3. Western blot analysis of microsomal EDTA extract before chromatography and elution from the fluphenazine affinity matrix

(1) 40 μl of fluphenazine-column-eluted microsomal proteins; (2) 40 ul of microsomal proteins eluted from a calmodulin-Sepharose column; (3), 40 μl of microsomal extract before chromatography; (4), (5) and (6), 40, 80 and 120 μl respectively of standard chicken gizzard calmodulin (0.09 mg/ml); (7), 40 μl of aldolase (1 mg/ml). (From Ref. 25).

The mechanism of the hormonal stimulation was not established. Because the microsomal fraction was known to possess enzymes of phospholipid metabolism we explored the possibility that the hormonal effects are mediated by stimulation of phospholipid methylation. Epinephrine and glucagon treatment indeed stimulated phospholipid methylation (28). However, careful examination by the use of stimulators and inhibitors of phospholipid methylation did not support the notion that the processes are functionally connected; namely, that phospholipid methylation occurs first, resulting in increased Ca^{2+} uptake. The most pertinent data are presented in Table 3. They show that addition of S-adenosyl methionine (SAM) to the isolated microsomal fraction stimulated phospholipid methylation as expected; however, the stimulation of phospholipid methylation was not associated with increased Ca^{2+} uptake. A lack of correlation between the two processes was also shown using S-adenosyl homocysteine (SAHC), an inhibitor of the methylation process (Table 3, Ref. 29).

Studies on cyclic-AMP stimulated phosphorylation also gave inconclusive results. While cyclic AMP did increase the phosphorylation of microsomal proteins, the phosphorylation, at least in our experiments, was not associated with a specific protein but seemed to be uniformly increased (unpublished data.)

Another possibility which has to be considered is that the increase in the V_{max} of the Ca^{2+} uptake process is connected with the hormonal stimulation of Ca^{2+} efflux from the endoplasmic reticulum. Recent studies have indicated that the endoplasmic reticulum is the major Ca^{2+} storage site and a compartment from which Ca^{2+} is released upon hormonal stimuli (30). It was shown previously that glucagon and catecholamines release Ca^{2+} from the liver (31,32). It is possible that following the exposure of the liver to glucagon or epinephrine, Ca^{2+} is released from the endoplasmic reticulum. The microsomal fraction which is subsequently isolated might be then more depleted of Ca^{2+} than the microsomal fraction prepared from untreated livers. This might then result in increased uptake. This explanation is in line with the observation that only the V_{max} of Ca^{2+} uptake is stimulated while the hormonal treatment has no effect on the Ca^{2+} ATPase activity (6). Clearly, the exact mechanisms by which hormones affect microsomal Ca^{2+} sequestering is not yet known.

Table 3. Phospholipid methylation rates and Ca^{2+} uptake in isolated microsomal vesicles

Additions (μM) SAM or SAHC	Methylation pmol/mg/min		^{45}Ca uptake nmoles/mg min	
	SAM	SAHC*	SAM	SAHC
0	-	94	0.37	0.72
5	110	14	0.50	0.68
10	127	11	0.50	0.74
50	181	5	0.49	0.74

*Phospholipid methylation and $^{45}Ca^{2+}$ uptake were measured simultaneously as described in ref. 29. The pH of the assay medium was 7.4, which accounts for the low rate of uptake.
SAM = S-adenosyl-t-methionine
SAHC = S-adenosyl-homocysteine
*SAHC, 5 μM SAM was also present.

REFERENCES

1) Moore, L., Chen, T., Knapp, H.R. Jr. and Landon E.J. Energy-dependent calcium sequestration activity in rat liver, microsomes. J. Biol. Chem. 250, 4562-4568, 1974.
2) Bygrave, F.L. Properties of energy-dependent calcium transport by rat liver microsomal fraction as revealed by initial-rate measurements. Biochem J. 170, 87-91, 1978.
3) Dawson, A.P. Kinetic properties of the Ca^{2+} accumulation system of a rat liver microsomal fraction. Biochem. J. 206, 73-79, 1982.
4) Famulski, K. and Carafoli, E. Ca^{2+} transporting activity of membrane fractions isolated from the post mitochondrial supernatant of rat liver. Cell Calcium 3, 263-281, 1982.
5) Andia-Waltenbaugh, A.M. and Friedmann, N. Hormone sensitive calcium uptake by liver microsomes. Biochem. Biophys. Res. Comm. 82, 603-608, 1978.
6) Andia-Waltenbaugh, A.M., Lam, A. Hummel, L. and Friedmann, N. Characterization of the hormone-sensitive Ca^{2+} uptake activity of the hepatic endoplasmic reticulum. Biochim. Biophys. Acta 630, 165-175, 1980.

7) Fleschner, C.R., Kraus-Friedmann, N. and Wibert, G.J. Phosphorylated intermediates of two hepatic microsomal ATPase. Biochem. J. 226, 839-845, 1985.

8) Fleschner, C.R. and Kraus-Friedmann, N. The effect of Mg^{2+} on hepatic microsomal Ca^{2+} and Sr^{2+} transport. Eur. J. Biochem. 154, 313-320, 1986.

9) De Meis, L.D. and Inesi, G. The transport of calcium by sarcoplasmic reticulum and various microsomal preparations. In: Membrane Transport of Calcium (E. Carafoli, ed.), pp. 141-186, Academic Press, London, 1982.

10) Martonosi, A. and Feretos, R. Sarcoplasmic reticulum. II. Correlation between adenosine triphosphatase activity and Ca^{2+} uptake. J. Biol. Chem. 239, 659-668, 1964.

11) Heilmann, C., Spanner, C. and Gerok, W. The calcium pump in rat liver endoplasmic reticulum. Demonstration of the phosphorylated intermediate. J. Biol. Chem. 259, 11139-11144, 1984.

12) Fleschner, C.R. and Kraus-Friedmann, N. Inhibition of rat liver microsomal Ca^{2+} ATPase by fluorescein S-isothiocyanate. (Submitted).

13) Lin, S.-H. Novel ATP-dependent calcium transport component from rat liver plasma membranes. J. Biol. Chem. 260, 7850-7856, 1985.

14) Lin, S.-H. and Fain, J.N. Purification of $(Ca^{2+}-Mg^{2+})$-ATPase from rat liver plasma membranes. J. Biol. Chem. 259, 3016-3020, 1984.

15) Racker, E. and Eytan, E. A coupling factor from sarcoplasmic reticulum required for the translocation of Ca^{2+} ions in a reconstituted Ca^{2+} ATPase pump. J. Biol. Chem. 250, 7533-7534, 1975.

16) Leonard, S.K., and Kutchai, H. Coupling of Ca^{2+} transport to ATP hydrolysis by Ca^{2+} ATPase of sarcoplasmic reticulum potential role of the 53-kilodalton glycoprotein. Biochemistry 24, 4876-4884, 1985.

17) Pick, U. Interaction of fluorescein isothiocyanate with nucleotide-binding sites of the Ca^{2+}-ATPase from sarcoplasmic reticulum. Eur. J. Biochem. 121, 187-195 (1981).

18) Mitchinson, C., Wilderspin, A.F., Tinnamann, B.J. and Green, N.M. Identification of a labeled peptide after stoichiometric reaction of fluorescein isothiocyanate with the Ca^{2+} dependent adenosine triphosphatase of sarcoplasmic reticulum. FEBS Lett. 146, 87-92, 1982.

19) Chiesi, M. and Carafoli, E. Role of calmodulin in skeletal muscle sarcoplasmic reticulum. Biochemistry 22, 985-993, 1983.

20) Campbell, K.P. and MacLennan, D.H. A calmodulin-dependent protein kinase system from skeletal muscle sarcoplasmic reticulum. J. Biol. Chem. 257, 1238-1246, 1982.

21) Tuana, B.S. and MacLennan, D.H. Calmidazolium and compound 48/80 inhibit calmodulin-depend protein phosphorylation and ATP-dependent Ca^{2+}-uptake but not Ca^{2+} ATPase activity in skeletal muscle sarcoplasmic reticulum. J. Biol. Chem. 259, 6979-6983, 1984.

22) Louis, C.F. and Maffitt, M. Characterization of calmodulin-mediated phosphorylation of cardiac muscle sarcoplasmic reticulum. Arch. Biochem. Biophys. 218, 109-118, 1982.

23) Kirchberger, M.A. and Antoneta, T. Calmodulin-mediated regulation of calcum transport and $(Ca^{2+} + Mg^{2+})$ activated ATPase activity in isolated cardiac sarcoplasmic reticulum. J. Biol. Chem. 257, 5685-5691, 1982.

24) Plank, B., Wyskowsky, W., Helmann, G. and Suko, J. Calmodulin-dependent elevation of calcium-transport associated with calmodulin dependent phosphorylation in cardiac sarcoplasmic reticulum. Biochim. Biophys. Acta. 732, 99-109, 1983.

25) Moore, P.B. and Kraus-Friedmann, N. Hepatic microsomal Ca^{2+} ATPase. Biochem. J. 214, 69-75, 1983.

26) Famulski, K.F. and Carafoli, E.   Calmodulin-dependent protein phosphorylation and calcium uptake in rat-liver microsomes. Eur. J. Biochem. 141, 15-20, 1984.

27) Dawson, A.P. and Fulton, D.W. Some properties of the Ca^{2+}-stimulated ATPase of a rat liver microsomal fraction. Biochem. J. 210, 405-410, 1983.

28) Kraus-Friedmann, N. and Zimniak, P.   Glucagon and epinephrine stimulated phospholipid methylation in hepatic microsomes.   Life Sciences 28:1483-1488, 1981.

29) Kraus-Friedmann, N. and Zimniak, P. $^{45}Ca^{2+}$ uptake and phospholipid methylation in isolated rat liver microsomes.   Cell Calcium 4, 139-150, 1983.

30) Burgess, G.M., Godfrey, P.P., McKinney, J.S., Berridge, M.J., Irvine, R.F. and Putney, J.W., Jr.   The second messenger linking receptor activation to internal Ca release in liver.   Nature, 309, 63-66, 1984.

31) Friedmann, N. and Park, C.R.   Early effects of 3-5'AMP on the fluxes of calcium and potassium in the perfused liver of normal and adrenalectomized rats.   Proc. Natl. Acad. Sci.   USA 61, 504-508, 1968.

32) Kraus-Friedmann, N.   Hormonal regulation of hepatic gluconeogenesis.   Physiol. Rev. 64, 170-259, 1984.

REGULATION OF LIVER PLASMA MEMBRANE Ca^{2+} PUMP

Sophie Lotersztajn, Catherine Pavoine, Ariane Mallat and Françoise Pecker

Unité INSERM 99
hôpital Henri Mondor
94010 Créteil

INTRODUCTION

In mammalian tissues, Na^{2+}/Ca^{2+} exchange and ATP-dependent Ca^{2+} pump supported by a (Ca^{2+}-Mg^{2+})ATPase, both located in the plasma membranes, are the two mechanisms responsible for extrusion of Ca^{2+} out of the cell against its electrochemical gradient (for a review, see ref. 1). The extracellular free Ca^{2+} concentration is about 10^4 times that of intracellular free Ca^{2+} (50-200 nM). Therefore, the maintenance of a low intracellular free Ca^{2+} level is critical to preserve the integrity of the cell and its responsiveness to multiple external stimuli. It is now well established that a wide variety of hormones and neurotransmitters exert their effects by mobilizing Ca^{2+} from intracellular stores, namely endoplasmic reticulum[1]. The resulting increase in free cytosolic Ca^{2+} is supposed to be the signal which initiates cellular responses[1]. However, considering the limited capacity of intracellular stores and the maintenance of elevated Ca^{2+} after the stimulus, one may assume that inhibition of the liver Ca^{2+} pump by Ca^{2+} mobilizing hormones explain the prolonged physiological responses. The purpose of the present report is to make the point on our recent results concerning the liver plasma membrane Ca^{2+} pump and its regulation.

MATERIALS AND METHODS

ATPase[2] and phosphorylation[3] assays were carried out as previously described, using rat liver plasma membranes prepared from 100-120 g female albino Wistar rats according to Neville[4] up to step 11. Calcium uptake was measured, as described in[3] according to Chan and Junger[5], in plasma membrane vesicles prepared according to Pilkis et al[6]. Reconstitution of purified (Ca^{2+}-Mg^{2+})ATPase into phospholipid vesicles was performed as described in ref. 7 and Ca^{2+} uptake and (Ca^{2+}-Mg^{2+})ATPase activity in reconstituted vesicles were measured under the same assay conditions, as decribed in ref. 7. Inhibitor activity was assayed as described in ref. 8 on the basis of its ability to inhibit the activity of the partially purified liver (Ca^{2+}-Mg^{2+})ATPase measured in the presence of activator. One unit of inhibitor was defined as the amount of inhibitor that caused 50% of maximal inhibition. Highly purified porcine glucagon and insulin

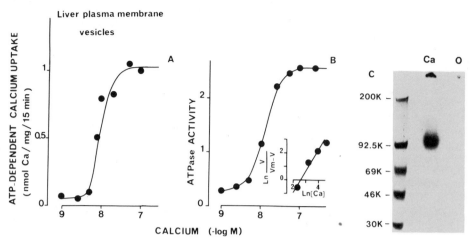

Fig. 1. Definition of the three kinetics components of the liver Ca²⁺ pump. (A) The ATP-dependent calcium uptake was measured in liver plasma membrane vesicles prepared according to Pilkis[6], as described in[3], in the presence of 10 mM MgCl₂. (B) (Ca²⁺-Mg²⁺)ATPase activity was measured in liver plasma membranes prepared according to Neville[4], as described in[2] in the absence of exogenously added magnesium. (C) Plasma membranes (80 ug of protein) were phosphorylated at 30°C for 10 sec., in the absence or in the presence of 0.1 uM free Ca²⁺[3].The precipitated proteins were solubilized and electrophoresed in the SDS-polyacrylamide gel system[3]. The molecular weight markers are shown on the left.

were obtained from Novo Laboratories, and glucagon derivatives were prepared as described in[3]. C₁₂E₈ was from Kouyoh Lab (Japan). Cholera toxin was from Sigma (Saint-Louis, MO). IAP was from List Biological (Campbell, Ca).

CHARACTERIZATION AND PURIFICATION OF THE LIVER PLASMA MEMBRANE Ca²⁺ PUMP. RECONSTITUTION OF THE PURIFIED (Ca²⁺-Mg²⁺)ATPase INTO PHOSPHOLIPID VESICLES

Definition of the plasma membrane Ca²⁺ pumps relies on three criteria presented by Penniston[9]: (i) the pump is of plasma membrane origin, (ii) the pump has a high affinity Ca²⁺ stimulated ATPase activity; (iii) the pump shows a high Ca²⁺affinity Ca²⁺ transport activity. In addition, phosphorylated intermediates of the Ca²⁺ pump enzymes have been described in several systems which share the following properties: they are formed from the gamma-phosphorus of ATP in the presence of Ca²⁺, are easily discharged by a pulse of ATP, and are labile to hydroxylamine or alkali treatment. Briefly, three main kinetics components define the Ca²⁺ pump systems: ATP hydrolysis activity, Ca²⁺ pumping activity and formation of the phosphorylated intermediate.

Characterization of the liver plasma membrane Ca^{2+} pump

We have shown that liver plasma membranes possessed a high affinity $(Ca^{2+}-Mg^{2+})$ATPase responsive to nanomolar concentrations of free calcium[2]. As shown in Fig. 1B, calcium activation of ATPase activity followed a cooperative mechanism (Hill number = 1.2), half-maximal activation occurring at 14 ± 5 nM free calcium. Enzyme activity was dependent on micromolar concentrations of ATP ($K_{0.5}$ for ATP was 21 ± 9 uM) and two interacting catalytic sites were involved in the activation mechanism[2].

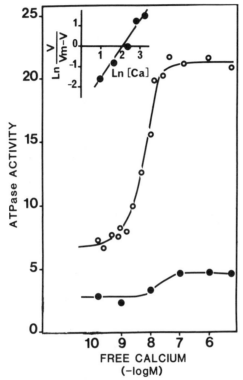

Fig. 2. Dependence of the purified $(Ca^{2+}-Mg^{2+})$ATPase on free Ca^{2+} concentration. $(Ca^{2+}-Mg^{2+})$ATPase activity eluted from DE-52 chromatography[2] was assayed in the absence (●) or in the presence (○) of activator, with total calcium varying between 21 or 31 and 400 uM in the presence of 0.4 mM EGTA. The inset represents the best fitting linear form of the Hill equation using data points between 2,5 and 25 nM. Two separate determinations yielded a Hill number of 1.4 and $K_{0.5}$ of 13 ± 5 mM with a correlation coefficient of 0.99. From ref 2.

The ATP-dependent calcium transport characterized in liver plasma membrane vesicles[6] exhibed kinetics and substrate specificity similar to those of the $(Ca^{2+}-Mg^{2+})$ATPase activity[3, 5, 10]. The dependence on free calcium concentration of the ATP-dependent calcium uptake by liver plasma membranes is shown in Fig. 1A. As described by Chan and Junger[5], the calcium uptake exhibited saturable kinetics reaching a maximum at a free calcium concentration of approximately 50 nM, with a $K_{0.5}$ of 17 ± 5 nM.

A calcium-sensitive phosphoprotein could be identified in the liver plasma membranes which has several characteristics that satisfy criteria for a phosphorylated intermediate of the $(Ca^{2+}-Mg^{2+})$ATPase[3, 5]. Fig. 1C shows an autoradiograph of SDS gel of plasma membranes which were incubated for 10 seconds at 25°C with (^{32}P)ATP in the presence and absence of 0.1 uM free calcium. In these conditions, in full agreement with the observation of Chan and Junger[5], a single major (^{32}P) labelled polypeptide with a molecular weight of 110,000 ± 10,000 was observed.

Purification of the $(Ca^{2+}-Mg^{2+})$ATPase was achieved after solubilization of the liver plasma membranes by a non ionic detergent, octaethylene-glycol-dodecyl-ether $(C_{12}E_8)$ followed by a chromatography of the solubilized proteins on concanavalin A Ultrogel. The glycoprotein peak containing $(Ca^{2+}-Mg^{2+})$ATPase activity was then applied on a DE-52 column where the purified enzyme could be separated from an activator protein[2]. In the absence of activator, the enzyme fraction displayed a low activity, partly responsive to Ca^{2+}. In the presence of activator, the $(Ca^{2+}-Mg^{2+})$ATPase activity assayed as a function of free Ca^{2+} concentrations, was maximally activated by 0.1 uM free Ca^{2+}, half maximal activation being obtained for 13 nM free Ca^{2+} (Fig. 2). As described above for the enzyme in its native liver plasma membrane environment, a Hill plot of the data yielded a slope of 1.4 which possibly suggests a cooperative mechanism for the Ca^{2+} activation, involving two Ca^{2+} ions. Characterization of the activator of $(Ca^{2+}-Mg^{2+})$ATPase indicated that this protein is distinct from calmodulin[2]. Furthermore, it should be pointed out that the purified $(Ca^{2+}-Mg^{2+})$ATPase was neither activated by calmodulin, nor it was inhibited by calmodulin inhibitors[2]. This lack of sensitivity to calmodulin is shared with the $(Ca^{2+}-Mg^{2+})$ATPases in corpus luteum[11], osteosarcoma[12], stomach smooth muscle[13], and neutrophil plasma membranes[14].

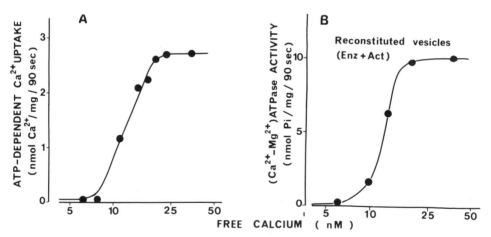

Fig. 3. **Dependence of ATP-dependent Ca^{2+} uptake and $(Ca^{2+}-Mg^{2+})$ATPase activity on free Ca^{2+} concentrations.** (A) ATP-dependent Ca^{2+} uptake into vesicles reconstituted with purified $(Ca^{2+}-Mg^{2+})$-ATPase and its activator, and (B) $(Ca^{2+}-Mg^{2+})$ATPase activity of same vesicles were assayed with varying total Ca^{2+} concentration between 202 to 364 uM, giving a free Ca^{2+} concentration varying between 5 to 50 nM. From ref 7.

Reconstitution of the purified enzyme into phospholipid vesicles

The $(Ca^{2+}-Mg^{2+})$ATPase and its activator purified as described above[2] were inserted together into asolectin vesicles, after elimination of non-ionic detergent by chromatography on an Extracti-gel D column, as described in Ref. 7. Reconstituted vesicles exhibited an ATP-dependent Ca^{2+} uptake maximally stimulated by 20 nM free Ca^{2+}, half-maximal extent of Ca^{2+} accumulation being attained at 13 ± 3 nM free Ca^{2+} (Fig. 3A). Addition of the Ca^{2+} ionophore A-23187 caused an immediate and complete release of the accumulated Ca^{2+} indicating that this ion is actively sequestered into the reconstituted vesicles[7]. This correlates with the dependence on calcium of ATP-dependent Ca^{2+} transport in native membrane vesicles[3, 5, 15] (Fig. 1A). The $(Ca^{2+}-Mg^{2+})$ATPase activity of reconstituted vesicles was assayed in parallel with Ca^{2+} uptake, under the same assay conditions, namely in the presence of 3 mM $MgCl_2$, 1 mM ATP and 5 to 50 nM free Ca^{2+}. As shown in Fig. 3 (B), the $(Ca^{2+}-Mg^{2+})$ATPase activity of reconstituted vesicles was maximally activated by 20 nM free Ca^{2+}, half-maximal activation occurring at 13 nM free Ca^{2+}. This dependence of ATPase activity on Ca^{2+} was parallel with that of Ca^{2+} uptake, and at each Ca^{2+} concentration the stoichiometry of Ca^{2+} transport vs ATP hydrolysis was 0.3-1. The Ca^{2+} ionophore A-23187 caused a 5- to 7-fold activation of $(Ca^{2+}-Mg^{2+})$ATPase activity of reconstituted vesicles (not shown). Such a stimulatory effect of the ionophore A-23187 on ATPase activity has been also reported in various reconstituted systems[16, 17] and has been attributed to uncoupling of ATP hydrolysis from Ca^{2+} transport.

It can be concluded that the high affinity $(Ca^{2+}-Mg^{2+})$ATPase in liver plasma membranes, supports Ca^{2+} transport and therefore can be considered as the enzymatic activity of the Ca^{2+} pump.

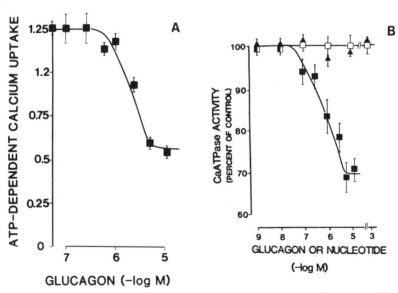

Fig. 4. Effect of glucagon on the ATP-dependent calcium uptake by liver plasma membrane vesicles and on $(Ca^{2+}-Mg^{2+})$ATPase activity in liver plasma membranes. (A) the ATP-dependent calcium uptake was measured in the presence of 199 uM total $CaCl_2$ (0.25 uM free Ca^{2+}). (B) $(Ca^{2+}-Mg^{2+})$ATPase was assayed in the presence of 393 uM total $CaCl_2$ (0.1 uM free Ca^{2+}). Results are expressed as percent of the control activity (1.2 $\pm$ 0.2 umol Pi/mg of protein/10 min.).

INHIBITION OF THE LIVER PLASMA MEMBRANE Ca^{2+} PUMP BY GLUCAGON

The effect of glucagon on ATP-dependent calcium uptake was assayed in liver plasma membrane inside out vesicles prepared according to Pilkis et al[6]. Addition of 6.5 uM glucagon to the plasma membrane vesicles resulted in a 55% decrease in maximal calcium uptake (Fig. 4A). The inhibitory effect of glucagon was concentration dependent, half-maximal inhibition occurring in the presence of 2.5 uM glucagon (Fig. 4A). In parallel to the inhibition of ATP-dependent Ca^{2+} uptake we observed a 25-35% maximal decrease in (Ca^{2+}-Mg^{2+})ATPase activity in the presence of 10 uM glucagon added <u>in vitro</u> to the assay medium, the half maximal inhibition occurring in the presence of 0.7 ± 0.3 uM glucagon (Fig. 4B). Kinetic studies of (Ca^{2+}-Mg^{2+})ATPase activity in the presence and absence of glucagon showed that the hormone did not affect the apparent affinity of the enzyme for either the substrate ATP, or Ca^{2+}, but caused a decrease in the maximal velocity of the reaction (not shown). This effect was mimicked neither by cyclic AMP, nor by dibutyryl cyclic AMP (1 nM - 1 mM) (Fig. 4B). A study of the structure activity relationship of six glucagon derivatives demonstrated the specificity of glucagon action, since only two analogs markedly altered the (Ca^{2+}-Mg^{2+})ATPase activity and two were potent antagonists of glucagon inhibition[3]. The study of the potencies of these analogs demonstrated the total absence of correlation between adenylate cyclase activation and (Ca^{2+}-Mg^{2+})ATPase inhibition by these glucagon derivatives (Table 1).

CHARACTERIZATION AND PURIFICATION OF AN INHIBITOR OF THE LIVER CALCIUM PUMP

Dependency on magnesium of the purified (Ca^{2+}-Mg^{2+})ATPase and its activator was studied in parallel with that of the enzyme in native liver plasma membranes. As shown in Fig. 5A, 100 uM Mg^{2+} maximally activated the purified (Ca^{2+}-Mg^{2+})ATPase activity, half maximal activation being observed for 10 uM Mg^{2+}. In contrast, Mg^{2+} caused a dramatic inhibition of (Ca^{2+}-Mg^{2+})ATPase activity in native liver plasma membranes (Fig. 5B). A possible explanation was the presence in the plasma membranes of an inhibitor of the (Ca^{2+}-Mg^{2+})ATPase which would render the enzyme sensitive to inhibition Mg^{2+}. In fact, after ammonium sulfate washing of liver plasma membranes followed by a chromatography on an AcA-44 Ultrogel, we obtained a protein fraction which caused an inhibition of the purified (Ca^{2+}-Mg^{2+})-ATPase supplemented with its activator, only in the presence of Mg^{2+}[18].

Table 1.   Potencies of glucagon derivatives for stimulating adenylate cyclase and inhibiting CaATPase

Derivative	Potencies relative to glucagon[a]	
	Adenylate cyclase	CaATPase
Arginine-substituted glucagon	100	0
Guanidyl glucagon	17	0
Carbomoyl glucagon	6	15
Cyanogen bromide glucagon	5	0
N^{alpha}-Trinitrophenyl glucagon	0.1	0
Glycinamide glucagon	0.004	50

[a]Potencies are relative to glucagon (defined as 100);   see ref. 3 for Experimental details.

The $(Ca^{2+}-Mg^{2+})$ATPase of the partially purified enzyme measured in the presence of activator was studied as a function of increasing amount of inhibitor fraction, in the absence 'or in the presence of 1 mM added Mg^{2+} (Fig. 6). In the absence of added Mg^{2+}, no significant inhibition was detected. In contrast, in the presence of 1 mM $MgCl_2$, maximal amounts (5 ug) of inhibitor caused a 60% inhibition of $(Ca^{2+}-Mg^{2+})$ATPase activity. Also, we observed that an excess of activator reversed the effect of the inhibitor[18]. These data suggest that the purified $(Ca^{2+}-Mg^{2+})$ATPase is sensitive to inhibition by Mg^{2+} only in the presence of the inhibitor[18]. We conclude that the dramatic inhibition of the enzyme by micromolar concentrations of Mg^{2+} in the native liver plasma membranes is probably due to the presence of the inhibitor in these membranes, and reflects its interaction with the $(Ca^{2+}-Mg^{2+})$ATPase.

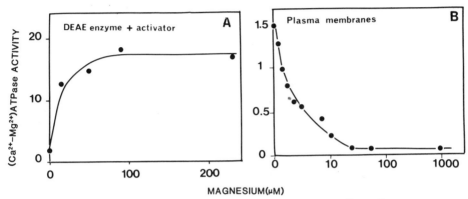

Fig. 5. **Comparative effect of magnesium on the $(Ca^{2+}-Mg^{2+})$ATPase of the purified system and of the enzyme in native liver plasma membranes.** $(Ca^{2+}-Mg^{2+})$ATPase activity was assayed in the purified system consisting of the enzyme eluted from DE-52 and its activator and (B) in the native liver plasma membranes.

The presence of the $(Ca^{2+}-Mg^{2+})$ATPase inhibitor was assayed in the 100,000 g supernatant of liver homogenate, after ammonium sulfate washing and gel filtration on AcA 54-Ultrogel. It appeared that the inhibitor was present in the 100,000 g liver supernatant (cytosol) in amount large enough to allow its purification from this fraction[8]. The purified protein was a single polypeptide with an apparent molecular weight of 30,000[8], similar to that previously determined by gel filtration and sucrose gradient for the inhibitor associated with the plasma membranes[18].

Role of the $(Ca^{2+}-Mg^{2+})$ATPase inhibitor in the glucagon and Mg^{2+} inhibition processes

Since biochemical studies of the purified inhibitor indicated its sensitivity to N-ethyl maleimide (NEM)[8], we used this sulfhydryl reagent to examine the possible role of the inhibitor in the regulation of the $(Ca^{2+}-Mg^{2+})$ATPase by glucagon and Mg^{2+}. When liver plasma membranes were treated with 50 mM NEM for 60 min. at pH 7, the $(Ca^{2+}-Mg^{2+})$ATPase loss its sensitivity to inhibition by both (2.5-3.5) uM glucagon and 10 uM Mg^{2+} as compared to 55 and 25% inhibitions observed respectively in control membranes (treated with beta-mercaptoethanol alone) (Fig. 7). In contrast, no alteration of the basal $(Ca^{2+}-Mg^{2+})$ATPase activity, measured in the absence of glucagon or Mg^{2+}, was observed in NEM-treated membranes as compared to control. Addition of the purified inhibitor to NEM-treated membranes restored both the inhibitions of the $(Ca^{2+}-Mg^{2+})$ATPase by glucagon and Mg^{2+} (Fig. 7): 55% and 25% inhibitions were observed in the presence of 10 uM Mg^{2+} and (2.5-3.5) uM glucagon, respectively. Optimal reconstitution occurred in the presence of 0.2 ug of the purified inhibitor and 2 to 6 ug of NEM-treated membranes (not shown). At this ratio of inhibitor to plasma membranes, the $(Ca^{2+}-Mg^{2+})$ATPase activity in control membranes was unaffected by the purified inhibitor. However, higher amounts of the inhibitor caused inhibition of the basal activity of the enzyme (not shown). Thus, it appeared that the $(Ca^{2+}-Mg^{2+})$ATPase inhibitor could fully restore the sensitivity of the enzyme to both Mg^{2+} and glucagon inhibitions in NEM-treated membranes. It can be concluded that the $(Ca^{2+}-Mg^{2+})$ATPase ihnibitor not only confers its sensitivity of the enzyme to Mg^{2+}, but also mediates the inhibition of this system by glucagon.

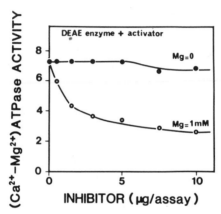

Fig. 6. Magnesium dependence of the effect of the inhibitor on the purified $(Ca^{2+}-Mg^{2+})$ATPase. $(Ca^{2+}-Mg^{2+})$ATPase activity of the purified enzyme was assayed in the presence of its activator as described in[2] and in the absence (●) or in the presence (○) of 1 mM $MgCl_2$.

ROLE OF A Gs-LIKE PROTEIN IN THE HORMONAL CONTROL OF THE $(Ca^{2+}-Mg^{2+})$ATPase ACTIVITY

The role of guanine nucleotide binding (G) proteins has been demonstrated not only in the hormonal stimulation (G_s) or inhibition (G_i) of adenylate cyclase activity[19] but also, more recently, in effects not linked to adenylate cyclase[20]. Purification of G proteins has shown that they all are comprised of three subunits, alpha, beta, and gamma[20]. The alpha subunits bind guanine nucleotides and some are specifically ADP-ribosylated by either cholera toxin ($alpha_s$), or pertussis toxin ($alpha_i$, $alpha_o$), or both toxins (alpha subunit of transducin)[19]. The sensitivity of alpha components to both toxins and/or their guanine nucleotide binding activity have been used as a means to infer the role of G proteins in the mediation of hormonal responses. Since GTP acts as a substrate of $(Ca^{2+}-Mg^{2+})$ATPases[2], its role in regulation of this system was difficult to examine. Therefore, we have investigated the influence of cholera toxin and pertussis toxin on liver plasma membrane $(Ca^{2+}-Mg^{2+})$ATPase as a way to test the possible involvement of a G protein in the hormonal regulation of this enzyme system.

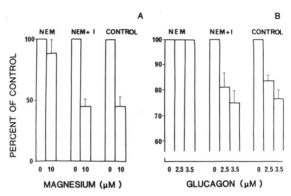

Fig. 7. **Reconstitution of Mg^{2+} and glucagon-inhibited $(Ca^{2+}-Mg^{2+})$ATPase activity in NEM-treated plasma membranes by addition of the purified inhibitor.** Liver plasma membranes were preincubated with 50 nM NEM for 60 min., or Tris-HCl 50 mM, pH 7, as control. $(Ca^{2+}-Mg^{2+})$ATPase activity was assayed in control or NEM-treated membranes (2-6 ug protein/assay) in the absence or in the presence of 250 ng of the purified inhibitor, (A) with or without Mg^{2+}, or (B) with or without glucagon diluted in 0.01% serum albumin. Results are expressed as percent of control activity (0.7 umol/mg/10 min.). From ref. 8.

In a first series of experiments, we studied the response of the $(Ca^{2+}-Mg^{2+})$ATPase to glucagon after treatment of the liver plasma membranes with cholera toxin. In control membranes, addition of 4 uM glucagon resulted in a 14 ± 2% maximal decrease in $(Ca^{2+}-Mg^{2+})$ATPase activity, with half-maximal inhibition occurring in the presence of 2 uM glucagon (Fig. 8A). By contrast, in cholera toxin-treated membranes no inhibition by glucagon was observed. It is known that cholera toxin treatment, which inhibits the GTPase activity of the alpha subunit of G_s, leads to a persistent activation of adenylate cyclase activity[19]. In order to ensure that the effect of cholera toxin on $(Ca^{2+}-Mg^{2+})$ATPase was not due to the production of cyclic AMP, we preincubated liver plasma membranes with 1 mM cyclic AMP instead of cholera toxin. Unlike results obtained with cholera toxin, treatment of membranes with cyclic AMP did not suppress the inhibition of $(Ca^{2+}-Mg^{2+})$ATPase by glucagon (Fig. 8B). The effectiveness of cholera toxin treatment was estimated by measuring adenylate cyclase activity in control and in treated membranes. As previously observed by several authors[19], cholera toxin induced a 2 ± 0.3 fold increase in basal adenylate cyclase activity as compared to its activity in control membranes. In addition, activation of adenylate cyclase activity by 10 mM NaF, which is known to stimulate G_s[19], was reduced to 4 ± 0.5 fold in cholera toxin-treated membranes as compared to 8 ± 2 fold in control membranes, due to the increase in "basal" activity[21]. Also, we used SDS polyacrylamide gel electrophoresis to verify that, in the conditions we used, cholera toxin effectively stimulated ADP-ribosylation of two specific proteins of 52,000 and 42,000 Da, identified as two forms of the alpha subunit of Gs[19]. However, no ADP-ribosylation of proteins, which would be the $(Ca^{2+}-Mg^{2+})$ATPase (110,000 Da, Fig. 2) or its inhibitor (30,000 Da[8]) respectively, was detected (not shown).

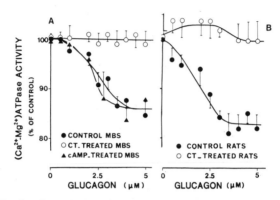

Fig. 8. **Effect of in vitro treatment of liver plasma membranes or in vivo treatment of rats with cholera toxin.** (A) liver plasma membranes were subjected to an in vitro treatment with cholera toxin (O), cyclic AMP (▲) or vehicle as control (●). (B) Rats were injected with cholera toxin and killed 26 hours after treatment. Liver plasma membranes were then prepared from control (●) or treated rats (O). $(Ca^{2+}-Mg^{2+})$-ATPase activity was assayed as a function of increasing concentrations of glucagon diluted in 50 mM Tris-HCl pH 8, containing 0.01% bovine serul albumin. Results are expressed as percent of control activity in the absence of glucagon. (A) 3.0 ± 0.14, 2.8 ± 0.14, and 2.9 ± 0.3 umol Pi/mg/10 min., for cholera toxin-treated, cyclic AMP-treated and control membranes, respectively. (B) 1.4 ± 0.4 and 1.42 ± 0.3 umol Pi/mg/10 min. for control rats or cholera toxin treated rats). Results are the mean ± S.E.M. of four experiments.

We next examined the effects of in vivo treatment of rats with an intraperitoneal injection of cholera toxin. Liver plasma membranes were prepared from rats injected with cholera toxin and killed 26 hours later. As shown in Fig. 8B, addition of 4 uM glucagon to control membranes resulted in a 18 ± 3% inhibition of $(Ca^{2+}-Mg^{2+})$ATPase activity, half-maximal inhibition being observed with 2 uM glucagon. In plasma membranes obtained from cholera toxin-treated rats, the inhibition of $(Ca^{2+}-Mg^{2+})$ATPase by glucagon (0.5-5 uM) did not occur. When plasma membranes obtained from control rats were ADP-ribosylated in vitro with cholera toxin, specific labeling of proteins of Mr 39,000, 42,000 and 52,000 Da occurred. In contrast, these bands were only faintly visible in membranes obtained from cholera toxin-treated rats and then ADP-ribosylated with cholera toxin in vitro[21].

In a second series of experiments, liver plasma membranes were subjected to treatment with pertussis toxin in the presence of 10 uM NAD, under conditions which induce ADP-ribosylation of a 41,000 Da protein, identified as the alpha subunit of G_i[19]. In pertussis-toxin treated membranes, 4 uM glucagon caused a 21 ± 2% maximal inhibition of $(Ca^{2+}-Mg^{2+})$ATPase which was comparable to the 19 ± 1.5% inhibition observed in control membranes. The apparent affinity of glucagon for the enzyme was similar under both conditions (2.5 and 1.5 uM, respectively)[21].

Taken together, these results strongly suggest that the inhibition of the liver $(Ca^{2+}-Mg^{2+})$ATPase by glucagon depends on a G protein that is sensitive to cholera toxin but not to pertussis toxin. This effect of cholera toxin would not seem to be caused by a G_s-mediated activation of adenylate cyclase, since the action of the toxin is not mimicked by cyclic AMP (Fig. 8A). These observations suggest that a protein which is a substrate for cholera toxin, perhaps G_s or a G_s-like protein, regulates the inhibition of the liver Ca^{2+} pump by glucagon. It might be predicted, therefore, that cholera toxin treatment would stabilize $(Ca^{2+}-Mg^{2+})$ATPase in an activated state and thereby lead to a loss of sensitivity of the enzyme activity to hormonal inhibition.

CONCLUSIONS

A high affinity $(Ca^{2+}-Mg^{2+})$ATPase has been identified in liver plasma membranes. Until very recently, the identity between this activity and the calcium transport activity were very controversial since in a previous report[22], Lin failed to demonstrate that the enzyme reconstituted into artificial liposomes supports Ca^{2+} transport. On the basis of the present reconstitution experiments, it is now evident that the $(Ca^{2+}-Mg^{2+})$ATPase activity in liver plasma membranes is the enzymatic support of Ca^{2+} transport. Ca^{2+} pump systems have now been identified in plasma membranes of a wide variety of cells[1], and activation by submicromolar concentration of free Ca^{2+} appears to be a common feature of all these systems. The Ca^{2+} pump in erythrocyte plasma membrane was the first to be identified[23], purified as a 138,000 Da protein and reconstituted into phospholipid vesicles[16]. This system is now accepted as a reference. However, Carafoli[16] has suggested that the liver plasma membrane Ca^{2+} pump belong to a class of Ca^{2+} pump distinct from that of erythrocyte, on the basis of its absence of sensitivity to calmodulin[2, 10, 24, 25] and its lower molecular weight[3, 5]. Further work is needed to establish conclusively the existence of two classes of plasma membrane Ca^{2+} pumps. Also, it could be asked whether distinct classes of $(Ca^{2+}-Mg^{2+})$ATPases could coexist in plasma membranes of liver and other cells since contradictory reports suggests the existence of distinct Ca^{2+} pumps in different plasma membrane regions of hepatocyte[24, 26, 27]. Therefore, the respective role of these Ca^{2+} pumps remain to be elucidated.

We report that glucagon added in vitro inhibits both calcium uptake and $(Ca^{2+}-Mg^{2+})$ATPase activity. A major observation of this study is that inhibition of $(Ca^{2+}-Mg^{2+})$ATPase and activation of adenylate cyclase by glucagon are two independent processes. This is indicated not only by the absence of effect of cyclic AMP on $(Ca^{2+}-Mg^{2+})$ATPase activity, but also by the total absence of correlation between the interaction of glucagon derivatives with the adenylate cyclase system and their action on

$(Ca^{2+}-Mg^{2+})$ATPase (Table 1). Also, inhibition of the liver calcium pump by glucagon cannot be related to the activation of phospholipase C observed in the presence of nanomolar concentrations of glucagon[28]. There is a difference of three orders of magnitude between the glucagon concentrations effective for activation of phospholipase C[28] and those required for inhibition of the calcium pump. Our recent data indicate that a proteolytic fragment of glucagon would be responsible for the inhibition of the liver calcium pump observed in the presence of glucagon. The mechanism by which this peptide exerts inhibition of $(Ca^{2+}-Mg^{2+})$ATPase activity appears to be quite different from the inhibitory mechanism of vasopressin, angiotensin II and alpha$_1$-adrenergic effectors on the liver calcium pump[15, 29]. Indeed, while the inhibition induced by the glucagon fragment can be observed directly on isolated plasma membranes, the effect of vasopressin and alpha$_1$-adrenergic effectors can be demonstrated only in liver plasma membrane preparations obtained either from isolated hepatocytes which have been incubated with the hormones prior to membrane isolation[29] or from perfused liver[15].

The role of regulatory proteins in different inhibition/activation processes of hormonal action is a well known phenomenon[19-20]. Our results indicate that the inhibition of the liver plasma membrane $(Ca^{2+}-Mg^{2+})$ATPase involves a Mg^{2+}-dependent inhibitor and a guanine nucleotide regulatory protein sensitive to cholera toxin, which may be G_s or a G_s-like protein. The activator of the liver plasma membrane $(Ca^{2+}-Mg^{2+})$ATPase might be a candidate as the alpha subunit of this G_s-like protein, since it activates the enzyme by direct interaction[2]. In this hypothesis, interaction of the activator with a beta-gamma like subunit would result in the deactivation of $(Ca^{2+}-Mg^{2+})$ATPase. One could postulate that the inhibitor, which reverses the stimulation of the $(Ca^{2+}-Mg^{2+})$ATPase induced by the activator[18] and mediates the inhibitory signal produced by glucagon[8] (Fig. 7), plays the role of a beta-gamma like subunit[19].

Several reports have established the multiple role of G_i-like proteins in hormonal action in cAMP-dependent[19], as well as in cAMP independent pathways[20]. Implication of G_s-like proteins in metabolic responses which are independent of adenylate cyclase have also been evoked in chemotaxis[30], insulin action[31], regulation of the T-cell antigen receptor[32], and inhibition of glucagon-stimulated phospholipase C[28]. In none of these systems, could the precise role of G_s-like proteins in regulation of specific enzymes be defined. The present data suggest that the plasma membrane $(Ca^{2+}-Mg^{2+})$ATPase with its activator and inhibitor proteins provide a useful system to examine enzymatic regulation by G proteins.

REFERENCES

1. H. Rasmussen, The calcium messenger system (first of two parts), New. Engl. J. Med., 314:1094-1101 (1986).

2. S. Lotersztajn, J. Hanoune, and F. Pecker, A high affinity calcium-stimulated magnesium-dependent ATPase in rat liver plasma membranes, J. Biol. Chem., 256:11209-11215 (1981).

3. S. Lotersztajn, R. Epand, A. Mallat, and F. Pecker, Inhibition by glucagon of the calcium pump in liver plasma membranes, J. Biol. Chem., 259:8195-8201 (1984).

4. D.M. Neville, Isolation of an organ specific protein antigen from cell-surface membrane of rat liver, Biochim. Biophys. Acta., 154: 540-552 (1968).

5. K.M. Chan, and K.D. Junger, Calcium transport and phosphorylated intermediate of $(Ca^{2+}-Mg^{2+})$ATPase in plasma membranes of rat liver, J. Biol. Chem., 258:4404-4410 (1983).

6. S.J. Pilkis, J.H. Exton, R.A. Johnson, and C.R. Park, Effects of glucagon on cyclic AMP and carbohydrate metabolism in livers from diabetic rats, Biochim. Biophys. Acta., 343:250-267 (1974).

7. C. Pavoine, S. Lotersztajn, A. Mallat, and F. Pecker, The high affinity $(Ca^{2+}-Mg^{2+})$ATPase in liver plasma membranes is a Ca^{2+} pump. Reconstitution of the purified enzyme into phospholipid vesicles, Submitted for publication.

8. S. Lotersztajn, A. Mallat, C. Pavoine, and F. Pecker, The inhibitor of liver plasma membrane $(Ca^{2+}-Mg^{2+})$ATPase. Purification and identification as a mediator of glucagon action, J. Biol. Chem., 260:9692-9696 (1986).

9. J.T. Penniston, Plasma membrane Ca^{2+}-ATPases as active Ca^{2+} pumps, in: "Calcium and Cell Function", W.Y. Cheung, ed., Academic Press, New York 4:99-151 (1983).

10. N. Kraus-Friedmann, J. Biber, H. Murer, and E. Carafoli, Calcium uptake in isolated hepatic plasma membrane vesicles, Eur. J. Biochem., 129:7-12 (1982).

11. A.K. Verma, and J.T. Penniston, A high affinity Ca^{2+}-stimulated and Mg^{2+}-dependent ATPase in rat corpus luteum plasma membrane fractions, J. Biol. Chem., 256:1269-1275 (1981).

12. E. Murray, J.P. Gorski, and J.T. Penniston, High affinity Ca^{2+}-stimulated and Mg^{2+} dependent ATPase from rat osteosarcoma plasma membranes, Biochem. Int., 6:527-533 (1983).

13. C.Y. Kwan, and P. Kostka, A Mg^{2+}-independent high affinity Ca^{2+}-stimulated adenosine triphosphatase in the plasma membrane of rat stomach smooth muscle, Biochim. Biophys. Acta., 776:209-216 (1984).

14. D.L. Ochs, and P.W. Reed, Ca^{2+}-stimulated Mg^{2+}-dependent ATPase activity in neutrophil plasma membrane vesicles. J. Biol. Chem., 259:102-106 (1984).

15. V. Prpic, K.C. Green, P.F. Blackmore, and J.H. Exton, Vasopressin-angiotensin II- and alpha$_1$-adrenergic-induced inhibition of Ca^{2+} transport by rat liver plasma membrane vesicles. J. Biol. Chem., 259:1382-1385 (1984).

16. E. Carafoli, Calmodulin-sensitive calcium-pumping ATPase of plasma membranes: isolation, reconstitution and regulation, Fed. Proc., 43:3005-3010.

17. H. Haaker, and E. Racker, Purification and reconstitution of the Ca^{2+}ATPase from plasma membranes of pig erythrocytes, J. Biol. Chem., 254:6598-6602.

18. S. Lotersztajn, and F. Pecker, A membrane-bound protein inhibitor of the high affinity CaATPase in rat liver plasma membranes. J. Biol. Chem., 257:6638-6641 (1982).

19. A.G. Gilman, G proteins and dual control of adenylate cyclase, Cell, 36:577-579 (1984).

20. H.R. Bourne, One molecular machine can transduce diverse signals, Nature, 321:814-816 (1986).

21. S. Lotersztajn, C. Pavoine, A. Mallat, and F. Pecker, Cholera toxin blocks glucagon-mediated inhibition of the liver plasma membrane $(Ca^{2+}-Mg^{2+})ATPase$, Submitted for publication.

22. S.H. Lin, The rat liver plasma membrane high affinity $(Ca^{2+}-Mg^{2+})ATPase$ is not a calcium pump, J. Biol. Chem., 260: 10976-10980 (1985).

23. H.J. Schatzmann, and G.L. Rossi, $(Ca^{2+}-Mg^{2+})$-activated membrane ATPase in human red cells and their possible relations to cation transport, Biochim. Biophys. Acta., 241:379-392 (1971).

24. O. Bachs, K.S. Famulski, F. Mirabelli, and E. Carafoli, ATP-dependent Ca^{2+} transport in vesicles isolated from the bile cana-licular region of the hepatocyte plasma membrane, Eur. J. Biochem., 147:1-7 (1985).

25. Y. Iwasa, T. Iwasa, K. Higashi, K. Matsu, and E. Migamoto, Demonstration of a high affinity Ca^{2+}-ATPase in rat liver plasma membranes, Biochem. Biophys. Res. Commun., 105:488-494 (1982).

26. R. Lester, G. Hugentobler, C. Evers, P. Omaj, P.J. Meier, and H. Murer, The liver plasma membrane calcium pump is located at the basolateral surface of rat hepatocytes, Hepatol., N6:58 (1986).

27. S.H. Lin, Novel, ATP-dependent calcium transport component from rat liver plasma membranes. The transporter and the previously reported $(Ca^{2+}-Mg^{2+})ATPase$ are different proteins, J. Biol. Chem., 260:7850-7856 (1985).

28. M.J.O. Wakelam, G.J. Murphy, G.J. Hruby, and M.D. Houslay, Acti-vation of two signal-transduction systems in hepatocytes by glucagon, Nature, 323:68-71 (1986).

29. S.H. Lin, M.A. Wallace, and J.N. Fain, Regulation of $(Ca^{2+}-Mg^{2+})ATPase$ activity in hepatocyte plasma membranes by vasopressin and phenylephrine, Endocrinol., 113: 2268-2275 (1982).

30. R.P. Aksamit, P.S.Jr. Backlund, and G.L. Cantoni, Cholera toxin inhibits chemotaxis by a cAMP-independent mechanism, Proc. Natl. Acad. Sci., 82:7475-7479 (1985).

31. C.M. Heyworth, A.D. Whetton, S. Wong, B.R. Martin, and M.D. Houslay, Insulin inhibits the cholera toxin-catalysed ribosyla-tion of a Mr 25,000 protein in rat liver plasma membranes, Biochem. J., 228:593-603 (1985).

32. J.B. Imboden, D.M. Shoback, G. Pattison, and J.D. Stobo, Cholera toxin inhibits the T-cell antigen receptor-mediated increases in inositol triphosphate and cytoplasmic free Ca^{2+}, Proc. Natl. Sci., 83:5673-5677 (1986).

PURIFICATION OF Ca^{2+}-ATPase FROM RAT PANCREATIC ACINAR PLASMA MEMBRANES USING CALMODULIN-AFFINITY CHROMATOGRAPHY

M. Bridges, R. Mahey, W. Lau, M. Hampong and S. Katz

Division of Pharmacology and Toxicology, Faculty of
Pharmaceutical Sciences, University of British Columbia
Vancouver, Canada

Although a great deal is known about the stimulatory role of calcium in stimulus-secretion coupling, little is known about the mechanism by which intracellular calcium is regulated. The free calcium concentration in the acinar cell cytoplasm is typically between 10^{-5}-10^{-7} M, in contrast to the much higher levels of calcium (approximately 10^{-3} M) in the extracellular space (Peterson, 1982). Calcium therefore penetrates into cells continuously down its electrochemical gradient by passive diffusion. In order to maintain a homeostatic environment in the cell and assure proper cell function, free calcium must be continuously removed.

In most cell types, the plasma membrane plays an important role in the maintenance of intracellular calcium homeostasis. The two most important mechanisms appear to be a Na^{+}/Ca^{2+} exchange system and the Ca^{2+}-ATPase. Where the two systems have been compared directly it appears that they are complementary, the exchanger being a low affinity, high capacity transporting system and the Ca^{2+} pumping ATPase, a higher affinity but low capacity system (Penniston, 1982).

Our laboratory has recently described a high affinity Ca^{2+}-ATPase activity in purified rat pancreatic acinar plasma membrane preparations (Ansah et al., 1984). This activity had characteristics similar to Ca^{2+}-transport ATPases from other tissues, including a K_{Ca2+} of 1.7 µM free, an apparent Mg^{2+} requirement and an associated hydroxylamine-sensitive Ca^{2+}-dependent phosphoprotein intermediate. In addition, it was demonstrated that the Ca^{2+}-ATPase activity was stimulated by calmodulin and this stimulation could be blocked by micromolar concentrations of trifluoperazine.

Attempts to further characterize this high-affinity Ca^{2+}-ATPase activity which may underlie Ca^{2+}-transport in pancreatic acinar plasma membranes have been plagued by the presence of an active Ca^{2+}- or Mg^{2+}-activated ATP phosphohydrolase activity in this organelle (Hamlyn and Senior, 1983; Forget and Heisler, 1976). It was therefore attempted to isolate this enzyme activity from other membrane ATPases by using calmodulin affinity chromatography.

MATERIALS AND METHODS

Pancreatic acinar cells were prepared from female Sprague-Dawley rats (175-200g) by the method of Kondo and Schulz (1976) as modified by Chauvelot et al. (1979). This method involves collagenase digestion of minced pancreases at 37°, mechanical dissociation of acinar cells from connective tissues, filtration, centrifugation through 4% (w/v) bovine serum albumin-containing buffer and collection of the cell pellet. The plasma membrane fraction of these cells was prepared by the method of Svoboda (1976) which involved sequential differential and sucrose gradient centrifugation. The plasma-membrane-enriched cellular fraction was collected at the 27-35% (w/v) sucrose interface. These membranes were then washed with EDTA-containing buffer to remove endogenous calmodulin.

The acinar plasma membranes were solubilized with 0.5% (w/v) Triton X-100, subjected to ultracentrifugation (150,000 x g for 20 minutes) and the supernatant applied in the presence of 50 μM Ca^{2+} to a calmodulin-affinity column. The calmodulin-bound fraction of the membrane solubilizate was washed exhaustively with buffer containing 0.05% (w/v) Tween 20 and was eluted with 2 mM EDTA. The purified product was assayed for protein by a fluorometric method (Bridges et al., 1986). ATPase activity was determined by the radiometric method of Blostein (1968).

RESULTS

Table 1 indicates the percentage of total acinar plasma membrane protein eluted from the calmodulin-affinity column by EDTA-buffer. The results show that the Ca^{2+}-ATPase fraction of total protein in acinar plasma membranes is similar to that present in erythrocyte membranes (Penniston, 1982).

Table 1

No. of Prep'ns	% Protein Recovered (w/w)
3	0.155 ± 0.01% (Mean ± SE)

SDS gel electrophoretic studies have determined that three bands of protein are present in the EDTA buffer eluant. They represent proteins of 33.5, 91 and 110 KDa.

Table 2 compares the specific activity in the presence of 0.2 μM free Ca^{2+} of the Ca^{2+}-ATPase purified by calmodulin-affinity chromatography to that activity present in the purified plasma membranes. Asolectin, 0.02% (w/v), a soybean phospholipid mixture rich in acidic species, was present in the purified enzyme assay media.

Table 2

	Specific Activity (μmol/mg/h)		% Enhancement
	-Calmodulin	+Calmodulin	by Calmodulin
Plasma membranes	1.4	2.9	110%
Purified enzyme	139	166	20%

DISCUSSION

The aim of this study is to isolate and characterize a high affinity Ca^{2+}-ATPase activity that we have found to be present in pancreatic acinar cell plasma membranes and determine if this activity is associated with the regulation of intracellular Ca^{2+}. Calmodulin-affinity chromatography was chosen as the isolation procedure due to the observation that this Ca^{2+}-ATPase activity is stimulated by calmodulin and that calmodulin bound to a protein of similar molecular weight to the phosphoprotein intermediate of the Ca^{2+}-ATPase (Ansah et al., 1984).

Passage of solubilized preparations of purified pancreatic plasma membranes through a calmodulin affinity column revealed the presence of three calmodulin binding proteins. The 110 KDa protein appears to correspond to the acyl phosphoprotein formed in the presence of Ca^{2+} in purified plasma membrane preparations and presumed to be the intermediate of the Ca^{2+}-transport ATPase (Ansah et al., 1984).

The studies to date have shown that the high affinity Ca^{2+}-ATPase present in rat pancreatic acinar plasma membranes can be isolated and partially purified by calmodulin affinity chromatography. The enzyme activity obtained is stimulated by submicromolar concentrations of calcium. The relatively low calmodulin-stimulatory capacity of the enzyme is probably due to the competitive activation by acidic phospholipids present in the asolectin added to the assay medium. The specific activity of the purified Ca^{2+}-ATPase, representing 10-15% of the levels seen in erythrocyte membranes (Graf et al., 1982), is probably not maximal.

This study indicates that by using calmodulin-affinity chromatography, the acinar plasma membrane Ca^{2+}-ATPase present can be enriched 60-100 fold. Studies aimed at maximizing the yield, the activity and the purity of this enzyme are currently in progress.

ACKNOWLEDGEMENT

We gratefully acknowledge the Canadian Cystic Fibrosis Foundation for the support to carry out these studies. R.M. is a recipient of a Canadian Cystic Fibrosis Studentship.

REFERENCES

Ansah, T-A, Molla, A. and Katz, S. 1984 J. Biol. Chem. 259:13442-13450.
Bridges, M.A., McErlane, K.M., Kwong, E., Katz, S. and Applegarth, D.A. 1986. Clin. Chim. Acta 157:73-80.
Blostein, R. 1968 J. Biol. Chem. 243:1957-1965.
Chauvelot, L., Heisler, S., Huot, J. and Gagnon, D. 1979 Life Sci. 25: 913-920.
Forget, G., Heisler, S. 1976 Clin. Exp. Pharmacol. Physiol. 3:67-72.
Graf, E., Verma, A.K., Gorski, J.P., Lopaschuk, G., Niggli, V., Zurini, M., Carafoli, E. and Penniston, J.T. 1982 Biochemistry 21:4511-4516.
Hamlyn, J.M. and Senior, A.E. 1983 Biochem. J. 214:59-68.
Kondo, S. and Schulz, I. 1976 Biochim. Biophys. Acta 419:76-92.
Penniston, J.T. 1982 Ann. N.Y. Acad. Sci. 402:296-303.
Peterson, O.H. 1982 Biochim. Biophys. Acta 694:163-184.
Svoboda, M., Robberecht, P., Camus, J., Deschodt-Lanckman, M. and Christophe, J. 1976 Eur. J. Biochem. 69:185-193.

THE RELATIVE IMPORTANCE OF CALCIUM INFLUX AND EFFLUX

VIA NA-CA EXCHANGE IN CULTURED MYOCARDIAL CELLS

William H. Barry, and John H. B. Bridge

From the Cardiology Division, and the Nora Eccles Harrison
Cardiovascular Research and Training Institute, University
of Utah School of Medicine, Salt Lake City, UT 84132

INTRODUCTION

In the intact myocardial cell, Ca homeostasis consists of several
interrelated processes: Ca influx across the sarcolemma; Ca uptake and
release by intracellular organelles, notably sarcoplasmic reticulum and
mitochondria; Ca binding to and release from intracellular Ca binding
proteins; and transsarcolemmal Ca efflux. Since the work of Niedergerke[1]
it been recognized that Ca influx and efflux increase with electrical
activation. Voltage clamp studies have suggested that some of the Ca
influx involved in the activation of contraction occurs via the slow Ca
channel.[2] This Ca is believed to trigger release of Ca from intracellular
Ca stored within the sarcoplasmic reticulum,[3] resulting in a rise of free-
Ca ion sufficient to produce contraction of the myofilaments. It is
possible that Ca may enter the cell under some circumstances via the Na-Ca
exchange carrier.[4] However, the relative magnitudes of Ca influx into the
cell via the slow Ca channel, and via Na-Ca exchange during normal
excitation-contraction coupling, have not been established.

To prevent progressive Ca accumulation, an amount of Ca equal to that
entering the cell during each depolarization must be extruded before the
next contraction-relaxation cycle. Reuter and Seitz in 1967[5] showed that
efflux of ^{45}Ca in guinea pig myocardium was sensitive to the ratio of external Na and Ca concentrations, and suggested that Na and Ca could participate in exchange diffusion. Blaustein and Hodgkin [6], working with squid
axon, concluded that the inward Na gradient provided the necessary energy
for extrusion of Ca from the cell via a Na-Ca exchange mechanism. Na-Ca
exchange appears to be wide spread, and has been documented in a variety of
excitable tissues, including squid giant axon, barnacle muscle fibers, frog
skeletal muscle, and some smooth muscle cells. In addition to Na-Ca
exchange, there exists an ATP-dependent Ca-pump in the sarcolemma of myocardial cells[7] which can contribute to Ca efflux.

In this discussion we will consider recent experimental data obtained
in layer cultures of chick embryo ventricular cells. We have attempted to
investigate the relative magnitudes of Ca influx via the Na-Ca exchanger
and via the slow Ca channel; and Ca efflux via Na-Ca exchange, and the Ca-
ATPase Ca pump, during the normal contraction-relaxation cycle of the cell.

METHODS

Tissue Culture

Spontaneously contracting layers of chick embryo ventricular cells were prepared by trypsinization of ventricular fragments obtained from 10 day old embryos.[8] Cells were cultured for 3-4 days in 6% fetal calf serum-containing medium in a 5% CO_2 atmosphere. This method results in a sheet of synchronously contracting cells which beat at rates of 60-120/min., and in which approximately 80% of the cells are myocytes.

Measurement of Cell Motion

Contraction and relaxation of myocytes in culture was quantitated using a video motion detector system.[8] This permits continuous monitoring of the amplitude and velocity of contraction and relaxation of a single cell within the layer culture, during continuous superfusion of the culture at physiologic temperature.

Membrane Potential Recording

Intracellular potentials were measured using 80-90 M glass capillary electrodes.[8] Cell penetration was achieved with a Burleigh Instruments Inchworm Controller, mounted on a conventional micro-manipulator. Potentials were obtained from the same cells from which motion was recorded, or from the immediately adjacent cell.

Ion Fluxes and Contents

One of the advantages of layer cultures of heart cells is that the diffusion barriers are relatively insignificant, permitting rapid exchange of the extracellular fluid space. This permits measurements of transsarcolemmal ion fluxes using radioactive isotopes. For ^{45}Ca uptake experiments, cells were first exposed to ^3H leucine to label cell protein and permit convenient normalization of ^{45}Ca uptake relative to cell protein. Individual coverslips with attached layers of cells were immersed in uptake medium containing ^{45}Ca for periods ranging from 1 second to 2 hours. Individual coverslips were subsequently removed and washed for 30 seconds in ice cold balanced salt solution, containing EGTA. The ice cold temperature prevents significant loss of intracellular label, while allowing essentially complete removal of extracellular ^{45}Ca from the extracellular fluid space, and from superficial binding sites on the cell membrane. After washing, the cells were dissolved and subsequently counted in a liquid scintillation spectrometer. From the measured CPM for ^{45}Ca and ^3H, uptake data were calculated as nmols of Ca/mg of cell protein[9].

For Ca efflux experiments, cells were labeled to equilibrium (2 hours) in ^{45}Ca. Individual coverslips were then washed for 15-30 seconds to remove extracellular tracer and submerged serially in known volumes of efflux solution at 37°. ^{45}Ca lost into these efflux volumes over known time periods were determined, and ^{45}Ca efflux calculated as fractional efflux, after determination of the total ^{45}Ca counts remaining in the cells after the end of the efflux period.[8]

Contents of Ca and Na were measured using atomic absorption spectroscopy methods.[7]

Measurement of Intracellular Free Ca Ion Concentration

We have used the new fluorescent Ca^{2+} probe, Indo-1,[10] to estimate phasic changes in Ca^{2+} concentration within these cultured cells. To load the cells with the Ca^{2+}-sensitive form of the dye, cells were exposed to the membrane permeable ester form, Indo-1-AM, 10 uM, for 15 minutes. Within the cell, the ester group is cleaved by intracellular esterases, leaving the free dye Indo-1 to react with Ca^{2+}. After washing the cells for 1 hour, which allowed contractility to return to normal, Indo-1 within the cells was excited with 360 nm light. Fluorescence was detected at 410 nm (increases with increasing Ca^{2+}), and at 480 nm (decreases with increasing Ca^{2+}) simultaneously using 2 photomultiplier tubes.[11] Using an epifluorescence system, cell motion was measured simultaneously with $[Ca^{2+}]_i$ transients. Calibration of the $[Ca^{2+}]$ is achieved in vivo using a nonfluorescent Ca^{2+}-ionophore, bromo A23187, and extracellular Ca^{2+}-buffered solutions.[11]

RESULTS

As discussed by Mullins[12], the direction and magnitude of Ca movement via the Na-Ca exchange process depends upon the Na and Ca electrochemical gradients, the stoichiometry of the exchange process and the membrane potential. Thus, when $n(E_{Na} - E_M) = (E_{Ca} - E_M)$, the electrochemical gradients are balanced, the exchange is at equilibrium, and no net Na-Ca exchange will occur. In this expression n is the coupling ratio for Na-Ca exchange, E_{Na} and E_{Ca} are the equilibrium potentials for Na and Ca, and E_M is the membrane potential. At equilibrium, E_M is the reversal potential of the Na-Ca exchange, and is designated E_{rev}. Provided there are no kinetic restraints, membrane potentials positive to E_{rev} will produce Ca influx linked to Na extrusion and potentials negative to E_{rev} will produce net Na entry with Ca extrusion. Thus, if one knows the value of these thermodynamic variables during the contraction-relaxation cycle in the myocardial cell, the direction of the Na-Ca exchange can be predicted. A knowledge of the direction of the exchange, combined with its magnitude, will allow estimation of the relative contributions of the exchange to Ca influx and efflux.

We have investigated the Na-Ca exchange stoichiometry in these cultured cells by measuring the ratio of cellular Na lost to Ca gained in Na loaded myocardial cells after abrupt removal of extracellular Na, and substitution by choline chloride.[13] In these experiments, net movements of Na and Ca were measured using atomic absorption spectroscopy, avoiding the potential complication of Ca-Ca exchange.[14] The stoichiometric coefficient of the exchanger in these cultured myocardial cells was 3. This value agrees with that reported recently by Reeves and Hale in sarcolemmal membrane vesicles.[15]

We have measured the concentration gradients of Na and Ca across the cell membrane. The extracellular Na concentration in the experiments we have performed is 140 mM. Intracellular Na content determined by isotope labelling, or by atomic absorption spectroscopy is approximately 100 nmols/mg/protein. Measurements of cell water using ^3H-O-methyl-glucose have yielded values of 6.5 ul of cell water/mg protein. This results in an intracellular Na concentration of approximately 15 mM, corresponding intracellular Na^+ activity of approximately 10 mM. This value agrees well with measurements in isolated ventricular cells using Na^+-sensitive microelectrodes.[16] We assume that the Na concentration within the cells does not change significantly during the normal excitation contraction coupling interval.

The extracellular Ca concentration is 1.8 mM. The intracellular Ca concentration in these cells, as measured with Indo-1, ranges from approximately 300 nM at end diastole, to 800-900 nM at peak levels attained early in systole. The onset of the $[Ca^{2+}]_i$ transient precedes the onset of

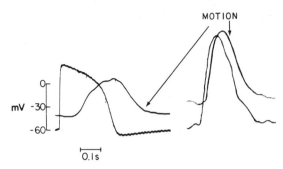

MOTION

Fig. 1   Simultaneous membrane potential and motion (left) and $[Ca^{2+}]_i$-transient and motion (right). Recordings were made in different cultures, but the time base for recordings was identical. Membrane depolarization preceded contraction by about 50 msec., and the $[Ca^{2+}]_i$ transient preceded motion by about 20 msec. $[Ca]_i$ at end diastole was 300 nM, and at peak during systole was 800 nM.

motion by approximately 25 msec and peaks before motion peaks. The relative relationships between membrane potential and cell motion, and the $[Ca^{2+}]_i$ transient and motion in these cells are shown in Fig 1.

For a 3 Na to 1 Ca exchange stoichiometry, the reversal potential, $E_{rev} = 3E_{Na} - 2E_{Ca}$. In these cells, using the above values at end diastole, $E_{Na} = 66mV$ and $E_{Ca} = 108.7$ mV. Therefore, $E_{rev} = 198$ mV $- 217.4$ mV or -19.4 mV. This indicates that at end diastole, since the membrane potential is well negative to this value, the Na-Ca exchanger should function in a Na-in, Ca-out mode. With the onset of depolarization, membrane potential rises to approximately +20 mV, or well positive to the reversal potential of the Na-Ca exchanger. This indicates that during the early phase of the action potential, the exchanger could function to bring Ca into the cell in exchange for intracellular Na. Recent studies in perfused, voltage-clamped single ventricular cells[18] suggest that the response time of the exchanger is sufficiently rapid that this could occur before the $[Ca^{2+}]_i$ begins rising 20-30 msec. after the onset of the action potential. This rise in Ca^{2+}, probably due chiefly to release of Ca from sarcoplasmic reticulum[17], causes the reversal potential for the Na-Ca exchanger to increase, and to exceed the membrane potential approximately 70 msec. after the onset of depolarization. This is illustrated in Fig. 2. When the reversal potential for the exchanger is positive to the membrane potential (after 70msec) the exchanger should again function in a Na-in, Ca-out mode, thus extruding Ca from the cell.

The maximum Na-Ca exchange flux has been estimated at 30 pmoles per cm^2/sec.,[19] or 2.1 pmoles/cm^2/70msec, which would be equivalent in this analysis to 2.1 pmoles/cm^2/beat. This is roughly equivalent to estimated values of Ca influx via the slow Ca channel by voltage clamp methods in a variety of other myocardial preparations, in the presence of 1.8 mM[20]. However, the driving force for the operation of the exchanger under physiologic conditions is far from maximum. Phillipson and Ward[21] have measured vesicular exchange rates under more physiologic conditions. In their studies, under conditions approximating those at the onset of membrane depolarization in our studies (3 mM intracellular Mg, 16 mM Na, 1.5 mM extracellular Ca, 140 mM extracellular Na, and E_M = 0mV) Ca "influx" via the exchanger was only 0.7nmol/mg/sec, or about 15% of the maximum Na-Ca exchange flux. Based on these results, and our findings (Fig.2) we

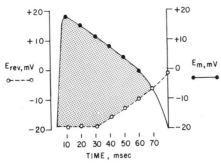

Fig. 2 Changes in the calculated reversal
potential for the Na-Ca exchanger (E_{rev}, dotted
line) and the membrane potential (E_M, solid
line) with time, after initial membrane depolarization. When E_M is > E_{rev} (cross-hatched area)
the Na-Ca exchanger should function to bring
Ca^{2+} into the cell. The magnitude of the difference $E_{rev}-E_M$ is the driving force for Na-Ca
exchange. The sign of this difference indicates
the direction of exchange.

estimate that the Ca influx via Na-Ca exchange during the initial 70 msec
of the action potential is no more than 0.2 pmoles/cm^2/beat, or only about
25% of that estimated to occur via the Ca channel[9].

This fraction of Ca influx expected to occur via Na-Ca exchange is
smaller than previously estimated by measuring the difference in rapid ^{45}Ca
uptake in the presence and absence of 10^{-6} M verapamil[9], as shown in Fig.
3. Only about 30% of the rapid uptake could be inhibited by verapamil and
the remainder was inhibited by lanthanum, suggesting that Ca uptake via Na-
Ca exchange contributed significantly (2/3 of total) to Ca uptake in these
cells. However, subsequent studies[22] have shown that verapamil induces depolarization (to-40 mV) of these cells. Since the Na-Ca exchanger is voltage sensitive[15], depolarization in combination with a decrease in $[Ca^{2+}]_i$,
could increase the rate of influx and decrease the rate of efflux of ^{45}Ca,
relative to control conditions. This could cause an underestimation of the
true magnitude of Ca influx via the slow Ca channel during spontaneous
beating, and therefore an _overestimation_ of the influx component due to Na-
Ca exchange. Furthermore, Ca-Ca exchange does occur in these cells[8]. This
would tend also to cause some overestimation also of the magnitude of Ca
influx via the Na-Ca exchange, since Ca-Ca exchange is also inhibited by
lanthanum.

The above analysis makes it obvious that the Na-Ca exchanger is
functioning in a Na-in, Ca-out mode during the major portion (all but
70msec) of the excitation-contraction coupling cycle. The importance of
the Na-Ca exchanger in providing for Ca efflux in these cells is
illustrated by the results shown in Fig. 4. In this experiment, a
contracture was induced in cells in the presence of zero Na and nominal
zero Ca by abrupt exposure to caffeine. Relaxation of this contracture, as
well as the efflux of ^{45}Ca, was significantly greater if extracellular Na
concentration was restored coincident with caffeine exposure. These
results do demonstrate however, that relaxation and Ca extrusion in these
cells does occur in the absence of extracellular Na, consistent with the
presence of a Ca-ATPase Ca-pump[8]. However, the rate of relaxation which
can be produced by the Ca pump is very slow (T1/2 = 8.6 seconds) relative
to that which can be produced by extracellular Na (T1/2 = 770 msec).

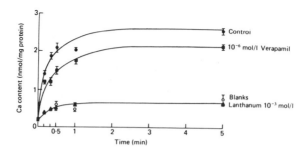

Fig. 3 Effect of verapamil and La^{3+} on Ca^{2+}
influx. Control uptake of Ca^{2+} is the upper
curve. After exposure of spontaneously con-
contracting cells to verapamil 10^{-6}M, uptake was
depressed. Lanthanum completely inhibited uptake.
It is possible that verapamil, by causing depolarization of the cells, increased Ca^{2+} uptake via
Na-Ca exchange (La-inhibitable component), thus
causing an apparent decrease in the estimated
influx occurring via the slow Ca channel (difference between control and verapamil curves) and an
overestimation of the component due to Na-Ca exchange. See text. From Barry W.H., and Smith,
T.W., J. Physiol 325:243, 1982, with permission of
the publisher.

Interestingly, this rate of relaxation is only slightly slower than
that which occurs between beats of spontaneously contracting cells[23], and
which is associated with a fall in [Ca^{2+}]$_i$ (see Fig 1). We conclude from
these experiments that the Na-Ca exchanger is important in beat-to-beat
relaxation in these cells, and provides rapid extrusion of Ca, thus
maintaining Ca homeostasis. The Ca pump may also contribute to Ca homeostasis, although its capacity for Ca extrusion is 5 times less than the
maximum capacity of the Na-Ca exchanger, and it does appear to be able to
contribute significantly to beat-to-beat relaxation in this tissue.[8]

DISCUSSION

Our results, and the analysis of the thermodynamics of Na-Ca exchange in cultured chick embryo ventricular cells, indicate that Ca influx
via the Na-Ca exchanger early during depolarization can occur. However, it
is unlikely to be greater than 25% of the Ca influx occurring via the Ca
channel. Under conditions of increased intracellular Na con- centration,
as occur during exposure to cardiac glycosides, this comp- onent could be
somewhat larger. However, studies using extracellular dyes by Cleeman et
al.[24] have not shown evidence of extracellular Ca depletion during EC-
coupling when a positive inotropic effect was induced by Na pump
inhibition, suggesting that this effect is relatively small. A relatively
insignificant contribution of Na influx via the Na-Ca ex- changer during
normal EC-coupling is also suggested by the fact that exposure to Ca
channel blockers such as nifedipine can completely inhibit contraction at a
time when membrane depolarization and action potential generation is still
occurring[22]. This indicates that the magnitude of Ca influx via the Na-Ca
exchange mechanism only is inadequate to trigger release of Ca from
sarcoplasmic reticulum, and/or inadequate to maintain sarcoplasmic
reticulum stores.

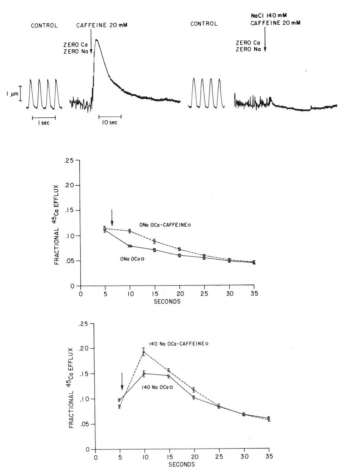

Fig. 4. Effects of abrupt exposure to caffeine
(verticle arrow) with and without resupply of external Na, on cultured cell motion (top) and ^{45}Ca efflux
(middle and bottom). From Barry W.H., et al., J. Gen.
Physiol. 88: 393, 1986 with permission of the
publisher.

Significant Ca influx via the Na-Ca channel exchanger may occur under
pathological conditions. For example, after prolonged ischemia the
increase in intracellular Na may be quite marked. Experiments performed in
our laboratory in cultured chick embryo ventricular cells have demonstrated a rise in cell Na content from 107nmol/mg/protein to 672 nmol per
mg/protein after 3 hours of metabolic inhibition with cyanide and 2-
deoxyglucose. Such massive Na gain coupled with a membrane depolarization could lead to significant Ca influx via Na-Ca exchange, and may
contribute to the marked increase in Ca content noted under these conditions.[25]

It seems that the Na-Ca exchange system is of primary importance in
producing Ca extrusion, and may contribute to diastolic relaxation of
tension in some myocardial cells. Thus, elevation of intracellular Na
produced by cardiac glycosides, or by increases in heart rate, probably
bring about an inotropic effect by slowing Ca extrusion from the cell, and
thus "priming" of the sarcoplasmic reticulum, augmenting sarcoplasmic
reticulum Ca content, and thus increasing Ca released during EC-coupling.

Na-Ca exchange is electrogenic, and may contribute to a portion of the inward current during the action potential plateau as Ca^{2+} is extruded (26). Our analysis also suggests that early after depolarization, it could generate an outward current [? a component of i_{to} (26)], due to Ca^{2+} influx with Na^+ extrusion.

Further studies of the precise role of the Na-Ca exchanger in EC-coupling would be greatly aided by a specific inhibitor. Unfortunately, trivalent cations such as lanthanum, although they are potent inhibitors of the Na-Ca exchange, also block the slow Ca channel, and alter the function of ATPases. The amiloride derivative dichlorabenzamil, recently determined to be a Na-Ca exchange inhibitor[27], also blocks the slow Ca channel and this effect is manifest at a lower concentration than is required to inhibit the exchanger.[28]

REFERENCES

1. Niedergerke, R., Movement of Ca in beating ventricles of the frog heart, J. Physiol. (Lond.) 167:551 (1963).
2. Reuter, H. The dependence of slow inward current in Purkinje fibers on the extracellular calcium concentration, J. Physiol. (Lond.) 192:479 (1967).
3. Fabiato, A., Myoplasmic free calcium concentration reached during the twitch of an intact isolated cardiac cell and during calcium-induced release of calcium from the sarcoplasmic reticulum of a skinned cardiac cell from the adult rat or rabbit ventricle, J. Gen. Physiol. 78:457 (1981).
4. Glitsch, H.G., Reuter, H., Scholtz, H., The effect of the internal sodium concentration on calcium flux in isolated guinea pig ventricles, J. Physiol. (Lond.) 209:25 (1970).
5. Reuter, H., and Seitz, N., The dependence of calcium efflux from cardiac muscle on temperature and external ion composition, J. Physiol. (Lond.) 195:451 (1968).
6. Blaustein, M.P., and Hodgkin, A.L., The effect of cyanide on the efflux of calcium from squid axons, J. Physiol. (Lond.) 200:497 (1969).
7. Caroni, P., and Carafoli, E., An ATP-dependent Ca^{2+} pumping system in dog heart sarcolemma, Nature 283:765 (1980).
8. Barry, W.H., Rasmussen, C.A.F., Jr., Ishida, H., and Bridge, J.H.B., External Na-independent Ca extrusion in cultured ventricular cells, J. Gen. Physiol. 88:393, (1986).
9. Barry, W.H., and Smith, T.W., Mechanisms of transmembrane calcium movements in cultured chick embryo ventricular cells, J. Physiol. (Lond.) 324:243 (1982).
10. Grynkiewicz, G., Poenie, M., and Tsien, R.Y., A new generation of Ca^{2+} indicators with greatly improved fluorescence properties, J. Biol. Chem. 260:3440 (1985).
11. Peeters, G.A. and Barry, W.H., Changes in $[Ca^{2+}]_i$ during spontaneous contraction and zero $[Na]_o$ -induced contracture in cultured ventricular cells detected with indo-1, J. Gen. Physiol. 88:46a (1986).
12. Mullins, L.T., The generation of electric currents in cardiac fibers by a Na-Ca exchange, Am. J. Physiol. 236:C103 (1979).
13. Bridge, J.H.B., Ishida, H., Menlove, R.L., and Barry, W.H. An estimate of the stoichiomatic coefficient of Na-Ca exchange in intact cultured ventricular cells, Submitted.
14. Eisner, D.A., and Lederer, W.J., Na-Ca exchange stoichiometry and electrogenicity, Am. J. Physiol. 248:C189 (1985).
15. Reeves, J.P. and Hale, C.C., Stoichiometry of the cardiac Na-Ca exchange system, J. Biol. Chem. 259:7733 (1984).

16. Desilets, M. and Baumgarten, C.M., Measurements of K+, Na+, and Cl activities in myocytes isolation rabbit heart, Biophys. J. 47:462a (1985).

17. Rasmussen, C.A.F., Jr., Sutko., J.L., and Barry, W.H., Effects of ryanodine and caffeine on contractility, membrane voltage, and calcium exchange in cultured heart cells, Circ. Res. (1987) In Press.

18. Nako, M., Shepherd, N., Bridge, J.H.B, and Gadsky, D.C., Membrane currents generated by Na-Ca exchange is isolated heart cells, Fed. Proc. 45(4):770 (1986).

19. Chapman R.A., Coray, A., and McGuigan, J.H.S., Sodium/calcium exchanger in mammalian ventricular muscle: a study with sodium-sensitive microelectrodes, J. Physiol. (Lond.) 343:253 (1983).

20. Reuter, H., Divalent cations as charge carriers in excitable membranes, Prog. Biophys. Mol. Biol. 26:7 (1973).

21. Phillipson, K.D. and Ward, R., Ca^{2+} transport capacity of sarcolemmal Na^+-Ca^{2+} exchange. Extra-polation of vesicle data to in vivo conditions, J. Mol. Cell. Cardiol. 18:943 (1986).

22. Hasin, Y., and Barry, W.H., Comparison of simultaneous electrophysiologic and mechanical effects of verapamil and nifedipine in cultured chick embryo ventricular cells, J. Mol. Cell. Cardiol. In Press.

23. Miura, D.S., Biedert, S. and Barry, W. H., Effects of calcium overload on relaxation in cultured heart cells, J. Mol. Cell. Cardiol. 13:949 (1981).

24. Cleeman L., Pizarro, G., and Morad, M., Optical measurements of extra-cellular calcium depletion during a single heart beat, Science 226:172 (1984).

25. Murphy, E., Wheeler, D.M., Le Furgey, A., Jacob, R., Lobaugh, L.A., and Liebermann, M., Coupled sodium-calcium transport in cultured chick heart cells, Am. J. Physiol. 250:C442 (1986).

26. Noble, D., The surprising heart: a recent review of progress in cardiac electrophysiology, J. Physiol (Lond.) 353:1 (1984).

27. Siegl, P.K.S., Cragoe, E.J., Jr., Trumble, M.J. and Kaczorowski, G.J., Inhibition of Na^+-Ca^{2+} exchange in membrane vesicle and papillary muscle preparations from guinea pig heart by analogs of amiloride. Proc. Natl. Acad. Sci. 81:3238 (1984).

28. Bielefeld D.R., Hadley, R.W., Vassile , P.M., and Hume, J.R., Membrane electrical properties of vesicular Na-Ca exchange inhibitors in single atrial myocytes, Circ. Res. 59:381 (1986).

NA-CA EXCHANGE IN CARDIAC SARCOLEMMAL VESICLES

Carole A. Bailey, Philip Poronnik, and John P. Reeves

Roche Institute of Molecular Biology
Roche Research Center
Nutley NJ 07110 USA

Every second of a heart cell's existence is characterized by large fluctuations in the cytoplasmic concentration of calcium ions. Accordingly, heart cells exhibit a very sophisticated mechanism for the regulation of their cytoplasmic calcium concentration ($[Ca^{2+}]_i$), a system which involves the coordinated interaction of Ca^{2+} channels and pumps in the plasma membrane and intracellular organelles as well as Ca-binding proteins in both the cytoplasm and, of course, the myofibrillar apparatus itself. One element of this complex mechanism for regulating $[Ca]_i$ is the Na-Ca exchange system, a carrier-mediated transport process in which the movement of Ca^{2+} in one direction across the membrane is directly coupled to the movement of Na^+ in the opposite direction. It is a component of the cardiac plasma membrane (sarcolemma) and mediates Ca^{2+} movements in either direction between the cell cytoplasm and the extracellular fluid. As discussed in detail elsewhere (1,2), its primary physiological role is probably to serve as a Ca^{2+} pump, i.e. to effect the net efflux of Ca^{2+} from the myocardial cell, although it seems likely that under some circumstances it can bring about the net entry of Ca^{2+} as well.

Its existence was first postulated in 1958, by Lüttgau and Niedergerke (3), who observed that extracellular Na^+ antagonized the effects of Ca^{2+} on tension development in frog ventricular strips. The first experimental demonstrations of exchange activity came approximately 10 years later, through the efforts of two groups of investigators (4,5) who were studying the Na-dependence of Ca^{2+} fluxes in squid axons and in guinea pig atria. Their findings showed that Ca^{2+} influx was antagonized or promoted by extra- and intracellular Na^+, respectively, and that an opposite relation held for Ca^{2+} efflux. Baker *et al.* (4) suggested that this system might be responsible for mediating the inotropic effects of cardiac glycosides.

Today much is known, on a phenomenological level, about the operation and regulation of the Na-Ca exchange system (reviewed in ref.1). In addition to catalyzing Na-Ca exchange, the exchanger also conducts Na-Na and Ca-Ca exchanges; the latter is stimulated by alkali metal ions, including Na^+ at low concentrations. The stoichiometry of Na-Ca exchange appears to be 3 Na^+ per Ca^{2+} (cf.below); with this stoichiometry, each turnover of the exchange carrier results in the translocation of a positive charge across the membrane and its activity would therefore be expected to generate a current and to respond in an appropriate fashion to changes in the membrane potential. By and large, these predictions have been confirmed, although some unusual and perplexing features of the voltage dependency of exchange activity have been reported (6). Studies with internally perfused or dialyzed squid axons indicate that the exchange system is kinetically asymmetric, with a K_m for Ca^{2+} that differs by 2 or 3 orders of magnitude between the extracellular and intracellular membrane surfaces (4,7,8). Moreover, the K_m for Ca^{2+} at the intracellular surface, and that for Na^+ at the extracellular surface, appear to be regulated by an ATP-dependent mechanism, since ATP depletion increases both values (7,9). For example, in squid axons, the inclusion of ATP in the internal dialysis fluid reduces the K_m for cytoplasmic Ca^{2+} from 10-20 μM to 1-2 μM (7). In addition, the operation of the exchange system in the so-called "reverse mode" (Na_i-dependent Ca^{2+} influx) appears to depend upon the presence of *both* ATP and Ca^{2+} (10). It has been suggested that these observations may reflect the regulation of the exchange system by a Ca-calmodulin dependent protein kinase (11).

Cardiac Sarcolemmal Vesicles

Work in our laboratory has been directed toward studying the Na-Ca exchange system in a subcellular preparation consisting of osmotically sealed cardiac sarcolemmal vesicles (12). These are prepared by homogenizing cardiac ventricular tissue and isolating a highly enriched preparation of sarcolemmal membranes by differential and density gradient centrifugation. The vesicles are devoid of cytoplasmic constituents and internal organelles but retain many of the transport characteristics of the intact cell. They are a mixed population topologically, with 30-50% of the vesicles being of the "inside-out" orientation (13), i.e. with the cytoplasmic membrane surface forming the external surface of the vesicle. The inside-out subpopulation exhibits ATP-dependent Na^+ transport *via* the Na-K-ATPase as well as ATP-dependent Ca^{2+} transport *via* the sarcolemmal Ca-activated ATPase; the latter is a different enzyme than the Ca-ATPase of the sarcoplasmic reticulum, and exhibits a different molecular weight, substrate specificity and regulatory properties (14,15).

Na-Ca exchange activity is measured by diluting vesicles loaded internally with 160 mM NaCl 50- to 100-fold into an isosmotic Na-free medium (e.g. 160 mM KCl) containing $^{45}Ca^{2+}$. The outwardly directed concentration gradient of Na^+ drives the accumulation of $^{45}Ca^{2+}$ into the vesicles *via* the Na-Ca exchange system. Appropriate control experiments have demonstrated that the $^{45}Ca^{2+}$ is indeed transported into the vesicle interior and is not simply bound to sites on the external surface (12). Ca^{2+} accumulation under these conditions requires the presence, specifically, of Na^+ in the vesicle interior and is blocked by high concentrations of external Na^+.

Stoichiometry of Na-Ca Exchange

The experimental use of membrane vesicles has contributed in an important way to delineating the fundamental characteristics of the exchange process. Early measurements of Na^+ and Ca^{2+} fluxes in sarcolemmal vesicles were consistent with a stoichiometry of 3:1 for the exchange process (16). Other studies showed that Na-Ca exchange activity resulted in changes in the membrane potential in the vesicles, suggesting that the exchange process is electrogenic (17). More recent results have unambiguously confirmed this conclusion by establishing that changes in the membrane potential can drive net Ca^{2+} movements via Na-Ca exchange in the absence of a concentration gradient for Na^+ (18). The stoichiometry of the exchange process was determined using a thermodynamic approach which involved balancing the membrane potential against an offsetting Na^+ gradient such that no net Ca^{2+} movement occurred. The theoretical balance point in such an experiment differs for different assumed stoichiometries and the results yielded an average value of 2.97 ± 0.03 (N=9). Energetic considerations suggest that with a stoichiometry of 3 Na^+ per Ca^{2+}, the exchange system is theoretically capable of reducing $[Ca^{2+}]_i$ to 10-50 nM in resting mammalian myocardial cells; this is actually somewhat lower than values measured with Ca-selective microelectrodes.

Kinetics of Na-Ca Exchange

Vesicles would seem to be the ideal system for precise measurement of the kinetics of the exchange process since there are no internal compartments other than the intravesicular space itself (but see below) and the ionic compositions of the internal and external media can be controlled experimentally. However, the kinetic parameter of primary interest, the exchanger's K_m for Ca^{2+}, shows a high degree of variability from preparation to preparation; reported values range from 1.5 µM to more than 200 µM. Part of this variability is probably a reflection of the large number of factors that affect the K_m for Ca^{2+} in the vesicle system; a partial list is given in Table 1. A particularly important influence is the effect of intravesicular Ca^{2+}, and this will be considered in detail in the following paragraphs.

The data in Table 2 show that the initial rate of Ca^{2+} uptake by bovine sarcolemmal vesicles could be stimulated 3-fold by preincubating the vesicles in the presence of 0.5 mM $CaCl_2$ in 160 mM NaCl; conversely, the addition of 0.1 mM ethylenebis(oxyethylenenitrilo)tetraacetic acid (EGTA) to the NaCl medium to chelate endogenous Ca^{2+} resulted in a 34% inhibition. The effect of added $CaCl_2$ developed gradually over a preincubation period of more than 40 min. in 160 mM NaCl, a time course which correlates with the slow rate of Ca^{2+} entry into the vesicles under these conditions. Stimulation of exchange activity developed more quickly when Ca^{2+} accumulated rapidly in the vesicle interior, as in the usual assay for Na-Ca exchange activity. As shown in Table 3, when Na-loaded vesicles were diluted into a KCl medium containing 20 µM $^{40}CaCl_2$, the initial rate of $^{45}Ca^{2+}$ uptake (measured by adding 3 sec. pulses of $^{45}Ca^{2+}$ to the medium) increased nearly 3-fold within 1 min. Thus, the rate of acceleration in transport activity was related to the rate at which Ca^{2+} entered the vesicles, suggesting that it was the presence of Ca^{2+} within the vesicle *interior* that stimulated exchange activity. The effect of intravesicular Ca^{2+} was not due to Ca-Ca exchange; indeed, the latter activity could not be detected under these conditions, presumably because the high concentration of internal Na^+ competes with intravesicular Ca^{2+} for binding to the exchange carrier. The stimulatory effect of intravesicular Ca^{2+} was shown to be due to a reduction in the K_m for extravesicular Ca^{2+}; vesicles preincubated in 160 mM NaCl containing either 0.2 mM $CaCl_2$ or 0.1 mM EGTA exhibited K_m values of 33 µM and 200 µM respectively (19).

The mechanism by which intravesicular Ca^{2+} stimulates Na-Ca exchange activity is uncertain at present. The various possibilities are discussed in detail in ref. 19. The most appealing explanation is that the binding of Ca^{2+} to sites on the intravesicular membrane surface accelerates a rate limiting step in the exchange cycle, perhaps by influencing the electrostatic field within the membrane. This interpretation is supported by the observations that certain other cationic substances that bind strongly to biological membranes, such as quinacrine and tetraphenyl-phosphonium, also stimulate exchange activity when preincubated with the vesicles (20).

Whatever its mechanism or physiological significance, the stimulatory effect of intravesicular Ca^{2+} on exchange activity has disturbing

Table 1. Treatments that Stimulate Na-Ca Exchange Activity in Cardiac Sarcolemmal Vesicles

Treatment	Reference
Proteolysis	33
Phospholipases C and D	34, 35
Anionic Amphiphiles	36, 37
Membrane Phosphorylation	15
Redox Reagents	24
Intravesicular Ca^{2+}	19

Table 2. Vesicles Pretreated with $CaCl_2$ or EGTA: Effect on Na-Ca Exchange

Treatment	Ca^{2+} uptake (nmol/mg protein/sec)	% Control
Control	1.8 ± 0.2	100
EGTA	1.2 ± 0.1	66 ± 6
$CaCl_2$	5.5 ± 0.4	296 ± 18

Vesicles were incubated in 160 mM NaCl with either 0.1 mM EGTA, 0.5 mM $CaCl_2$ or no additions (Control) for 60 min at 37°C and then assayed for Na-Ca exchange activity. The results are the means of three separate experiments conducted with different vesicle preparations. Data taken from ref.19.

Table 3. Stimulation of Unidirectional Ca^{2+} Influx during Ca^{2+} Accumulation by Na-Ca Exchange

Time (sec)	Ca^{2+} Influx (nmol/mg protein/3 sec)	% Increase
0	4.2	-
10	6.9	65
20	8.3	98
40	10.1	142
60	11.0	170

Vesicles loaded internally with 160 mM NaCl were diluted 50-fold into 160 mM KCl containing 20 μM $CaCl_2$ plus 0.5 μM valinomycin at 25°C. At intervals after the dilution step, 12 μM $^{45}CaCl_2$ was added and the reaction was terminated by filtration 3 sec later. The data represent the quantity of Ca^{2+} accumulated during the 3 sec pulse with $^{45}CaCl_2$. The results are the average values obtained in two separate experiments, where the points for each experiment were measured in triplicate. Cumulative Ca^{2+} uptake by the vesicles at 10, 20, 40 and 60 sec was 10, 20, 35 and 49 nmol/mg protein, respectively. The % increase refers to the increase in Ca^{2+} influx over that observed at t=0. For additional details, see ref. 19.

implications for kinetic measurements in vesicles. The levels of intravesicular Ca^{2+} attained during 1 sec. initial rate measurements of activity (2-10 nmol/mg protein) are sufficient to alter the kinetics of the exchange process itself; thus, true initial rate conditions are unlikely to prevail during these measurements so that the kinetic parameters obtained may not accurately reflect the true properties of the system. Another implication of the results is that variations in the amount of endogenous Ca^{2+} present among different preparations or storage conditions may produce corresponding variations in kinetic properties of the vesicles; this may account for at least a portion of the variability in K_m values for Ca^{2+} in the literature.

The variety of treatments that stimulate exchange activity (Table 1) suggests that the exchanger is in a metastable, kinetically malleable state in the vesicles. In part, this may reflect the loss of regulatory mechanisms during vesicle preparation which are responsible for maintaining the kinetic asymmetry of the system *in vivo*. As mentioned previously, experiments with internally perfused or dialyzed squid axons suggest that the K_m values for Ca^{2+} at the inner and outer membrane surfaces differ by 2 or 3 orders of magnitude (4,7,8). While the kinetic properties of the cardiac exchange system *in vivo* have not been studied as thoroughly, it seems likely that a similar asymmetry might prevail. In cardiac vesicles, however, the exchange system appears to be nearly symmetric (21), suggesting that the exchanger may have "relaxed" from a highly constrained, kinetically asymmetric state *in vivo* to a more symmetric, but kinetically malleable, state during vesicle preparation.

However, vesicles from other tissues do not necessarily display the same stimulatory responses to the treatments in Table 1 as cardiac vesicles. Adrenal medulla plasma membrane vesicles, for instance, are unaffected by chymotrypsin, redox reagents or intravesicular Ca^{2+}, treatments which stimulate exchange activity in cardiac vesicles several fold (22). Similarly, vesicles from tracheal smooth muscle fail to respond to chymotrypsin or redox reagents (23). These observations indicate that the variability of exchange kinetics in the cardiac system is not due solely to artifacts introduced by vesicle preparation procedures. Perhaps the plasticity of the cardiac system *in vitro* is a manifestation of an *in vivo* cardiac regulatory process which is required to meet the special demands imposed by the continual fluctuations in $[Ca]_i$ in heart cells, and the need to regulate total cellular Ca^{2+} content in a highly adaptive, yet rigorously controlled, manner.

Redox modification and sulfhydryl groups

Na-Ca exchange activity can be stimulated up to 10-fold by treating the vesicles with certain combinations of redox reagents (24). Both an oxidant and a reductant are required and their effects are mediated by transition metal ions such as Fe^{2+}. Combinations of redox reagents that stimulate exchange activity include dithiothreitol (1 mM) plus H_2O_2 (0.1 mM), Fe^{2+} (1 μM) plus H_2O_2 (0.1 mM), glutathione plus glutathione disulfide (2 mM each) and superoxide generated by xanthine oxidase. Full experimental details have been presented in ref. 24. The issue to be considered here is the possible involvement of protein sulfhydryl groups in this process. The fact that redox stimulation is promoted by Na^+ and antagonized by Ca^{2+} suggests that the redox reagents interact directly with the exchange carrier. It was postulated that the mechanism of stimulation might involve thiol-disulfide interchange among the sulfhydryl groups of the exchange carrier (24).

To test this possibility, the effects of sulfhydryl reagents on exchange activity were examined (25). Most of the sulfhydryl regents

Table 4. Inhibition of Na-Ca Exchange by pCMBS in Native and Redox-Activated Vesicles

[pCMBS]	Ca^{2+} Uptake		Residual Activity	
	Control	Fe-H$_2$O$_2$	Control	Fe-H$_2$O$_2$
(µM)	(nmol/mg protein/sec)		(%)	
0	2.1	7.6	100	100
20	2.0	6.9	94	91
40	1.8	5.7	85	75
80	0.7	0.5	34	7
120	0.7	0.4	34	5

Redox activated vesicles were incubated for 30 min at 37°C in 160 mM NaCl containing 1 µM FeSO$_4$ plus 0.1 mM H$_2$O$_2$, then diluted with 10 vol of ice-cold 160 mM NaCl and collected by centrifugation; control vesicles were treated similarly except that the FeSO$_4$ and H$_2$O$_2$ were omitted. Each set of vesicles were then incubated for 30 min at 37°C in 160 mM NaCl containing the indicated concentrations of pCMBS and then assayed for Na-Ca exchange activity. Data from a representative experiment are shown.

tested partially inhibited exchange activity and the organomercurial p-chloromercuribenzenesulfonic acid (pCMBS) was selected for further study. As shown in Table 4, pCMBS inhibited exchange activity in native vesicles and in vesicles pretreated with Fe-H$_2$O$_2$ over a similar concentration range (20-100 µM). However, the extent of inhibition by pCMBS was much greater in the redox-activated vesicles than in the native vesicles (Table 4). A similar result was obtained when native vesicles and chymotrypsin-activated vesicles were compared; i.e. the latter show a much greater sensitivity to inhibition by organomercurials. Interestingly, however, vesicles in which exchange activity was stimulated by intravesicular Ca^{2+} did not exhibit an increased sensitivity to pCMBS; 300 µM pCMBS inhibited exchange activity to 26% and 29% of controls for Ca-treated and EGTA-treated vesicles, respectively. Moreover, in vesicles pretreated with 100 µM pCMBS, residual exchange activity could no longer be stimulated with redox reagents or chymotrypsin, although it remained responsive to the stimulatory effects of intravesicular Ca^{2+}.

The results are consistent with the participation of sulfhydryl groups in the stimulation of exchange activity by redox reagents or chymotrypsin. The most general explanation is that these treatments induce a conformational change in the exchange carrier that is blocked by the prior addition of pCMBS and reversed by the subsequent addition of this agent. This conformational change could involve thiol-disulfide interchange within the exchange carrier, as originally postulated (24); other possiblities, such as the removal of an inhibitory regulatory protein, are also consistent with the data. In any event, it seems clear that the stimulation of exchange activity by intravesicular Ca^{2+} reflects a fundamentally different process than stimulation by redox reagents or chymotrypsin since the former does not involve alterations in the exchanger's sensitivity to sulfhydryl reagents while the latter does.

Identification of the Exchange Carrier

The identification and eventual purification of the exchange carrier itself is a central goal of current research efforts on the biochemistry of Na-Ca exchange. Progress in this area has been hampered by the lack of a specific high-affinity probe or inhibitor that could be used to label the carrier. Consequently, one must rely upon measurements of transport activity in reconstituted proteoliposomes to assay for the presence of the exchange carrier. Earlier work from this laboratory had led to the suggestion that the exchange carrier was an 82 kDa glycoprotein that was highly resistant to proteolysis (26). Subsequent experiments, however, showed that the 82 kDa protein bound to a column of immobilized Concanavalin A (a lectin with a high affinity for α-mannose residues) but that exchange activity did not (27,28). These and other observations indicate that the 82 kDa glycoprotein is not the exchange carrier. The exchanger is a glycoprotein, however, as indicated by the fact that it interacts with a different lectin, wheat germ agglutinin, which has a high affinity for N-acetylglucosamine residues. Serial chromatographic treatment of solubilized vesicle extracts with Concanavalin A and wheat germ agglutinin has allowed us to isolate a glycoprotein fraction which binds to the latter lectin but not to the former. This fraction shows substantial enrichment in Na-Ca exchange activity in reconstituted proteoliposomes and a greatly reduced number of protein species compared to native vesicles. Lectin affinity chromatography, therefore, will undoubtedly be an important tool in the eventual purification of the exchange carrier.

Work in other laboratories has led to the identification of polypeptides at 70 kDa (29) and 33 kDa (30) as possible candidates for the Na-Ca exchange carrier. Proof that either of these proteins (or any other candidate) is indeed the exchange carrier must await their complete purification in an active state and the development of specific antibodies against them.

A report which initially seemed to be a major breakthrough claimed that monoclonal antibodies developed against a particular surface antigen of lymphocytic cell lines inhibited Na-Ca exchange activity in cardiac sarcolemmal vesicles (31,32). However, subsequent studies in several different laboratories, including ours, failed to confirm these findings. Thus, it seems unlikely that these antibodies will serve as useful probes for the Na-Ca exchange carrier or its activity.

Conclusions

The use of cardiac sarcolemmal vesicles has contributed in an important way to our understanding of the fundamental attributes of the Na-Ca exchange process, such as its electrogenicity and stoichiometry. The results of kinetic studies with the vesicles, however, are difficult to reconcile with the properties of the exchange system in more physiological systems such as perfused heart cells, barnacle muscles and squid axons. Perhaps this reflects the absence, in the vesicles, of cytoplasmic regulatory processes that are responsible for maintaining the asymmetry of the system *in vivo* or for regulating the system's activity over a wide range of cytoplasmic calcium concentrations. The identification and purification of the exchange carrier, and the development of specific antibodies against it will be a crucial step in resolving these issues.

REFERENCES

1. Reeves, J.P., *Curr. Topics Membr. Transp.* 25:77-127 (1985).
2. Reeves, J.P., *in* Stone, H.L. and Weglicki, W.B. (eds) "Pathobiology of Cardiovascular Injury". (Martinus Nijhoff, Boston), pp. 232-244 (1985).
3. Lüttgau, H.C. and Niedergerke, R., *J. Physiol. (London)* 143:486-505 (1958).
4. Baker, P.F., Blaustein, M.P., Hodgkin, A.L. and Steinhardt, R.A. *J. Phsiol. (London)* 200:431-458 (1969).
5. Reuter, H. and Seitz, N., *J. Physiol. (London)* 195:451-470 (1968)

6. Baker, P.F. and Allen, T.J.A., *in* Bronner, F. and Peterlik, M. (eds) "Calcium and Phosphate Transport Across Biomembranes, Proceedings 2nd International Workshop". (Liss, New York) pp. 89-94 (1984).
7. Blaustein, M.P. *Biophys. J.* **20**:79-111 (1977).
8. Baker, P.F. and McNaughton, P.A., *J. Physiol. (London)* **276**:127-150 (1978).
9. Baker, P.F. and Glitsch, H.G., *J. Physiol. (London)* **233**:44P-46P (1973).
10. DiPolo, R., *J. Gen. Physiol.* **73**:91-113 (1979).
11. Caroni, P. and Carafoli, E. *Eur. J. Biochem.* **132**:451-460 (1983).
12. Reeves, J.P. and Sutko, J.L., *Proc. Natl. Acad. Sci. U.S.A.* **76**:590-594 (1979).
13. Trumble, W.R., Reeves, J.P. and Sutko, J.L., *Life Sci.* **27**:207-214 (1980).
14. Trumble, W.R., Sutko, J.L. and Reeves, J.P., *J. Biol. Chem.* **256**:7101-7104 (1981).
15. Caroni, P. and Carafoli, E., *J. Biol. Chem.* **256**:3263-3270 (1981).
16. Pitts, B.J R., *J. Biol. Chem.* **254**:6232-6235 (1979).
17. Reeves, J.P. and Sutko, J.L., *Science* **208**:1461-1464 (1980).
18. Reeves, J.P. and Hale, C.C., *J. Biol. Chem.* **259**:7733-7739 (1984).
19. Reeves, J.P. and Poronnik, P., *Am. J. Physiol.* (in press) (1987).
20. de la Peña, P. and Reeves, J.P., *Am. J. Physiol.* (in press) (1987).
21. Philipson, K.D., *Biochim. Biophys. Acta* **821**:367-376 (1985).
22. Bailey, C.A. and Reeves, J.P., *Fed. Proc.* (in press) (1987).
23. Slaughter, R., Welton, A. and Morgan, D., *Biophys. J.* **49**:546a (1986).
24. Reeves, J.P., Bailey, C.A. and Hale, C.C., *J. Biol. Chem.* **261**:4948-4955 (1986).
25. Bailey, C.A. and Reeves, J.P., *Biophys. J.* **49**:345a (1986)
26. Hale, C.C., Slaughter, R.S., Ahrens, D. and Reeves, J.P., *Proc. Natl. Acad. Sci. U.S.A.* **81**:6569-6573 (1984).
27. Carafoli, E., (personal communication).
28. Reeves, J.P., (unpublished observations).
29. Barzilai, A., Spanier, R. and Rahamimoff, H., *Proc. Natl. Acad. Sci. U.S.A.* **81**:6521-6525 (1984).
30. Soldati, L., Longoni, S. and Carafoli, E., *J. Biol. Chem.* **260**:13321-13327 (1985).
31. Michalak, M., Quackenbush, E. J. and Letarte, M., *J. Biol.Chem.* **261**:92-95 (1986).
32. Letarte, M., Quackenbush, E.J., Baumal, R. and Michalak, M., *Biochem. Cell Biol.* **64**:1160-1169 (1986).
33. Philipson, K.D. and Nishimoto, A.Y., *Am. J. Physiol.* **243**:C191-C195 (1982).
34. Philipson, K.D. and Nishimoto, A.Y., *J. Biol. Chem.* **257**:5111-5117 (1983).
35. Philipson, K.D. and Nishimoto, A.Y., *J. Biol. Chem.* **259**:16-19 (1984).
36. Philipson, K. D., *J. Biol. Chem.* **259**:13999-14002 (1984).
37. Philipson, K.D. and Ward, R., *J. Biol. Chem.* **260**:9666-9671 (1985)

SODIUM-CALCIUM EXCHANGE IN PLATELET PLASMA MEMBRANE VESICLES

Appavoo Rengasamy and Harold Feinberg

Department of Pharmacology
University of Illinois College of Medicine at Chicago
Chicago, Illinois

INTRODUCTION

Unstimulated platelets maintain submicromolar concentration of cytosolic Ca^{2+} ($\sim$100 µM) and a steep plasma membrane Ca^{2+} gradient. Since passive inward diffusion of Ca^{2+} will cause platelet activation, mechanisms in addition to Ca^{2+} sequestration by endoplasmic reticulum must exist to remove Ca^{2+} from cytosol. In other tissues low cytosolic Ca^{2+} is achieved, in part, by plasma membrane ATP-dependent Ca^{2+} efflux[1,2] and Na^+-Ca^{2+} exchange[3,4]. Although platelets possess $Ca^{2+}-Mg^{2+}$-ATPase activity, the available evidence suggests that this enzyme is present only in the inner membranes[5,6]. Whether Na^+-Ca^{2+} exchange activity occurs in platelets is not known. We investigated the involvement of Na^+-Ca^{2+} exchange in this process. This study establishes that platelet membranes enriched in plasma membrane markers exhibited Na^+-Ca^{2+} exchange activity.

MATERIALS AND METHODS

Isolation of Plasma Membranes

Platelet plasma membranes were prepared following the method of Mauco et al.[7] with some modifications. Platelets were collected from platelet rich plasma by differential centrifugation and washed three times with Ca^{2+}-free Ardlie buffer (pH 6.5). Platelets were resuspended in 25 mM Tris-HCl (pH 7.4), 100 mM NaCl and 3 mM $MgCl_2$ and sonicated. The homogenate was centrifuged at 1,500 x g for 10 min. The supernatant was fractionated on Percoll gradients at pH 7.4 and at pH 9.6 as described by Mauco et al.[7]. The plasma membrane fraction was mixed with equal volume of sonication buffer and centrifuged at 160,000 x g for 1 hr. The membranes were resuspended in 10 mM Tris-HCl (pH 7.4) containing 140 mM KCl or NaCl.

Ca^{2+} Uptake Measurements

A small volume (5 µl) of vesicles loaded with 140 mM NaCl were diluted 41-fold into 10 mM Mops-Tris (pH 7.4, 37°C), 140 mM KCl and 40 mM $^{45}CaCl_2$ (Ca^{2+} uptake medium). The reaction was terminated by the addition of equal volume of ice-cold 5 mM Mops-Tris (pH 7.4) containing 140 mM KCl and 5 mM $LaCl_3$ (stopping solution). Ca^{2+} uptake for less than 10 sec were measured by using a computer system to control the addition of Ca^{2+} uptake medium

Table 1. Dependence of Na^+-dependent Ca^{2+} uptake on intravesicular Na^+ concentration

Intravesicular Na^+ concentration (mM)	14	28	46.6	80	112	140
Ca^{2+} uptake (pmol/mg/30 sec)	62	120	168	274	441	558

Vesicles loaded separately with 140 mM NaCl or KCl were mixed in appropriate ratios to obtain the desired concentration of intravesicular Na^+. The vesicles were equilibrated at 4°C overnight and at 37°C for 30 min before the assay. Ca^{2+} uptake was determined as described in "Materials and Methods".

and stopping solution. The vesicles were filtered on Millipore filters (0.45 µm) and washed twice with 2.5 ml of 5 mM Mops-Tris (pH 7.4), 140 mM KCl and 2 mM $LaCl_3$. The Na^+-dependent Ca^{2+} uptake was obtained by subtracting the Ca^{2+} uptake obtained after dilution of Na^+ containing vesicles with a medium containing NaCl instead of KCl. Protein was determined according to the method of Bradford[8].

RESULTS AND DISCUSSION

The platelet plasma membranes prepared by Mauco et al.[7] are enriched in surface membrane markers e.g. con A (6-fold), 1-monoacylglycerol lipase (5-fold), 2-monoacylglycerol lipase (3-fold) and exhibits no enrichment in antimycin-insensitive NADH-cytochrome c reductase, an endoplasmic reticulum marker[9]. We prepared platelet plasma membranes by a modification of this method and found that the membranes were enriched in Na^+,K^+-ATPase (15-fold)

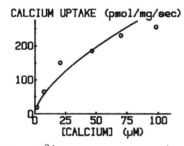 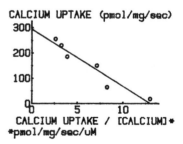

Fig. 1A. Ca^{2+} dependence of Na^+-dependent Ca^{2+} uptake. Vesicles (5 µl) loaded with 10 mM Tris-HCl (pH 7.4), 140 mM NaCl were diluted 41-fold into a medium containing 10 mM Mops-Tris (pH 7.4), 140 mM KCl or NaCl and various concentrations of $^{45}CaCl_2$. Ca^{2+} uptake was measured for 1 sec as described in "Materials and Methods".

1B. Eadie-Hofstee plot of the data in Fig. 1A. The Km for Ca^{2+} was 22 µM and the Vmax 290 pmol/mg/sec.

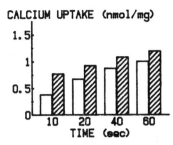
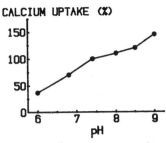

Fig. 2A. Effect of valinomycin on Na^+-dependent Ca^{2+} uptake. Ca^{2+} uptake
was determined by diluting vesicles loaded with 140 mM NaCl into
Ca^{2+} uptake medium containing 0.25% ethanol (open bar) or 1 μM
valinomycin (right hatched bar).

2B. Effect of pH on Na^+-dependent Ca^{2+} uptake. Vesicles were loaded
with 10 mM Tris-HCl (pH 7.4) and 140 mM NaCl and diluted into
Ca^{2+} uptake medium containing 10 mM Tris-maleate buffer at
different pH values, 140 mM NaCl or KCl and 40 μM $^{45}CaCl_2$.

without enrichment of antimycin-insensitive NADH-cytochrome c reductase (data
not shown). Na^+-Ca^{2+} exchange activity in this membrane fraction was
enriched 7-fold compared to homogenate (data not shown).

The Na^+-dependent Ca^{2+} uptake was linear up to 4 sec and plateaued
thereafter (data not shown). The dependency of Ca^{2+} uptake on the intravesicular concentration of Na^+ is shown in Table 1. An approximately linear
increase of Ca^{2+} uptake was observed as intravesicular Na^+ rose. When Ca^{2+}
was loaded into vesicles by Na^+-Ca^{2+} exchange for about 2-3 min, the addition
of 50 mM NaCl but not KCl caused a release of Ca^{2+} (about 65-70% in 5 min)
indicating that the exchange system operates reversibly (data not shown).
Vesicles loaded with Ca^{2+} showed a rapid loss (about 65-75% in 1.5 min) of
Ca^{2+} in the presence of 1 μM A23187 (data not shown); an indication that the
Ca^{2+} released was intravesicular.

Fig. 1A shows the initial rate of Na^+-dependent Ca^{2+} uptake as a
function of extravesicular Ca^{2+} concentration. The high Km for Ca^{2+} (22 μM)
suggests that Na^+-Ca^{2+} exchange is either a less efficient system or that the
Km is not appropriate for in vivo conditions. It is possible that phosphorylation[10], redox conditions[11] and the action of phospholipases and
proteases[12] may regulate Na^+-Ca^{2+} exchange by lowering the in vivo Km for
Ca^{2+}. Although the Vmax (290 pmol/mg/sec) is less than that reported for
cardiac membranes[13], it is comparable to skeletal mucle sarcolemmal
vesicles[14] and rat brain microsomes[15].

Cardiac sarcolemmal vesicles exchange 3 Na^+ for 1 Ca^{2+} hence a net
outward movement of positive charge which inhibits Na^+-Ca^{2+} exchange[16]. An
inward movement of K^+ induced by valinomycin can be used to compensate this
effect and stimulate Na^+-Ca^{2+} exchange. As shown in Fig. 2A platelet plasma
membrane vesicles loaded with Na^+ also exhibited an electrogenic exchange as
Ca^{2+} uptake was increased in the presence of valinomycin. Fig. 2B shows
Na^+-Ca^{2+} exchange activity is sensitive to pH, thus alteration in pH may
regulate cytosolic Ca^{2+} concentration.

In summary we have shown that isolated partially purified plasma membrane vesicles obtained from human platelets exhibit electrogenic Na^+-Ca^{2+} exchange activity.

REFERENCES

1. H. J. Schatzmann, The red cell calcium pump, Ann. Rev. Physiol. 45:303 (1983).
2. P. Caroni, and E. Carafoli, An ATP-dependent Ca^{2+}-pumping system in dog heart sarcolemma, Nature 283:765 (1980).
3. H. Reuter, and Sietz, The dependence of calcium efflux from cardiac muscle on temperature and external ion composition, J. Physiol. 195:451 (1968).
4. J. P. Reeves, and J. L. Sutko, Sodium-calcium ion exchange in cardiac membrane vesicles, Proc. Natl. Acad. Sci. USA 76:590 (1979).
5. L. S. Robblee, D. Shepro, and F. A. Belamarich, Calcium uptake and associated adenosine triphosphatase activity of isolated platelet membranes, J. Gen. Physiol. 61:462 (1973).
6. S. Menashi, K. S. Authi, F. Carey, and N. Crawford, Characterization of Ca^{2+}-sequestering process associated with human platelet membranes isolated by free-flow electrophoresis, Biochem. J. 222:413 (1984)
7. G. Mauco, J. Fauvel, H, Chap, and L. Douste-Blazy, Studies on enzymes related to diacylglycerol production in activated platelets II.Subcellular distribution, enzymatic properties and positional specificity of diacylglycerol- and monoacylglycerol-lipases, Biochim. Biophys. Acta 796: 169 (1984).
8. M. M. Bradford, A rapid and sensitive method for the quantitation of microgram quantities of protein utilizing the principle of protein-dye binding, Anal. Biochem. 72:248 (1976).
9. J. Fauvel, H. Chap, U. Rogues, S. Levy-Toledano, and L. Douste-Blazy, Biochemical characterization of plasma membranes and intracellular membranes isolated from human platelets using Percoll gradients, Biochim. Biophys. Acta 856:155 (1986).
10. P. Caroni, and E. Carafoli, The regulation of sodium-calcium exchanger of heart sarcolemma, Eur. J. Biochem. 132:451 (1983).
11. J. P. Reeves, C. A. Bailey, and C. C. Hale, Redox modifications of sodium-calcium exchange activity in cardiac sarcolemmal vesicles, J. Biol. Chem. 261:4948 (1986).
12. J. P. Reeves, and J. L. Sutko, Competitive interactions of sodium and calcium with the sodium-calcium exchange system of cardiac sarcolemmal vesicles, J. Biol. Chem. 258:3178 (1983).
13. K. D. Philipson, Sodium-calcium exchange in plasma membrane vesicles, Ann. Rev. Physiol. 47:561 (1985).
14. J. R. Gilbert, and G. Meissner, Sodium-calcium exchange in skeletal muscle sarcolemmal vesicles, J. Memb. Biol. 69:77 (1982).
15. G. D. Schellenberg, and P. D. Swanson, Sodium-dependent and calcium-dependent calcium transport by rat brain microsomes, Biochim. Biophys. Acta 648:13 (1981).
16. B. J. R. Pitts, Stoichiometry of sodium-calcium exchange in cardiac sarcolemmal vesicles-coupling to the sodium pump, J. Biol. Chem. 254:6232 (1979).

EFFECT OF Ca^{2+} CHANNEL BLOCKERS ON PASSIVE CALCIUM INFLUX INTO RESEALED

HUMAN RED BLOOD CELL GHOSTS

Basil D. Roufogalis* and Anar Virji

Laboratory of Molecular Pharmacology
Faculty Pharmaceutical Sciences
University of B.C.
Vancouver. B.C. Canada

INTRODUCTION

Red blood cells exhibit a slow but measurable inward leak of calcium (approx. 50 μmoles per hour per litre cells), which is easily compensated by an active Ca^{2+} efflux fueled by a powerful plasma membrane calcium pump (Lew et al., 1982). While there is considerable information on the calcium pump mechanism at the molecular level, mostly derived from the study of the coupled Ca^{2+}-ATPase activity in the isolated plasma membrane (see Schatzmann, 1982), the nature of the passive Ca^{2+} influx mechanism, is not well understood. It is generally agreed that passive Ca^{2+} uptake into intact human erythrocytes occurs by a carrier-mediated passive diffusion mechanism (Ferreira and Lew, 1977; Varecka and Carafoli, 1982; Gárdos et al., 1980). The influx may occur through a protein channel, as it is inhibited by various sulphydryl agents and divalent cations (Varecka et al., 1986) and other Ca^{2+} channel blockers (Locher et al., 1984). The Ca^{2+} influx mechanism appears to proceed by the discharge of the transmembrane K^+ gradient (Varecka and Carafoli, 1982), but it does not appear to be entirely the result of hyperpolarization induced by activation of the Ca^{2+}-activated K^+ channel (Varecka et al., 1986). By contrast to the low passive Ca^{2+} permeability of intact erythrocytes, resealed erythrocyte "ghosts" produced by hypotonic lysis of red cells show a considerably enhanced calcium permeability (Lew and Ferreira, 1977; Porzig, 1972). Because of the high haemoglobin content of red cells, photochromic calcium dyes cannot be readily used to study Ca^{2+} uptake in intact cells, but such methods have been used to study passive Ca^{2+} uptake into resealed white erythrocyte ghosts (Yingst and Hoffman, 1978). In the present study we have examined the effects of Ca^{2+} channel blockers and K^+ on the passive uptake of Ca^{2+} into resealed ghosts and compared the properties of the Ca^{2+} influx mechanism to those in intact cells.

METHODS

Resealed ghosts were prepared and loaded with Arsenzo III by a procedure similar to that reported by James-Kracke and Freedman (1985).

---

*Current address: Department of Biochemistry, University of Sydney, Sydney. N.S.W. Australia.

Freshly collected human red blood cells were washed three times at 4°C in an isotonic solution (100 mM NaCl, 5 mM KCl, 5 mM glucose, 50 mM sodium-HEPES, pH 6.0). After centrifugation, the cells were concentrated to 8 volumes and incubated with 100 μM Arsenazo III at 4°C before being resealed in isotonic KCl, pH 7.4 (adjusted by the addition of 5 mM HEPES) at 37°C for 6 min. The resealed ghosts were stored on ice for 10 min, washed four times in an isotonic buffer (145 mM NaCl, 5 mM KCl, 2 mM MgCl$_2$ and 5 mM sodium-HEPES, pH 7.4) and resuspended to an approx. 1% haematocrit for subsequent Ca^{2+} uptake measurements. Passive Ca^{2+} uptake was measured at 37°C by following the difference in absorption with time at the wavelength pair of 675nm-695nm in an SLM/Aminco DW-2C spectrophotometer equipped with magnetic stirring.

RESULTS AND DISCUSSION

Ca^{2+} uptake increased exponentially in the first 20 min, and thereafter reached a slower rate during the next 30 min of observation. The initial rate of Ca^{2+} uptake increased with increasing extracellular CaCl$_2$ concentration from 0.10 to 1.0 mM, whereas the later slow component rate appeared to be essentially independent of the extracellular Ca^{2+} concentration. The CaCl$_2$ dependence tended towards a plateau at the highest CaCl$_2$ concentration examined. At 1 mM CaCl$_2$ the initial Ca^{2+} uptake rate was similar both in ghosts prepared with KCl or NaCl in the loading/resealing medium (not shown). In ghosts prepared in KCl, changing the KCl concentration in the external medium from 5 mM to 20 mM or 50 mM had little effect on the initial Ca^{2+} uptake rate. These results differ from those in intact ghosts, where increasing the external KCl concentration (and hence decreasing the KCl gradient) decreased the Ca^{2+} uptake rate (Varecka and Carafoli, 1982). In resealed ghosts the Ca^{2+} uptake mechanism therefore appears to be largely independent of the KCl gradient.

The effect of various classes of Ca^{2+} channel blockers and a Ca^{2+} channel "agonist" on the initial Ca^{2+} uptake rate were examined. The results are presented in Table 1.

Table 1. Effect of Various Agents on Passive Calcium Influx into Resealed Erythrocyte Ghosts

Drug	Concentration	$\dfrac{\Delta A}{Time}$ (min-1) x 10^5
Control (DMSO)		28.2 - 39.9
Verapamil	100 μM	30.6
Nifedipine	1 μM	40.2
	10 μM	36.0
Nitrendipine	20 μM	33.9
Nicardipine-(+)	20 μM	0
	10 μM	0
	5 μM	8.4
	4 μM	7.5
Nicardipine-(-)	4 μM	5.9
Bay K-8644	1 μM	30.0
Trifluoperazine	20 μM	30.0

All drugs were added in dimethylsulfoxide and the rates of Ca^{2+} uptake (expressed as $\Delta A_{675-695nm}$/min) were compared to corresponding controls in the same concentration of dimethylsulfoxide (1%) in the absence of drug.

Verapamil (100 μM) had no effect on the initial rate of Ca^{2+} uptake, in contrast to the inhibition reported at this concentration in intact red blood cells (Varecka and Carafoli, 1982). The classical Ca^{2+} channel blockers examined of the 1,4-dihydropyridine group (Nifedipine and Nitrendipine) also failed to inhibit Ca^{2+} uptake, even up to 20 μM concentrations (Table 1). These results again differ from those in intact red blood cells, where Nitrendipine showed a dose-dependent inhibition of influx with a K_i of around 1.5 μM (Locher et al., 1984). The Ca^{2+} channel agonist, Bay K 8644 (1 μM) also failed to affect the initial Ca^{2+} uptake rate, while it was reported to inhibit Ca^{2+} uptake into intact red cells at all concentrations tested from 10 nM to 50 μM (Stimpel et al. 1984).

By contrast to the above results, the 1,4-dihydropyridine, Nicardipine, was found to inhibit initial Ca^{2+} uptake into resealed ghosts in a dose-dependent manner (Table 1). However, the inhibition was apparently not stereoselective, as both (+)-Nicardipine and (-)-Nicardipine inhibited to a similar extent when tested at 4 μM, in contrast to the stereoselectivity exhibited by Nicardipine towards skeletal muscle binding sites (Glossmann et al., 1984). This observation, together with the high concentration required for Ca^{2+} influx inhibition relative to its affinity for Ca^{2+} channel binding sites in excitable tissues (Glossmann et al., 1984), suggests that Nicardipine may block passive Ca^{2+} influx into revealed ghosts by interacting nonspecifically at membrane sites. This interaction may be the result of the large hydrophobic group in the ester substitutent of Nicardipine, which is absent in the other 1,4-dihydropyridines examined. Nicardipine was also found to be the most potent of a series of 1,4-dihydropyridines examined as calmodulin antagonists, which may also reflect nonspecific interactions at a hydrophobic site (Minocherhomjee and Roufogalis, 1984). On the other hand, another antagonist of calmodulin, trifluoperazine, failed to inhibit Ca^{2+} influx at similar concentrations to those that inhibit calmodulin actions and cause membrane perturbations (Table 1).

Conclusions

The use of entrapped Arsenazo III has allowed the continuous monitoring of Ca^{2+} uptake into resealed ghosts by following the change in absorption of the Ca^{2+}-dye complex over time at a suitable wavelength pair. An ititial rapid uptake of Ca^{2+} was found to depend on extracellular $CaCl_2$ levels. The initial rate of Ca^{2+} uptake was independent of the K^+ gradient across the resealed ghosts, a result which contrasts with the uptake of Ca^{2+} into intact red blood cells. The Ca^{2+} influx was also insensitive to various Ca^{2+} channel blockers, including Verapamil, Nifedipine and Nitrendipine, as well as to a Ca^{2+} channel agonist, which also contrasts to results reported for the uptake of Ca^{2+} into intact red blood cells. The exception was the effect of Nicardipine, which inhibits the initial Ca^{2+} influx into resealed ghosts, but this inhibition was non-stereoselective and probably reflects a nonspecific effect on the membrane. Nevertheless, this effect of Nicardipine may be useful in preventing pathological passive Ca^{2+} influx into cells, and warrants further investigation. These results indicate that the larger Ca^{2+} influx in resealed ghosts occurs through membrane mechanisms that differ from those responsible for the normal physiological leak in intact red cells, which probably occurs through channels similar to those in excitable cells. Alternatively, however, it is possible that the process of hypotonic lysis of red cells during ghost formation may remove a regulatory component responsible for Ca^{2+}-channel antagonist binding (Poggioli et al., 1985) and possibly the control of the Ca^{2+} influx rate (Porzig, 1977). Heterogeneity of Ca^{2+} uptake in resealed ghosts has been previously reported (Yingst and Hoffmann, 1984) and it was recently shown that certain divalent cations and sulphydryl reagents induce a new pathway for Ca^{2+} entry in intact human red blood cells (Varecka et *al.*, 1986). Whatever the explanation, it is clear from these results that the resealed human erythrocyte ghosts cannot be used as a model for the Ca^{2+} uptake mechanism in intact cells.

ACKNOWLEDGEMENTS

Supported by the MRC of Canada and the Canadian Heart Foundation.

REFERENCES

Ferreira, H.G., and Lew, V.L., 1977, Passive calcium transport and cytoplasmic Ca buffering in intact red cells, in: "Membrane Transport in Red Cells", J.C. Ellory, ed., Academic Press, New York.

Gárdos, G., Szász, I., Sarkadi, B. and Szebeni, J., 1980, Various pathways for passive Ca transport in red cells, in: "Membrane Transport in Erythrocytes", U.V. Lassen, H.H. Ussing and J.O. Weith, eds., Munksgaard, Copenhagen.

Glossmann, H., Ferry, D.R., Goll, A., and Rombusch, M., 1984, Molecular pharmacology of the calcium channel: evidence for subtypes, multiple drug-receptor sites, channel subunits, and the development of a radioiodinated 1,4-dihydropyridine calcium channel label, [^{125}I]Iodipine. J. Cardiovasc. Pharmacol., 6, Suppl. 4:S608.

James-Kracke, M.R., and Freedman, J.C., 1985, Calcium transport in red-cell ghosts monitored by Quin-2 fluorescence, Fed. Proc., 44:1595

Lew, V.L., and Ferreira, H.G., 1978, Calcium transport and the properties of a calcium-activated potassium channel in red cell membranes in: "Current Topics in Membranes and Transport", Vol. 10, F. Bronner and A. Kleinzeller, eds., Academic Press, New York.

Lew, V.L., Tsien, R.Y., Miner, C. and Bookchin, R.M., 1982, Physiological [Ca^{2+}]$_i$ level and pump-leak turnover in intact red cells measured using an incorporated Ca chelator, Nature, 298:478.

Locher, R., Neyses, L., Stimpel, M., Küffer, B., and Vetter, W., 1984, The cholesterol content of the human erythrocyte influences calcium influx through the channel, Biochem. Biophys. Res. Comm., 124:822.

Minocherhomjee, A.-e-V., and Roufogalis, B.D., 1984, Antagonism of calmodulin and phosphodiesterase by Nifedipine and related calcium entry blockers, Cell Calcium, 5:57.

Poggioli, J., Mauger, J.-P., Guedson, R., and Claret, M., 1985, A regulatory calcium-binding site for calcium channel in isolated rat hepatocytes, J. Biol. Chem., 260:3289.

Porzig, H., 1972, ATP-independent calcium net movements in human red cell ghosts, J. Membr. Biol., 8:237.

Porzig, H., 1977, Studies on the cation permeability of human red cell ghosts. Characterization and biological significance of two membrane sites with high affinities for Ca. J. Membr. Biol., 31:317.

Schatzmann, H.J., 1982, The plasma membrane calcium pump of erythrocytes and other animal cells, in: "Membrane Transport of Calcium," E. Carafoli, ed., Academic Press, London.

Stimpel, M. Neyses, L, Locher, R., Groth, H., and Vetter, V., 1984, J. Hypertension, 2, Suppl. 3:577.

Varecka, L. and Carafoli, E., 1982, Vanadate-induced movements of Ca^{2+} and K^+ in human red blood cells, J. Biol. Chem., 257:7417.

Varečka, L., Peterajová, E., and Pogády, J., 1986, Inhibition by divalent cations and sulphydryl reagents of the passive Ca^{2+} transport in human red blood cells observed in the presence of vanadate, Biochim. Biophys. Acta, 856:585.

Yingst, D.R., and Hoffmann, J.F., 1978, Changes of intracellular Ca^{2+} as measured by Arsenazo III in relation to the K permeability of human erythrocyte ghosts, Biophys. J., 23:463.

Yingst, D.R., and Hoffman, J.F., 1984, Passive Ca Transport in human red blood cell ghosts measured with entrapped Arsenazo III, J. Gen. Physiol., 83:1.

ALTERED CALCIUM HOMEOSTASIS AND MEMBRANE INTEGRITY IN MYOCARDIAL CELL INJURY

L. Maximilian Buja, Karen P. Burton, Kenneth R. Chien, and
James T. Willerson

Departments of Pathology, Physiology, and Internal Medicine
(Cardiology Division) The University of Texas Health Science
Center at Dallas
5323 Harry Hines Blvd., Dallas, Texas   75235

INTRODUCTION

Coronary occlusion leads to contractile arrest of ischemic myocardium
and progressive metabolic derangements and ultrastructural alterations,
which if of sufficient duration and severity, lead to irreversible myocardial
injury. Based on a number of experimental observations, we and others have
put forward the following general hypothesis regarding the pathogenesis of
irreversible myocardial injury[1,2]. Myocardial ischemia causes oxygen depri-
vation which leads to depressed energy metabolism resulting in a reduced ATP
level, increased lactate, and decreased pH. The metabolic changes are followed by discrete alterations in energy dependent membrane transport systems
which lead to altered ionic composition of the cell, including an increase in
cytosolic calcium. These membrane alterations may include altered ionic flux
across the sarcolemma as well as release of calcium from mitochondria and
sarcoplasmic reticulum. The elevated cytosolic calcium concentration has
the potential to activate catabolic enzymes, including phospholipases. This
may lead to acceleration phosphlipid degradation, increased membrane permeability, and further electrolyte derangements, including calcium accumulation. The excess cellular calcium load may also lead to ATP depletion by
activation of calcium-dependent ATPases as well as by mitochondrial calcium
accumulation which occurs at the expense of continued energy production.
Thereafter, a vicious cycle of membrane injury and ATP depletion may ensue
which terminates in irreversible cell injury. Observations pertinent to this
hypothesis are reviewed in this chapter.

PATHOBIOLOGY OF MYOCARDIAL INFARCTION

Irreversible injury first develops in the most severely ischemic sub-
endocardial region of the myocardium at approximately 40 to 60 minutes after
the onset of coronary occlusion. Irreversible injury then spreads to involve
peripheral, predominately subepicardial tissue in the bed-at-risk, with the
major extent of necrosis completed within approximately 3 to 6 hours after
the onset of coronary occlusion [3]. In association with the development of
irreversible injury, myocytes exhibit marked clumping of nuclear chromatin,
mitochondria with disrupted cristae and amorphous matrix (focculent) den-
sities formed by denatured protein and lipid, and disruption of the tri-
laminar plasma membrane[2-4]. In peripheral infarct regions, necrotic myocytes

show additional changes characterized by disrupted myofibrils, contraction bands, and electron dense deposits, indicative of marked calcium overloading in the mitochondria[2-4]. Such calcium overloading also occurs with temporary coronary occlusion and reperfusion[2-4].

Clinically, acute myocardial infarcts may be identified by myocardial imaging with various radiopharmaceuticals, including technetium 99-m pyrophosphate[4]. This agent selectively accumulates in myocardium with some residual perfusion and irreversibly injured, calcium-loaded myocytes. These observations regarding the pathobiology of myocardial infarction indicate that excess calcium accumulation occurs in ischemic myocardium during the evolution of myocardial infarction and that the degree of calcium accumulation is influenced by the degree and duration of the ischemia. These observations also have led to more basic investigations aimed at elucidating the role of altered calcium homeostasis in the development of myocardial injury.

PATHOPHYSIOLOGY OF MEMBRANE INJURY

Cell swelling with intracellular edema is an early manifestation of ischemic membrane dysfunction[5,6]. In studies performed in an isolated blood perfused canine heart preparation, significant inhibition of sodium, potassium ATPase activity was measured in membrane homogenates from both the ischemic subendocardium and subepicardium after 60 minutes of permanent coronary occlusion or 40 minutes of temporary coronary occlusion and 20 minutes of reflow[5]. The approximately 20% decrease in sodium, potassium ATPase activity was associated with multifocal swelling of myocytes, but occurred prior to the onset of extensive cell necrosis as judged by morphologic criteria and the lack of reduction in creatine kinase activity in this model. The relatively mild cell injury after 60 minutes of ischemia was related to non-working in vitro model used for these experiments. In addition to the sodium, potassium pump, other specific ion transport systems likely are involved during the evolution of myocyte injury[7]. The mechanisms of inhibition of these transport systems may involve both reduction in ATP pools as well as direct injury to the transport proteins.

The cellular effects of membrane dysfunction have been evaluated in studies performed using myocardial tissue slices obtained from dogs subjected to coronary occlusion for 30 to 60 minutes[6]. Responses of normal myocardium and ischemic myocardium to cold shock were evaluated. Measurements were made of total tissue water as well as inulin diffusible and impermeable spaces (Figure 1). Control tissue slices exhibited reversible increases in total tissue water and inulin impermeable space without a change in inulin diffusible space. These changes were indicative of intracellular swelling following cold-induced inhibition of energy metabolism and a return to normal cell volume upon rewarming. In contrast, ischemic tissue slices exhibited persistent increases in total tissue water, inulin impermeable space, and inulin diffusible space. Upon incubation of the ischemic slices with hyperosmolar media, there was a reduction in total tissue water primarily as a result of the decrease in the inulin impermeable space with minimal change in the inulin diffusible space. These experiments indicated that the ischemic tissue exhibited defective cell volume regulation which was accompanied by an increase in membrane permeability as reflected by expansion of the inulin diffusible space. The partial responsiveness of the ischemic slices to hyperosmolar incubation suggested the presence of a mixed population of myocytes: one with intact plasma membranes responsive to hyperosmolar exposure and a second with structural defects in the plasma membranes that remained swollen and permeable to inulin and was not subject to modification by exposure to hyperosmolar medium. Ultrastructural observations confirmed the presence of these two populations of cells.

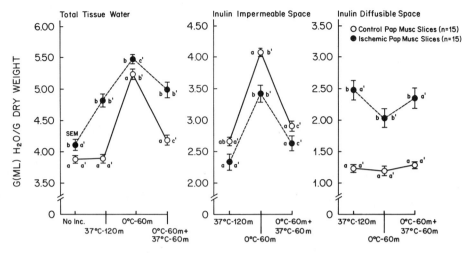

Figure 1. Response to various _in vitro_ experimental conditions of control and ischemic papillary muscle tissue slices from dogs after 60 minutes of coronary occlusion. Statistical differences between control and ischemic slices under a given experimental condition are shown by the a, b, c series. From Buja et al[6].

Functional membrane alterations were further explored in isolated myocardial preparations using an ionic lanthanum probe technique[8,9]. Lanthanum is an electron dense trivalent ion with properties similar to those of calcium. Lanthanum has an extracellular location in normal muscle, so that intracellular lanthanum accumulation can serve as a marker of altered membrane permeability. The technique was used to evaluate membrane permeability changes during the course of hypoxia with and without reoxygenation in isolated cat papillary muscle and ischemia with reflow in the perfused rabbit intraventricular septal preparation. In both preparations, abnormal intracellular lanthanum deposits indicative of a membrane permeability defect to multivalent ions developed in temporal association with the onset of persistent functional depression. Abnormal lanthanum accumulation was identified not only in severely damaged muscle cells, but also in a significant proportion of the muscle cells with only mild structural damage.

The analytical electron microscopic technique of electron probe x-ray microanalysis was used to measure changes in cellular electrolytes which develop in association with altered membrane permeability in isolated myocardial preparations[10]. The perfused rabbit intraventricular septal preparation was modified so that the small right ventricular papillary muscles were left attached to the septum for subsequent rapid freezing, cryosectioning, and elemental analysis. Studies were performed on controls and muscles maintained under hypoxic conditions, using a nitrogenous atmosphere and perfusion with 95% nitrogen and 5% carbon dioxide. These early electron probe studies were complicated by some elemental redistribution which resulted in relatively high sodium and chloride values. Nevertheless, it was possible to measure relative changes in different groups. Analysis of the hypoxic muscles revealed two populations of muscle cells. The majority of the muscle cells exhibited more severe changes in these elements as well as evidence of calcium overloading with formation of electron dense inclusions in the mitochondria. Mitochondrial uptake is dependent upon electron transport, and total anoxia inhibits this process. Thus, it is likely that mito-chondrial calcium accumulation in this model was due to exposure of the cells to a state of less than total anoxia but of hypoxia significant enough to injure the cells without preventing calcium accumulation. Furthermore, the levels of calcium and phosphorus which accumulated in the mitochondria ex-ceeded the levels which have been previously shown to produce severe damage to isolated mitochondrial preparations[11]. Thus, these studies showed that progressive impairment of membrane function occurs during the course of hypoxic and ischemic myocardial injury and that a membrane permeability de-fect to calcium develops in association with the transition from reversible to irreversible myocardial injury.

In addition to alterations in ion transport and permeability, ischemic myocardium develops alterations in adrenergic receptors as another manifesta-tion of membrane dysfunction. After one hour of coronary occlusion, ischemic myocardium exhibited an approximately 60% increase in the number of beta adrenergic receptors without a change in receptor affinity[12,13]. Para-doxically, the receptor increase occurred during the time when ischemic tissue developed an altered distribution of catecholamines with release of catecholamines from nerve terminals into the ischemic myocardium[14]. Corr et al. have reported that the number of alpha adrenergic receptors in feline heart increases after 30 minutes of coronary occlusion[15]. When the increased numbers of beta adrenergic receptors in ischemic canine myocardium were stim-ulated by isoproterenol or epinephrine during reperfusion, the ischemic tissue developed increased levels of cyclic AMP and activated phosphory-lase[13]. No change in muscarinic cholinergic receptors occurred in the canine model[12]. Similar increases in beta adrenergic receptors have been produced in cultured myocytes subjected to metabolic inhibition[16], suggesting the possibility of unmasking of latent receptors or alterations in cycling of receptors as the cause of the increase in membrane-associated receptors [16,17]. The in vitro studies also indicated that the increase in beta adre-nergic receptors developed during the reversible stage of injury. It is likely that relatively mildly injured cells in the periphery of the myo-cardial zone are responsible for the changes observed in the intact animal. The alterations in the adrenergic system may contribute to the progression of cell injury and arrhythmogenesis during the course of myocardial ischemia. The relationship of these adrenergic alterations to altered calcium homeo-stasis requires further study.

ROLE OF PHOSPHOLIPID ALTERATIONS

The observations reviewed above suggest that ischemic membrane injury involves an early phase of discrete alterations in membrane transport sys-tems, a later stage with a more generalized change in membrane permeability, and a final phase with actual structural defects in the membrane. There is evidence to support the concept that progressive alterations in membrane phospholipids contribute importantly to the functional and structural mem-brane derangements. Altered membrane phospholipid composition can influence the function of membrane enzymes involved in membrane transport systems, whereas more severe alterations may lead to membrane permeability defects[18]. The myocardium contains both phospholipase A and phospholipase C activities, which may be susceptible to activation by an increase in calcium concentra-tion[19,20]. Thus, it is possible that subtle derangements in calcium homeo-stasis may be involved in the activation of membrane-associated phospholi-pases with subsequent accelerated phospholipid degradation. Changes in total phospholipids and phospholipid species in ischemic myocardium were relatively small compared to those observed in a liver ischemia model[21,22]. Chien et al. reported, after one hour of permanent coronary occlusion in the dog, a 3.3 percent reduction in total phospholipids in the ischemic subendocardium with a significant 5 percent decrease in phosphotidyl ethanolamine and a slight decrease of phosphotidyl choline. After 3 hours of coronary occlusion, there was a significant 10.8 percent decrease in total phospholipids associated with 11.6 percent decreases in both phosphotidyl ethanolamine and phosphotidyl choline. Further evidence of accelerated phospholipid degradation was sought by measurement of phospholipid degradation products[23]. It was found that a several fold increase in free fatty acids, including arachidonic acid, in the ischemic myocardium occurred after 40 to 60 minutes of coronary occlusion in the dog model (Figure 2). Since arachidonic acid is normally stored in membrane phospholipids, accumulation of free arachidonate serves as a marker of accelerated phospholipid degradation. Similar changes have been observed with global ischemia in an isolated rat heart model[24]. In order to evaluate the functional significance of these changes, myocardial microsomal vesicles were prepared from normal canine myocardium and loaded with calcium-45 by sodium, calcium exchange. Treatment of these vesicles with either phospholipase C or phospholipase A (0.01 mg/ml) resulted in a marked acceleration of calcium efflux[22]. The marked calcium permeability defect was associated with relatively small (10 percent) changes in total phospholipids and phospholipid species. These observations indicate that: a) significantly altered membrane permeability occurs with small measurable changes in total phospholipids and b) accumulation of free fatty acids, including arachidonic acid, is a more sensitive marker of significant membrane phospholipid perturbation than is a change in total phospholipids.

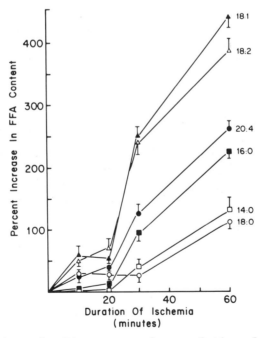

Figure 2. Time course of accumulation of unesterified fatty acids in ischemic canine myocardium. From Chien et al[23].

A cultured neonatal rat cardiac myocyte model has also been used to pursue the role of membrane phospholipid alterations[25-29]. This is a system in which the effects of specific components of ischemia can be evaluated directly in a uniform population of myocytes without the complexities of in vivo ischemia which involves multiple cell types, regional variations in collateral blood flow, and the influence of the autonomic nervous system. Specifically, relationships between impaired energy metabolism and membrane phospholipid alterations have been studied. Measurements were made ot subcellular concentrations of calcium and other elements by electron probe x-ray microanalysis, intracellular free calcium by the fura-2 technique, tritiated arachidonic acid as a marker of membrane phospholipid degradation, and ATP content of the cells (Table 1). Impaired energy metabolism was produced by a variety of metabolic inhibitors, including iodoacetate and combinations of deoxyglucose and oligomycin or cyanide. Iodoacetate treatment resulted in a progressive decrease of myocyte ATP content with mild reduction after one hour and marked reduction after two or more hours. The severe ATP reduction was associated with the development of hypercontraction and marked surface blebbing of myocytes. These myocytes exhibited significant elemental alterations characterized by an elevation of sodium and chloride, a decrease in potassium in the cytosol and mitochondria, and calcium accumulation, particularly in the mitochondria. Cytosolic free calcium was also elevated in these cells. The morphologic changes and calcium overloading correlated temporally with progressive release of tritiated arachidonic acid from the myocytes. In recovery studies, there was significant recovery of ATP after one hour of iodoacetate treatment but not after two to four hours. Similar results were obtained with other metabolic inhibitors. The data indicated that, when a threshold level of approximately 50% ATP reduction was reached, there was progressive arachidonate release indicative of accelerated phospholipid degradation and associated cellular calcium overloading.

In other studies, normal myocytes were subjected to inhibition of the sodium potassium pump by incubation in a zero potassium medium[28,29]. Sodium accumulation, potassium loss and elevation in total and cytosolic calcium were confirmed by analytical electron microscopy and fura-2 measurements. The calcium-loaded myocytes became arrested in a contrated state. They exhibited increased arachidonate release which commenced as early as 30 minutes and progressively increased thereafter. In contrast to metabolically inhibited cells, the sodium pump inhibited cells exhibited only moderate ATP reduction and considerable recovery, at least after the first hour of this process. However, after 2 to 3 hours of pump inhibition, a significant proportion of myocytes developed persistent depression of contractile activity and ultrastructural evidence of damage. These data indicate that calcium overloading leads to accelerated phospholipid degradation with increased release of free arachidonic acid, but that the degree of impaired energy metabolism associated with calcium loading is an important determinant of the potential for recovery of calcium loaded cardiac myocytes.

The findings in these studies were consistent with the concept of an important deacylation-reacylation cycle involving myocardial phospholipids[23]. The data indicate that calcium overloading leads to accelerated phospholipid degradation with release of free fatty acids. This may be due to activation of a phospholipase A or other phospholipases, but other mechanisms, including direct effects of calcium on phospholipids also may be operative. Reacylation of membrane phospholipids involves energy dependent reactions. Thus, when ATP levels are partially preserved, reacylation of phospholipids may occur allowing preservation of membrane integrity. This may explain why normal myocytes can withstand a period of calcium overlaoding without developing extensive irreversible injury. However, when energy deficient myocytes develop a prominent increase in cytoplasmic calcium, accelerated phospholipid degradation occurs in association with an impaired ability to reacylate membrane phospholipids. The result is net loss of phospholipids,

Table 1. Effect Of Metabolic Inhibition With 3×10^{-5}M Iodoacetic Acid (IAA) On Various Parameters In Cultured Rat Cardiac Myocytes.

Measurement*	Control	IAA,1Hr	IAA,2-3 Hrs
^{3}H-arach. release (cpm/mg prot. $\times 10^{-2}$)	11.6 + 1.9	13.1 + 2.1	41.4 + 5.6
Mito. Ca (mmoles/kg dry weight)**	-2.8 + 0.5	47 + 28	199 + 62
Intracellular free Ca^{2+} (nM)	80 + 6.6	56 + 6.3	496 + 116
ATP (nmoles/mg prot.) - end treatment	35.1 + 2.1	27.2 + 2.6	13.3 + 4.2
ATP (nmoles/mg prot.) - 24 hrs recovery	36.4 + 1.7	33.7 + 3.8	4.6 + 0.7

* $\bar{x}$ + SEM, n = 5 or more cultures

** A cell by cell analysis of the electron probe x-ray microanalysis data showed elevated calcium in mitochondria of 2 of 23 myocytes in the 1 hr IAA group versus 14 of 16 myocytes in the 2 hr IAA group.

impaired membrane integrity, the potential for severe calcium overloading, and cell death.

To further test the importance of membrane phospholipid degradation in irreversible myocyte injury, experiments were performed using agents with phospholipase inhibitory properties. Previously, in the isolated perfused septal preparation, it was found that pretreatment of animals with chlorpromazine was associated with a decrease in abnormal intracellular lanthanum accumulation and better functional recovery of ischemic myocardium[9]. Das et al. have recently reported a protective effect of mepacrine in an intact pig model of temporary myocardial ischemia and reperfusion[30]. More recently we have tested the effects of a synthetic sterol agent which inhibits pancreatic phospholipase A activity. This agent was used in the myocyte culture model. It was found that, while this agent did not prevent the reduction of ATP levels in response to metabolic inhibition, it did prevent tritiated arachidonate release and ultrastructural evidence of severe myocardial damage[31]. These various studies suggest that the inhibition of accelerated membrane phospholipid degradation is associated with protection against the development of irreversible injury. In contrast, the onset of membrane phospholipid damage and calcium overloading are associated with the development of irreversible injury in energy depleted myocytes.

OTHER MECHANISMS OF MEMBRANE INJURY

Other mechanisms have been postulated to contribute to the progression of membrane and cellular injury in ischemia. One such mechanism involves the accumulation of amphiphiles in ischemic myocardium[18,32]. These include lysophospholipids as well as fatty acids, long chain fatty acyl co-A and long chain acylcarnitine. Corr et al. have shown a transient, quantitatively small increase in lysophospholipids early in the course of myocardial ischemia in the cat[32]. These lysophospholipids have arrhythmogenic properties. However, progressive accumulation of lysophospholipids in myocardium apparently does not occur, probably because of the action of lysophospholipases which degrade these compounds. Thus, the appearance of lysophospholipids occurs early during the reversible phase of injury and does not appear to be responsible for the late changes associated with the development of irreversible injury. We and others have shown progressive accumulation of free fatty acids, the potential toxic effects of which require further elucidation[18,33]. Long chain acylcarnitine does not accumulate in severely ischemic canine myocardium but may contribute to injury in less severely ischemic tissue. Another potential mechanism involves free radical effects leading to lipid peroxidation. This phenomenon may be particularly important during the reflow phase of injury[34,35]. It is possible that free radical effects could act in concert with the effects of phospholipase mediated accelerated phospholipid degradation. Steenbergen and associates have recently suggested another potential mechanism of membrane injury which initially may involve an ultrastructural inapparent membrane permutation followed by the physical effects of cell swelling leading to structural membrane defects[36]. Stennbergen et al. have suggested that the initial event may be activation of a calcium sensitive protease which causes disruption of the cytoskeletal-membrane connections, thereby making the membrane more prone to the effects of swelling. Steenbergen et al. have not detected early changes in total phospholipids in their model of in vitro ischemia. However, our studies have shown that myocardial ischemia in the intact animal is associated with a small decrease in total phospholipids associated with marked increases in free fatty acids. Reasons to suggest that these changes are significant are discussed above. It is possible that calcium-mediated activation of both proteases and phospholipases contribute to membrane damage in ischemia.

FUTURE DIRECTIONS

Thus, future work should focus in several areas. There is a need to characterize further the deacylation-reacylation cycle of membrane phospholipids in the myocardium. Another area is defining the exact timing of subtle changes in altered calcium homeostasis vis-a-vis the onset of membrane phospholipid injury. Finally, it will be important to isolate and characterize specific phospholipases of the myocardium in order to determine which of these enzymes are involved in key degradative reactions and to develop inhibitors of their actions.

ACKNOWLEDGEMENTS

This work was supported by NIH Ischemic Heart Disease SCOR Grant HL17669, NIH Grants HL30570 and HL01806, and the Moss Heart Fund, Dallas, Texas.

REFERENCES

1. W.G. Nayler, The role of calcium in the ischemic myocardium, Am. J. Pathol. 102:262 (1981).
2. J.T. Willerson, A. Mukherjee, K. Chien, C. Ezquierdo, and L.M. Buja, Calcium and acute myocardial infraction, in: "Calcium Antagonists and Cardiovascular Disease", L.H. Opie, ed., Raven Press, New York, p 257 (1984).
3. K.A. Reimer and R.B. Jennings, The "wavefront phenomenon" of myocardial ischemic cell death. II. Transmural progression of necrosis within the framework of ischemic bed size (myocardium at risk) and collateral blood flow, Lab. Invest. 40:633 (1979).
4. L.M. Buja, A.J. Tofe, P.V. Kulkarni, A. Mukherjee, R.W. Parkey, M.D. Francis, F.J. Bonte, and J.T. Willerson, Sites and mechanisms of localization of technetium-99m phosphorus radiopharmaceuticals in acute myocardial infarcts and other tissues, J. Clin. Invest. 60:724 (1977).
5. J.T. Willerson, F. Scales, A. Mukherjee, M.R. Platt, G.H. Templeton, G.C. Fink, and L.M. Buja, Abnormal myocardial fluid retention as an early manifestation of ischemic injury, Am. J. Pathol. 87:159 (1977).
6. L.M. Buja and J.T. Willerson, Abnormalities of volume regulation and membrane integrity in myocardial tissue slices after early ischemic injury in the dog: Effects of mannitol, polyethylene glycol and

propranolol, Am. J. Path. 103:79 (1981).

7. K.I. Shine, Ionic events in ischemia and anoxia, Am. J. Pathol. 102:256 (1981).

8. K.P. Burton, H.K. Hagler, G.H. Templeton, J.T. Willerson, and L.M. Buja, Lanthanum probe studies of cellular pathophysiology induced by hypoxia in isolated cardiac muscle, J. Clin. Invest. 60:1289 (1977).

9. K.P. Burton, H.K. Hagler, J.T. Willerson, and L.M. Buja, Relationship of abnormal intracellular lanthanum accumulation to progression of ischemic injury in isolated perfused myocardium; effect of chlorpromazine, Am. J. Physiol. 241:H714 (1981).

10. L.M. Buja, K.P. Burton, H.K. Hagler, and J.T. Willerson, Alterations of elemental composition of individual myocytes in hypoxic rabbit myocardium: a quantitative x-ray microanalytical study, Circ. 68:872 (1983).

11. A. Mukherjee, T.M. Wong, G.H. Templeton, L.M. Buja, and J.T. Willerson, Influence of volume dilution, lactate, phosphate and calcium on mitochondrial functions, Am. J. Physiol. 237:H224 (1979).

12. A. Mukherjee, T.M. Wong, L.M. Buja, R.J. Lefkowitz, and J.T. Willerson, Beta adrenergic and muscarinic cholinergic receptors in canine myocardium: Effects of ischemia, J. Clin. Invest. 64:1423 (1979).

13. A. Mukherjee, L. Bush, K.E. McCoy, R.J. Duke, H.K. Hagler, L.M. Buja, and J.T. Willerson, Relationship between B-adrenergic receptor numbers and physiologic responses during experimental canine myocardial ischemia, Cir. Res. 50:735 (1982).

14. K.H. Muntz, H.K. Hagler, H.J. Boulas, J.T. Willerson, and L.M. Buja, Redistribution of catecholamines in the ischemic zone of the dog heart, Am. J. Pathol. 114:64 (1984).

15. P.B. Corr, J.A. Shayman, J.B. Kramer, and R.J. Kipnis, Increased alpha adrenergic receptors in ischemic cat myocardium: a potential mediator of electrophysiological derangements, J. Clin. Invest. 67:1232 (1981).

16. L.M. Buja, H.K. Muntz, T. Rosenbaum, Z. Haghani, D.K. Buja, A. Sen, K.R. Chien, and J.T. Willerson, Characterization of a potentially reversible increase in beta adrenergic receptors in isolated, neonatal rat cardiac myocytes with impaired energy metabolism, Cir. Res. 57:640 (1985).

17. A.S. Maisel, H.J. Motulsky, P.A. Insel, Externalization of B-adrenergic receptors promoted by myocardial ischemia, Science 230:183 (1985).

18. A.M. Katz and F.C. Messineo, Lipid-membrane interactions and the pathogenesis of ischemic damage in the myocardium, Circ. Res. 48:1 (1981).

19. R. Franson, D.C. Pang, D.W. Towle, W.B. Weglicki, Phospholipase A activity of highly enriched preparations of cardiac sarcolemma from hamster and dog, J. Mol. Cell. Cardiol. 10:921 (1978).

20. K.Y. Hostetler, and L.B. Hall, Phospholipase C activity of rat tissues, Biochem. Biophys. Res. Comm. 96:388 (1980).

21. K.R. Chien, J. Abrams, A. Serroni, J.T. Martin, and J.L. Farber, Accelerated phospholipid degradation and associated membrane dysfunction in irreversible, ischemic liver cell injury, J. Biol. Chem. 253:4809 (1978).

22. K.R. Chien, J.P. Reeves, L.M. Buja, F.J. Bonte, R.W. Parkey, and J.T. Willerson, Phospholipid alterations in canine ischemic myocardium. Temporal and topographical correlations with Tc-99m-PPi accumulation and an in vitro sarcolemmal Ca^{2+} permeability defect, Cir. Res. 48:711 (1981).

23. K.R. Chien, A. Han, A. Sen, L.M. Buja, and J.T. Willerson, Accumulation of unesterified arachidonic acid in ischemic canine myocardium: relationship to a phosphatidylcholine deacylation-reacylation cycle and depletion of membrane phospholipids, Cir. Res. 54:313 (1984).

24. K.P. Burton, L.M. Buja, A. Sen, J.T. Willerson, and K.R. Chien, Accumulation of arachidonate in triacylglycerols and unesterified fatty acids during ischemia and reflow in the isolated rat heart: correlation with the loss of contractile function and the development of

calcium overload, _Am. J. Pathol._ 124:238 (1986).

25. L.M. Buja, H.K. Hagler, D. Parsons, K. Chien, R.C. Reynolds, and J.T. Willerson, Alterations of ultrastructure and elemental composition in cultured neonatal rat cardiac myocytes following metabolic inhibition with iodoacetic acid, _Lab. Invest._ 53:397 (1985).

26. K.R. Chien, A. Sen, R.C. Reynolds, A. Chang, Y. Kim, M.D. Gunn, L.M. Buja, and J.T. Willerson, Release of arachidonate from membrane phospholipids in cultured myocardial cells during ATP depletion: correlation with the progression of cell injury, _J. Clin. Invest._ 75:1770 (1985).

27. M.D. Gunn, A. Sen, A. Chang, J.T. Willerson, L.M. Buja, and K.R. Chien, Mechanisms of accumulation of arachidonic acid in cultured myocardial cells during ATP depletion, _Am. J. Physiol._ 249:H1188 (1985).

28. L.M. Buja, P.K. Williams, D.K. Buja, K.R. Chien, and J.T. Willerson, Comparative effects of cardiac myocyte injury induced by inhibition of the Na^+, K^+ pump and intermediary metabolism, _Clin. Res._ 34:627A (1986).

29. A.C. Morris, P.K. Williams, F.A. Lattanzio, D.J. Bellotto, H.K. Hagler, J.T. Willerson, and L.M. Buja, Altered calcium homeostasis induced by Na^+, K^+ pump inhibition in cultured ventricular myocytes, _Circulation_ 74 (Suppl II): II-418 (1986).

30. D.K. Das, R.M. Engleman, J.A. Rousou, R.H. Breyer, H. Otani, and S. Lemeshow, Role of membrane phospholipids in myocardial injury induced by ischemia and reperfusion, _Am. J. Physiol._ 251:H71 (1986).

31. K. Chien, A. Sen, Y. Kim, K. Burton, L.M. Buja, and J.T. Willerson, Biochemical characterization of a new synthetic myocardial phospholipase inhibitor: effects on myocardial cells during ATP depletion, _Circulation_ 70 (Suppl II): II278 (1984).

32. P.B. Corr, R.W. Gross, and B.E. Sobel, Amphipathic metabolites and membrane dysfunction in ischemic myocardium, _Circ. Res._ 55:135 (1984).

33. K.R. Chien, A. Sen, L.M. Buja, and J.T. Willerson, Fatty acylcarnitine accumulation and membrane injury in ischemic canine myocardium, _Am. J. Cardiol._ 52:893 (1983).

34. K.P. Burton, Superoxide dismutase enhances recovery following myocardial ischemia, _Am. J. Physiol._ 248:H637 (1985).

35. S.W. Werns, M.J. Shea, and B.R. Lucchesi, Free radicals and myocardial injury: pharmacologic implications, _Circulation_ 74:1 (1986).

36. C. Steenbergen, M.L. Hill, and R.B. Jennings, Volume regulation and plasma membrane injury in aerobic, anaerobic, and ischemic myocardium _in vitro_: effects of osmotic cell swelling on plasma membrane integrity, _Circ. Res._ 57:864 (1985).

CELLULAR Ca^{2+} DYSHOMEOSTASIS IN THE

LIVER IN ENDOTOXIC SHOCK

Mohammed M. Sayeed and Subir R. Maitra

Department of Physiology
Loyola University Stritch School of Medicine
Maywood, IL

INTRODUCTION

Cellular Ca^{2+} homeostasis is understood to be maintained by three membrane systems viz. the plasma membrane, the inner mitochondrial and the endoplasmic reticular membranes. Each of these membranes possesses distinctive Ca^{2+} transport processes by means of which it regulates cytosolic Ca^{2+} concentration.[1] While Ca^{2+} mobilization into the cytosolic compartment subsequent to cell activation plays an important role in the elicitation of various normal cellular responses, an inappropriate elevation of intracellular Ca^{2+} causes cell damage. Although the precise mechanism of cell damage remains to be understood, it could result from Ca^{2+} induced activation of cytolytic processes[2,3] and altered regulation of enzymes required for cellular metabolism and ion transport.[4,5] Several studies have implicated altered cellular Ca^{2+} regulation in cell damage within various organ systems of animals in septic and endotoxic shock.[6,7,8] In our laboratory, we have evaluated alterations in the regulation of hepatic intracellular Ca^{2+} in endotoxic animals. These evaluations included measurements of (1) cellular Ca^{2+} efflux and its modulation by norepin- ephrine, (2) Ca^{2+} uptake by endoplasmic reticulum, and (3) cytoplasmic exchangeable Ca^{2+}. In addition, cytosolic free Ca^{2+} concentrations were measured under basal and hormone stimulated conditions.

METHODS

Endotoxic shock was produced in rats by giving them intravenous injection of saline suspensions of <u>Salmonella enteritidis</u> lipopolysaccharide (LPS) (Difco Laboratory, Detroit, MI) in doses of 15-20 mg/kg. Five hrs after LPS injections, rats became hypoglycemic and hyperlacticacidemic and their bowels showed hemorrhagic lesions. These signs marked the onset of the shock syndrome. Saline injected (control) and LPS injected (endotoxic) rats were killed 5 hours after injections and their livers excised. Tissue slices (0.3 mm thick), isolated hepatocytes or endoplasmic reticular vesicles (ER) were prepared from the livers using standard procedures. Hepatic cellular Ca^{2+} efflux was measured in liver slices which were initially loaded with ^{45}Ca at 37°C for 60 minutes in a radioisotope-containing oxygenated (95% O$_2$ + 5% CO$_2$) Krebs-Ringer-bicarbonate (KRB) medium. Liver slices were then washed in ^{45}Ca-free KRB for successive duration of 5 or 10 minutes each to quantitate ^{45}Ca efflux.[9] Cytosolic Ca^{2+} concentration was measured in isolated heptocytes using the quin 2 fluorescence technique. Details of measurement of cytosolic free Ca^{2+} in isolated hepatocytes and ^{45}Ca uptake by ER have been described elsewhere.[9,10]

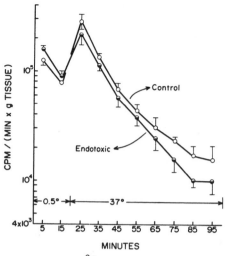

Fig. 1. Ca^{2+} from liver slices
of control (n=11) and endotoxic
rats (n=7). Effluxes (mean ± SE)
were measured during successive
washouts of 10 min. durations.

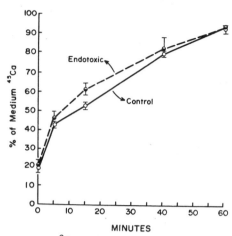

Fig.2. Ca^{2+} uptake (mean ± SE) by
hepatic endoplasmic reticulum of
control (n=6) and endotoxic rats
(n=6).

RESULTS AND DISCUSSION

Fig. 1 shows ^{45}Ca efflux from liver slices of endotoxic rats was not
different from controls. ^{45}Ca efflux from control liver slices was found
to be dependent on cellular metabolic activity. Firstly, it was enhanced
with an increase in washout temperature (from 0.5° to 37°C) so that the
Q_{10} value for the temperature effect was approximately 2. Secondly, the
enhancement of efflux with the change of temperature was abolished when
iodoacetate was added to the washout medium. Thus, active movement of
Ca^{2+} across the plasma membrane was maintained during endotoxic shock.
Fig. 2 shows that there was also no effect of endotoxic shock on active
hepatic ER uptake of ^{45}Ca. ^{45}Ca uptake by ER, from both control and
endotoxic rat livers, was dependent on ATP. In control rat livers, ER
^{45}Ca uptake decreased from 65 ± 2 (% medium $^{45}Ca/hr$) (mean ± SE) in the
presence of ATP (5mM) to 15 ± 2 in ATP's absence.

In contrast to the lack of effect of endotoxic shock on active Ca^{2+}
movements across plasma membrane and ER, we found endotoxic shock to significantly alter the intracellular exchangeable Ca^{2+} in liver cells. We
determined exchangeable Ca^{2+} from ^{45}Ca washout in liver slices previously
incubated to radioisotopically label the extracellular and the cytoplasmic
Ca^{2+} compartments.[9] The cytoplasmic compartment consisted of mainly the
ER and mitochondria. The cytoplasmic exchangeable Ca^{2+} pool size, quantitated by extrapolating the slower phase of the ^{45}Ca washout curves (see
Fig. 3), was significantly higher in endotoxic (553 ± 23 nmol/g) than in
control rat livers (413 ± 17). The increase in the cytoplasmic exchangeable Ca^{2+} in endotoxic rats was parallel to an increase in cytosolic free
Ca^{2+} concentration measured in isolated hepatocytes. The cytosolic Ca^{2+}
increased from 146 ± 23 nM in controls to 525 ± 92 in endotoxic rat
hepatocytes (p<.05). The increase in both the cytoplasmic exchangeable
Ca^{2+} and the cytosolic free Ca^{2+} support a cellular calcium overload in
liver cells during endotoxic shock. The overload of calcium was presumably
not due to any change in active Ca^{2+} movements across the plasma membrane
of ER.

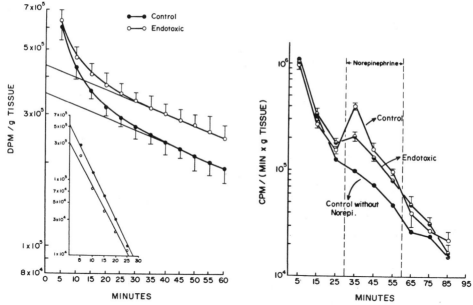

Fig. 3. ^{45}Ca remaining in control (n=15) and endotoxic (n=9) rat liver slices after successive washouts of 5 min durations each. Fig. shows visual extrapolations of slower phases of washout curves to approximate y-intercepts. Inset shows calculated shows calculated values of tissue ^{45}Ca during the initial, faster phase of ^{45}Ca washout representing washout from the extracellular pool.

Fig. 4. Effect of norepinephrine on Ca^{2+} efflux (mean ± SE) from liver slices of control (n=7) and endotoxic (n=5) rats.

Since a heightened release of catecholamine occurs during endotoxic shock[11] and since catecholamines act as Ca^{2+} mobilizing agonists in the liver,[1] we evaluated the effectiveness of exogenous catecholamines on liver slices and hepatocytes from endotoxic rats. In liver slices from endotoxic rats, we found a gross attenuation of the norepinephrine (NE) induced enhancement of Ca^{2+} efflux (Fig. 4). In control liver cells, NE mobilizes Ca^{2+} from the intracellular pool (viz. endoplasmic retiulum) and subsequently increases Ca^{2+} efflux.[13,14] The attenuation of NE-induced Ca^{2+} efflux in livers of endotoxic rats could be due to an inadequate release of Ca^{2+} from the endoplasmic reticulum pool. It is possible that during endotoxic shock, high concentrations of circulating catecholamines impinge on liver cells to cause excessive Ca^{2+} mobilization from endoplasmic reticulum and thus to a depletion of this calcium pool. The depletion of ER Ca^{2+} would imply that the observed increase in cytoplasmic exchangeable Ca^{2+} was due mainly to accumulation of Ca^{2+} by mitochondria.

In our studies, we also found an impaired ability of endotoxic rat hepatocytes to respond to epinephrine. While control rat hepatocytes responded to epinephrine ($10^{-6}M$) by elevating their cytosolic Ca^{2+} concentration from 146 ± 23 (nM) to 324 ± 65 (p<.05), endotoxic rat hepatocyte cytosolic Ca^{2+} in the presence of $10^{-5}M$ epinephrine (600 ± 96) was not significantly different from that in its absence (525 ± 92). The lack of effect of exogenous epinephrine on cytosolic Ca^{2+} in endotoxic rat hepatocytes further supports the concept of an exhaustion of endoplasmic reticulum Ca^{2+} pool in livers of rats during shock.

The adrenoreceptor stimulation of control hepatocytes presumably elevates cytosolic free Ca^{2+} not only via mobilization of Ca^{2+} from endoplasmic reticulum but also by an increase in influx of Ca^{2+} across the plasma membrane.[14,15] The latter mechanism may be important in supporting physiologic cellular responses in the liver such as glycogenolysis and gluconeogenesis.[16,17] However, an excessive catecholamine stimulation of liver cells as might occur in endotoxic shock could lead to both an exhaustion of endoplasmic reticulum Ca^{2+} pool and a persistent elevation of the cytoplasmic exchangeable and cytosolic free Ca^{2+} as wasobserved in our studies. These alteration in hepatic calcium homeostasis could adversely affect hepatic metabolic functions viz. glycogenolysis and gluconeogenesis and contribute to a Ca^{2+} mediated cellular damage.

ACKNOWLEDGEMENT

This research was supported by National Institute of Health Grants GM-32288 and HL 31163. Fig. 1-4 are taken from reference #9 with the permission of the American Journal of Physiology. The authors thank Julie Guszcza for assistance in the prepartion of this manuscript.

REFERENCES

1. H. Rasmussen and P.Q. Barrett. Calcium messenger system: an integrated view. Physiol. Rev. 64:938-984 (1984).
2. V. Baracos, R.E. Greenberg, and A.L. Goldberg. Influence of calcium and other divalent cations on protein turnover in rat skeletal muscle. Am. J. Physiol. 250:E702-E710 (1986).
3. M. Joffe, N. Savage, and H. Isaacs. Increased muscle calcium: a possible cause of mitochondrial dysfunction and cellular necrosis in denervated rat skeletal muscle. Biochem. J. 196:663-667 (1981).
4. E. Carafoli. Membrane transport and the regulation of the cell calcium levels. In: Pathophysiology of Shock, Anoxia, and Ischemia. Eds. R.A. Cowley and B.F. Trump. Baltimore; Williams and Wilkins, (1982).
5. W. Rummel, E. Seifen, and J. Baldauf. Influence of calcium and ouabain upon the potassium efflux in human erythrocytes. Biochem. Pharmacol. 12:557-563 (1963).
6. M.L. Hess, M.E. Soulsby, J.A. Davis, and F.N. Briggs. The influence of venous return on cardiac mechanical and sarcoplasmic reticulum function during endotoxemia. Circ. Shock 4:143-152 (1977).
7. K.M. Nelson and J.A. Spitzer. Alterations of adipocyte calcium homeostasis by Escherichia Coli endotoxin. Am. J. Physiol. 248:R331-R338 (1985).
8. I.V. Deaciuc and J.A. Spitzer. Rat liver free cytosolic calcium and glycogen phosphorylase in endotoxicosis and sepsis. Am. J. Physiol. 251:R984-R995 (1986).
9. M.M. Sayeed. Alterations in cellular calcium regulation in the liver in endotoxic shock. Am. J. Physiol. 19:R884-R891 (1986).
10. M.M. Sayeed and S.R. Maitra. Effect of diltiazem on altered cellular calcium regulation during endotoxic shock. Submitted (1986).
11. S.B. Jones and F. Romano. Plasma catecholamines in the conscious rat during endotoxicosis. Circ. Shock 14:189-201 (1984).
12. S. Kimura, N. Kugai, R. Tada, I Kojima, K. Abe and E. Ogata. Sources of calcium mobilized by alpha-adrenergic stimulation in perfused rat liver. Horm. Metab. Res. 14:133-137 (1982).
13. P.F. Blackmore, J.P. Dehaye and J.H. Exton. Studies on alpha-adrenergic activation of hepatic glucose output. J. Biol. Chem. 254:6945-6950 (1979).
14. J.R. Williamson, R.H. Cooper, S.K. Joseph and A.P. Thomas. Inositorl trisphosphate and diacylglycerol as intracellular second messengers in liver. Am. J. Physiol. 248:C203-C216 (1985).
15. J.P. Manger, J. Poggioli, F. Guesdon and M. Claret. Noradrenaline, vasopressin, and angiotensin increases calcium influx by opening a common pool of calcium channels in isolated rat liver cell. Biochem. J. 221:121-127 (1984).

16. J.C. Garrison and M.K. Borland. Regulation of mitochondrial pyruvate carboxylation and gluconeogenesis in rat hepatocytes via an alpha-adrenergic, adenosine 3',5' mono-phosphate-independent mechanism. J. Biol. Chem. 254:1129-1133 (1979).

17. D.A. Hems and P.D. Whitton. Stimulation by vasopressin of glycogen breakdown and gluconeogenesis in the perfused rat liver. Biochem. J. 136:705-709 (1973).

EVIDENCE FOR HEXAGONAL II PHASE

LIPID INVOLVEMENT IN MITOCHONDRIAL Ca^{2+} MOVEMENTS

Paul Wolkowicz

Department of Medicine
Division of Cardiovascular Disease
University of Alabama
School of Medicine at Birmingham
Birmingham, Alabama 35294

INTRODUCTION

The release of matrix Ca^{2+} from mitochondria is induced by a variety of compounds, eg. palmitoyl-CoA (P-CoA) (1). Addition of these compounds to mitochondria which contain Ca^{2+} produces a period of mitochondrial Ca^{2+} release and reaccumulation, i.e. Ca^{2+} cycling, followed by large amplitude swelling, inner membrane depolarization and net Ca^{2+} release (2). These phenomena occur only if inorganic phosphate is in the reaction medium (3). Whether these observations are related to the mechanism(s) through which the mitochondrion contributes to Ca^{2+} homeostasis in the normal cell remains to be determined. However, under pathological conditions such as ischemia this process of Ca^{2+} release may relate to matrix Ca^{2+} content and mitochondrial volume changes observed (4).

Phosphate-dependent net release of matrix Ca^{2+} has not been dissociated from large amplitude swelling and these two processes may be fundamentally related. Understanding the cause(s) of swelling under these conditions then may aid in delineating one mechanism of mitochondrial Ca^{2+} release. Large amplitude mitochondrial swelling may be caused by (i) alterations in monovalent cation transport activity (5, 6), (ii) phospholipase induced alteration in membrane integrity (7) or (iii) free-radical induced peroxidation of membrane lipids followed by loss of membrane integrity (8). Experiments investigating the latter possibility were performed by determining the effects of a hydrophobic free-radical scavenger, butylated hydroxytoluene (BHT), on the process of net mitochondrial Ca^{2+} release and swelling.

Materials and Methods

Rat liver mitochondria were isolated as previously described (9). All spectrophotometric results reported were obtained from an Aminco DW-2 split and dual wavelength spectrophotometer as previously described (9). All oxygen related parameters were measured on a Yellow Springs Instrument Model 53 oxygen monitor as previously described (9).

Isatoic anhydride (ITA) modification of mitochondria was obtained either by preincubation of mitochondria for 2-3 minutes at 30°C in the Ca^{2+}

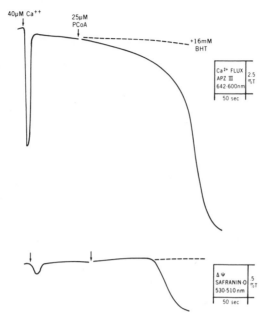

Figure 1: BHT Prevents P-CoA Induced Phosphate-
Dependent Mitochondrial Calcium Release and
Depolarization
UPPER TRACE: Mitochondria (0.7 mg/ml) were incubated
at 30° C in a Ca^{2+} uptake medium as previously described (9). Where indicated 40 μM Ca^{2+}, 25 μM P-CoA
were added. The solid trace indicates mitochondria
with no BHT, the dashed trace indicates mitochondria
pretreated with 16 μM BHT. Ca^{2+} dependent changes
in antipyryllazo III absorbance were measured with
the wavelength pair of 642-600 nm and a downward
deflection indicate an increase of Ca^{2+} in the medium.
LOWER TRACE: Mitochondria were incubated as above
but containing 3 μM Safranin-0. Ca^{2+} and P-CoA were
added as in the upper panel to mitochondria that were
(dashed line) or were not (solid line) preincubated
with BHT. Membrane potential was monitored at the
wavelength pair 530-510 nm and a downward deflection
indicates depolarization.

uptake medium or by addition of ITA to mitochondrial suspensions in the DW2
following Ca^{2+} accumulation but prior to P-CoA or BHT addition. ITA stock
solutions of 14 or 140 mM were used.

All reagents and chemical were from commercial sources.

Results and Discussion

Mitochondria accumulate Ca^{2+} into their matrix space using a membrane
potential driven electrophoretic uniporter (10). Addition of P-CoA to
mitochondria loaded with Ca^{2+} in the presence of phosphate results in the
release of this Ca^{2+} into the incubation medium (Fig. 1). BHT added either
prior to Ca^{2+} or P-CoA results in concentration dependent suppression of
mitochondrial Ca^{2+} release, membrane depolarization (Fig. 1) uncoupling and
large amplitude swelling (Fig. 2) observed during net Ca^{2+} release. In
these experiments, the interruption of P-CoA induced Ca^{2+} release by BHT was

132

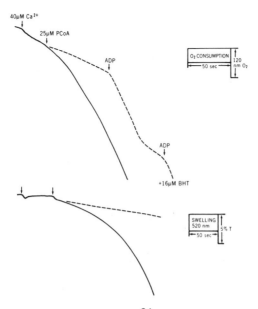

Figure 2: BHT Prevents Ca^{2+} and P-CoA Induced,
Phosphate Dependent, Mitochondrial Uncoupling and
Swelling.
UPPER TRACE: Mitochondria were incubated as in
Figure 1 in a YSI Model 53 oxygen monitor with
Ca^{2+} and P-CoA being added where indicated. Mitochondria were (dashed line) or were not (solid line)
preincubated with 16μM BHT. A downward deflection
indicates a decrease in oxygen tension.
LOWER TRACE: Mitochondria were incubated in the
medium of Figure 1 in the absence of dye in an
Aminco DW-2 in the split beam mode at 520 nm.
Ca^{2+} and P-CoA were added where indicated in the
absence (solid line) or presence (dashed line) of
16 μM BHT. A downward deflection indicates an
increase in matrix volume.

not separated from the alterations in membrane integrity evidenced by
swelling and membrane depolarization. Similar results are observed using
acetoacetate or t-butyl hydroperoxide as Ca^{2+} release agent. Introduction
of BHT to mitochondrial suspensions during the process of net Ca^{2+} release
results in a time-dependent reversal of Ca^{2+} release and depolarization
(Fig. 3). The time dependence of this effect may relate to the extent of
large amplitude swelling which occurs prior to BHT addition. That is, as
release proceeds and the mitochondrial matrix volume increases, eventually
alterations in membrane integrity occur which cannot be halted or reversed
by BHT.

P-CoA induced Ca^{2+} release from mitochondria occurs only if phosphate
is in the incubation medium (3, 11). However, while BHT suppresses
phosphate dependent Ca^{2+} release it stimulates a dramatically increased
release of Ca^{2+} from mitochondria incubated in the presence of lactate or
acetate as permeant anion (Fig. 4). This BHT-induced Ca^{2+} release is
accompanied by mitochondrial swelling and uncoupling but a hyperpolarization
is observed (Fig. 5) using the Safranin-O technique. Further experiments
demonstrate that the BHT induced Ca^{2+} release in the absence of phosphate
is rapidly reversed by the addition of phosphate during the release process

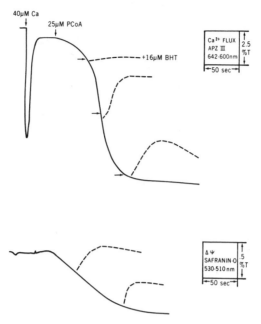

40μM Ca

25μM PCoA

+16μM BHT

Ca²⁺ FLUX
APZ III
642-600 nm
2.5 %T
←50 sec→

Δ Ψ
SAFRANIN-O
530-510 nm
.5 %T
←50 sec→

Figure 3: BHT Reverses P-CoA Induced, Phosphate-Dependent Mitochondrial Ca^{2+} Release and Depolarization.
UPPER TRACE: Mitochondria were incubated and Ca^{2+} flux measured as in Figure 1. Ca^{2+} and P-CoA were added where indicated, 16 μM BHT was added at either of the places indicated by an arrow resulting in a dashed line.
LOWER TRACE: Mitochondria were incubated and membrane potential measured as in Figure 1. Ca^{2+} and P-CoA were added as in the upper trace and 16 μM BHT was added at the place indicated by the dashed line.

(Fig. 5). This phosphate reversal of BHT induced Ca^{2+} release is sensitive to ruthenium red (Fig. 5) and mersalyl indicating that it requires the Ca^{2+} uniporter and transmembrane movements of phosphate on the phosphate carrier (12).

These experiments demonstrate that although Ca^{2+} release may be dissociated from a requirement for medium phosphate or membrane depolarization it cannot be separated from large amplitude swelling of the inner membrane. Attempts to measure a possible free-radical origin for the persistent large amplitude swelling proved negative as malondialdehyde production was not significant under any experimental condition. Therefore, alternate explanations for these observations were sought.

Recently Sokolove and Shinaberry (13) reported that duramycin, an antibiotic which interacts with lipids capable of hexagonal II phase (HII phase) formation (e.g. phosphatidylethanolamine (PE)), is an effective inhibitor of P-CoA induced Ca^{2+} release. Also, Cheng et al. (14) reported that BHT lowered the bilayer to HII phase transition temperature for PE from 55° to 35° C. These reports raise the possibility that BHT interaction with HII phase forming lipids in the mitochondrial inner membrane may be responsible for the alterations observed in Ca^{2+} transport.

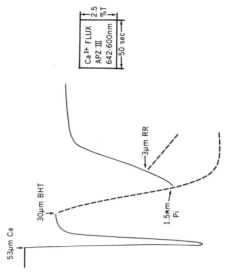

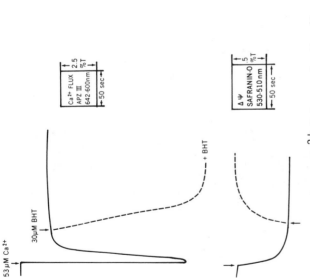

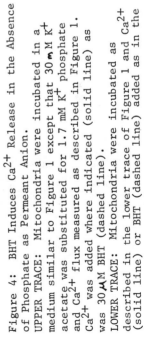

Figure 4: BHT Induces Ca^{2+} Release in the Absence of Phosphate as Permeant Anion.
UPPER TRACE: Mitochondria were incubated in a medium similar to Figure 1 except that 30 mM K$^+$ acetate was substituted for 1.7 mM K$^+$ phosphate and Ca^{2+} flux measured as described in Figure 1. Ca^{2+} was added where indicated (solid line) as was 30 μM BHT (dashed line).
LOWER TRACE: Mitochondria were incubated as described in the lower trace of Figure 1 and Ca^{2+} (solid line) or BHT (dashed line) added as in the upper trace.

Figure 5: BHT Induced Ca^{2+} Release is Reversed by Transmembrane Phosphate Movements.
Mitochondria were incubated as described in the upper trace of Figure 4. Ca^{2+} was added followed by 30 μM BHT (dashed line). K$^+$ phosphate (1.5 mM) was added (solid line) during release and ruthenium red (RR) at 3 μM was added as indicated.

135

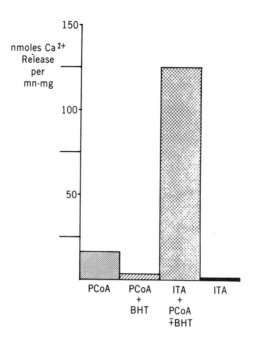

Figure 6: Isatoic Anhydride Stimulates the Rate
of P–CoA Induced Ca^{2+} Release Independent of BHT.
Mitochondria were incubated as in Figure 1. Rates
of P–CoA ($25 \mu M$) induced Ca^{2+} release in the absence
(▨▨▨) or presence of (▨▨▨) $16 \mu M$ BHT are
reported. Mitochondria were preincubated for three
minutes at $30° C$ with $600 \mu M$ ITA and Ca^{2+} uptake
and P–CoA induced release measured in the absence
or presence of $16-30 \mu M$ BHT (▨▨▨). Basal rates
of Ca^{2+} release in ITA treated mitochondria are
given in the final column.

To investigate this hypothesis experiments were performed measuring
the effect of modification of mitochondrial amines (e.g. PE headgroups)
on mitochondrial Ca^{2+} transport. Mitochondria were incubated with isatoic
anhydride (ITA), an amine reactive compound (15), either prior to or
following Ca^{2+} addition and the rates and BHT sensitivity of P–CoA induced
Ca^{2+} release were measured. Mitochondria not exposed to ITA undergo P–CoA
induced Ca^{2+} release at a rate of 15 nm Ca^{2+} per minute-milligram (Figure 6)
which is BHT sensitive. In contrast, mitochondria treated with $500-700 \mu M$
ITA demonstrate a rate of P–CoA induced Ca^{2+} release of 125 nm Ca^{2+} per
minute-milligram and this release is insensitive to BHT. ITA alone did not
affect Ca^{2+} accumulation or basal rates of release. The ITA concentration
dependence of this stimulation of P–CoA induced Ca^{2+} release demonstrates a
half-maximal value of $200 \mu M$ (Fig. 7). These results indicate an involvement of amine-reactive molecules in both P–CoA induced Ca^{2+} release and
the BHT effects upon this process.

One interpretation of the BHT and ITA results could be that the process
of P–CoA induced release of Ca^{2+} may be modulated by alterations in the
packing state of the lipids in the inner mitochondrial membrane. BHT which
can modulate HII phase formation is shown here to alter the Ca^{2+} release
process while ITA modification of mitochondrial amines, presumably PE,
results in both a stimulation of the process of P–CoA induced Ca^{2+} release
and removal of its BHT sensitivity. HII phase forming lipids (PE or

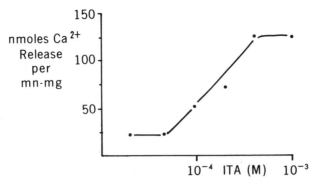

Figure 7: The Concentration Dependence of ITA Activation of P–CoA Induced Ca^{2+} Release. Mitochondria were incubated as described in Figure 1 in a medium containing varying concentrations of ITA (abscissa). The rate of P–CoA ($25 \mu M$) induced Ca^{2+} release was measured.

cardiolipin) may act as one factor in the Ca^{2+} release process and disruption of these lipids by Ca^{2+} release agents (e.g. P–CoA, acetoacetate, t–butylhydroperoxide) or by phospholipase activation may induce Ca^{2+} cycling and eventually a general increase in inner membrane permeability and net Ca^{2+} release. BHT may act to inhibit these phenomena by inducing or stabilizing the organization of HII phase forming lipids. Modification of PE headgroups by ITA may stimulate P–CoA induced Ca^{2+} release because the number of HII phase forming lipids is decreased by chemical modification resulting in an increased sensitivity of the mitochondria to Ca^{2+} release agents as well as an insensitivity to BHT. While HII phase forming lipids may be involved in the Ca^{2+} release process the lack of effect of ITA alone on Ca^{2+} release indicates that an interaction of factors (HII phase forming lipids and a Ca^{2+} release pathway) is required. The effect of anions on BHT induced Ca^{2+} reaccumulation or release suggests that the lipid packing state and its effect on a Ca^{2+} release pathway are altered by the matrix ionic composition. This ion–dependent switching of inner membrane lipid state and the general question of HII phase forming lipids in mitochondrial metabolism/energetics will be under further investigation in our laboratory.

References

(1) Asimakis, G.R. and Sordahl, L.A. (1977) Arch. Biochem. Biophys. 179, 200–210.

(2) Wolkowicz, P.E. and McMillin–Wood, J.B. (1980) Biochem. J. 186, 257–266.

(3) Wolkowicz, P.E. and McMillin–Wood, J.B. (1980) J. Biol. Chem. 255, 10348–10353.

(4) Henry, P.D., Shuchleib, R., Davis, J., Weiss, S. and Sobel, B.E. (1977) Am. J. Physiol. 233, H677–684.

(5) Jung, D.W. and Brierly, G.P. (1981) J. Biol. Chem. 256, 10490–10496.

(6) Nakashima, R.A., Dordick, R.S. and Garlid, R.D. (1982) J. Biol. Chem. 257, 12540–12545.

(7) Beatrice, M.D., Palmer, J.W. and Pfeiffer, D.R. (1980) J. Biol. Chem. 8663–8669.

(8) Leung, H.W., Vang, M.J. and Mavis, R.D. (1981) Biochem. Biophys. Acta 664, 266–272.

(9) Wolkowicz, P.E. and McMillin-Wood, J.B. (1981) Arch. Biochem. Biophys. 209, 408–422.

(10) Reynafarje, B. and Lehninger, A.L. (1977) Biochem. Biophys. Res. Commun. 77, 1273–1279.

(11) Bardsley, M.E. and Brand, M.D. (1982) Biochem. J. 202, 197–201.

(12) Coty, W.A. and Pedersen, P.L. (1975) Mol. and Cell. Biochem. 9, 109–124.

(13) Sokolove, P.M. and Shinaberry, R.G. (1986) Biophys. J. 49, 94a.

(14) Cheng, K.H., Yeagle, P.L., Lepock, J.R. and Hui, S.W. (1986) Biophys. J. 49, 324a.

(15) Moorman, A.R. and Abeus, R.H. (1982) J. Amer. Chem. Soc. 104, 6785–6788.

ABNORMAL Ca^{2+} TRANSPORT CHARACTERISTICS OF

HEPATOMA MITOCHONDRIA AND ENDOPLASMIC RETICULUM

Anne N. Murphy and Gary Fiskum

Department of Biochemistry
George Washington University School of Medicine
Washington, D.C., 20037 U.S.A.

INTRODUCTION

The oncogenic transformation of cells from a normal to malignant phenotype is associated with a variety of experimentally discernible changes in the pattern of metabolism. Many of these alterations involve processes modulated by the intracellular level and distribution of calcium. In addition to increased growth rates, Ca^{2+} may play a specific role in the increased rates of aerobic glycolysis (Cittadini et al., 1981), elevated rates of cholesterol synthesis (Beg et al., 1985), and alterations in cytoskeletal organization and function (Ben-Ze'ev, 1985). Given these and other observations of alterations of cellular processes associated with malignancy, the general hypothesis has surfaced that tumor cell calcium metabolism is abnormal.

Whether alterations in the transport or effects of calcium are the primary mechanism by which malignant cells dictate their high growth rate or whether they are the manifestation of some other transforming characteristic is unknown at this time. Regardless of this lack of resolution, a variety of alterations in Ca^{2+} metabolism have been experimentally noted. Among these is the observation that tumor cells are capable of proliferating in media containing calcium levels which are 10 to 100 fold less than those required by the corresponding non-malignant cells (Swierenga, 1978). Tumor cells, as well as tumor mitochondria generally contain abnormally high levels of endogenous Ca^{2+} (Hickie and Kalant, 1967, Fiskum and Cockrell, 1985). Elevated levels of the Ca^{2+}-dependent regulatory protein calmodulin have also been found to be a common characteristic in tumor cells (Means et al., 1982). Alterations of calcium transport across tumor cell membranes include altered Ca^{2+} influx and efflux across the plasma membrane (Cittadini et al., 1982, Ohnishi, et al., 1982) and unusual Ca^{2+} uptake capacities by tumor cell mitochondria (Villalobo and Lehninger, 1980, Fiskum and Cockrell, 1985).

In terms of general cellular metabolism, mitochondrial Ca^{2+} transport appears to be involved primarily in the physiological regulation of intramitochondrial levels of Ca^{2+} (Hansford, 1985), whereas transport activities at the plasma membrane and endoplasmic reticulum are thought to play primary roles respectively in regulation of basal levels and transient changes in the cytosolic Ca^{2+} concentration. However, mitochondrial Ca^{2+} uptake and release may assume a more critical role in regulating cytosolic Ca^{2+} under metabolically stressful conditions, such as during ischemia and reperfusion. Conditions of variable oxygen and substrate availability have special significance to tumor growth given that a large and variable proportion of the viable cells comprising solid tumors are severely hypoxic (Moulder and Rockwell, 1984). The probability also exists that mitochondrial Ca^{2+} uptake functions to buffer transient increases in cytosolic Ca^{2+} that occur in response to extracellular stimuli.

Recent studies in our laboratory have addressed a number of calcium transport properties in preparations of AS-30D ascites hepatoma cells (Smith et al., 1970), in comparison to corresponding preparations of normal rat liver. The level of extramitochondrial free Ca^{2+} that can be buffered by mitochondria from either tissue has been compared, as well as the capacities for Ca^{2+} accumulation. The regulation of Ca^{2+} efflux from isolated AS-30D and rat liver mitochondria by the oxidation-reduction state of pyridine nucleotides has also been examined. In addition, the buffering capacity and responsiveness to inositol trisphosphate of vesicles of the endoplasmic reticulum of both AS-30D hepatoma and rat liver have been studied. The observed differences in Ca^{2+} transport properties and their potential relationship to the malignant phenotype will be described in the following sections.

MITOCHONDRIAL Ca^{2+} ACCUMULATION

A typical calcium electrode experiment measuring maximal Ca^{2+} uptake by isolated AS-30D tumor mitochondria is presented in Fig. 1. Mitochondria were suspended in a medium which resembles the ionic composition of the cytosol with respect to potassium, sodium, phosphate, and magnesium. Results were obtained in the absence of ATP to simulate cellular ATP-depletion such as that which occurs following a period of ischemia, and in the presence of ATP to mimic fully energized conditions. Oxidizable substrates were included to provide for respiration-dependent electrophoretic uptake of calcium by the mitochondria. Addition of mitochondria to a medium devoid of ATP which contains approximately 1.6 μM free Ca^{2+} results in transient uptake of Ca^{2+} by the mitochondria followed by release to a free Ca^{2+} level not significantly different from 1.6 μM. The addition of 25 nmoles Ca^{2+} per mg of mitochondrial protein to the medium causes an initial rapid rise in the free Ca^{2+} concentration, followed by mitochondrial Ca^{2+} uptake which returned the medium free Ca^{2+} concentration to initial steady state levels. Successive pulses of Ca^{2+} lead to similar results until at a total level of 125 nmoles Ca^{2+} mg^{-1} protein the mitochondria can no longer maintain the steady state buffer point of 1.6 μM and spontaneously release the sequestered Ca^{2+}. At this level of accumulated Ca^{2+}, the mitochondria become irreversibly damaged and are unable to carry out oxidative phosphorylation (Fiskum and Lehninger, 1982).

Comparisons of mitochondrial Ca^{2+} uptake capacities between AS-30D and normal rat liver mitochondria are presented in Table I. In the presence or absence of ATP and in the presence of either NAD^+-linked or FAD-linked oxidizable substrates, tumor mitochondria demonstrate significantly greater uptake capacity. Similar results were also obtained with digitonin-permeabilized cells, in which the plasma membrane of the cells are made leaky to ions and molecules with a minimal amount of digitonin in order to measure the function of organelles without having to

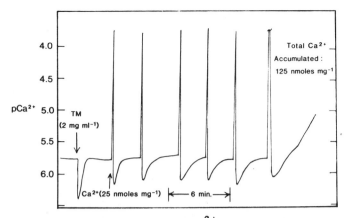

Fig. 1 Respiration-dependent Ca^{2+} uptake by AS-30D hepatoma mitochondria. Isolated tumor mitochondria (TM) were added to a medium (2.3 ml total volume, 30°C) which contained 125 mM KCl, 1mM $MgCl_2$, 2mM KH_2PO_4, 5mM malate, 5 mM glutamate, and 20 mM HEPES (pH 7.0). Each Ca^{2+} addition was 25 nmoles $CaCl_2$ mg^{-1} mitochondrial protein. The free Ca^{2+} concentration (pCa^{2+}) was monitored with an Ionetics Calcium Stat Electrode (Costa Mesa, CA).

subject them to the potential alterations elicited by even the best of isolation procedures (Fiskum, 1985). These results confirm that the observed distinction in uptake capacities are not artifactual results from the different procedures necessary for isolating hepatoma and liver mitochondria. The largest relative differences in uptake capacity is observed in the absence of ATP during which tumor mitochondria can accumulate approximately four times the amount of Ca^{2+} accumulated by rat liver mitochondria. The variations in calcium uptake maintained in the presence or absence of ATP indicate that the increased Ca^{2+} accumulating ability of tumor mitochondria is not due to differences in endogenous levels of adenine nucleotides, which are known to protect mitochondria from Ca^{2+}-induced damage and therefore potentiate Ca^{2+} accumulation (Fiskum and Lehninger, 1982).

The high level of Ca^{2+} accumulation demonstrated by AS-30D and rat liver mitochondria would not be expected to assume physiological significance under normal metabolic conditions. However, the ability to accumulate a large quantity of Ca^{2+} could be advantageous to physiologically stressed cells, such as those exposed to ischemia, which results in a large net influx of Ca^{2+} across the plasma membrane, followed by reoxygenaton, which activates respiration-dependent mitochondrial Ca^{2+} uptake. An elevated Ca^{2+} uptake capacity may provide a protective function by maintaining a low cytosolic Ca^{2+} concentration, thereby avoiding or minimizing the activation of Ca^{2+} sensitive degradative enzymes, e.g. phospholipases and proteases, which may initiate irreversible cell damage (Farber, 1982). This may be important to the survival of tumor cells in light of their potentially frequent or extended periods of ischemia involving fluctuations in the degree of oxygenation and availability of substrates (Kennedy, et al., 1980).

Table 1. Maximum Ca^{2+} Uptake Capacities of Rat Hepatoma and Rat Liver Mitochondria

| | Ca^{2+} Accumulated (nmoles mg^{-1} mitochondrial protein)[1] | | | |
| | Malate + Glutamate | | Succinate (+rotenone) | |
	−ATP	+ATP	−ATP	+ATP
Isolated Mitochondria				
AS-30D Hepatoma (n=8)	150 ± 25	1300 ± 200	250 ± 50	2200 ± 350
Normal Liver (n=7)	30 ± 5	720 ± 85	80 ± 20	1200 ± 175
Permeabilized Cells				
AS-30D Hepatoma (n=6)	180 ± 30	1550 ± 250	330 ± 40	2450 ± 300
Normal Hepatocytes (n=4)	45 ± 10	680 ± 70	100 ± 25	1250 ± 200

[1]The accumulation of added Ca^{2+} was followed with a Ca^{2+} electrode in experiments such as the one shown in Fig. 1. When permeabilized cells were used, the conditions were similar to those described by Fig. 4.

The factors responsible for differences in Ca^{2+} uptake capacities of different types of mitochondria appears to vary with the type of mitochondria analyzed. Recent studies indicate that an elevated endogenous level of Mg^{2+} is responsible for protection against Ca^{2+} induced membrane damage in Ehrlich ascites tumor mitochondria (Fiskum and Cockrell, 1985). However, atomic absorption measurments indicate that AS-30D tumor mitochondria contain similar endogenous levels of Mg^{2+} (25.9 ± 3.9 nmoles mg^{-1} protein) to those of rat liver mitochondria (23.5 ± 3.8 nmoles mg^{-1} protein). Other experiments indicate that AS-30D tumor mitochondria exhibit only 50% of the phospholipase A_2 activity of rat liver mitochondria (G. Fiskum and D. Pfeiffer, unpublished results). Mitochondrial phospholipase A_2 activity has been associated with mitochondrial membrane disruption and is known to potentiate the loss of accumulated Ca^{2+} stores (Broekemeier et al., 1985).

Another factor potentially providing tumor mitochondria with the ability to accumulate large amounts of Ca^{2+} is their elevated level of membrane cholesterol (Parlo and Coleman, 1984, Woldegiorgis and Shrago, 1985). Elevated cholesterol levels play a role in the abnormal adenine nucleotide transport activities (Lau et al., 1984) and increased rates of citrate export (Parlo and Coleman, 1984) across the inner membrane of various tumor mitochondria. AS-30D mitochondria contain approximately three times the total amount of cholesterol of rat liver mitochondria (6.9 ± 1.4 versus 2.3 ± 0.6 µg mg^{-1} protein). Furthermore, AS-30D tumor mitoplasts (mitochondria from which the outer membrane has been removed) possess over 10 times the amount of cholesterol present in rat liver mitoplasts (4.0 ± 0.9 versus 0.3 ± 0.1 µg mg^{-1} protein). In addition to the alteration of Ca^{2+} uptake capacities, the possibility also exists that this abnormality in membrane lipid composition could contribute to a change in the level at which mitochondria buffer exogenous free Ca^{2+} concentrations.

MITOCHONDRIAL STEADY STATE BUFFERING OF AMBIENT FREE Ca^{2+}

Differences between the levels at which tumor and rat liver mitochondria maintain, or buffer, the extramitochondrial free Ca^{2+} concentration are shown in Table 2. In the presence of 3 mM ATP and low (6mM) Na^+, the Ca^{2+} buffer point of tumor mitochondria is greater than that maintained by rat liver mitochondria by at least 0.5 µM free Ca^{2+}. The addition of 20mM Na^+ to the medium, which increases the total Na^+ concentration to approximately the upper level of $\underline{in}$ $\underline{vivo}$ intracellular conditions, results in an increase of the differences in buffer points to over 1 µM. At the low concentration of Na^+ and in the presence of a physiological concentration of the polyamine spermine, the differences in Ca^{2+} buffer points between tumor and rat liver mitochondria largely disappear, and buffer points are decreased to values approaching those maintained by corresponding microsomal (endoplasmic reticulum) vesicles. Physiological concentrations of spermine (0.5-1.0 mM) had previously been shown to increase the net affinity for Ca^{2+} uptake by isolated rat liver mitochondria and saponin-permeabilized hepatocytes (Nichitta and Williamson, 1984). At high concentrations of Na^+ in the presence of 0.5 mM spermine, the hepatoma mitochondria buffer Ca^{2+} at approximately 1.8 µM, a level significantly higher than the buffer point of rat liver mitochondria.

As evidenced by the data in Table 2, AS-30D hepatoma and normal rat liver mitochondria demonstrate different sensitivities to Na^+. This difference may be explainable by different rates at which the mitochondrial Na^+/Ca^{2+} antiport efflux mechanism operates in the two mitochondrial types. Steady state Ca^{2+} influx-efflux cycling rates are reflected by the initial rate of Ca^{2+} efflux by mitochondria to which ruthenium red, a specific inhibitor of mitochondrial Ca^{2+} uptake, is added. When such experiments were performed at a low Na^+ concentration (6 mM), the rate of Ca^{2+} efflux by AS-30D tumor mitochondria (2.5 ± 0.6 nmoles min^{-1} mg^{-1}) was approximately twice as fast as that obtained with rat liver

Table 2. Steady-State Buffering of Ambient Free Ca^{2+} by Normal
Rat Liver and AS-30D Hepatoma Mitochondria

Medium	µM free Ca^{2+}	
	Normal Liver	Hepatoma
No additions[1]	0.8 ± 0.2[2]	1.6 ± 0.3
+ 20mM Na^+	0.9 ± 0.2	2.4 ± 0.4
+ 0.5mM spermine	0.2 ± 0.1	0.4 ± 0.1
+ 20mM Na^+ 0.5mM spermine	0.2 ± 0.1	1.8 ± 0.4

[1] Electrode measurements of the ambient free Ca^{2+} concentration maintained in suspensions of mitochondria (2 mg/ml) at 30°C in medium similar to that described in Fig. 4.

[2] The values represent the means $\pm$ standard deviations of results obtained from at least 4 different preparations.

mitochondria (1.3 nmoles $\text{min}^{-1}\text{mg}^{-1}$). At a higher Na^+ concentration
(26 mM), ruthenium red-induced Ca^{2+} efflux by the hepatoma mitochondria
(9.7 ± 2.6 nmoles $\text{min}^{-1}\text{mg}^{-1}$) was over six times faster than that
observed with rat liver mitochondria (1.5 ± 0.3 nmoles $\text{min}^{-1}\text{mg}^{-1}$).
Similar data on Ca^{2+} buffer points and Na^+ sensitive Ca^{2+} cycling
have been obtained with digitonin-permeabilized tumor cells and hepatocytes.
These data, along with the observation that Ehrlich ascites tumor mitochondria posseses substantial Na^+-dependent Ca^{2+} efflux (Fleschner et
al., 1983) suggest that an elevated Na^+/Ca^{2+} transport activity may be
common to highly malignant tumor cells.

In summary, hepatoma mitochondria appear to buffer ambient free
Ca^{2+} at levels higher than normal rat liver mitochondria and demonstrate
increased Na^+ sensitivity to Ca^{2+} efflux. Given that the measured
cytosolic Ca^{2+} concentrations of tumor cells and normal cells have been
estimated to be similar and lower than the mitochondrial Ca^{2+} buffer
points (Arslan et al., 1985), it is unlikely that an elevated free Ca^{2+}
buffer point for tumor mitochondria would be of significance under basal
steady state conditions. Depending on the physiological concentrations of
regulatory factors (e.g. Na^+ and spermine) the buffering of elevations
in cytosolic Ca^{2+} elicited by extracellular stimuli could be
significantly different in hepatoma cells versus hepatocytes due to
alterations in the mitochondrial Ca^{2+} buffer points. In addition, the
altered rate of Ca^{2+} influx- efflux cycling across hepatoma mitohondria
suggests that the regulation of intramitochondrial free Ca^{2+} as well as
extramitochondrial Ca^{2+} may be abnormal. Any alteration of
intramitochondrial Ca^{2+} could, in turn, affect the activity of certain
key Ca^{2+}-regulated enzymes such as pyruvate, isocitrate, and
α-ketoglutarate dehydrogenases (Hansford, 1985).

REGULATION OF MITOCHONDRIAL Ca^{2+} RELEASE BY THE REDOX STATE OF PYRIDINE NUCLEOTIDES

Recent studies have revealed that in contrast to normal rat liver
mitochondria, AS-30D hepatoma mitochondria are insensitive to the Ca^{2+}
releasing effects of t-butyl hydroperoxide (Fiskum and Pease, 1986).
Tert-butyl hydroperoxide (tBH), when added to suspensions of rat liver
mitochondria respiring on succinate, induces the oxidation of reduced
glutathione followed by the oxidation of NADPH (Fig. 2). NADH also becomes
oxidized as a result of the activity of the pyridine nucleotide
transhydrogenase. As previously observed (Lehninger et al., 1978, Fiskum
and Lehninger, 1979, Lotscher et al., 1979), pyridine nucleotide oxidation
results in the release of accumulated Ca^{2+} from rat liver mitochondria.
However, in AS-30D tumor mitochondria respiring on succinate, pyridine
nucleotides remain reduced in the presence of tBH due to the activity of a
mitochondrial malic enzyme which reduces either $NADP^+$ or NAD^+ during
carboxylation of malate to form pyruvate. This isozyme is virtually absent
from rat liver mitochondria but in hepatomas and other tumors it exhibits
activities that have been correlated with cellular growth rates (Sauer et
al, 1980). When ascorbate plus tetramethyl-p-phenylenediamine is used as an
artificial non-malate generating system for donating electrons to the
respiratory chain, tBH induces NAD(P)H oxidation and release of Ca^{2+}
from AS-30D as well as rat liver mitochondria. These findings demonstrate
that the pyridine nucleotide redox state-modulated Ca^{2+} efflux system is
present in hepatoma as well as rat liver mitochondria and that the system is
normally inoperative in hepatoma mitochondria due to their rapid
re-reduction of oxidized pyridine nucleotides. In vitro experiments
suggest that sustained release of accumulated Ca^{2+} upon oxidation of
pyridine nucleotides does not occur unless the extramitochondrial

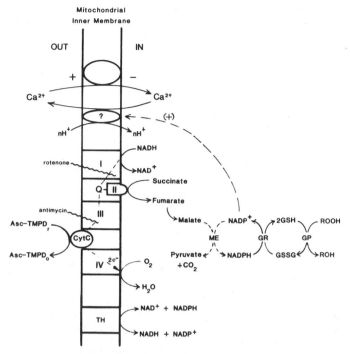

Fig. 2   Pathways of Ca^{2+} transport and pyridine nucleotide
metabolism in rat liver and hepatoma mitochondria. GP (glutathione
peroxidase), GR (glutathione reductase), ME (malic enzyme), TH
(transhydrogenase), GSH (reduced glutathione), GSSG (oxidized
glutathione), Asc-TMPD (ascorbate plus tetramethyl
-p-phenylenediamine), I,II,III,IV (mitochondrial electron transport
chain complexes) (From Fiskum and Pease, 1986).

concentration of Ca^{2+} is high, and ATP and ADP levels are low (Nicholls
and Brand, 1980, Bernardes et al., 1986). Such conditions might arise _in
vivo_ after prolonged substrate and oxygen depletion wherein cytosolic
Ca^{2+} concentrations may be elevated and adenine nucleotide levels
reduced. The unusual resistance to net oxidation of pyridine nucleotides
suggests that tumor mitochondria might be somewhat better adapted for
avoiding or minimizing the potentially damage-inducing release of
accumulated Ca^{2+} to the cytosol during post-ischemic reperfusion.
However, _in situ_ protection of tumor cell viability resulting from this
difference in Ca^{2+} transport remains to be documented.

MICROSOMAL Ca^{2+} BUFFERING

AS-30D hepatoma cells and normal rat liver have also been compared in
terms of their microsomal Ca^{2+} buffering properties. Microsomal
fractions from both tissues, obtained from 100,000 x g centrifugation of
post-mitochondrial supernatants, were tested for maximal initial rates of
ATP-dependent Ca^{2+} uptake (Fig. 3) in the presence of mitochondrial
inhibitors rotenone and oligomycin. In the presence of a high concentration
of extramicrosomal Ca^{2+} (10 µM), the rate of Ca^{2+} uptake by AS-30D
microsomes is approximately twice as fast as that observed with rat liver
microsomes (respectively 13.9 ± 3.2 vs. 7.0 ± 2.1 nmoles min^{-1}

mg^{-1}). Similar differences are obtained with a medium free Ca^{2+} concentration of 1 μM. In the absence of added Ca^{2+}, the buffer points of AS-30D and rat liver microsomes are surprisingly similar (respectively, 0.18 ± 0.11 vs. 0.25 ± 0.12 μM).

Comparable microsomal buffer points are also observed using digitonin-permeabilized hepatoma cells and hepatocytes in the presence or absence of mitochondrial inhibitors. Figure 4 represents a Ca^{2+} electrode tracing of digitonin-permeabilized AS-30D hepatoma cells and hepatocytes in the absence of mitochondrial inhibitors. The initial buffer points established in both cell types prior to the addition of exogenous Ca^{2+} are similar to one another and comparable to those of the respective isolated microsomes. However, after saturating the non-mitochondrial Ca^{2+} uptake capacity by the addition of exogenous Ca^{2+}, the new buffer point established in hepatoma cells was approximately 1 μM higher than the level maintained by hepatocytes. The buffer points obtained at high total Ca^{2+} for hepatoma cells and hepatocytes are very similar to those obtained with isolated AS-30D and rat liver mitochondria under similar conditions, as previously discussed.

One of the most interesting differences in Ca^{2+} transport properties between rat liver and AS-30D hepatoma is in the responsiveness of their isolated microsomes to the Ca^{2+} releasing effects of inositol 1,4,5 trisphosphate (IP$_3$). IP$_3$ is generated upon activation of phospholipase C from the membrane phospholipid phosphatidylinositol 4,5 bisphosphate in response to mitogens, hormones and other stimuli (Berridge and Irvine, 1984). IP$_3$ functions to transduce these extracellular signals into increases in cytosolic Ca^{2+}. As other researchers have observed (Joseph et al., 1984), the release of Ca^{2+} from isolated rat liver microsomes that occurs in response to the addition of IP$_3$ is extremely limited (Fig. 5). In fact, 5–10 μM IP$_3$ fails to elicit a maximum rise in free Ca^{2+} greater than 0.1 μM. However, as little as

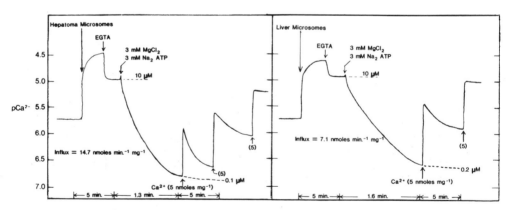

Fig. 3 Ca^{2+} uptake by isolated rat liver and AS-30D hepatoma microsomes. The conditions were the same as those described in Fig. 1 except that malate and glutamate were omitted and rotenone (4μM) and oligomycin (1 μg ml^{-1}) were included. Microsomal protein was 0.5–1.0 mg ml^{-1}. Ca^{2+} uptake was initiated by the addition of 3mM Na$_2$ATP plus 3mM MgCl$_2$. The numbers in parentheses refer to subsequent additions of CaCl$_2$ in nmoles mg^{-1} microsomal protein.

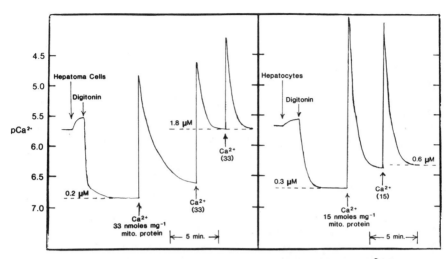

Fig. 4 Regulation of the steady-state ambient free Ca^{2+} concentration by digitonin-permeabilized AS-30D hepatoma cells and normal rat hepatocytes. The conditions were the same as those described in Fig. 1 except that 3mM Na_2 ATP, 3mM $MgCl_2$, and 0.005-0.010% digitonin were included. AS-30D cells and rat hepatocytes were present at 4×10^7 cells ml^{-1} and 1×10^7 cells ml^{-1} respectively.

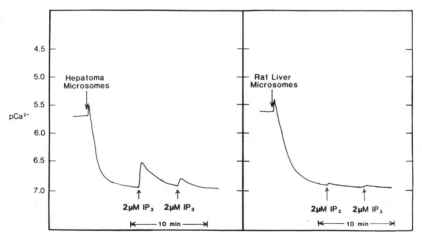

Fig. 5 Release of Ca^{2+} by inositol 1,4,5 trisphosphate (IP_3) from AS-30D hepatoma and rat liver microsomes. The conditions were the same as those described in Fig. 3.

0.1 μM IP_3 induces significant Ca^{2+} release from AS-30D microsomes, followed by Ca^{2+} reuptake in the presence of ATP.

In experiments with digitonin-permeabilized hepatocytes and hepatoma cells, the responsiveness of the non-mitochondrial Ca^{2+} pool is significantly greater than that of the respective isolated microsomal fractions. Furthermore, the difference in IP_3-induced Ca^{2+} release from the permeabilized hepatocytes and hepatoma cells is much less than that observed with the isolated microsomes, possibly suggesting the loss of a responsive fraction in the rat liver microsomal preparation. Evidence that mitochondria can participate in the buffering of transient rises in cytosolic Ca^{2+} resulting from the release of Ca^{2+} stores in the endoplasmic reticulum have also come from experiments with digitonin-permeabilized cells. The maximum levels to which the ambient free Ca^{2+} rises in response to IP_3 stimulation of AS-30D microsomes is dampened in the absence of inhibitors of the mitochondrial respiratory chain and ATP synthetase (G. Fiskum, unpublished results).

In summary, AS-30D microsomes have been found to have a faster rate of Ca^{2+} uptake and an increased sensitivity to IP_3 in comparison to rat liver microsomes. However, the malignant and normal organelles appear to buffer Ca^{2+} at the same resting level. If the in vivo response of hepatoma endoplasmic reticulum to IP_3 is actually greater than that in rat liver, this observation suggests important consequences to the malignant phenotype, especially with respect to the cellular response to growth factors and modulation of IP_3 generation by the products of various oncogenes.

CONCLUSIONS AND PROSPECTUS

A number of Ca^{2+} transport activities in AS-30D mitochondria and microsomes have been found to significantly differ from the corresponding fractions from rat liver. Hepatoma mitochondrial Ca^{2+} uptake capacity, Ca^{2+} cycling and buffer points are elevated in comparison to normal rat liver mitochondria. These tumor mitochondria also demonstrate insensitivity to the Ca^{2+} releasing effects of t-butyl hydroperoxide due to the pyridine nucleotide reducing activity of a mitochondrial malic enzyme present in tumor but not liver mitochondria. These altered Ca^{2+} transport characteristics are possibly a survival-oriented adaptation by tumor cells to withstand the hypoxic or ischemic environment to which they are often exposed. Such adaptive mechanisms may allow the maintenance of cytosolic Ca^{2+} at levels compatible with cell function under conditions of decreased ATP production during partial ischemia or during the initial stages of reperfusion following complete ischemia. Efforts to determine how these alterations might interact to provide protection to tumor cells under hypoxic conditions and how they might provide a selective mechanism for cancer therapy are in progress.

The possibility that tumor cell endoplasmic reticulum possesses enhanced sensitivity to the Ca^{2+} releasing effects of IP_3 may play an important role in elucidating the mechanisms involved in the stimulated growth rates associated with malignancy. An increased sensitivity to IP_3 could promote cellular responses to mitogens resulting in elevated basal Ca^{2+} levels or protracted Ca^{2+} transients. Attention directed toward the involvement of src, ros, abl, and fps oncogene products which may enhance IP_3 release (Macara, 1985) from membrane phospholipides in warrented.

ACKNOWLEDGEMENTS

This review article was written while G. Fiskum was supported by grant CA32946 from the National Institutes of Health. Part of the work described herein was supported by the same grant.

REFERENCES

Arslan, P., DiVirgilio, F., Beltrame, M., Tsien, R. and Pozzan, T., 1985, Cytosolic Ca^{2+} homeostasis in Erhlich and Yoshida carcinomas, J. Biol. Chem. , 260: 2719-2727.

Beg, Z.H., Stonik, J.A. and Brewer, H.B., Jr., 1985, Phosphorylation of hepatic 3-hydroxy-3-methylglutaryl coenzyme A reductase and modulation of its enzymic activity by calcium-activated and phospholipid-dependent protein kinase, J. Biol. Chem. , 260: 1682-1687.

Ben-Ze'ev, A., 1985, The cytoskeleton in cancer cells, Biochem. Biophys. Acta, 780: 197-212.

Bernardes, C.F., da Silva, L.P. and Vercesi, A.E., 1986, t-Butylhydroperoxide-induced Ca^{2+} efflux from liver mitochondria in the presence of physiological concentrations of Mg^{2+} and ATP, Biochem, Biophys.Acta, 850: 41-48.

Berridge, M.J. and Irvine, R.F., 1984, Inositol trisphosphate, a novel second messenger in cellular signal transduction, Nature , 312: 315-321.

Broekemeier, K.M., Schmid, P.C., Schmid, H.H.O., and Pfeiffer, D.R., 1985, Effects of phospholipase inhibitors on ruthenium red-induced Ca^{2+} release from mitochondria, J. Biol. Chem., 260:105-113.

Cittadini, A., Bossi, D., Dani, A.M., Calviello, G., Wolf, F. and Terranova, T., 1981, Lack of effect of the Ca^{2+} ionophore A23187 on tumor cells, Biochem, Biophys, Acta, 645: 177-182.

Cittadini, A., Dani, A.M., Wolf, F., Bossi, D. and Calviello, G., 1982, Calcium permeability of Ehrlich ascites tumor cell plasma membrane in vivo, Biochem. Biophys. Acta, 686: 27-35.

Farber, J.L., 1982, Biology of disease: membrane injury and calcium homeostasis in the pathogenesis of coagulative necrosis, Lab Invest. , 47: 114-123.

Fiskum, G., 1985, Intracellular levels and distribution of Ca^{2+} in digitonin-permeabilized cells, Cell Calcium, 6: 25-37.

Fiskum, G. and Cockrell, R.S., 1985, Uncoupler-stimulated release of Ca^{2+} from Ehrlich ascites tumor cell mitochondria, Arch. Biochem. Biophys., 240: 723-733.

Fiskum, G. and Lehninger, A.L., 1979, Regulated release of Ca^{2+} release from mitochondria by Ca^{2+}/2H^{+} antiport, J. Biol. Chem., 254: 6236-6239.

Fiskum, G. and Pease, A., 1986, Hydroperoxide-stimulated release of calcium from rat liver and AS-30D hepatoma mitochondria, Canc. Res., 46: 3459-3463.

Fleschner, C.R., Martin, A.P., Vorbeck, M.L, Darnold, J.R. and Long, J.W., Jr., 1983, Ca^{2+} release from energetically campled tumor mitochondria, Biochem, Biophys. Res. Commun., 115: 430-436.

Hansford, R.G., 1985, Relation between mitochondrial calcium transport and control of energy metabolism, Rev. Physiol. Biochem. Pharmacol., 102: 1-72.

Hickie, R.A. and Kalant, H., 1967, Calcium and magnesium content of rat liver and Morris hepatoma 5123tc, Canc. Res., 27: 1053-1057.

Joseph, S.K., Williams, R.J., Corkey, B.E., Matschinsky, F.M. and

Williamson, J.R., 1984, The effect of inositol trisphosphate on Ca^{2+} fluxes in insulin secreting tumor cells, J. Biol. Chem., 259: 12952-12955.

Kennedy, K.A., Teicher, B.A., Rockwell, S. and Sartorelli, A.C., 1980, The hypoxic tumor cell: a target for selective cancer chemotherapy, Biochem. Pharm., 29: 1-8.

Lau, B.W.C., Weber, L, Maggio, M. and Chan, S.H.P., 1984, Elevated content of cholesterol affects adenine nucleotide transport in tumor mitochondria, Fed. Proc., 43: 1876.

Lehninger, A.L., Vercesi, A. and Bababunmi, E.A., 1978, Regulation of Ca^{2+} release from mitochondria by the oxidation-reduction state of pyridine nucleotides, Proc. Natl. Acad. Sci. USA, 75: 1690-1694.

Lotscher, H.R., Winterhalter, K.H., Carafoli, E. and Richter, C., 1979, Hydroperoxides can moderate the redox state of pyridine nucleotides and the calcium balance in rat liver mitochondria, Proc. Natl. Acad. Sci. USA, 76: 4340-4344.

Macara, I.G., 1985, Oncogenes, ions, and phospholipids, Am. J. Physiol., 248: C3-C11.

Means, A.R., Tash, J.S. and Chafouleas, J.G., 1982, Physiological implications of the presence, distribution and regulation of calmodulin in eukaryotic cells, Physiol. Rev., 62: 1-39.

Moulder, J.E. and S.J. Rockwell, 1984, Hypoxic fractions of solid tumors: experimental techniques, methods of analysis, and a survey of existing data, Int. J. Radiat. Oncol. Biol. Phys., 10: 695-772.

Nichitta, C.V. and Williamson, J.R., 1984, Spermine: a regulator of mitochondrial calcium cycling, J. Biol. Chem., 259: 12978-12983.

Nicholls, D.G. and Brand, M.D., 1980, The nature of the calcium ion efflux induced in rat liver mitochondria by the oxidation of endogenous nicotinamide nucleotides, Biochem. J., 188: 113-118.

Ohnishi, T., Suzuki, Y. and Ozawa, K., 1982, A comparative study of plasma membrane Mg^{2+} ATPase activities in normal, regenerating and malignant cells, Biochim. Biophys. Acta, 684: 67-74.

Parlo, R.A. and Coleman, P.S., 1984, Enhanced rate of citrate export from cholesterol-rich hepatoma mitochondria: the tuncated Krebs cycle and other metabolic ramifications of mitochondrial membrane cholesterol, J. Biol. Chem., 259: 9997-10003.

Sauer, L.A., Dauchy, R.T., Nagel, W.O. and Morris, H.P., 1980, Mitochondrial $NAD(P)^{+}$-dependent malic enzyme activity and malate-dependent pyruvate formation are progression-linked in Morris hepatomas, J. Biol. Chem., 255: 3844-3848.

Smith, D.F., Walborg, E.F. Jr., Chang, J.P, 1970, Establishment of a transplantable ascites variant of a rat hepatoma induced by 3'-methyl-4-dimethylaminoazobenzene, Canc. Res., 30: 2306-2309.

Swierenga, S.H.H., Whitfield, J.F. and Karasaki, S., 1978, Loss of proliferative calcium dependence: simple in vitro indicator of tumorigenicity, Cell Biology, 75: 6069-6072.

Villalobo, A. and Lehninger, A.L., 1980, Inhibition of oxidative phosphorylation in ascites tumor mitochondria and cells by intramitochondrial Ca^{2+}, J. Biol. Chem., 255: 2457-2464.

Woldegiorgis, G. and Shrago, E., 1985, Adenine nucleotide translocase activity and sensitivity to inhibitors, J. Biol. Chem., 260: 7585-7590.

ALKYLATING TOXINS AND THE LIVER PLASMA MEMBRANE CALCIUM PUMP/CALCIUM ATPASE

Janice O. Tsokos-Kuhn, Helen Hughes, Charles V. Smith,
and Jerry R. Mitchell

Department of Medicine
Baylor College of Medicine
Houston, Texas 77030

INTRODUCTION

The role of altered calcium homeostasis as a possible unifying mechanism of acute lethal cell injury by chemical toxins, ischemia, and other agents has attracted much interest (Trump and Berezesky, 1984; Schanne et al., 1979; Jewell et al., 1982; Lowrey et al., 1981; Bellomo and Orrenius, 1985). Clearly, many cellular processes are regulated or influenced by the cytosolic free calcium concentration, which in turn is controlled by calcium transport systems of the plasma membrane, the endoplasmic reticulum, and the mitochondria. Moore and coworkers (1976) first showed over 10 years ago that liver microsomes isolated 30 or more minutes after administration of CCl_4 to Sprague-Dawley rats had virtually lost the capacity for ATP-dependent Ca^{2+} uptake. They postulated that inhibition of the liver endoplasmic reticulum Ca^{2+} pump might be the initial insult disrupting Ca^{2+} homeostasis sufficiently to produce an injury allowing massive Ca^{2+} influx into the cell (Moore et al., 1976).

CCl_4 is one example of a considerable array of hepatotoxic chemicals. These can be organized into several classes by reference to the types of reactive intermediates they yield, the cellular protection systems effective against them, and the chemical lesions they produce in the liver (Mitchell et al., 1984). Figure 1 illustrates the four main classes with some examples, and indicates some of the salient characteristics of these hepatotoxins.

In the work to be described here, we undertook to compare the effects of acetaminophen and bromobenzene, toxins that deplete glutathione and alkylate cellular protein molecules, with those of CCl_4, which does not give rise to a substrate for glutathione S-transferase, and which produces lipid peroxidation as well as alkylation of macromolecules in vivo. We examined the Ca^{2+} transport functions of the three liver cell membrane systems responsible for Ca^{2+} homeostatic regulation after administration of hepatotoxic doses of acetaminophen, CCl_4, and bromobenzene to test the hypothesis that calcium homeostatic regulation may be disturbed by alkylating chemical toxins.

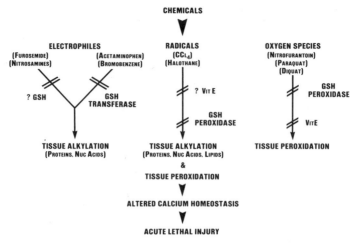

CHEMICALS

ELECTROPHILES
(Furosemide) (Acetaminophen)
(Nitrosamines) (Bromobenzene)

? GSH   GSH
               TRANSFERASE

TISSUE ALKYLATION
(Proteins, Nuc Acids)

RADICALS
(CCl₄)
(Halothane)

? Vit E

GSH
PEROXIDASE

TISSUE ALKYLATION
(Proteins, Nuc Acids, Lipids)
&
TISSUE PEROXIDATION

OXYGEN SPECIES
(Nitrofurantoin)
(Paraquat)
(Diquat)

GSH
PEROXIDASE

Vit E

TISSUE PEROXIDATION

ALTERED CALCIUM HOMEOSTASIS

ACUTE LETHAL INJURY

Figure 1.

METHODS

Male Sprague-Dawley rats were induced with phenobarbital or 3-methyl-cholanthrene (for acetaminophen), fasted overnight, and dosed with CCl_4, bromobenzene or acetaminophen as previously described (Tsokos-Kuhn et al., 1985). Animals were sacrificed 4 hours or 2.5 hours (acetaminophen) after dose and liver microsomes, mitochondria, or plasma membranes were isolated by standard procedures as described (Tsokos-Kuhn et al., 1985). Calcium transport was measured by a Millipore filtration method using ^{45}Ca, or by a spectrophotometric method utilizing the calcium indicator antipyrylazo III (mitochondria). Passive calcium efflux was monitored by a Millipore method after overnight loading at 4° in 1 mM $CaCl_2$ (Tsokos-Kuhn et al., in press). Calcium content of isolated membranes was measured by atomic absorption spectrophotometry. Neuraminidase-releasable sialic acid was measured by a thiobarbituric acid method as previously described (Tsokos-Kuhn et al., in press).

RESULTS

None of the three hepatotoxins significantly influenced succinate-driven Ca^{2+} uptake by mitochondria isolated after dosing in vivo (Fig. 2). Ruthenium red-insensitive mitochondrial Ca^{2+} efflux was also unaffected (data not shown). Similarly, ATP-dependent Ca^{2+} uptake by liver microsomal fractions was unchanged after bromobenzene or acetaminophen administration (Fig. 3). Only CCl_4, as thoroughly documented by others (Moore et al., 1976; Lowrey et al., 1981) was highly effective in inhibiting microsomal Ca^{2+} uptake.

In contrast, however, all three model hepatotoxins produced significant inhibition of ATP-dependent Ca^{2+} uptake of liver plasma membrane vesicles isolated after toxin administration (Fig. 4). Plasma membrane calcium uptake was virtually abolished after CCl_4 administration, and lesser, but still highly significant amounts of inhibition were observed after acetaminophen and bromobenzene.

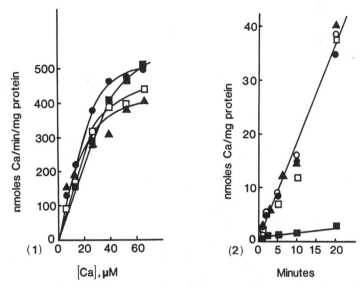

Figure 2. (left) Effect of hepatotoxins in vivo on the rate of succinate-supported liver mitochondrial Ca^{2+} uptake. (●) control; (▲) bromobenzene; (□) acetaminophen; (■) CCl_4 (from Tsokos-Kuhn et al., 1985).

Figure 3. (right) Effect of hepatotoxins on ATP-dependent microsomal Ca^{2+} uptake. Symbols as in Figure 2 except (○) 3-methylcholanthrene control (from Tsokos-Kuhn et al., 1985).

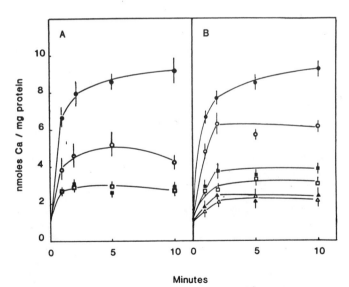

Figure 4. Effect of hepatotoxins in vivo on Ca^{2+} uptake by liver plasma membrane vesicles. A. 3-methylcholanthrene control: (●) + ATP, (■) - ATP; acetaminophen: (○) + ATP, (□) - ATP. B. phenobarbital control: (●) + ATP, (■) - ATP; bromo-benzene: (○) + ATP, (□) - ATP; CCl_4 (▲) + ATP, (△) - ATP (from Tsokos-Kuhn et al., 1985).

Table 1. Proportions of Right-Side-Out Vesicles in Preparations
from Toxin-Treated or Control Rats

	Right-Side-Out Vesicles	
	Control	Toxin-Treated
Acetaminophen	67.8 ± 6.9	72.6 ± 9.2
Bromobenzene	71.2 ± 8.5	75.0 ± 6.7
CCl₄	62.6 ± 4.5	97.1 ± 7.2

The proportion of right-side-out vesicles is estimated as the
ratio of sialic acid released by neuraminidase from vesicles
incubated in the absence of detergent to that released in the
presence of 0.05% Triton X-100. Data are the mean ± standard
error for three separate preparations.

To examine the possibility that the decreased calcium uptake was
caused by altered vesicle sidedness, we looked at neuraminidase-releasable
sialic acid contents in control and toxin membranes in the absence and the
presence of detergent (Table 1). The ratio of these values estimates the
percent of right side out vesicles. Neither bromobenzene nor acetaminophen
significantly changed the right side out:inside out vesicle distribution.
CCl₄ gave a puzzling result appearing to suggest either that all vesicles
were right side out or that there was significant permeability of the
vesicles to neuraminidase. Both seem unlikely, but it is possible that
CCl₄ vesicles have altered membranes (see below) that may become permeable
to neuraminidase during incubation with the enzyme.

We also looked for changes in percent contamination by other
membranes. Neither CCl₄, bromobenzene, nor acetaminophen plasma membrane
preparations exhibited increased glucose-6-phosphatase or azide-sensitive
ATPase activities, suggesting there was no increase in the distribution of
contaminating endoplasmic reticulum or mitochondrial membranes into the
plasma membrane fraction after toxin treatment (data not shown).

Further studies were focused primarily on the CCl₄ and acetaminophen
models. First we were concerned to establish whether CCl₄ vesicles, in
particular, were more permeable to Ca^{2+} than controls, which could explain
their virtual inability to accumulate Ca^{2+}. Vesicles were passively
loaded in the presence of 1 mM ^{45}Ca, subsequently diluted 30-fold with
ice-cold medium containing 2 mM EGTA, and efflux of Ca from the vesicles
was followed as a function of time (Fig. 5, top). Zero time values were
determined separately on samples of the loading suspension. CCl₄ vesicles
had lower Ca^{2+} content at zero time, markedly increased rates of Ca^{2+} loss
from the vesicles, and lower A23187-insensitive Ca^{2+} content, in addition.
A semilog plot of the first five minutes of efflux (Fig. 5, bottom) shows
the biphasic character of the process. The first order rate constants of
efflux were 0.27 min^{-1} for control, 1.78 min^{-1} for CCl₄ in the first
phase, 0.052 min^{-1} and 0.17 min^{-1} , respectively, in the second phase.
Thus, in the first phase, the rate constant for efflux was increased more
than six-fold after CCl₄.

154

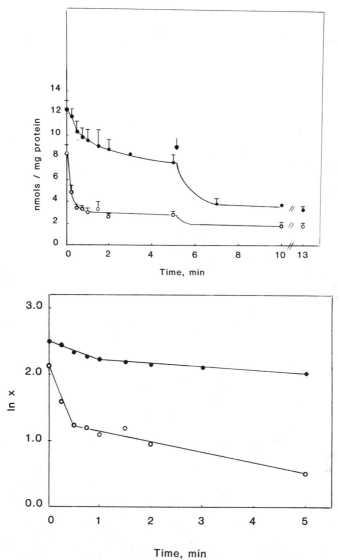

Figure 5. Efflux of Ca^{2+} from passively loaded plasma membrane vesicles.
(●) control, (○) CCl_4. At arrow, ionophore A23187 (2 µM) was
introduced. Bottom, semilog plot of first two minutes of
efflux. First order rate constants of the first phase of
efflux are 0.27 and 1.78 min^{-1} for control and CCl_4 vesicles,
respectively (from Tsokos-Kuhn et al., in press).

Table 2. Calcium Content of CCl₄ Plasma Membrane Vesicles

	Millipore Method	Ion Exchange Method	Ca^{2+} Content of
	Zero Time Ca^{2+} Content After Passive Loading		Freshly Isolated Vesicles Measured by Atomic Absorption Spectrometry
	nmol/mg protein		
Control	12.3 ± 0.8 (5)	11.2 ± 1.8 (3)	17.4 ± 2.0 (5)
CCl₄	8.3 ± 0.8 (5)	8.1 ± 0.4 (3)	10.9 ± 1.2 (5)

Table 2 summarizes the zero time Ca^{2+} contents measured by two different methods and also includes data obtained by atomic absorption analysis of freshly isolated membranes. In both cases the CCl₄ membranes had significantly decreased bound Ca^{2+}. The A23187-insensitive Ca content was also significantly lower in CCl₄ vesicles (Fig. 5, top). The intravesicular volume of plasma membrane vesicles after CCl₄ was significantly greater than control (5.1 versus 3.1 µl/mg protein) so the decreased zero time content in CCl₄ vesicles is unlikely to be the result of a lesser loading volume. Rather it probably reflects in part a rapid efflux occurring during sampling for zero time measurements, and partly a lower content of bound Ca^{2+}.

In other experiments, K^+ permeability of the vesicles was tested, using the technique of Garty et al. (1983). CCl₄ vesicles also exhibited greater permeability to K^+, although the difference from controls was less than seen in the case of Ca^{2+} (Tsokos-Kuhn et al., in press).

After CCl₄, both plasma membranes and microsomes contained significantly increased amounts of 11-, 12-, and 15-hydroxyeicosatetraenoic acids (HETEs), measured by the highly specific and sensitive GC-MS assay developed in our laboratories as an index of lipid peroxidation (Hughes et al., 1986). Time courses of decreased Ca^{2+} accumulation and increased Ca^{2+} efflux of liver plasma membranes after CCl₄ dosing indicate that both are well established by 30 minutes after dose, as is true for liver microsomes. It is well-known that the liver endoplasmic reticulum membranes undergo early peroxidative changes in CCl₄ intoxication and we have found that CCl₄ microsomes also exhibit increased passive Ca^{2+} permeability. Thus both plasma membranes and microsomes undergo similar structural and functional changes in CCl₄ intoxication. The ionophoretic properties of certain oxygenated polyunsaturated fatty acids (Serhan et al., 1981; Deleers et al., 1985), probably not including the HETEs but perhaps one or more of the numerous other lipid oxidation products present in peroxidized membranes, suggest a possible mechanism for the increased ion permeability observed after CCl₄ intoxication.

Acetaminophen and bromobenzene provide a contrast to the CCl₄ situation. Effects of acetaminophen on Ca^{2+} uptake of plasma membranes are established early (Tsokos-Kuhn et al., 1985), as is true with CCl₄. But plasma membranes isolated after acetaminophen or bromobenzene do not exhibit altered permeability or altered Ca^{2+} content. Vesicle volumes are

156

not different from controls after acetaminophen or bromobenzene, and compare very well with those of the control vesicles in the CCl_4 experiments. Furthermore, no accumulation of specific lipid oxidation products has been detected in plasma membranes of acetaminophen-treated rats.

If the decrease in Ca^{2+} accumulation by plasma membranes after acetaminophen cannot be explained even in part by membrane lipid peroxidation or increased ion permeability, the calcium pump itself seems a likely target of the toxic electrophilic intermediate(s) of acetaminophen. We measured Ca^{2+}-dependent ATPase in the absence of added Mg^{2+}, as described by Lotersztajn et al. (1981), and found a significant decrease of ATPase activity after acetaminophen, although not to the very marked extent that Ca^{2+} transport was inhibited.

CONCLUSIONS

To summarize, liver plasma membrane Ca^{2+} transport is susceptible to early and profound inhibition by chemical hepatotoxins. In the case of CCl_4, a major effect appears to be altered cation permeability in conjunction with lipid peroxidation and decreased Ca^{2+} binding. Both plasma membrane and microsomes are subject to these changes. The ionophoretic activity of certain oxygenated fatty acids (Serhan et al., 1981; Deleers et al., 1985) suggests a mechanism for the ion permeability increase observed in CCl_4 membranes undergoing peroxidative changes. Acetaminophen does not produce membrane lipid peroxidation or alter plasma membrane permeability but instead may act by direct alkylation of susceptible thiols of the ATP-dependent Ca^{2+} pump, or possibly of a related regulatory protein.

Thus both of these differently acting hepatotoxic chemicals exhibit the potential to alter calcium homeostatic regulation in vivo. Different mechanisms of action are involved, but these are entirely consistent with the chemistry of the postulated reactive metabolites of CCl_4 and acetaminophen. These results provide further support for the hypothesis that altered calcium homeostasis plays a general role in toxic cell injury.

REFERENCES

1. Bellomo, G. and Orrenius, S., 1985, Altered thiol and calcium homeostasis in oxidative hepatocellular injury. Hepatology, 5:876.
2. Deleers, M., Grognet, P., and Baasseur, R., 1985, Structural considerations for calcium ionophoresis by prostaglandins. Biochem. Pharmacol., 34:3831.
3. Garty, H., Rudy, B., and Karlish, S.J.D., 1983, A simple and sensitive procedure for measuring isotope fluxes through ion-specific channels in heterogenous populations of membrane vesicles. J. Biol. Chem., 258:13094.
4. Hughes, H., Smith, C.V., Tsokos-Kuhn, J.O., and Mitchell, J.R., 1986, Quantitation of lipid peroxidation products by gas chromatography-mass spectrometry. Anal. Biochem., 152:107.
5. Jewell, S.A., Bellomo, G., Thor, H., Orrenius, S., and Smith, M.T., 1982, Bleb formation in hepatocytes during drug metabolism is caused by disturbances in thiol and calcium ion homeostasis. Science, 271:1257.
6. Lotersztajn, S., Hanoune, J., and Pecker, F., 1981, A high-affinity calcium-stimulated magnesium-dependent ATPase in rat liver plasma membranes. J. Biol. Chem., 256:11209.

7. Lowrey, K., Glende, E.A., Jr., and Recknagel, R.A., 1981, Destruction of liver microsomal calcium pump activity by carbon tetrachloride and bromotrichloromethane. Biochem. Pharmacol., 30:135.

8. Mitchell, J.R., Smith, C.V., Lauterburg, B.H., Hughes, H., Corcoran, G.B., and Horning, E.C., 1984, Reactive metabolites and the pathophysiology of acute lethal cell injury, in: "Drug Metabolism and Drug Toxicity," J.R. Mitchell and M.G. Horning, eds., Raven Press, New York.

9. Moore, L., Davenport, G.R., and Landon, E.J., 1976, Calcium uptake of a rat liver microsomal subcellular fraction in response to in vivo administration of carbon tetrachloride. J. Biol. Chem., 251:1197.

10. Schanne, F.A.X., Kane, A.B., Young, E.E., and Farber, J.L., 1979, Calcium dependence of toxic cell death: a final common pathway. Science, 206:700.

11. Serhan, C., Anderson, P., Goodman, E., Dunham P., and Weissmann, G., 1981, Phosphatidate and oxidized fatty acids are calcium ionophores: studies employing arsenazo III in liposomes. J. Biol. Chem., 256:2736.

12. Trump, B.F. and Berezesky, I.K., 1984, Role of sodium and calcium regulation in toxic cell injury, in: "Drug Metabolism and Drug Toxicity," J.R. Mitchell and M.G. Horning, eds., Raven Press, New York.

13. Tsokos-Kuhn, J.O., Smith, C.V., Mitchell, J.R., Tate, C.A., and Entman, M.L., Evidence for increased membrane permeability of plasmalemmal vesicles from livers of CCl_4-intoxicated rats. Molec. Pharmacol., In Press.

14. Tsokos-Kuhn, J.O., Todd, E.L., McMillin-Wood, J.B., and Mitchell, J.R., 1985, ATP-dependent calcium transport in rat liver plasma membrane vesicles: effect of alkylating hepatotoxins in vivo. Molec. Pharmacol., 28:56.

ROLE OF ATP AND NA+ IN THE REGULATION OF

CYTOSOLIC FREE CALCIUM IN KIDNEY CELLS

André B. Borle

Department of Physiology
University of Pittsburgh School of Medicine
Pittsburgh, PA 15261

Cytosolic free calcium ($Ca_i{}^{2+}$) is controlled by several calcium transporters located at the plasma membrane, the inner membrane of the mitochondria and in the endoplasmic reticulum. Fig. 1 shows the various ATP-dependent pumps and antiporters involved in the control of $Ca_i{}^{2+}$ and $Na_i{}^+$ (In this figure, the plasmalemmal Na^+-Ca^{2+} antiporter is conventionally assumed to operate in the forward mode i.e. Ca^{2+} efflux energized by Na^+ influx). Since Ca^{2+} transport out of the cell can be energized by ATP or by the Na^+ electrochemical potential $\Delta\mu Na^+$, a fall in cellular ATP or a drop in $\Delta\mu Na^+$ would be expected to depress Ca^{2+} efflux, raise $Ca_i{}^{2+}$ and increase the cell Ca^{2+} content. In recent experiments (1,2) performed with cultured monkey kidney cells (LLC-MK$_2$), my collaborators Dr. K.W. Snowdowne, C.C. Freudenrich and I found that only one of these three predictions was proved correct. Lowering cellular ATP from 2 to 0.1 mM by exposing the cells to anoxia and removing

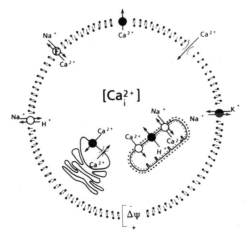

Fig. 1   Pathways of calcium transport in epithelial cells. Na^+-Ca^{2+} exchange is shown operating in the forward mode.

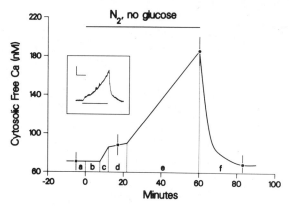

Fig. 2   Effect of anoxia and removal of substrate on Ca_i^{2+} in kidney
cells. (Reproduced from Snowdowne et al (1) with permission
from J. Biol. Chem 260, 11619, 1985. Copyright 1985 by the
American Society of Biological Chemists Inc.)

metabolic substrates increased Ca_i^{2+} 3 fold (Fig. 2). Lowering $\Delta\mu Na^+$ by
decreasing the extracellular Na^+ concentration (Na_o^+) with
tetramethylamonium (TMA) as substituting ion increased Ca_i^{2+} 6 folds
(Fig. 3) when measured with aequorin (3). The rise in Ca_i^{2+} was
proportional to the fall in Na_o^+ (Fig. 4). However, Ca^{2+} efflux was not
decreased. Contrary to the predictions, Ca^{2+} efflux was significantly
stimulated 3 to 5 folds (Fig. 5 and 6) both by anoxia and by low Na_o^+,
and cellular Ca^{2+} content was unchanged in both conditions. These
results indicate that the rise in Ca_i^{2+} was not caused by a decreased

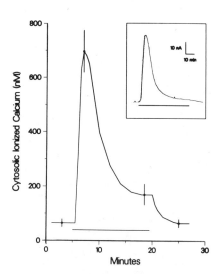

Fig. 3.   Effect of substituting TMA for extracellular Na^+ on Ca_i^{2+} in
kidney cells. (Reproduced from Snowdowne and Borle (2) with
permission from J. Biol Chem 260, 14998, 1985. Copyright 1985
by the American Society of Biological Chemists Inc)

160

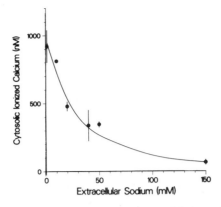

Fig. 4. Relation between the fall in extracellular Na^+ and the rise in Ca_i^{2+} (Reproduced from Snowdowne and Borle with permission from J. Biol Chem 260, 14998, 1985. Copyright 1985 by the American Society of Biological Chemists Inc)

Ca^{2+} efflux out of the cells; rather, we have to conclude that the increase in Ca^{2+} efflux was a consequence of the rise in Ca_i^{2+}. These results also suggest that calcium influx into the cells must have been markedly stimulated since the cell Ca^{2+} content did not change in spite of a 3 to 5-fold increase in Ca^{2+} efflux. And indeed, ^{45}Ca uptake was significantly enhanced both by anoxia and by Na_o^+-free conditions (1,2). It is always difficult to assess the relative contribution of calcium influx from the extracellular fluids and of calcium mobilization from intracellular organelles to an elevation in Ca_i^{2+}. Nevertheless, our experiments clearly show that the mobilization of Ca^{2+} from intracellular sources did not play a significant role in raising Ca_i^{2+}. First,

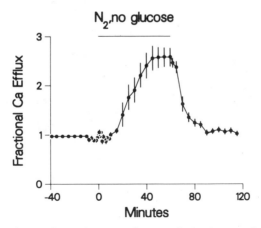

Fig. 5. Effect of anoxia and removal of substrate or fractional calcium efflux from kidney cells. (Reproduced from Snowdowne et al with permission from J Biol Chem 260, 11619, 1985. Copyright 1985 by the American Society of Biological Chemists Inc)

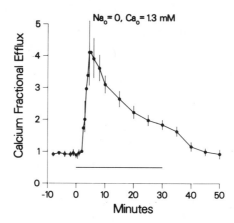

Fig. 6.   Effect of substituting TMA for extracellular Na+ on fractional
           calcium efflux from kidney cells. (Reproduced from Snowdowne
           and Borle with permission from J Biol Chem 260, 14998, 1985.
           Copyright 1985 by the Americal Society of Biological Chemists
           Inc)

lowering extracellular Ca^{2+} (Ca_o^{2+}) decreases the rise in Ca_i^{2+} induced
either by anoxia or by low Na_o^+ (Fig. 7); second, below $10^{-5}M$ Ca_o^{2+}, no
elevation in Ca_i^{2+} can be detected; and third, substitution of Ca_o^{2+} with
Sr^{2+} or addition of La^{3+} to the medium abolish the rise in Ca_i^{2+}[1,2].
Thus it appears that the principal source of calcium responsible for the
rise in Ca_i^{2+} is extracellular.   We propose that anoxia (with its
concomittant fall in ATP) or a reduction in $\Delta\mu Na^+$ could increase Ca^{2+}
influx on the Na^{2+}-Ca^{2+} antiporter operating in the reverse mode. During
anoxia, the ATP concentration falls to 0.1 mM which is below the $K_{0.5}$ for
ATP of the (Na^+-K^+) ATPase (0.2-0.3 mM) but above the $K_{0.5}$ for ATP of the
(Ca^{2+}-Mg^{2+}) ATPase (10-20 μM).   Consequently Na_i^+ can be expected to
rise progressively and decrease $\Delta\mu Na^+$, without affecting Ca^{2+} efflux on

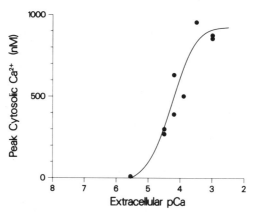

Fig. 7.   Effect of lowering the extracellular calcium concentration on
           the peak rise in Ca_i^{2+} induced by substituting TMA for
           extracellular Na+. (Reproduced from Snowdowne and Borle with
           permission from J Biol Chem 260, 14998, 1985. Copyright 1985
           by the American Society of Biological Chemists Inc)

the ATP-dependent plasmalemmal Ca^{2+} pump. And indeed, Mason et al (4) found that Na_i increases more than 4 folds in less than 20 min following renal ischemia. Because $\Delta\mu Na^+$ is significantly decreased by a high $Na_i{}^+$ in anoxia or by a low $Na_o{}^+$ in Na^+-free media, the Na^+-Ca^{2+} antiporter can be expected to operate in the reverse mode, i.e. Ca^{2+} influx vs Na^+ efflux. Two observations support this hypothesis: 1) Na^+ efflux increases when extracellular Na^+ is removed but not when both Na^+ and Ca^{2+} are removed from the extracellular medium (2); and 2) reduction of $Na_o{}^+$ from 132 to 18 mM hyperpolarizes cultured kidney cells from -51 to -65 mV (5) as would be expected from the activation of the electrogenic Na^+-Ca^{2+} antiporter operating in the reverse mode.

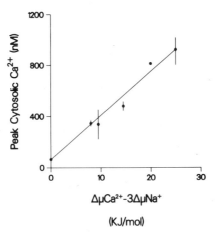

Fig. 8.   Relation between the calculated net driving force for Ca^{2+} influx on the Na^+-Ca^{2+} antiporter ($\Delta\mu Ca^{2+}$ -3 $\Delta\mu Na^+$) and the peak rise in $Ca_i{}^{2+}$ observed at various extracellular Na^+ concentrations. (Reproduced from Snowdowne and Borle with permission from J Biol Chem 260, 14998, 1985. Copyright 1985 by the American Society of Biological Chemists Inc)

Energetically, such a reversal is quite possible in kidney cells. Assuming a membrane potential E_m of -60 mV, $Na_i{}^+$ = 14 mM, Na_o^+ = 140 mM, Ca_i^{2+} 10^{-7} M, and Ca_o^{2+} = 10^{-3} M, the electrochemical potential for calcium $\Delta\mu Ca^{2+}$ is exactly three times greater than $\Delta\mu Na^+$ or 35 vs 11.5 kJ/mol, respectively. If one postulate an antiporter stoichiometry of 3 Na^+ for 1 Ca^{2+}, the driving forces for calcium influx and for sodium influx would be exactly the same. In anoxia, since Ca_i^{2+} rises to 2 x 10^{-7} M and Na_i^+ to 70 mM (4), $\Delta\mu Na^+$ decreases from 11.5 to 7.5 kJ/mol, and $\Delta\mu Ca^{2+}$ falls from 35 to 33 kJ/mol. Thus, the $\Delta\mu Ca^{2+}$ of 33 kJ/mol would be about 50% larger than the driving force for Na^+ influx (3 X 7.5 = 22.5 kJ/mol). In these conditions, calcium influx would increase and energize the uphill transport of Na^+ out of the cell. In experiments where Na_o^+ is decreased at various levels, the peak Ca_i^{2+} obtained should be proportional to the driving force for Ca^{2+} influx on the Na^+-Ca^{2+} antiporter $\Delta\mu Ca^{2+}$-$3\Delta\mu Na^+$. Our experiments show that there is an excellent correlation between the peak Ca_i^{2+} measured at various Na_o^+ (Fig. 4) and the net driving force calculated assuming a Na_i^+ of 14 mM and a membrane potential of -60 mV. (Fig. 8).

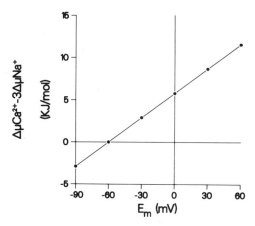

Fig. 9.   Effect of the cell membrane potential difference on the balance
           between the calcium and sodium electrochemical potentials. A
           positive number energizes calcium influx (reverse mode) and a
           negative number calcium efflux (forward mode)

        Theoretically, if one assumes that Na_i^+ = 14 mM, Ca_i^{2+} = 10^{-7}M and
E_m = -60mV, there is no net driving force for either Ca^{2+} influx or
efflux on the Na^+-Ca^{2+} antiporter since the Ca^{2+} -Na^+ electrochemical
potential balance $\Delta\mu Ca^{2+}$-$3\Delta\mu Na^+$ = 0.   In these conditions, one can
postulate that the Na^+-Ca^{2+} antiporter is inoperative or immobilized and
electrically silent.   Several perturbations may trigger its activation
either in the forward mode (when $\Delta\mu Ca^{2+}$-$3\Delta\mu Na^+$ has a negative value) or
in the reverse mode (when $\Delta\mu Ca^{2+}$-$3\Delta\mu Na^+$ has a positive value). Fig. 9
shows that a membrane depolarization below -60 mV would evoke calcium
influx on the antiporter operating in the reverse mode while a
hyperpolarization above -60 mV would cause calcium efflux on the
antiporter in the forward mode.   Fig. 10 shows that the Na^+ -Ca^{2+}
antiporter should be most sensitive to small changes in intracellular
Na^+. A small rise in Na_i^+ in the range observed with ouabain or with

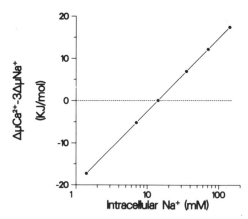

Fig. 10.   Effect of the intracellular Na^+ concentration on the balance
           between the calcium and sodium electrochemical potentials. A
           positive number energizes calcium influx (reverse mode) and a
           negative number of calcium efflux (forward mode)

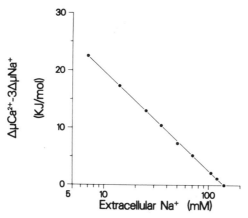

Fig. 11. Effect of extracellular Na^+ concentration on the balance
between the calcium and sodium electrochemical potentials. A
positive number energizes calcium influx (reverse mode) and a
negative number of calcium efflux (forward mode)

anoxia would trigger an immediate calcium influx, while a drop in Na_i^+
below 10 mM would allow the antiporter to operate in the forward mode as
a calcium efflux pathway. The antiporter is not very sensitive to small
changes in extracellular Na^+ (Fig. 11). Unless Na_o^+ is reduced much
below 100 mM, no significant calcium fluxes can be expected. Fig. 12
shows that fluctuations in intracellular free calcium within the
physiological range will generate smaller driving forces for calcium
influx or efflux than changes in Na_i^+. And finally physiological changes
in extracellular calcium will have practically no effect on the balance
of forces between Na^+ and Ca^{2+} (Fig. 13). Thus, in theory, the cell
membrane potential difference and intracellular Na^+ appear to have the
greatest influence on Ca_i^+ when modulated by the Na^+-Ca^{2+} antiporter.

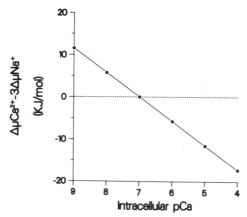

Fig. 12. Effect of intracellular free Ca^{2+} concentration on the balance
between the calcium and sodium electrochemical potentials. A
positive number energizes calcium influx (reverse mode) and a
negative number of calcium efflux (forward mode)

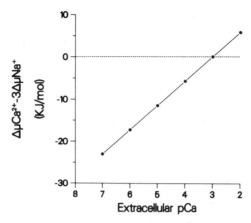

Fig. 13. Effect of the extracellular free Ca^{2+} concentration on the
balance between the calcium and sodium electrochemical
potentials. A positive number energizes calcium influx
(reverse mode) and a negative number of calcium efflux (forward
mode)

The question remains whether in physiological conditions the
antiporter operates in the forward or reverse mode. That would depend on
the relative magnitude of $\Delta\mu Na^+$ and of $\Delta\mu Ca^{2+}$ and principally on the
membrane potential E_m and on Na_i^+. Unless Na_i^+ is significantly less
than 14 mM or E_m significantly greater than -60 mV, $\Delta\mu Na^+$ is not great
enough to energize calcium efflux. If the Na^+ and Ca^{2+} potentials were
equal, Na^+-Ca^{2+} exchange would not be functioning. On the other hand, if
Na_i^+ was greater than 14 mM and E_m less than -60 mV, which is more likely
according to all the values published for kidney cells, the driving force
for Ca^{2+} influx would exceed that for Na^+ influx ($\Delta\mu Ca^{2+} > 3\Delta\mu Na^+$) and
the Na^+-Ca^{2+} antiporter would operate as a calcium influx pathway. The
reverse mode of Na^+-Ca^{2+} exchange could be the usual and physiological
mode as shown in Fig. 14. It is likely that in kidney cells the only

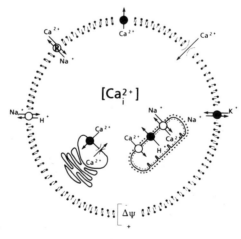

Fig. 14. Pathways of calcium transport in epithetial cells with the Na^+
-Ca^{2+} antiporter operating in the reverse mode as a calcium
influx pathway

transport mechanisms available for Ca^{2+} efflux is the $(Ca^{2+}\text{-}Mg^{2+})$-ATPase-dependent calcium pump. Only in hyperpolarized cells ($E_m > -60$ mV) or at very low Na^+ (< 10 mM) could $Na^+\text{-}Ca^{2+}$ exchange operate as a calcium efflux pathway. These considerations may bridge the differences between the proponents of $Na^+\text{-}Ca^{2+}$ exchange as an important Ca^{2+} transport system and those who challenge its importance as a Ca^{2+} efflux mechanism.

Appendix

The electrochemical potential gradient for Ca^{2+} is $\Delta\mu Ca^{2+} = zF(E_m -E_{Ca^{2+}})$ where z = ionic valence, F = Faraday constant 96,500 coulombs/eq, and E_m = membrane potential difference. $E_{Ca^{2+}}$ is the Nernst equilibrium potential (RT/zF) ln (Ca_o/Ca_i) where R = gas constant 8.3 J/mol and T = the absolute temperature, 300 ^{o}C. The electrochemical potential gradient for Na^+ is $\Delta\mu Na^+ = zF (E_m -E_{Na^+})$.

References

1. K. W. Snowdowne, C. C. Freudenrich and A. B. Borle. The effects of anoxia on cytosolic free calcium, calcium fluxes and cellular ATP levels in cultured kidney cells. J. Biol. Chem. 260, 11619-11626, 1985
2. K. W. Snowdowne and A. B. Borle. Effects of low extracellular sodium on cytosolic ionized calcium. Na^+ -Ca^{2+} exchange as a major calcium influx pathway in kidney cells. J. Biol. Chem. 260, 14998-15007, 1985
3. A. B. Borle and K. W. Snowdowne. The measurement of intracellular ionized calcium with aequorin. Method. Enzymol. 124, 90-116, 1986
4. J. Mason, F. Beck, A. Dörge, R. Rick and K. Thurau. Intracellular electrolyte composition following renal ischemia. Kidney Int. 20, 61-70, 1981
5. M. Paulmichl, F. Friedrich and F. Lang. Electrical properties of Madin-Darby-canine-kidney cells. Effects of extracellular sodium and calcium. Pflügers Arch. 407, 258-263, 1986

ROLE OF GUANINE NUCLEOTIDE REGULATORY PROTEINS AND INOSITOL PHOSPHATES IN

THE HORMONE INDUCED MOBILIZATION OF HEPATOCYTE CALCIUM

Peter F. Blackmore, Christopher J. Lynch, Ronald J. Uhing,
Thomas Fitzgerald, Stephen B. Bocckino and John H. Exton

Howard Hughes Medical Institute and
Department of Molecular Physiology and Biophysics
Vanderbilt University School of Medicine
Nashville, Tennessee   37232

INTRODUCTION

Many hormones and neurotransmitters exert their effects in the liver by increasing the concentration of free ionized Ca^{2+} in the cytoplasm.[1,2,3] Examples of such agonists are norepinephrine and epinephrine acting via α_1-adrenergic receptors, vasopressin acting on V_1 receptors, ATP and ADP acting on P_2 purinergic receptors and angiotensin II. Each agonist, after binding to its specific cell surface receptor, provokes the hydrolysis of PI 4,5-P_2 by a phospholipase C activity to give rise to DAG and Ins 1,4,5-P_3.[4,5] The DAG functions to activate protein kinase C while Ins 1,4,5-P_3 mobilizes Ca^{2+} from elements of the endoplasmic reticulum.[4,5] Recent studies have implicated the involvement of a guanine nucleotide binding protein which couples the various hormone receptors to the PI 4,5-P_2 specific phospholipase C[6]. The existence of a novel inositol phosphate ester, Ins 1,3,4,5-P_4, has also been described.[7] The purpose of this article is to present our data on these two aspects of hormone action in the liver.

GUANINE NUCLEOTIDE BINDING PROTEIN

A. HEPATOCYTE STUDIES USING AlF_4^-

There is evidence that a guanine nucleotide-binding protein is involved in the coupling of various receptors to the hydrolysis of PI 4,5-P_2 and the mobilization of Ca^{2+}. Such evidence includes showing that GTP inhibits the binding of hormones to their receptors[8] and that the introduction of GTP analogues into permeabilized cells such as mast cells will stimulate histamine release.[9] Also, calcium-mediated agonists stimulate guanine nucleotide hydrolysis or exchange in membranes[10,11].

It is also known that F^- in the presence of Al^{3+} modulates the activity of G_s, G_i and transducin, and the active ingredient is thought to be AlF_4^-.[12,13] Hepatocytes were thus treated with

AlF$_4^-$ to observe if the effects of the Ca^{2+} mobilizing hormones could be mimicked.[14,15] The data in Fig. 1 show that NaF produces a dose dependent hydrolysis of PI 4,5-P$_2$ with a concomitant increase in Ins P$_3$ and DAG the second messengers for Ca^{2+} mobilization and protein kinase C activation respectively. In these experiments cAMP levels declined, thus the mobilization of Ca^{2+} and activation of phosphorylase are not likely to be due to cAMP (Fig. 2).

The ability of NaF to produce its effects on calcium mobilization were potentiated by the addition of AlCl$_3$ (Fig. 2). Thus the observed effects of NaF on calcium mobilization are most likely due to AlF$_4^-$, the aluminum fluoride species which predominates when μM concentrations of Al^{3+} are added to mM concentrations of F$^-$.[12] The potentiating effects of Al^{3+} were blocked by the potent chelator of Al^{3+} deferoxamine (data not shown).[14]

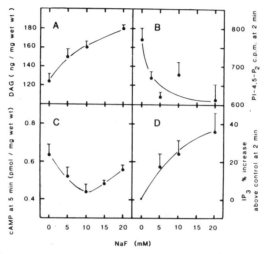

Fig. 1. Dose response of NaF to increase DAG (A), decrease PI 4,5-P$_2$ (B), alter cAMP levels (C), and increase Ins P$_3$ levels (D) in hepatocytes. After 8 min of incubation with NaF, 5 ml aliquots of cell suspensions (45 mg/ml, wet weight) were extracted with chloroform:methanol (1:2), and the DAG was measured by high pressure liquid chromatography.[14] Since changes in PI-4,5-P$_2$ were transient, the levels of [^{3}H]PI 4,5-P$_2$ and [^{3}H]Ins P$_3$ were measured at 2 min, when maximal changes were observed. Reproduced by permission of the authors and publisher.[14]

There is evidence in some systems that the agonist-stimulated Ins P$_3$ formation is mediated by G$_i$ or a G$_i$-like protein since the islet-activating protein (IAP), a <u>Bordetella pertussis</u> toxin, inhibits receptor-mediated PI 4,5-P$_2$ hydrolysis and Ca^{2+} mobilization.[16-20] In liver, however, the effect of the Ca^{2+} mobilizing agonist to increase [Ca^{2+}]$_i$ and activate phosphorylase were not modified following IAP treatment of hepatocytes (data not shown).[21] The ability of angiotensin II to inhibit glucagon mediated increases in cAMP was prevented however, thus IAP appeared to ADP ribosylate G$_i$ and inhibit its activity in rat liver.[21]

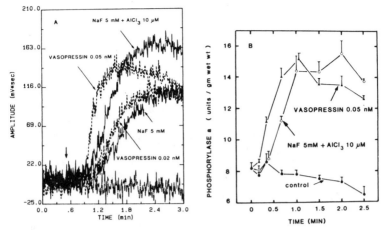

Fig. 2. Time course of NaF and vasopressin to raise $[Ca^{2+}]_i$ and activate phosphorylase. Hepatocytes were loaded with Quin 2, centrifuged once, and resuspended in low Ca^{2+}-containing media for the fluorescence measurements. The basal $[Ca^{2+}]_i$ was approximately 200 nM. This was increased to approximately 500 nM with 5 mM NaF plus 10 μM $AlCl_3$ (measured after 2.5 min). The arrow indicates the time at which the various agents were added (0.5 min). Each trace is the mean of triplicate incubations. The effects of two concentrations of vasopressin are included for comparison. In B, the effects of 0.05 nM vasopressin and 5 mM NaF plus 10 μM $AlCl_3$ on phosphorylase activation are shown for comparison with the fluorescence changes. Reproduced by permission of the authors and publisher.[14]

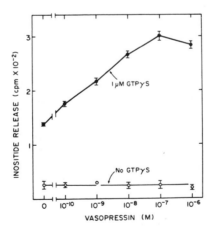

Fig. 3. Stimulation of inositide release by vasopressin. Plasma membranes were incubated in the presence of 25 mM Tris-HCl, pH 7.5, 0.5 mM EGTA, 10 mM $MgCl_2$, 300 nM free calcium, and the indicated concentrations of vasopressin. Incubations were in the absence (o) or presence (●) of 1 μM GTPγS. Reproduced by permission of the authors and publisher.[33]

171

B. HORMONE STIMULATED POLYPHOSPHOINOSITIDE BREAKDOWN IN RAT LIVER PLASMA MEMBRANES

Several studies have shown guanine nucleotide effects on PI 4,5-P_2 hydrolysis in broken cell preparations of mast cells, blowfly salivary glands, human polymorphonuclear leukocytes and liver.[22-24]

The data in Fig. 3 show the dose response of vasopressin to stimulate inositide release in the presence and absence of 1 μM GTPγS from plasma membranes <u>in vitro</u>. In the presence of GTPγS, vasopressin caused a dose-dependent increase in inositide release with a half-maximal effect being obvserved with 1 nM vasopressin. These effects were similar to those for [^{3}H]vasopressin binding to plasma membranes[25] and for stimulation of Ins P_3 formation in hepatocytes.[25] The effects of GTPγS and GTPγS plus vasopressin were dependent on the presence of Ca^{2+}. The data in Fig. 4 show that when the free Ca^{2+} was 1 nM (when 1 mM EGTA was added) there was no inositide release in the presence of GTPγS and/or vasopressin. When the Ca^{2+} concentration was 150 μM inositide release was stimulated, but GTPγS and/or vasopressin only produced modest increases. The largest effects of GTPγS and/or vasopressin were seen with Ca^{2+} concentrations of approx. 300 nM.

The GDP analog, GDPβS inhibited the stimulation of inositide release by GTPγS (Fig. 5). It was shown that GDP and GDPβS inhibited GTP stimulation of adenylate cyclase.[26,27] When plasma membranes were incubated with NAD and cholera toxin, inositide release by GTPγS or GTPγS plus vasopressin was not modified (data not shown). There were 70⁰/o fewer ADP-ribosylation sites available after pretreatment with cholera toxin as judged by a second ribosylation with cholera toxin in the presence of [^{32}P]NAD. There was also no difference in the ability of GTPγS or GTPγS plus vasopressin to stimulate inositide release from membranes isolated from rats injected with islet activating protein intraperitoneally for 24 h[21] (data not shown). These data suggest that the guanine nucleotide binding protein involved in polyphosphoinositide hydrolysis and inositide release in rat liver is not G_i or G_s.

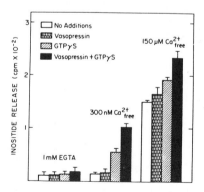

Fig. 4. Stimulation of inositide release by GTPγS and vasopressin at different concentrations of calcium. Plasma membranes were incubated in the presence of 25 mM Tris-HCl, pH 7.5, 10 mM $MgCl_2$, the indicated concentrations of free calcium, and no additions, 100 nM vasopressin, 1 μM GTPγS, or 1 μM GTPγS plus 100 nM vasopressin as indicated. Reproduced by permission of the authors and publisher.[33]

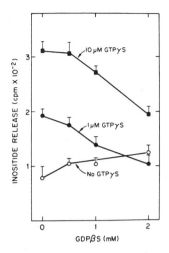

Fig. 5. Inhibition of GTPγS stimulation of inositide release by GDPβS.
Plasma membranes were incubated in the presence of 25 mM Tris–HCl, pH
7.5, 0.5 mM EGTA, 10 mM MgCl₂, 300 nM free calcium, the indicated
concentrations of GDPβS and no (o), 1 μM (●), or 10 μM (■) GTPγS.
Reproduced by permission of the authors and publisher.[33]

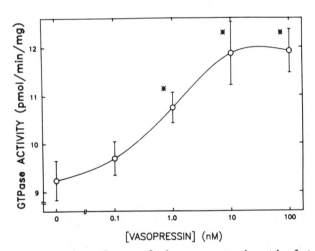

Fig. 6. Concentration dependency of the vasopressin–stimulated GTPase
activity. Plasma membranes were assayed for their GTPase activity in the
presence of the indicated concentrations of vasopressin.[28] The
incubation was at 30° for 10 min and the amount of [γ-³²P]GTP
hydrolyzed was quantitated. Reproduced by permission of the authors and
publisher.[28]

C. VASOPRESSIN STIMULATED GTPASE ACTIVITY IN RAT LIVER PLASMA MEMBRANES

The results in sections A and B suggest that the Ca²⁺ mobilizing
hormone receptors in liver are coupled to a polyphosphoinositide

phospholipase C through a GTP-binding protein distinct from G_i and G_s. The data in Fig. 6 show a dose response curve of vasopressin to stimulate GTPase activity in isolated plasma membranes.[28] The GTPase activity and was increased up to approx. 30% by 100 nM vasopressin. The vasopressin stimulated GTPase activity in plasma membranes was not modified by prior treatment with either cholera toxin or pertussis toxin (data not shown).

When plasma membranes were incubated with vasopressin and subsequently solubilized with digitonin there was an increase in GTPase activity compared to solubilized control membranes (Fig. 7). Angiotensin II also increased GTPase activity, and when membranes were incubated with both vasopressin and angiotensin II the GTPase activity was additive. These data suggest that the hormone receptors interact with GTP-binding protein(s) following solubilization with digitonin. When rat liver membranes were preincubated with [3H]vasopressin, solubilized with digitonin and the solubilized proteins sedimented through a sucrose gradient, a single peak of protein-bound [3H]vasopressin was observed (Fig. 8A). A peak of GTPase activity co-sedimented with the peak of protein bound [3H]vasopressin, with two minor peaks of GTPase activity sedimenting at a slower rate. When membranes were prelabeled with [α-32P]GDP and [3H]vasopressin, a peak of protein-bound [α-32P]GDP co-sedimented with the protein bound [3H]vasopressin (Fig. 8B). Most of the protein bound [α-32P]GDP had a slower sedimentation rate than the protein bound [3H]vasopressin (Fig. 8B). These data show that the GTPase activity which co-sediments with the protein bound [3H]vasopressin does not constitute the majority of guanine nucleotide binding activity. The addition of GTPγS (10 μM) to solubilized membranes labeled with [3H]vasopressin, prior to sucrose gradient sedimentation resulted in an approx. 90% decrease in the peak of [3H]vasopressin

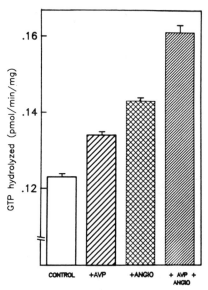

Fig. 7. Hormone-dependent stimulation of the GTPase activity in digitonin solubilized membranes. Plasma membranes were preincubated at 30° for 20 min with Hepes buffer (50 mM, pH 7.5), EGTA (1 mM), $Mg(CH_3CO_2)_2$ (10 mM), leupeptin (100 μg/ml), antipain (100 μg/ml) and in the presence or absence of the indicated hormone (0.1 μM). The membranes were collected by centrifugation and solubilized in 1% digitonin. The solubilized membranes were centrifuged at 100,000 x g for 1 h and then the GTPase activity of the supernatant was determined. Reproduced by permission of the authors and publisher.[28]

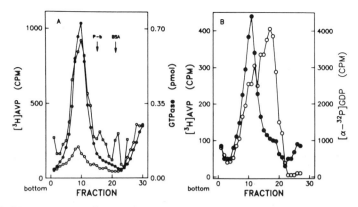

Fig. 8. Sedimentation of vasopressin-receptor through a sucrose density gradient. Plasma membranes were labeled with [³H]vasopressin (panel A) or [α-³²P]GDP and [³H]vasopressin (panel B). The plasma membranes were washed, solubilized and sedimented on sucrose gradients.[28] The gradients were fractionated and assayed for protein bound radioligands. Panel A, protein bound [³H]vasopressin (o,●) from gradients run in the presence (o), or absence (●), of GTPγS (10 μM). The fractions from the gradient run in the absence of GTPγS were assayed for GTPase activity ( ). Panel B, protein bound [³H]vasopressin (●) and protein bound [α-³²P]GDP (o). Reproduced by permission of the authors and publisher.[28]

(Fig. 8A). These data suggest that the protein bound [³H]vasopressin can be regulated by guanine nucleotides.

Using immuno detection in Western blots, 35 kDa β and 40 kDa α subunits of a GTP-binding protein(s) were found in the [³H]vasopressin peak in Fig. 8A (data not shown). The antisera used were prepared from peptides synthesized according to sequence information of the β subunit and the common amino acid sequence found in all α subunits. These results support the conclusion that liver plasma membranes contain a GTP-binding protein that can complex with the vasopressin receptor, and that this protein consists of a 35 kDa β subunit and a 40 kDa α subunit distinct from α_i, α_o and α_s.

AGONIST-INDUCED FORMATION OF INS 1,4,5-P₃, INS 1,3,4-P₃ and INS 1,3,4,5-P₄

Both [³H]Ins 1,3,4-P₃ and [³H]Ins 1,4,5-P₃ were identified in [³H]Ins-labeled hepatocytes by HPLC (Fig. 9).[7,29] The peak of radioactivity coeluting exactly with ATP between fractions 45 and 50 was presumed to be [³H]Ins 1,3,4-P₃. The peak of radioactivity appearing in fractions 50 to 56 coelutes with authentic [2-³H]Ins 1,4,5-P₃ (New England Nuclear). When commercial Ins P₅ (Calbiochem) was chromatographed on the HPLC system, the majority (measured by total phosphate) eluted between fractions 110 and 120, while a small amount of contaminating material eluted in fractions 80 to 85 and had a phosphate to inositol ratio of 4. The small peak of radioactivity eluting in fractions 80 to 85 was identified as [³H]Ins P₄ since it migrated with authentic [³H]Ins 1,3,4,5-P₄ (Amersham).

The data in Fig. 10 show that 10^{-7} M vasopressin increased Ins 1,4,5-P₃ 5-fold at 10 s, whereas the level of Ins 1,3,4-P₃ increased more slowly to reach a value 4-fold above the control at 1 min. Thus the

175

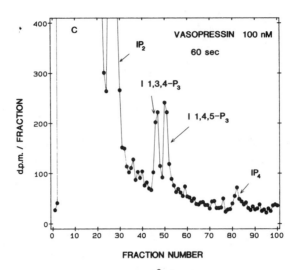

Fig. 9. HPLC analysis of hepatocyte [³H]Ins phosphates formed after 100 nM vasopressin stimulation. Hepatocytes labeled with [³H]Ins were incubated for 60 s with 100 nM vasopressin. One ml aliquots of incubated cells (approx. 40 mg/ml wet wt) were deproteinized and extracted with diethylether and then chromatographed by HPLC.[7,29]

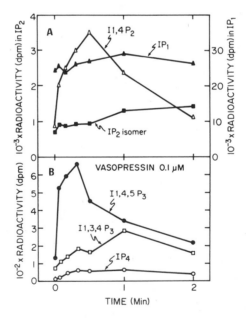

Fig. 10. Time course of 100 nM vasopressin on hepatocyte Ins P_2, Ins P_1, Ins 1,4,5-P_3, Ins 1,3,4-P_3 and Ins P_4. Eight ml of hepatocytes, labeled with [³H]Ins were incubated in 125 ml polypropylene Erlenmeyer flasks. At the indicated times 1 ml aliquots were removed into 0.2 ml of 100⁰/o TCA. Following removal of TCA, the samples were chromatographed by HPLC.

rate of increase in $[Ca^{2+}]_i$ induced by 10^{-7} M vasopressin[30] closely resembles the increase in Ins 1,4,5-P_3 and not Ins 1,3,4-P_3. The [^{3}H]compound identified as Ins P_4 also increased at early times.

Examination of the column profile in the bisphosphate region of the chromatogram revealed the presence of two peaks of radioactivity. One is designated Ins 1,4-P_2 since it coelutes with authentic [^{3}H]Ins 1,4-P_2 (Amersham). It possibly arose from the dephosphorylation of Ins 1,4,5-P_3 since it increased very rapidly, like Ins 1,4,5-P_3. The other peak of radioactivity which increased slowly may have been formed from the dephosphorylation of Ins 1,3,4-P_3 which also increased slowly.

When angiotensin II (10^{-7} M) was used as an agonist, Ins 1,4,5-P_3 increased rapidly and declined rapidly, whereas Ins 1,3,4-P_3 increased more slowly but remained elevated (data not shown). The level of Ins P_4 increased as rapidly as Ins 1,4,5-P_3 and remained elevated. Epinephrine (10^{-5} M) was the least effective of the agonists tested at increasing Ins 1,4,5-P_3 since it only increased this isomer approx. 2-fold at 20 s (data not shown). Ins 1,3,4-P_3 increased more slowly than Ins 1,4,5-P_3, whereas Ins P_4 increased very rapidly (data not shown). Ca^{2+}-mobilizing agents such as ATP and AlF_4^-,[14] and EGF[31,32] also increased the levels of all inositol phosphate esters (data not shown). PMA and insulin were inert.

The data in Fig. 11 show that vasopressin had only minimal effects on Ins P_1, whereas Ins P_2 (both bisphosphate isomers were added together in this experiment) only increased with 10^{-8} and 10^{-7} M vasopressin at 10 s. Small, but reproducible, increases in Ins 1,4,5-P_3 and Ins P_4 were seen with 10^{-10} M vasopressin at this time, with larger effects being observed with 10^{-9} M vasopressin and higher (Fig. 11). Vasopressin (10^{-7} M) increased Ins 1,4,5-P_3 8-fold whereas it elevated Ins 1,3,4-P_3 only approx. 2-fold. The half-maximally effective concentration of vasopressin to increase Ins 1,4,5-P_3 was 2 x 10^{-8} M.

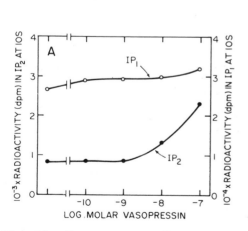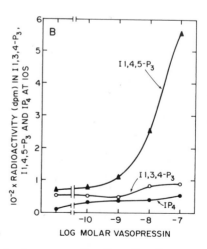

Fig. 11. Dose response of vasopressin to increase Ins P_1, Ins P_2 (panel A), Ins 1,4,5-P_3, Ins 1,3,4-P_3 and Ins P_4 (panel B) measured after 10 s. The equivalent of 1.0 ml of cell suspension was analyzed by HPLC for each hormone concentration used.

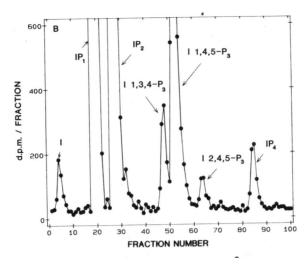

Fig. 12. HPLC analysis of the metabolism of $[2-^3H]$Ins 1,4,5-P$_3$ by digitonin permeabilized hepatocytes in the presence of ATP after 60 s of incubation.

To observe if Ins 1,4,5-P$_3$ could be converted to Ins 1,3,4-P$_3$ by liver enzymes in vitro, $[2-^3H]$Ins 1,4,5-P$_3$ was incubated with permeabilized hepatocytes in the presence or absence of ATP. When ATP was omitted from the incubations, $[2-^3H]$Ins 1,4,5-P$_3$ was rapidly dephosphorylated to $[^3H]$Ins P$_2$, $[^3H]$Ins P$_1$ and free $[^3H]$Ins. In the presence of ATP, however, $[^3H]$Ins 1,3,4-P$_3$ was formed, together with $[^3H]$Ins P$_4$ (Fig. 12) since it coeluted with the peak of radioactivity observed in hepatocytes labeled with $[2-^3H]$Ins and incubated with vasopressin (Fig. 9). The ATP-dependent formation of Ins 1,3,4-P$_3$ from Ins 1,4,5-P$_3$ (Figs. 12) would be consistent with phosphorylation of Ins 1,4,5-P$_3$ to Ins 1,3,4,5-P$_4$ then removal of the phosphate on position 5 by a phosphatase to form Ins 1,3,4-P$_3$.

SUMMARY

Treatment of isolated hepatocytes with F$^-$ produced a concentration-dependent activation of phosphorylase, efflux of Ca^{2+}, rise in [Ca^{2+}]$_i$, increase in Ins 1,4,5-P$_3$ levels, decrease in PI-4,5-P$_2$ levels, and increase in DAG levels.[14,15] The levels of intracellular cAMP were decreased by NaF.[14] The effects of NaF were potentiated by AlCl$_3$. This potentiation was abolished by the Al^{3+} chelator deferoxamine. These results illustrate that AlF$_4^-$ can mimic the effects of Ca^{2+}-mobilizing hormones in hepatocytes and suggest that the coupling of the receptors for these hormones to the hydrolysis of PI-4,5-P$_2$ is through a guanine nucleotide-binding regulatory protein.[14] This is because AlF$_4^-$ is known to modulate the activity of other guanine nucleotide regulatory proteins (G$_i$, G$_s$, and transducin).

Calcium-sensitive inositide release in a purified rat liver plasma membrane preparation was increased by calcium-mobilizing hormones in the presence of guanine nucleotides.[33] Vasopressin-stimulated inositide release was evident in the presence of GTP or GTPγS. The guanine nucleotide and hormonal stimulation was evident on both inositide production and PI 4,5-P$_2$ degradation. Treatment of plasma membranes with cholera toxin or islet activating protein or prior injection of animals with islet activating protein did not affect stimulation of inositide release by GTPγS or GTPγS plus vasopressin. The results suggest that calcium-mobilizing hormones stimulate polyphosphoinositide breakdown in rat liver plasma membranes through a novel guanine nucleotide binding protein.[33]

The GTPase activity of rat liver plasma membranes was stimulated 20% by 10^{-8} M vasopressin.[28] The vasopressin-stimulated GTPase activity was not inhibited in plasma membranes that had been ADP-ribosylated with either cholera toxin or pertussis toxin. When membranes that had been solubilized after preincubation with [^{3}H]vasopressin were subjected to sucrose gradient centrifugation, most of the protein-bound [^{3}H]vasopressin migrated as a single band, also, there was a GTPase activity that migrated with the bound [^{3}H]vasopressin. This peak of bound [^{3}H]vasopressin was decreased 90% when the sucrose gradient centrifugation was run in the presence of 10 M GTPγS. Direct evidence that a GTP-binding protein was present in the [^{3}H]vasopressin peak was obtained by the immuno-detection of a 35 kDa β subunit of a GTP-binding protein and a 40 kDa α subunit. These results support the conclusion that liver plasma membranes contain a GTP-binding protein that can complex with the vasopressin receptor.

Treatment of hepatocytes with vasopressin (10^{-7} M), produced a rapid and large (5-fold) increase in Ins 1,4,5-P_3 at 10 s. The level peaked at 20 s then slowly declined to approx. 2-fold basal at 2 min. Another inositol polyphosphate which was identified as Ins P_4 also increased rapidly. In contrast, the level of Ins 1,3,4-P_3 increased slowly to approx. 4-fold at 1 min and then declined. The increases in Ins 1,4,5-P_3 and Ins P_4 correlated temporally with the increase in $[Ca^{2+}]_i$. The dose response curves for vasopressin effects on Ins 1,4,5-P_3, Ins 1,3,4-P_3 and Ins P_4 were not similar at 10 s. Other Ca^{2+}-mobilizing agonists (ATP, EGF, angiotensin II, epinephrine and AlF$_4^-$) also increased Ins 1,4,5-P_3, Ins 1,3,4-P_3 and Ins P_4 to varying degrees. Incubation of digitonin-permeabilized hepatocytes with [2-^{3}H]Ins 1,4,5-P_3 in the presence of MgATP resulted in the formation of [^{3}H]Ins P_4 and [^{3}H]Ins 1,3,4-P_3. Phosphorylation of Ins 1,4,5-P_3 to Ins 1,3,4,5-P_4 by Ins 1,4,5-P_3 3-kinase followed by its dephosphorylation by a 5-phosphatase to form Ins 1,3,4-P_3 would account for the formation of these isomers in hepatocytes after hormonal stimulation.[34] The metabolic significance of these new compounds is not known but it is possible that they may play second message roles.

ABBREVIATIONS

Ins or I, myoinositol; PI 4,5-P_2, phosphatidylinositol 4,5-bisphosphate; EGTA, ethylene bis (oxyethylene nitrilo) tetraacetic acid; EGF, epidermal growth factor; PMA, 4 β phorbol 12 β-myristate 13 α-acetate; Hepes, 4-(2-hydroxyethyl)-1-piperazine ethane sulfonic acid; DAG, 1,2-diacylglycerol; Tris, tris (hydroxymethyl) aminomethane; $[Ca^{2+}]_i$, concentration of free Ca^{2+} in the cytoplasm; GTPγS, guanosine 5'-(3-0-thio)triphosphate; GDPβS, guanosine 5'-(2-0-thio)diphosphate; G_s, the stimulatory guanine nucleotide binding protein of adenylate cyclase; G_i, the inhibitory guanine nucleotide binding protein of adenylate cyclase.

REFERENCES

1. Williamson, J.R., Cooper, R.H., Joseph, S.K., and Thomas, A.P. Inositol triphosphate and diacylglycerol as intracellular second messengers in liver. Am. J. Physiol. 248:C203-C216 (1985).

2. Exton, J.H. Role of calcium and phosphoinositides in the actions of certain hormones and neurotransmitters. J. Clin. Invest. 73:1753-1757, 1985.

3. Blackmore, P.F. Effects of α-adrenergic agents on hepatic Ca^{2+} distribution. CRC Critical Rev. Biochem. (N. Kraus-Friedmann, ed.), Chemical Rubber Co., pp. 183-193, 1986.

4. Berridge, M.J. Inositol trisphosphate and diacylglycerol as second messengers. Biochem. J. 220:345-360 (1984).

5. Berridge, M.J. and Irvine, R.F. Inositol trisphosphate, a novel second messenger in cellular signal transduction. Nature 312:315-321 (1984).

6. Gomperts, B.D. Calcium shares the limelight in stimulus-secretion coupling. TIBS 11:290-292 (1986).

7. Batty, I.R., Nahorski, S.R., and Irvine, R.F. Rapid formation of inositol 1,3,4,5-tetrakisphosphate following muscarinic receptor stimulation of rat cerebral cortical slices. Biochem. J. 232:211-215 (1985).

8. Lynch, C.J., Charest, R., Blackmore, P.F., and Exton, J.H. Studies on the hepatic α_1-adrenergic receptor: modulation of guanine nucleotide effects by calcium, temperature, and age. J. Biol. Chem. 260:15393-1600 (1985).

9. Gomperts, B.D. Involvement of guanine nucleotide-binding protein in the gating of Ca^{2+} by receptors. Nature 306:64-66 (1983).

10. Hinkle, P.M. and Phillips, W.J. Thyrotropin-releasing hormone stimulates GTP hydrolysis by membranes from GH_4C_1 rat pituitary tumor cells. Proc. Natl. Acad. Sci. U.S.A. 81:6183-6187 (1984).

11. Lad, P.M., Olson, C.V., and Smiley, P.A. Association of the N-formyl-Met-Leu-Phe receptor in human neutrophils with a GTP-binding protein sensitive to pertussis toxin. Proc. Natl. Acad. Sci. U.S.A. 82:869-873 (1985).

12. Sternweis, P.C. and Gilman, A.G. Aluminum: a requirement for activation of the regulatory component of adenylate cyclase by fluoride. Proc. Natl. Acad. Sci. U.S.A. 79:4888-4891 (1982).

13. Kanaho, Y., Moss, J., and Vaughan, M. Mechanism of inhibition of transducin GTPase activity by fluoride and aluminum. J. Biol. Chem. 260:11493-11497 (1985).

14. Blackmore, P.F., Bocckino, S.B., Waynick, L.E. and Exton, J.H. Role of a guanine nucleotide-binding regulatory protein in the hydrolysis of hepatocyte phosphatidylinositol 4,5-bisphosphate by calcium-mobilizing hormones and the control of cell calcium: studies utilizing aluminum fluoride. J. Biol. Chem. 260:14477-14483 (1985).

15. Blackmore, P.F. and Exton, J.H. Studies on the hepatic calcium-mobilizing activity of aluminum fluoride and glucagon: modulation by cAMP and phorbol myristate acetate. J. Biol. Chem. 261:11056-11063 (1986).

16. Smith, C.D., Lane, B.C., Kusaka, I., Verghese, M.W., and Snyderman, R. Chemoattractant receptor-induced hydrolysis of phosphatidylinositol 4,5-bisphosphate in human polymorphonuclear leukocyte membranes: requirement for a guanine nucleotide regulatory protein. J. Biol. Chem. 260:5875-5878 (1985).

17. Nakamura, T., and Ui, M. Simultaneous inhibitions of inositol phospholipid breakdown, arachidonic acid release, and histamine secretion in mast cells by islet-activating protein, pertussis toxin: a possible involvement of the toxin-specific substrate in the Ca^{2+}-mobilizing receptor-mediated biosignaling system. J. Biol. Chem. 260:3584-3593 (1985).

18. Bokoch, G.M., and Gilman, A.G. Inhibition of receptor-mediated release of arachidonic acid by pertussis toxin. Cell 39, 301-308 (1984).

19. Molski, T.F.P., Naccache, P.H., Marsh, M.L., Kermode, J., Becker, E.L., and Sha'afi, R.I. Pertussis toxin inhibits the rise in the intracellular concentration of free calcium that is induced by chemotactic factors in rabbit neutrophils: possible role of the "G proteins" in calcium mobilization. Biochem. Biophys. Res. Commun. 124:644-650 (1984).

20. Volpi, M., Naccache, P.H., Molski, T.F.P., Shefcyk, J., Huang, C.-K., Marsh, M.L., Munoz, J., Becker, E.L., and Sha'afi, R.I. Pertussis toxin inhibits fMet-Leu-Phe- but not phorbol ester-stimulated changes in rabbit neutrophils: role of G proteins in excitation response coupling. Proc. Natl. Acad. Sci. U.S.A. 82:2708-2712 (1985).

21. Lynch, C.J., Prpic, V., Blackmore, P.F., and Exton, J.H. Effect of islet-activating pertussis toxin on the binding characteristics of Ca^{2+}-mobilizing hormones and on agonist activation of phosphorylase in hepatocytes. Mol. Pharmacol. 29:196-203, 1986.

22. Cockcroft, S. and Gomperts, B.D. Role of guanine nucleotide binding protein in the activation of polyphosphoinositide phosphodiesterase. Nature 314:534-536 (1985).

23. Litosch, I., Wallis, C., and Fain, J.N. 5-Hydroxytryptamine stimulates inositol phosphate production in a cell-free system from blowfly salivary glands: evidence for a role of GTP in coupling receptor activation to phosphoinositide breakdown. J. Biol. Chem. 260:5464-5471 (1985).

24. Uhing, R.J., Jiang, H., Prpic, V. and Exton, J.H. Regulation of a liver plasma memmbrane phosphoinositide phosphodiesterase by guanine nucleotides and calcium. FEBS Lett. 188:317-320, 1985.

25. Lynch, C.J., Blackmore, P.F., Charest, R., and Exton, J.H. The relationships between receptor binding capacity for norepinephrine, angiotensin II, and vasopressin and release of inositol trisphosphate, Ca^{2+} mobilization, and phosphorylase activation in rat liver. Mol. Pharmacol. 28:93-99 (1985).

26. Salomon, Y., Lin, M.C., Londos, C., Rendell, M., and Rodbell, M. The hepatic adenylate cyclase system: evidence for transition states and structural requirements for guanine nucleotide activation. J. Biol. Chem. 250:4239-4245 (1975).

27. Eckstein, F., Cassel, D., Levkovits, H., Lowe, M., and Selinger, Z. Guanosine 5'-O-(2-thiodiphosphate): an inhibitor of adenylate cyclase stimulation by guanine nucleotides and fluoride ions. J. Biol. Chem. 254:9829-9834 (1979).

28. Fitzgerald, T.J., Uhing, R.J., and Exton, J.H. Solubilization of the vasopressin receptor from rat liver plasma membranes: evidence for a receptor-GTP-binding protein complex. J. Biol. Chem. 261:(in press)(1986).

29. Blackmore, P.F., Bocckino, S., Jiang, H., and Exton, J.H. Agonist induced formation of myoinositol 1,4,5-P$_3$, myoinositol 1,3,4-P$_3$ and myoinositol-P$_4$ in rat liver parenchymal cells. Fed. Proc. 45:1688 (1986).

30. Charest, R., Prpic, V., Exton, J.H., and Blackmore, P.F. Stimulation of inositol trisphosphate formation in hepatocytes by vasopressin, adrenaline and angiotensin II and its relationship to changes in cytosolic free Ca^{2+}. Biochem. J. 227:79-90 (1985).

31. Johnson, R.M., Connelly, P.A., Sisk, R.B., Pobiner, B.F., Hewlett, E.L., and Garrison, J.C. Pertussis toxin or phorbol 12-myristate 13-acetate can distinguish between epidermal growth factor- and angiotensin-stimulated signals in hepatocytes. Proc. Natl. Acad. Sci. U.S.A. 83:2032-2036 (1986).

32. Bosch, F., Bouscarel, B., Slaton, J., Blackmore, P.F., and Exton, J.H. Epidermal growth factor mimics insulin effects in rat hepatocytes. Biochem. J. 239:523-530 (1986).

33. Uhing, R.J., Prpic, V., Jiang, H., and Exton, J.H. Hormone-stimulated polyphosphoinositide breakdown in rat liver plasma membranes: roles of guanine nucleotides and calcium. <u>J. Biol. Chem.</u> 261:2140-2146 (1986).

34. Irvine, R.F., Letcher, A.J., Heslop, J.P., and Berridge, M.J. The inositol tris/tetrakisphosphate pathway -- demonstration of Ins(1,4,5)P$_3$ 3-kinase activity in animal tissues. <u>Nature</u> 320:631-634 (1986).

FORMATION AND METABOLISM OF INOSITOL PHOSPHATES: THE INOSITOL

TRIS/TETRAKISPHOSPHATE PATHWAY

John R. Williamson, Carl A. Hansen,
Roy A. Johanson, Kathleen E. Coll and
Michael Williamson

Department of Biochemistry and Biophysics
University of Pennsylvania
Philadelphia, Pennsylvania 19104

INTRODUCTION

Many cell functions are modulated by receptor-activated mechanisms that act by increasing the free Ca^{2+} concentration in the cytosol (Williamson et al, 1981; Rasmussen and Barrett, 1984). Calcium mediates its effects by causing activity changes of a variety of proteins, including protein kinases, either directly or after binding to calmodulin or other Ca^{2+}-binding proteins (Cohen, 1985). A large number of studies have now established that a wide range of compounds, including hormones, secretagogues, neurotransmitters, chemoattractants and other cell activating subtances that involve Ca^{2+} mobilization, cause an activation of a phosphodiesterase (phospholipase C), which breaks down inositol lipids in the plasma membrane (Berridge and Irvine, 1984; Williamson et al., 1985; Hokin, 1985; Downes and Michell, 1985). However, unlike receptor-mediated activation of adenylate cyclase, which produces cAMP as the only second messenger, receptor-mediated inositol lipid breakdown serves a dual-signalling role with production of two second messengers having different functions. One of these compounds, myoinositol 1,4,5-trisphosphate ($Ins(1,4,5)P_3$), is responsible for eliciting intracellular Ca^{2+} mobilization (Berridge and Irvine, 1984; Williamson, 1986), while the second compound, 1,2-diacylglycerol (DAG), has as its primary signalling role the activation of protein kinase C (Nishizuka, 1986). Hence in principle, agents that interact with inositol lipid metabolism not only cause Ca^{2+} release with phosphorylation of proteins by Ca^{2+}-dependent protein kinases but also phosphorylation of a different set of proteins by activation of protein kinase C. However, most of these latter proteins have not been functionally characterized, and presently it is not clear whether receptor-mediated activation of protein kinase C via DAG production has as its physiological mode of action on cell function a synergistic role with Ca^{2+} or a negative feedback modulatory role (Williamson and Hansen, 1987). Probably both effects occur, depending on the cell type and the extent to which protein kinase C becomes activated (Nishizuka, 1986).

In addition to uncertainties concerning the role of protein kinase C in cell function, a number of novel inositol phosphate products and isomers have been identified in hormonally stimulated cells (Michell, 1986). In particular, Ins(1,4,5)P$_3$ can undergo further phosphorylation in the 3-position of the inositol ring to *myo*inositol(1,3,4,5) tetrakisphosphate (Ins(1,3,4,5)P$_4$). The identification of this intermediate in hormonally stimulated cells is of interest not only because it may have a unique second messenger role, but also because regulation of the inositol phosphate specific 3-kinase could be an important mechanism for controlling the concentration of Ins(1,4,5)P$_3$ and hence its role in Ca^{2+} signalling. In this paper we summarize recent findings concerning the formation and metabolism of novel inositol phosphates and the possible factors that may regulate the inositol tris/tetrakisphosphate pathway.

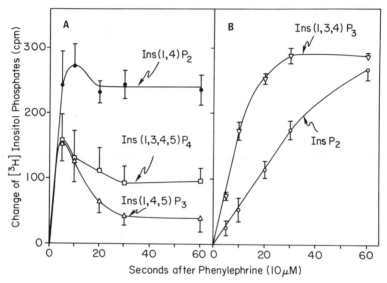

Fig. 1. Time course of the effects of phenylephrine (10 μM) on the accumulation of [^{3}H]inositol phosphates in rat hepatocytes. The experimental conditions for preparation of hepatocytes, incubation with [2-^{3}H]*myo*inositol, separation and analysis of the inositol phosphates were the same as described by Hansen et al. (1986). Control values were: Ins(1,4,5)P$_3$, 288 ± 26 cpm; Ins(1,3,4,5)P$_4$, 54 ± 8 cpm; Ins(1,4)P$_2$, 605 ± 5 cpm; Ins(1,3,4)P$_3$, 50 ± 3 cpm; InsP$_2$, 194 ± 6 cpm.

FORMATION OF INOSITOL POLYPHOSPHATES IN CELLS AND CELL EXTRACTS

Fig. 1 shows the kinetics of accumulation of different inositol phosphate isomers in isolated hepatocytes stimulated with the α_1-adrenergic agent phenylephrine. The hepatocytes were prelabeled with [^{3}H] inositol and the [^{3}H] inositol phosphates were extracted, separated and analysed by HPLC using a Whatman Partisil SAX column, as described by Hansen *et al.* (1986). Rapid and apparently simultaneous increases of Ins(1,4)P$_2$, Ins(1,4,5)P$_3$ and Ins(1,3,4,5)P$_4$ were observed (Fig. 1A), followed by slower accumulations of Ins(1,3,4)P$_3$ and an InsP$_2$ isomer that was distinct from Ins(1,4)P$_2$ (Fig. 1B). The accumulation of Ins(1,4,5)P$_3$ was characteristically biphasic, reaching a peak value 50% above the control level within 5 s, the earliest sampling time, before falling to a steady state level after 30 s which remained slightly above resting values. In contrast, Ins(1,4)P$_2$, the hydrolysis product of Ins(1,4,5)P$_3$ breakdown remained elevated close to its early peak value, while

184

Ins(1,3,4,5)P$_4$ levels followed a similar pattern to the changes of
Ins(1,4,5)P$_3$. From these changes alone, however, it is not possible to
deduce whether the major pathway for Ins(1,4,5)P$_3$ metabolism is via
hydrolysis to Ins(1,4)P$_2$ or phosphorylation to Ins(1,3,4,5)P$_4$.
Nevertheless, the relatively large and progressive accumulations of
Ins(1,3,4)P$_3$ and particularly of its InP$_2$ hydrolysis product (see later)
suggest that flux through the Ins(1,4,5)P$_3$ kinase may be appreciable. As
will be discussed later, regulation of the activity of this kinase may
account for the pronounced biphasic nature of Ins(1,4,5)P$_3$ accumulation.

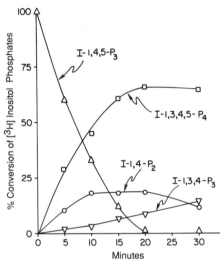

Fig. 2.   Phosphorylation of Ins(1,4,5)P$_3$ to Ins(1,3,4,5)P$_4$ by InsP$_3$
kinase.   The reaction medium (0.7 ml) contained 50 mM Tris, pH 8.0, 5 mM
ATP, 5 mM Mg^{2+}, 5 mM sodium pyrophosphate, 1 mM dithiothreitol, 50 μM
[^{3}H]Ins(1,4,5)P$_3$ (1000 cpm/nmol), and 2 mg of protein/ml of partially
purified InsP$_3$ kinase from liver.   Aliquots (0.1 ml) were removed at the
times shown, deproteinized with perchloric acid, and assayed by HPLC.

Measurements of the kinetics of accumulation of the individual
inositol phosphate isomers in cells after agonist stimulation illustrated
in Fig. 1 is typical of a number of recent studies with a variety of
agonists and cell types, and has provided a more realistic picture of
Ins(1,4,5)P$_3$ changes than obtained in previous studies where the InsP$_3$
measurements contained mixed Ins(1,4,5)P$_3$ and Ins(1,3,4)P$_3$ isomers (Thomas
et al., 1984; Charest et al., 1985).   Irvine et al. (1984) first showed
that the inositol trisphosphate pool produced by carbachol stimulation of
rat parotid glands for 15 min was heterogeneous and contained a large
proportion of Ins(1,3,4)P$_3$ in addition to Ins(1,4,5)P$_3$.   Further studies
with the rat parotid glands (Irvine et al., 1985) and with angiotensin II-
stimulated guinea pig hepatocytes and human HL-60 leukemia cells (Burgess
et al., 1985) showed that this second InsP$_3$ isomer accumulated after a
short delay, whereas the formation of Ins(1,4,5)P$_3$ was immediate.   The
predominance of the Ins(1,4,5)P$_3$ isomer at early times after hormonal
stimulation (see Fig. 1) accounts for the fact that in a number of studies
a good correlation between total InsP$_3$ production and the amount of Ca^{2+}
released from intracellular stores was seen under a variety of conditions
(Streb et al., 1985; Thomas et al., 1984; Vicentini et al., 1986).   On the
other hand, a poor correlation was observed between peak InsP$_3$
accumulation measured after 5 min and the maximum increase of cytosolic
free Ca^{2+} occurring after 10-30 s (Thomas et al., 1984; Charest et al.,
1985), due partly to an increased proportion of the Ins(1,3,4)P$_3$ isomer in
the total InsP$_3$ pool.

The recognition of a second InsP$_3$ isomer and its tentative identification as Ins(1,3,4)P$_3$ (Irvine et al., 1984; 1985), posed an intriguing question concerning its origin, since the phosphatidylinositol bisphosphate pool appeared not to be heterogeneous. This problem was solved by the detection of a more polar inositol polyphosphate in extracts from carbachol-stimulated brain slices eluting at 1.5 M ammonium formate/phosphoric acid, pH 3.7 on HPLC chromatographs, and which after isolation was degraded to Ins(1,3,4)P$_3$ by erythrocyte membrane inositol phosphate 5-phosphatase, suggesting that its structure was Ins(1,3,4,5)P$_4$ (Batty et al, 1985). The origin of Ins(1,3,4,5)P$_4$ was subsequently ascertained by the demonstration of a soluble ATP-dependent kinase in mammalian tissues that converted Ins(1,4,5)P$_3$ to Ins(1,3,4,5)P$_4$ (Irvine et al., 1986a; Hansen et al., 1986). Fig. 2 illustrates the conversion of Ins(1,4,5)P$_3$ to Ins(1,3,4,5)P$_4$ using a crude kinase preparation from a rat liver high speed supernatant. Approximately 70% of the added 50 μM [^{3}H] Ins(1,4,5)P$_3$ was converted to Ins(1,3,4,5)P$_4$ in the presence of MgATP^{2-}, while small amounts of Ins(1,4)P$_2$ and Ins(1,3,4)P$_3$ also accumulated due to the presence of inositol phosphate 5-phosphatase activity. Using a purified Ins(1,4,5)P$_3$ kinase from rat brain cortex, the more polar inositol polyphosphate product produced from Ins(1,4,5)P$_3$ has been isolated and unequivocally identified as Ins(1,3,4,5)P$_4$ by ^{1}H and ^{31}P nuclear magnetic resonance (NMR) spectroscopic analysis (Cerdan et al., 1986). Similarly, the product of hydrolysis of Ins(1,3,4,5)P$_4$ by purified rat brain 5-phosphatase has been isolated and characterized by NMR techniques as Ins(1,3,4)P$_3$ (Hansen et al., 1987).

A rapid formation of Ins(1,3,4,5)P$_4$, which is kinetically, but not necessarily quantitatively similar to the accumulation of Ins(1,4,5)P$_3$ and which is accompanied by a slower rate of formation of Ins(1,3,4)P$_3$, has also been observed in pancreatic islets stimulated with glucose (Turk et al., 1986), in rat parotid slices (Hawkins et al., 1986) and insulin secreting RIN m5F cells (Biden and Wollheim, 1986) after muscarinic receptor stimulation, in bradykinin-stimulated human A431 epidermoid carcinoma cells (Tilly et al., 1987) and in angiotensin II-stimulated rat adrenal glomerulosa cells (Balla et al., 1986). In other studies, the kinetics of formation of Ins(1,3,4)P$_3$ in hormonally stimulated RIN m5F cells (Wollheim and Biden, 1986), rat pituitary tumor GH$_3$ cells (Dean and Moyer, 1986), and rat pancreatic acinar cells (Merritt et al., 1986) was shown to be slow relative to that of Ins(1,4,5)P$_3$.

PATHWAYS OF INOSITOL PHOSPHATE METABOLISM

A schematic diagram of the intermediates and enzyme steps involved in the formation and metabolism of inositol phosphates in mammalian cells is shown in Fig. 3. The lipid precursors for the inositol polyphosphates are phosphatidylinositol 4-phosphate (PIP) and phosphatidylinositol 4,5-bisphosphate (PIP$_2$), which together represent less than 5% of a heterogeneously located total inositol lipid pool. Phospholipase C is responsible for cleavage of the inositol lipids to 1,2-diacylglycerol, where the fatty acid side chains R$_1$ and R$_2$ are predominantly stearic acid and arachidonic acid, respectively, and to the water soluble inositol phosphates Ins(1,4)P$_2$ and Ins(1,4,5)P$_3$. The activity of phospholipase C is controlled by agonist binding to specific receptors in the plasma membrane through the mediation of a GTP-binding protein, which although not yet isolated or characterized appears to be a novel member of the G-protein family (Gilman, 1984; Litosch and Fain, 1986; Williamson and Hansen, 1987). Ins(1,4,5)P$_3$ is uniquely formed from the breakdown of PIP$_2$, whereas Ins(1,4)P$_2$ is produced both by phospholipase C action on PIP and by 5-phosphomonoesterase activity on Ins(1,4,5)P$_3$. The rapid initial rate of formation of Ins(1,4)P$_2$ in hepatocytes after phenylephrine stimulation and the maintenance of elevated levels despite the fall of Ins(1,4,5)P$_3$ (Fig. 1A), suggests that PIP is the source of a major part of the Ins(1,4)P$_2$ accumulation.

186

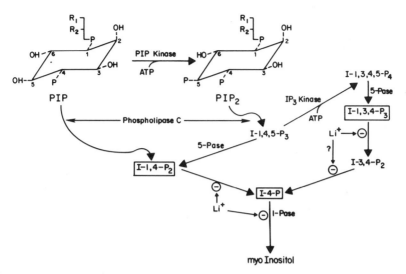

Fig. 3. Schematic diagram for the metabolism of inositol phosphates. Abbreviations used: PIP, phosphatidylinositol 4-phosphate; PIP_2, phosphatidylinositol 4,5-bisphosphate.

The second pathway for $Ins(1,4,5)P_3$ metabolism involves phosphorylation by a specific 3-kinase to $Ins(1,3,4,5)P_4$, and degradation of the latter intermediate by three or four different phosphatases. Of these only an inositol polyphosphate 5-phosphomonoesterase and an inositol monophosphate phosphatase have been characterized. As with $Ins(1,4,5)P_3$, the phosphate in the 5-position of $Ins(1,3,4,5)P_4$ is the most susceptible to hydrolysis, and the hydrolysis product, $Ins(1,3,4)P_3$, is further degraded to $Ins(3,4)P_2$ by a Li^+-sensitive 1-phosphomonoesterase that has been partially purified from a brain supernatant (see below). This enzyme also degraded $Ins(1,4)P_2$ to Ins 4-P, but did not further degrade $Ins(3,4)P_2$, suggesting that a different phosphatase is involved in $Ins(3,4)P_2$ metabolism. The further hydrolysis product of $Ins(3,4)P_2$ has not yet been identified and is assumed to be Ins 4-P in Fig. 3.

Several recent studies have also indicated that $Ins(1,4)P_2$ is metabolized to Ins-4-P (Balla et al., 1986; Dean and Moyer, 1986; Storey et al., 1984; Siess, 1985; Sherman et al., 1985), which accumulates in hormonally stimulated cells prior to Ins-1-P (Balla et al., 1986; Dean and Moyer, 1986). Most of the Ins-1-P accumulation in hormonally stimulated cells, particularly in the presence of Li^+, is probably derived from the delayed breakdown of phosphatidylinositol (Majerus et al., 1986), but its additional formation from $Ins(3,4)P_2$ hydrolysis is presently not excluded; Ins-1-P and Ins-3-P are structurally equivalent. With Li^+ pretreated cells, an accumulation of metabolites shown in boxes in Fig. 3, namely $Ins(1,3,4)P_3$, $Ins(1,4)P_2$ and Ins-4-P is observed (Burgess et al., 1985; Hansen et al., 1986; Balla et al., 1986; Siess, 1985; Morgan et al., 1987). These data suggest that the $Ins(1,4)P_2$ 1-phosphomonoesterase is Li^+ sensitive in addition to the InsP phosphatase characterized by Hallcher and Sherman (1980).

The identification of the hydrolysis product of $Ins(1,3,4)P_3$ as $Ins(3,4)P_2$, rather than $Ins(1,3)P_2$ as previously supposed (Hansen et al., 1986), was made by R. H. Michell and colleagues (personal communication) by taking advantage of the fact that $[^{32}P]Ins(1,4,5)P_3$ prepared by incubating human erythrocyte ghosts with $[^{32}P]$inorganic phosphate contains ^{32}P only in the 4 and 5 positions of the inositol ring (Downes et al., 1982). Fig. 4A shows the elution profile of a number of [^{3}H]inositol phosphate standards and [^{32}P]inorganic phosphate from the HPLC Partisil SAX column using four successive convex ammonium formate/phosphoric acid, pH 3.7 gradients. Fig. 4B shows that the hydrolysis products obtained by incubating a mixture of [^{3}H]inositol (1,4,5)P$_3$ and [4,5-^{32}P]Ins(1,4,5)P$_3$ with purified 5-phosphomonoesterase were [4-^{32}P]Ins(1,4)P$_2$ and [^{32}P]inorganic phosphate. It may be noted that the [^{3}H]/[^{32}P] ratio in Ins(1,4)P$_2$ was increased relative to that in the Ins(1,4,5)P$_3$ isotopic mixture, indicating that the relative ^{32}P specific activity in the 5-phosphate position was greater than that in the 4-phosphate position. The [4,5-^{32}P]Ins(1,4,5)P$_3$ after conversion to [4,5-^{32}P]Ins(1,3,4,5)P$_4$ by Ins(1,4,5)P$_3$ 3-kinase was hydrolysed to [4-^{32}P]Ins(1,3,4)P$_3$ by the purified 5-phosphomonoesterase as shown in Fig. C.

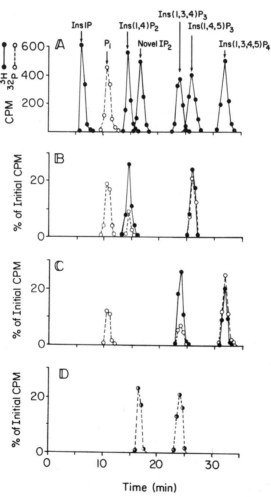

Fig. 4. Elution profiles of inositol phosphates by HPLC. A, Standards; B, degradation of [^{3}H] and [4,5-^{32}P]Ins(1,4,5)P$_3$; C, degradation of [^{3}H] and [4,5-^{32}P]Ins(1,3,4,5)P$_4$; D, degradation of [^{3}H] and [4-^{32}P]Ins(1,3,4)-P$_3$. The open and closed circles represent ^{32}P and ^{3}H, repectively.

The [4-^{32}P]Ins(1,3,4)P$_3$ was isolated, and when incubated with a brain supernatant phosphomonoesterase activity, which had been partially purified by phosphocellulose and DE52 cellulose column chromatography, caused hydrolysis to a [4-^{32}P]InsP$_2$ product (Fig. 4D). This compound had the same retention time on HPLC elution as the InsP$_2$ isomer that accumulated slowly in phenylephrine-stimulated (Fig. 1B) or vasopressin-stimulated (Hansen et al., 1986) hepatocytes. Similar experiments using [3-^{32}P]Ins(1,3,4)P$_3$ prepared by first synthesizing [3-^{32}P]Ins(1,3,4,5)P$_4$ from unlabeled Ins(1,4,5)P$_3$ and [γ-^{32}P]ATP and degrading it with purified 5-phosphomonoesterase, showed that the InsP$_2$ product of [3-^{32}P]Ins(1,3,4)P$_3$ hydrolysis contained ^{32}P in the 3-position. The novel InsP$_2$, therefore, must be Ins(3,4)P$_2$.

The pathway for the formation and metabolism of inositol phosphates is more complex than that schematized in Fig. 3 since inositol 1,2-cyclic phosphate compounds are also found in mammalian cells (reviewed by Majerus et al., 1986). It has been known for some time that the inositol phosphate products of phospholipase C action on phosphatidylinositol consist of a mixture of Ins-1-P and Ins 1,2(cyclic)-P, with the latter being converted to Ins 1-P by an inositol 1,2 cyclic phosphate hydrolase before further hydrolysis to free *myo*inositol (Dawson et al., 1971). However, attention has recently been refocussed on the inositol cyclic phosphates with the finding that hydrolysis of PIP and PIP$_2$ as well as PI by purified phospholipase C in phospholipid vesicles was associated with the formation of the 1,2-cyclic counterparts of Ins(1,4)P$_2$ and Ins(1,4,5)P$_3$ in various proportions with the noncyclic intermediates (Wilson et al., 1985a, 1985b). After taking precautions to extract cells under neutral rather than the normal acidic conditions, which opens the 1,2 cyclic bond leaving the phosphate in the inositol 1-positon, Ishi et al. (1986) demonstrated that the predominant InsP$_3$ isomer in platelets 10 s after thrombin addition was Ins 1,2(cyclic)4,5-P$_3$. The 1,2-cyclic phosphate forms of Ins-1-P, Ins(1,4)P$_2$ and Ins(1,4,5)P$_3$ have also been identified in pancreatic minilobules after muscarinic receptor stimulation (Dixon and Hokin, 1985, Sekar et al., 1987). Ins 1,2(cyclic)P has been shown to accumulate in large amounts in a Morris (7777) hepatoma tumor as well as in cultured cells derived from the turmor in the absence of agonist stimulation (Graham et al., 1987). Other cells, such as anterior pituitary GH$_3$ cells (Dean and Moyer, 1986) and fibrosarcoma cells (Majerus et al., 1986), however, apparently accumulate very little of the inositol 1,2(cyclic) phosphates.

Studies with homogenates of platelets and rat kidney have shown that the metabolism of the inositol 1,2(cyclic) phosphates follows the pathway: cyclic InsP$_3$ --> cyclic InsP$_2$ --> cyclic InsP --> Ins 1-P without formation of the noncyclic intermediates except at the final hydrolase step (Connolly et al., 1986b). The apparent Km of the platelet 5-phosphomonoesterase is 10-fold higher for Ins(1,2)cyclic 4,5-P$_3$ than for Ins(1,4,5)P$_3$ (Connolly et al., 1986b), while Ins(1,2)cyclic 4,5-P$_3$ is a very poor substrate for the 3-kinase (Connolly et al., 1987; Irvine and Moor, 1986). The biological effects of the cyclic and noncyclic forms of Ins(1,4,5)P$_3$ on Ca^{2+} release from permeabilized cells are very similar (Wilson et al., 1985b; Irvine et al., 1986b). At present, the factors regulating the relative amounts of cyclic and noncyclic inositol phosphates in different tissues after hormonal stimulation are unclear, as are the implications for physiological regulation of signalling processes. The unfavorable kinetic constants for Ins 1,2(cyclic)4,5-P$_3$ metabolism suggest that once formed it will have a longer lifetime and more prolonged effect on Ca^{2+} mobilization than Ins(1,4,5)P$_3$, which may account for some apparent anomalies between the amount of Ins(1,4,5)P$_3$ (cyclic and noncyclic) formed and the degree of Ca^{2+} mobilization observed with different agonists in hepatocytes (Williamson et al., 1987). In addition, the relative amounts of cyclic and noncyclic Ins(1,4,5)P_3 produced by the breakdown of PIP_2 could be a factor in regulating the amount of Ins(1,3,4,5)P_4 formed.

REGULATION OF THE INOSITOL TRIS/TETRAKISPHOSPHATE PATHWAY

The enzymes involved in the metabolism of inositol phosphates are only just beginning to be defined, but sufficient information is available to suggest that regulation of the inositol tris/tetrakisphosphate pathway is complex. A Mg^{2+}-dependent 5-phosphomonoesterase activity responsible for the hydrolysis of Ins(1,4,5)P_3 to Ins(1,4)P_2 has been described in a number of tissues where the bulk of the activity appears to be associated with the plasma membrane (for reviews see Downes and Michell, 1985; Majerus et al., 1986). However, in platelets the enzyme is mostly soluble and has been purified to apparent homogeneity (Connolly et al., 1985; 1986a) with a Mr of about 45,000 by SDS polyacrylamide gel electrophoresis (Majerus et al., 1986). As found with most studies using the particulate enzyme, the Km for Ins(1,4,5)P_3 of the platelet enzyme is rather high, 30 μM (Connolly et al., 1985) or 17μM (Connolly et al., 1986a) compared with values of 1-13 μM for Ins(1,4,5)P_3 concentrations reached in stimulated cells (Rittenhouse and Sasson, 1985; Meek, 1986; Bradford and Rubin, 1986). Studies on the purification of the 5-phosphomonoesterase from rat brain cortex in our laboratory (Hansen et al, 1987) have revealed three different activities, with different substrate specificities to Ins(1,4,5)P_3 and Ins(1,3,4,5)P_4. The bulk of the enzyme activity in the tissue (70%) is associated with the particulate fraction and has approximate Km's for Ins(1,4,5)P_3 and Ins(1,3,4,5)P_4 of 15 μM and 1.5 μM, respectively. Two soluble activities have been partially purified using phosphocellulose and DEAE chromatography; type I with Mr in the region of 40,000-60,000, a sharp pH optimum at 7.5 and Km values for Ins(1,4,5)P_3 and Ins(1,3,4,5)P_4 of 3 μM and 0.7 μM, respectively, and type II with a Mr of 175,000, a broad pH optimum between 6.5-7.0 and a Km for Ins(1,4,5)P_3 of about 15 μM but with a very poor affinity for Ins-(1,3,4,5)P_4. Despite the higher affinity of the particulate and type I enzyme for Ins(1,3,4,5)P_4, the Vmax was only about 10% of that with Ins(1,4,5)P_3. Similar relative kinetic constants have been reported for the platelet enzyme (Connolly et al., 1987), which may be the same as the brain type I enzyme. Calcium acts as a weak inhibitor presumably by interfering with the Mg^{2+}-binding site. The significance of the multiple Ins(1,4,5)P_3 5-phosphomonoesterase activities is presently unclear, but studies with the membrane bound enzyme of neutrophils have shown that it is partially an ectoenzyme and has the properties of an alkaline phosphatase suggesting that it may not be involved in Ins(1,4,5)P_3 metabolism (Badwey et al., 1986).

The kinetic properties of the soluble 5-phosphomonoesterase suggest that the relative rates of Ins(1,4,5)P_3 and Ins(1,3,4,5)P_4 hydrolysis will be commensurate at low substrate concentrations (< 1 μM) but that Ins(1,4,5)P_3 hydrolysis will be favored at higher concentrations. A similar situation applies for the relative rates of hydrolysis of Ins(1,4,5)P_3 to Ins(1,4)P_2 versus phosphorylation to Ins(1,3,4,5)P_4 since the Km for the 3-kinase is considerably lower than that for the 5-phosphomonoesterase. The purified 3-kinase from brain has a Km for Ins(1,4,5)P_3 of 0.2 μM, a broad pH optimum at 7.5 -8.0 (Johanson et al., 1987) but a total activity considerably less than that of the soluble 5-phosphomonoesterase. Thus, at intracellular Ins(1,4,5)P_3 concentrations of 0.1 to 1 μM, characteristic of the range of concentration in hormonally stimulated hepatocytes (Williamson and Hansen, 1987) and neutrophils (Bradford and Rubin, 1986), metabolism of Ins(1,4,5)P_3 by the 5-phosphomonoestearase and by the 3-kinase is likely to be approximately equal after the first few seconds of agonist stimulation. This split appears consistent with the pattern of inositol phosphate accumulations shown in Fig. 1.

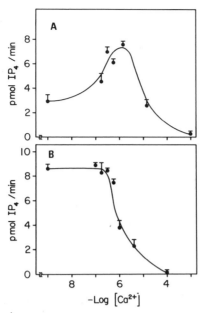

Fig. 5. Effect of Ca^{2+} on $InsP_3$ kinase activity. A, a 100,000 g supernatant of a 30% (w/v) homogenate of rat brain was diluted 1:10 in buffer pH 8.0 containing 100 mM KCl, 20 mM Tris, 5 mM EGTA, 1 mM dithiothreitol and 2 mM 2,3-diphosphoglycerol, with Ca^{2+} additions to achieve the required concentrations as measured with a Ca^{2+}-sensitive electrode. After a 2 min preincubation at 30° C, the kinase reaction was started by addition of 2 mM ATP and 2 μM $[^3H]Ins(1,4,5)P_3$. After quenching with perchloric acid, samples were assayed for $Ins(1,3,4,5)P_4$ by Dowex 1-x8 chromatography. B, partially purified $Ins(1,4,5)P_3$ 3-kinase from rat brain (specific activity 0.023 μmol/min.mg protein) was incubated as in A., except the pH was 7.1 and the $Ins(1,4,5)P_3$ concentration was 10 μM.

An unusual feature of the kinetics of $Ins(1,4,5)P_3$ accumulation after hormonal stimulation in many cells is its transience, with an initial peak after a few seconds being followed by a fall to a steady state value slightly above resting levels (e.g. the response to phenylephrine with hepatocytes shown in Fig. 1A). If the rate of production of $Ins(1,4,5)P_3$ remains constant over the first few minutes, this phenomenon may reflect an activation of the 5-phosphatase or the 3-kinase. In this respect it is of interest that Biden and Wollheim (1986) have reported that the $Ins(1,4,5)P_3$ kinase activity in a crude supernatant fraction from RIN m5F cells was activated by Ca^{2+} over the range from 0.2 to 10 μM with a change of Vmax but not of Km, while the 5-phosphatase activity was unaffected by Ca^{2+}. A similar activational effect of Ca^{2+} over a narrow concentration range of 0.1 to 2 μM on $Ins(1,4,5)P_3$ kinase has also been observed using a high speed supernatant fraction from rat brain (Fig. 5A). At higher concentrations, Ca^{2+} was inhibitory and only an inhibitory effect was observed with the purified enzyme, probably due to inhibition by $CaATP^{2-}$ (Fig. 5B). These data suggest that the activational effect of Ca^{2+} may require interaction of the enzyme with a Ca^{2+} binding protein. This may not be calmodulin since the Ca^{2+} activating effect on enzyme activity shown in Fig. 5A could not be prevented by a variety of calmodulin antagonists. Other studies have shown that calcium depletion caused relative increases of $Ins(1,4,5)P_3$ accumulation and decreases of $Ins(1,3,4)P_3$ accumulation in RIN m5F cells stimulated with carbamycholine

(Biden and Wollheim, 1986) and in human leukemic HL-60 cells stimulated with fMet-Leu-Phe (Lew *et al.*, 1987). A stimulation of Ins(1,4,5)P$_3$ kinase by Ca^{2+} is also suggested from the study by Rossier *et al.* (1986) who investigated the metabolism of Ins(1,4,5)P$_3$ in permeabilized adrenal glomerulosa cells as a function of the medium Ca^{2+} concentration. These studies suggest that an increase of cytosolic free Ca^{2+} induced by Ins(1,4,5)P$_3$ may provide a negative feedback signal to curtail the accumulation of Ins(1,4,5)P$_3$ by increasing its rate of disposal to Ins(1,3,4,5)P$_4$ and thence to Ins(1,3,4)P$_3$.

An alternative mechanism that may account for the unusual kinetics of Ins(1,4,5)P$_3$ accumulation is by a protein kinase C-mediated activation of the 5-phosphomonoesterase. The enzyme purified from human platelets has been shown to be phosphorylated by protein kinase C with a substantial increase of V*max* activity (Connolly et al., 1986a). Pretreatment of human platelets with diacylglycerol to activate protein kinase C *in situ* is also effective in causing an enhanced rate of hydrolysis of Ins(1,4,5)P$_3$ when added to subsequently permeabilized cells (Molina y Vedia and Lapetina, 1986). Preliminary studies with the purified 5-phosphomonoesterase from brain likewise show enhanced activity in the presence of activated protein kinase C (Williamson et al., 1987). At present the relative importance of these two mechanisms for regulation of Ins(1,4,5)P$_3$ levels in different cells after agonist stimulation is unclear.

BIOLOGICAL EFFECTS OF INS(1,3,4)P$_3$ AND INS(1,3,4,5)P$_4$

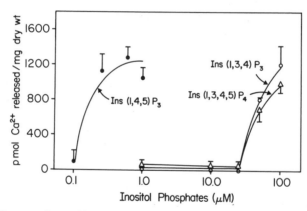

Fig. 6. Effects of Ins(1,4,5)P$_3$, Ins(1,3,4)P$_3$ and Ins(1,3,4,5)P$_4$ on Ca^{2+} release from permeabilized rat hepatocytes. The experimental conditions were as described by Joseph et al. (1984).

The physiological significance of the inositol tris/tetrakisphosphate pathway is presently unclear. One possibility discussed above is that phosphorylation of Ins(1,4,5)P$_3$ to Ins(1,3,4,5)P$_4$ may provide a primary mechanism for regulating Ins(1,4,5)P$_3$ levels and hence the extent of hormonally stimulated intracellular Ca^{2+} mobilization. An alternative possibility is that Ins(1,3,4,5)P$_4$, and possibly Ins(1,3,4)P$_3$, may have unique second messenger functions. Irvine et al. (1986b) have reported that Ins(1,3,4)P$_3$, unlike Ins(1,3,4,5)P$_4$, mobilized Ca^{2+} from permeabilized Swiss mouse 3T3 cells with a half-maximal effect at 9 μM compared with 0.3 μM for Ins(1,4,5)P$_3$, and suggested that because of the later accumulation of Ins(1,3,4)P$_3$ in hormonally stimulated cells it may contribute towards overall intracellular Ca^{2+} mobilization. However, as illustrated in Fig. 6, Ins(1,3,4)P$_3$ and Ins(1,3,4,5)P$_4$ were both very weak activators of Ca^{2+} mobilization in permeabilized hepatocytes, with half maximal effects at about 50 μM. Furthermore, neither compound when present at 50 μM affected the amount of Ca^{2+} released induced by a subsequent addition of 1 μM Ins(1,4,5)P_3 to permeabilized hepatocytes. It seems unlikely, therefore, that the inositol tetrakisphosphate pathway is involved in modulating intracellular Ca^{2+} mobilization.

Preliminary studies from the author's laboratory indicated that the Ins(1,3,4,5)P_4 increased the permeability of the plasma membrane to Ca^{2+} (Hansen et al., 1986). However, further studies with liver plasma membranes and brain synaptosomes showed that the effect was nonreproducible. Indirect evidence that Ins(1,3,4,5)P_4 may be affecting plasma membrane Ca^{2+} permeability has recently been obtained by the demonstration that co-injection of Ins(1,3,4,5)P_4 with Ins(2,4,5)P_3 (a weak Ca^{2+}-mobilizing agent) into sea urchin eggs caused a raising of the fertilization envelope in the presence but not in the absence of external Ca^{2+} (Irvine and Moor, 1986). Injection of either compound alone had no effect. The only report of effects of Ins(1,3,4,5)P_4 on plasma membrane ion currents is by Higashida and Brown (1986). These authors showed that injections of either Ins(1,3,4)P_3 or Ins(1,3,4,5)P_4 into neuroblastoma/glioma NG108-15 hybrid cells evoked an inward non-specific cation current with a reversal potential of -20 mV. In contrast, injection of Ins(1,4,5)P_3 activated an outward K^+ current with a reversal potential of -80 mV, probably as a secondary consequence of intracellular Ca^{2+} mobilization. Clearly further studies are required before Ins(1,3,4,5)P_4 can be assigned a mediator role.

ACKNOWLEDGMENT

This work was supported by NIH grants DK-15120 and AA-05662

REFERENCES

Badwey, J. A., Sadler, K. L., Robinson, J. M., Karnovsky, M.J. and Karnovsky, M. L., 1986, J. Cell. Biol. (Abstracts) 103: 506a.
Balla, T., Baukal, A. J., Guillemette, G., Morgan, R. O., and Catt, K. J., 1986, Proc. Natl. Acad. Sci. USA 83: 9323-9327.
Batty, I. R., Nahorski, S. R., and Irvine, R. F., 1985, Biochem. J. 232: 211-215.
Berridge, M. J. and Irvine, R. F., 1984, Nature (London) 312: 315-321.
Biden, T. J. and Wollheim, C. B., 1986, J. Biol. Chem. 261: 11931-11934.
Bradford, P. G. and Rubin, R. P., 1986, J. Biol. Chem. 261: 15644-15647.
Burgess, G. M., McKinney, J. S., Irvine, R. F., and Putney, J. W., 1985, Biochem. J. 232: 237-248.
Cerdan, S., Hansen, C. A., Johanson, R., Inubushi, T. and Williamson, J. R., 1986, J. Biol. Chem. 261: 14676-14680.
Charest, R., Prpic, V., Exton, J. H. and Blackmore, P. F., 1985, Biochem. J. 227: 79-90.
Cohen, P., 1985, Eur. J. Biochem. 151: 439-448.
Connolly, T. M., Bancal, V. S., Bross, T. E., Irvine, R. F., and Majerus, P. W., 1987, J. Biol. Chem. in press.
Connolly, T. M., Bross, T. E. and Majerus, P. W., 1985, J. Biol. Chem. 260: 7868-7874.
Connolly, T. M., Lawing, W. J. Jr., and Majerus, P. W., 1986a, Cell 46: 46: 951-958.
Connolly, T. M., Wilson, D. B., Bross, T. E. and Majerus, P. W., 1986b, J. Biol. Chem. 261: 122-126.
Dawson, R. M. C., Freinkel, N., Jungalwala, F. B. and Clarke, N., 1971, Biochem. J. 122: 605-607.
Dean, N. M. and Moyer, J. D., 1986, Proc. Natl. Acad. Sci. USA 83: 4162-4166.

Dixon, J. F. and Hokin, L. E., 1985, J. Biol. Chem. 260: 16068-16071.

Downes, C. P. and Michell, R. H., 1985, In: "Molecular Mechanisms of Transmembrane Signalling," P. Cohen and M. D. Houslay, eds., pp. 3-56, Elsevier Science Publ., Amsterdam.

Downes, C. P., Mussat, M. C., and Michell, R. H., 1982, Biochem. J. 203: 169-177.

Gilman, A. G., 1984, Cell 36: 577-579.

Graham, R. A., Meyer, R. A., Szwergold, B. S., and Brown, T. R., 1987, J. Biol. Chem. 262: 35-37.

Hallcher, L. M. and Sherman, W. R., 1980, J. Biol. Chem. 255: 10896-10901.

Hansen, C. A., Mah, S., and Williamson, J. R., 1986, J. Biol. Chem. 261: 8100-8103.

Hansen, C. A., Johanson, R., Williamson, M. T., and Williamson, J. R. 1987, manuscript in preparation.

Hawkins, P. T., Stephens, L. and Downes, C. P. 1986, Biochem. J. 238: 507-516.

Higashida, H. and Brown, D. A., 1986, FEBS Lett. 208: 283-286.

Hokin, L. E., 1985, Ann. Rev. Biochem. 54: 205-235.

Irvine, R. F., Letcher, A. J., Lander, D. J.and Downes, C. P. 1984, Biochem. J. 223, 237-243.

Irvine, R. F., Anggard, E. E., Letcher, A. J., and Downes, C. P. 1985, Biochem. J. 229, 505-511.

Irvine, R. F., Letcher, A. J., Heslop, J. P. and Berridge, M. J. 1986a, Nature (London) 320: 631-634.

Irvine, R. F., Letcher, A. J., Lander, D. J. and Berridge, M. J., 1986b Biochem. J. 240: 301-304.

Irvine, R. F. and Moor, R. M., 1986, Biochem. J. 240: 917-920.

Ishi, H., Connolly, T. M., Bross, T. E. and Majerus, P. W., 1986, Proc. Natl. Acad. Sci. 83: 6397-6401.

Johanson, R., Coll, K. E. and Williamson, J. R., 1987, manuscript in preparation.

Joseph, S. K., Thomas, A. P., Williams, R. J., Irvine, R. F. and Williamson, J. R., 1984, J. Biol. Chem. 259: 3077-3081.

Lew, P. D., Morad, A., Krause, K.-H., Waldvogel, F. A., Biden, T. J. and Schlegel, W. 1987, J. Biol. Chem. in press.

Litosch, I. and Fain, J. N., 1986, Life Sci. 39: 187-194.

Majerus, P. W., Connolly, T. M., Deckmyn, H., Ross, T. S., Bross, T. E., and Wilson, D. B., 1986, Science 234: 1520-1526.

Meek, J. L., 1986, Proc. Natl. Acad. Sci. USA 83: 4162-4166.

Merritt, J. E., Taylor, C. W., Rubin, R. P. and Putney, J. W. Jr., 1986b, Biochem. J. 238: 825-829.

Michell, R. H., 1986, Nature (London) 319: 176-177.

Molina y Vedia, L. M. and Lapetina, E. G., 1986, J. Biol. Chem. 261, 10493-10495.

Morgan, R. O., Chang, J. P. and Catt, K. J., 1987, J. Biol. Chem. 262: 1166-1171.

Nishizuka, Y., 1986, Science 233: 305-312.

Rasmussen, H. and Barrett, P. Q., 1984, Physiol Rev. 64: 938-984.

Rittenhouse, S. E. and Sasson, J. P., 1985, J. Biol. Chem. 260: 8657-8660.

Rossier, M. F., Dentand, I. A., Lew, P. D., Capponi, A.M. and Vallotton, M. B., 1986, Biochem. Biophys. Res. Commun. 139: 259-265.

Sekar, M. C., Dixon, J. F. and Hokin, L. E., 1987, J. Biol. Chem. 262: 340-344.

Sherman, W. R., Munsell, L. Y., Gish, B. G., and Honchar, M. P., 1985, J. Neurochem. 44: 798-807.

Siess, W., 1985, FEBS Lett. 185: 151-156.

Storey, D. J., Shears, S. B., Kirk, C. J. and Michell, R. H., 1984, Nature (London) 312: 374-376.

Streb, H., Heslop, J. P., Irvine, R. F., Schulz, I. and Berridge, M. J., 1985, J. Biol. Chem. 260, 7309-7315.

Thomas, A. P., Alexander, J., and Williamson, J. R., 1984, J. Biol. Chem. 259: 5574-5584.

Tilly, B. C., vanParidon, P. A., Wirtz, K. W. A., deLaat, S. W. and
    Moolenaar, W. H., 1987, <u>Biochem. J.</u> in press.
Turk, J., Wolf, B. A. and McDaniel, M. L., 1986, <u>Biochem. J.</u> 237: 259-
    263.
Vicentini, L. M., Ambrosini, A., DiVirgilio, F., Meldolesi, J. and
    Pozzan, T., 1986, <u>Biochem. J.</u> 234: 555-562.
Williamson, J. R., Cooper, R. H. and Hoek, J. B., 1981, <u>Biochim.</u>
    <u>Biophys. Acta</u> 639: 243-295.
Williamson, J. R., Cooper, R. H., Joseph, S. K., and Thomas, A. P.,
    1985, <u>Am. J. Physiol</u>. 248: C203-C216.
Williamson, J. R., 1986, <u>Hypertension</u> 8: II-140-II-156.
Williamson, J. R. and Hansen, C. A., 1987, <u>IN:</u> "Biochemical Actions
    of Hormones," G. Litwack, ed., Academic Press, New York, in press.
Williamson, J. R., Hansen, C. A., Verhoeven, A., Coll, K. E., Johanson,
    R., Williamson, M. T., and Filburn, C., 1987 <u>IN:</u> "Cellular Calcium
    and the Control of Membrane Transport," P. C. Eaton, and L. J.
    Mandel, Rockefeller Press, New York, in press.
Wilson, D. B., Bross, T. E., Sherman, W. R., Berger, R. A., and Majerus
    P. W., 1985a, <u>Proc. Natl. Acad. Sci.</u> USA 82: 4013-4017.
Wilson, D. B., Connolly, T. M., Bross, T. E., Majerus, P. W., Sherman,
    W. R., Tyler, A. N., Rubin, L. J., and Brown, J. E., 1985b, <u>J. Biol.</u>
    <u>Chem.</u> 260: 13496-13501.
Wollheim, C. B. and Biden, T. J., 1986, <u>J. Biol. Chem.</u> 261, 8314-8319.

POTENTIATION BY GTP OF INS(1,4,5)P$_3$-INDUCED Ca^{2+}

MOBILIZATION IN PERMEABILIZED HEPATOCYTES

Andrew P. Thomas

Department of Pathology and Cell Biology
Thomas Jefferson University
Philadelphia, Pennsylvania 19107

INTRODUCTION

The intracellular effects of a wide range of hormones and other agonists which bind to cell surface receptors are mediated by a rise in cytosolic free Ca^{2+}. In almost all cell types where hormones increase cytosolic Ca^{2+}, the primary source from which the Ca^{2+} is derived is an intracellular storage pool. While there has long been indirect evidence for a role of inositol phospholipids in the signaling mechanism through which this Ca^{2+} mobilization is brought about, it is only relatively recently that the key messenger components and their sites of action have been identified. It is now known that agonists stimulate an inositol lipid-specific phospholipase C which cleaves phosphatidylinositol 4,5-bisphosphate to yield inositol 1,4,5-trisphosphate (Ins(1,4,5)P$_3$) and diacylglycerol. Both of these compounds have important second messenger functions. Diacylglycerol activates protein kinase C leading to the phosphorylation of a range of intracellular proteins and Ins(1,4,5)P$_3$ has been shown to release Ca^{2+} from a specific intracellular storage pool.

The ability of Ins(1,4,5)P$_3$ to release Ca^{2+} was first demonstrated in a "leaky" preparation of pancreatic acinar cells (1). Similar results have subsequently been obtained with other permeabilized cell preparations including saponin-permeabilized liver cells (2). The Ins(1,4,5)P$_3$-sensitive Ca^{2+} pool sequesters Ca^{2+} in an ATP-dependent manner and is clearly distinct from the mitochondria. It has been suggested that this Ca^{2+} pool is a part of the endoplasmic reticulum (1-3). The Ca^{2+} release mechanism is very specific for Ins(1,4,5)P$_3$ with almost no Ca^{2+} release being elicited by other inositol polyphosphates at concentrations which normally occur in mammalian cells (3,4). Based on the limited temperature dependence of Ins(1,4,5)P$_3$-induced Ca^{2+} release and its requirement for permeant counter ions for charge neutralization, it appears that Ca^{2+} release is mediated by a ligand-activated channel.

Apart from Ins(1,4,5)P$_3$, the only other effector of the Ca^{2+} release system which has been reported is GTP. An effect of GTP was first shown by Dawson (5) who found that liver microsomes are very insensitive to Ins(1,4,5)P$_3$ under normal conditions but will release a significant proportion of their sequestered Ca^{2+} if they are pretreated with GTP and polyethylene glycol (PEG). However, in isolated microsome preparations GTP causes Ca^{2+} release even in the absence of Ins(1,4,5)P$_3$ and no effects are observed unless at least 3% PEG is added. It has also been shown that GTP can cause direct Ca^{2+} release from microsomes derived from a neuroblastoma cell line when incubated in the presence of PEG, with similar results being obtained in permeabilized preparations of these cells (6). In the studies described here we show that GTP increases the amount of Ca^{2+} available for release by $Ins(1,4,5)P_3$ in permeabilized hepatocytes without causing Ca^{2+} release in the absence of $Ins(1,4,5)P_3$ and without any requirement for PEG. It is suggested that hepatocytes may possess a GTP-dependent regulatory system which modulates the responsiveness to $Ins(1,4,5)P_3$.

EFFECTS OF GTP ON Ca^{2+} RELEASE IN PERMEABILIZED HEPATOCYTES

To examine the effect of GTP on Ca^{2+} release and resequestration in a more integrated cell model we have used a permeabilized hepatocyte preparation. For these studies liver cells were suspended in a Ca^{2+}-depleted KCl-based medium containing Quin2 (free acid) to buffer the medium free Ca^{2+} in the normal cytosolic range of 50-500 nM. The plasma membrane of the cells was permeabilized by adding a limited concentration of digitonin and then Ca^{2+} movements between the medium and intracellular organelles were followed by monitoring Quin2 fluorescence. For the experiment of Figure 1 isolated hepatocytes were permeabilized in the presence of oligomycin, rotenone and ruthenium red to prevent mitochondrial Ca^{2+} uptake. After cell permeabilization, the medium free Ca^{2+} was adjusted to about 250 nM and then ATP and a creatine phosphate/creatine kinase regenerating system was added to initiate Ca^{2+} uptake into non-mitochondrial pools (not shown in figure). Once a steady state level of Ca^{2+} uptake had been achieved, other additions were made as shown in Figure 1.

When $Ins(1,4,5)P_3$ was added in the absence of guanine nucleotides (Fig. 1A) a rapid release of Ca^{2+} was observed consistent with previous demonstrations of $Ins(1,4,5)P_3$-induced Ca^{2+} release in permeabilized hepatocytes (2,7). The concentration of $Ins(1,4,5)P_3$ added (1 μM) was a maximal dose as indicated by the failure to obtain any further Ca^{2+} release with a second $Ins(1,4,5)P_3$ addition. A subsequent addition of the iono-phore ionomycin resulted in the release of the remaining sequestered Ca^{2+}. The proportion of the total ATP-dependent intracellular Ca^{2+} pools which could be released by $Ins(1,4,5)P_3$ was about 25%, a value which we have found to be relatively constant over a large number of cell preparations. After pretreatment of the permeabilized hepatocytes with 50 μM GTP for 4 min, the amount of Ca^{2+} which could be released by $Ins(1,4,5)P_3$ was increased by almost 2 fold (Fig. 1B). Concomitant with this potentiation of $Ins(1,4,5)P_3$-induced Ca^{2+} mobilization there was a decrease in the residual Ca^{2+} available for release by ionomycin. Thus GTP increased the size of the $Ins(1,4,5)P_3$-releasable Ca^{2+} pool at the expense of the other $Ins(1,4,5)P_3$-insensitive Ca^{2+} pools. In contrast to the results obtained with isolated microsomes (5,6), the enhancement in the $Ins(1,4,5)P_3$ response brought about by GTP did not require PEG and was not associated with any direct release of Ca^{2+} by GTP alone. Over a series of 10 separate experiments GTP increased the proportion of the sequestered Ca^{2+} which could be released by $Ins(1,4,5)P_3$ from a control value of 26.3±2.2% to 51.2±1.6%.

The ability of GTP to potentiate $Ins(1,4,5)P_3$-induced Ca^{2+} release was not mimicked by non-metabolizable GTP analogues. As shown in Fig. 1C, a 4 min pretreatment with 50 μM GTP-γ-S did not alter the responsiveness to $Ins(1,4,5)P_3$ as compared with the control response in the absence of guanine nucleotides (Fig. 1C). This suggests that GTP hydrolysis may be required for the enhancement of Ca^{2+} release. The lack of effect of GTP-γ-S on the Ca^{2+} release system clearly distinguishes this effect from the activation of the inositol lipid-specific phospholipase C which is involved in the production of $Ins(1,4,5)P_3$ from endogenous substrates in the plasma membrane. The potentiation of $Ins(1,4,5)P_3$-induced Ca^{2+} release is specific for GTP, we have observed no effect with any other nucleoside triphosphate nor with other guanine nucleotides such as cyclic-GMP. Half-maximal effects of GTP on Ins(1,4,5)P$_3$-induced Ca^{2+} release are observed at about 5 μM GTP, with maximal activation at 50 μM GTP. The effect of GTP is time dependent, requiring a preincubation period of 3-4 min at optimal GTP concentrations.

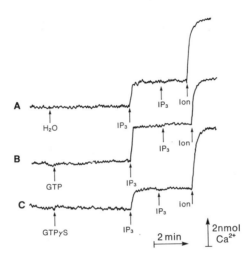

Figure 1. Isolated rat liver cells were permeabilized with digitonin (5 μg/mg cell protein) in KCl-based medium containing 75 μM Quin2 to allow simultaneous buffering and fluorometric measurement of medium Ca^{2+}. The cuvette chamber of the fluorimeter was maintained at 37°C and continuously stirred. After cell permeabilization the free Ca^{2+} concentration was adjusted to 250 nM and ATP was then added. After completion of ATP-dependent Ca^{2+} uptake the following additions were made as indicated: IP$_3$, 1 μM Ins(1,4,5)P$_3$; Ion, 5 μM ionomycin; GTP, 50 μM GTP; GTP-γ-S, 50 μM guanosine 5'-O-(3-thiotriphosphate).

Three potential mechanisms by which GTP might increase the responsiveness to Ins(1,4,5)P$_3$ are: 1. by decreasing Ca^{2+} reuptake and recycling through the ATP-dependent Ca^{2+} pump; 2. by increasing the activity of the Ins(1,4,5)P$_3$-sensitive Ca^{2+} channels; 3. by increasing the amount of Ca^{2+} available for release within the Ins(1,4,5)P$_3$-sensitive Ca^{2+} pool. In an attempt to investigate the role of the Ca^{2+} pump we have used *ortho*-vanadate to inhibit Ca^{2+} uptake. In the experiment of Figure 2, Ca^{2+} uptake was allowed to proceed to a steady state and then the permeabilized cells were further incubated in the presence or absence of 50 μM GTP. Subsequently 0.4 mM *ortho*-vanadate was added (sufficient to completely inhibit Ca^{2+} uptake) and Ca^{2+} release was initiated with Ins(1,4,5)P$_3$, followed by the addition of ionomycin to liberate residual Ca^{2+} pools. The rapid decrease in the signal after vanadate addition was due to a fluorescence quenching artifact which did not result from an alteration of the free or bound Ca^{2+}. As we have observed previously (7), the addition of vanadate did not alter the proportion of Ca^{2+} released by $Ins(1,4,5)P_3$ (Fig. 2A). It is also apparent from Fig. 2B that the ability of GTP to enhance the response to a subsequent $Ins(1,4,5)P_3$ addition was not reduced in the vanadate-treated cells. These data indicate that GTP does not act by inhibiting Ca^{2+} recycling via the uptake pathway. Furthermore, the finding that the basal level of $Ins(1,4,5)P_3$-induced Ca^{2+} release was not increased by vanadate strongly suggests that $Ins(1,4,5)P_3$ completely empties the $Ins(1,4,5)P_3$-sensitive Ca^{2+} pool even in the absence of GTP. If this is the case then GTP could not act by increasing the activity of pre-existing Ca^{2+} channels. Thus it appears most likely that GTP either unmasks latent Ca^{2+} channels, converting a previously $Ins(1,4,5)P_3$-insensitive Ca^{2+} pool into an $Ins(1,4,5)P_3$-sensitive Ca^{2+} pool or GTP may facilitate Ca^{2+} movement between Ca^{2+} pools such that a greater proportion of the sequestered Ca^{2+} is accessible to $Ins(1,4,5)P_3$-activated Ca^{2+} channels. Whatever the precise mechanism by which GTP acts, it is possible that this system may play a role within the intact cell by setting the level of the Ca^{2+} signal in response to a given degree of hormonal stimulation and $Ins(1,4,5)P_3$ formation.

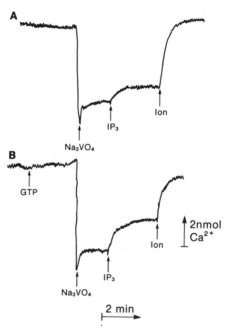

Figure 2. Permeabilized hepatocytes were incubated as described for Fig. 1. After ATP-dependent Ca^{2+} loading the cells were treated without (A) or with 50 μM GTP (B) followed by the addition of 0.4 mM *ortho*-vanadate (Na_3VO_4), 1 μM $Ins(1,4,5)P_3$ (IP_3), and 5 μM ionomycin (Ion).

Acknowledgements: This work was supported by U.S. Public Health Service grants AA07186 and AA07215.

REFERENCES

1.   H. Streb, R.F. Irvine, M.J. Berridge, and I. Schulz, Nature 306:67-69 (1983).

2.   S.K. Joseph, A.P. Thomas, R.J. Williams, R.F. Irvine, and J.R. Williamson, J. Biol. Chem. 259:3077-3081 (1984).

3.   M.J. Berridge and R.F. Irvine. Nature 312:315-321 (1984).

4.   R.F. Irvine, A.J. Letcher, D.J. Lander, and M.J. Berridge. Biochem. J. 240:301-304 (1986).

5.   A.P. Dawson, FEBS Lett. 185:147-150 (1985).

6.   T. Ueda, S. Chueh, M.W. Noel, and D.L. Gill, J. Biol. Chem. 261:3184-3192 (1986).

7.   A.P. Thomas, S.K. Joseph, and J.R. Williamson, in: "Hormones and Cell Regulation," J. Nunez, et al, eds, John Libbey, London. pp 81-93 (1986).

AGEPC: A POTENT CALCIUM-DEPENDENT CHEMICAL MEDIATOR IN THE LIVER

Rory A. Fisher, Denis B. Buxton, David S. Lapointe, Donald J. Hanahan, and Merle S. Olson

Department of Biochemistry
The University of Texas Health Science Center
San Antonio, Texas

INTRODUCTION

AGEPC (i.e. 1-O-alkyl-2-acetyl- sn -glycero-3-phosphocholine) or platelet activating factor is a unique phosphoglyceride first described as a fluid phase mediator of platelet aggregation during immunoglobulin E-induced anaphylaxis in the rabbit (1,2). AGEPC is produced in response to various stimuli in a variety of cells including neutrophils, basophils, monocytes and mast cells (3-7), and is among the most potent mediators formed and released by biological tissues. AGEPC induces aggregation and degranulation of platelets and neutrophils at subnanomolar concentrations (8,9) and is thought to act by interaction with specific receptors (10-13). In platelets, AGEPC-induced aggregation is associated with the turnover of inositol phospholipids, production of phosphatidic acid and protein phosphorylation (12-15). Additional studies have indicated that AGEPC possesses diverse biological actions including contraction of smooth muscles (16-18), negative inotropic cardiac effects (19,20), vasoconstriction (21,22), and exocrine gland stimulation (23). We have recently found that AGEPC possesses a powerful regulatory effect on hepatic metabolism which is the subject of this report.

RESULTS AND DISCUSSION

Our inquiry into the hepatic effects of AGEPC was prompted by studies of this lipid agonist in platelets demonstrating that AGEPC stimulates phosphoinositide turnover and the production of phosphatidic acid (15,24). In initial experiments, effects of AGEPC on phosphoinositide metabolism in isolated hepatocytes were examined (Fig. 1). Within 10 s after addition of AGEPC to hepatocytes labeled to equilibrium with [^{32} P]-orthophosphate, nearly a 40% decrease in the ^{32} P content of phosphatidylinositol 4,5-bisphosphate (PIP $_2$) was evident. The ^{32} P content of phosphatidylinositol 4-phosphate (PIP) decreased approximately 25% within 60 s and there were minor decreases in labeling of phosphatidylinositol (PI) during this period. Thus, at concentrations comparable to those reported to exert maximal effects on platelets, AGEPC caused a rapid and extensive turnover of hepatocyte phosphoinositides. Because of the close association between phosphoinositide turnover and the glycogenolytic action of calcium-mobilizing hormones in the liver, the effect of this lipid agonist on hepatic glycogenolysis was investigated. Glycogenolysis in the liver was monitored by following the rate of glucose output by perfused livers from fed

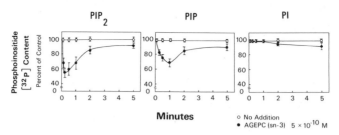

Fig. 1. AGEPC-induced changes in levels of PIP$_2$, PIP, and PI of rat hepatocytes (for details see reference below). Reprinted by permission from: Shukla, S.D., Buxton, D.B., Olson, M.S., and Hanahan, D.J. The Journal of Biological Chemistry 258: 10212-10214 (1983).

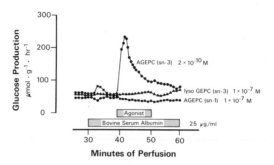

Fig. 2. Effects of sn-3-AGEPC, sn-1-AGEPC, and sn-3-lyso-GEPC on glucose output from the perfused rat liver (for details see reference in Fig. 1). Reproduced as described in Fig. 1.

rats. Fig. 2 illustrates that AGEPC (sn-3) exerts a potent glycogenolytic action in the liver, whereas the biologically inactive sn-1 stereoisomer and lyso-derivative were without significant effects at 500-fold greater concentrations. These latter findings argue strongly that AGEPC interacts with the liver in a specific manner to elicit the glycogenolytic response, likely via a receptor-mediated mechanism. Stimulation of hepatic glucose output in the perfused liver was associated with a significant activation of glycogen phosphorylase (22).

To characterize further the mechanisms involved in the glycogenolytic action of AGEPC in the liver, several experiments were initiated with isolated hepatocytes. However, quite surprisingly, AGEPC did not stimulate glucose output in hepatocytes (Fig. 3). Concentrations of AGEPC as high as 10^{-6} M had no effect on glucose production in these cells. To consider the possibility that AGEPC stimulates glycogenolysis in a transient manner which may be undetectable by measuring glucose accumulation in the medium, the effect of AGEPC on the activity of glycogen phosphorylase was assessed. In parallel experiments, the effects of AGEPC and several glycogenolytic agonists on PIP$_2$ metabolism and the activity of glycogen phosphorylase in hepatocytes were compared (Fig. 4). Contrary to the action of the calcium-mobilizing agonists epinephrine and vasopressin, AGEPC-stimulated degradation of PIP$_2$ was not accompanied by activation of glycogen phosphorylase. No activation of glycogen phosphorylase was apparent at times as early as 10 s following AGEPC addition or at concentrations of AGEPC as high as 10^{-7} M. This finding was somewhat of an enigma for two reasons. First, AGEPC represented the first agonist that induced hepatic PIP$_2$ degradation without promoting the calcium-dependent activation of glycogen phosphorylase. Recent studies have indicated that the inital response

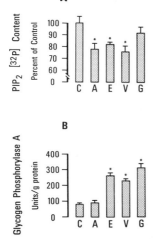

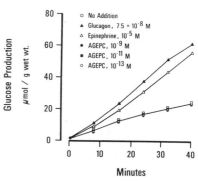

Fig. 3. Effects of AGEPC, epinephrine, and glucagon on the time course of glucose output from rat hepatocytes (for details see reference below). Reprinted by permission from: Fisher, R.A., Shukla, S.D., DeBuysere, M.S., Hanahan, D.J., and Olson, M.S. The Journal of Biological Chemistry 259: 8685-8688 (1984).

Fig.4. Effects of AGEPC and various glycogenolytic agonists on the level of phosphatidylinositol 4,5-bisphosphate (Panel A) and glycogen phosphorylase a (Panel B) in rat hepatocytes. C, control; A, 10^{-9} M AGEPC; E, 10^{-5} M epinephrine; V, 10^{-7} M vasopressin; G, 10^{-7} M glucagon (for details see reference in Fig. 3). Reproduced as described in Fig. 3

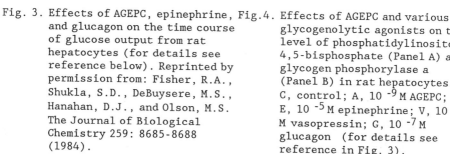

of hepatocytes to calcium-mobilizing hormones is the breakdown of PIP_2 to 1,2-diacylglycerol and inositol-1,4,5 triphosphate (IP_3) and much evidence has accumulated indicating that IP_3 represents the "second messenger" which mediates intracellular calcium mobilization of various agonists in the liver (25-29). If IP_3 is responsible for the effects of such agonists in the liver, these results suggested that AGEPC does not lead to increases in IP_3 in hepatocytes. In keeping with this suggestion is a recent study by Charest et al (30) in which evidence was presented indicating that hepatocyte IP_3 levels were not increased by AGEPC. If AGEPC stimulates PIP_2 hydrolysis via a phospholipase C reaction it is curious why increased levels of IP_3 do not accompany the degradation of PIP_2. Therefore, it is likely that the hydrolysis of PIP_2 observed in response to AGEPC occurs via another mechanism, such as phospholipase A action on the phosphoinositides. In this regard, it is of interest that a possible role of phospholipase A_2 in AGEPC-stimulated degradation of rabbit platelet phospholipids has been suggested (31). Second, the absence of AGEPC-stimulated glycogenolysis in hepatocytes suggested that elements of the intact liver may be essential for stimulation of hepatic glucose output by AGEPC. Glucose output from the liver is thought to be controlled at the level of the parenchymal cells (i.e. hepatocytes) since these cells comprise approximately 90% of the liver volume and constitute the primary storage site for glycogen. Among several likely possibilities, AGEPC may exert its glycogenolytic action in the perfused liver by an indirect effect on parenchymal cells following interaction with non-parenchymal cells in the liver. Of note is the observation that infusion of [^{3}H] AGEPC into perfused livers results in localization of radioactivity primarily in the portal sinusoids with little or no label appearing in the parenchyma (32).

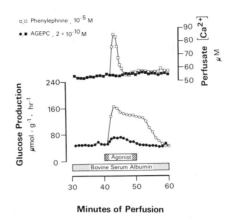

Fig. 5. Comparison of the effects of AGEPC and phenylephrine on stimulation of
glucose output and calcium efflux from the perfused rat liver at reduced
perfusate calcium concentration (for details see reference below).
Reprinted by permission from: Buxton, D.B., Shukla, S.D., Hanahan, D.J.,
and Olson, M.S. The Journal of Biological Chemistry 259: 1468-1471
(1984).

Several experiments were performed to elucidate a possible mechanism
for the observed stimulation of glycogenolysis upon AGEPC infusion into the
perfused liver. Hormones which stimulate glycogenolysis by mechanisms involving
intracellular calcium mobilization (e.g. alpha-adrenergic agonists, vasopressin,
and angiotensin II) cause a transient efflux of calcium from the liver upon
infusion (33,34). In Fig. 5, the effects of the alpha agonist phenylephrine and
AGEPC on perfusate calcium efflux and glycogenolysis are compared in experiments
in which the perfusate calcium concentration was reduced to 50 uM to facilitate
measurement of changes in calcium levels in the effluent perfusate. It can be
seen that the increase in glucose output in response to AGEPC was reduced
significantly by lowering the perfusate calcium concentration to 50 uM (i.e.
compare Fig. 2 and Fig. 5) and was not associated with efflux of calcium from
the liver as seen with phenylephrine. Removal of perfusate calcium (i.e. 1.25
mM) 5 min prior to infusion of AGEPC resulted in a similar significant
diminution of the glycogenolytic response to AGEPC. Thus, it seems that
extracellular calcium is important in the glycogenolytic response to AGEPC and
that inhibition of this response is not due to depletion of intracellular
calcium stores. Consistent with this concept is the observation that the calcium
channel blocker verapamil inhibits the glycogenolytic response of the liver to
AGEPC (22). However, it should be noted that verapamil has been shown to
interfere with AGEPC binding to platelets (35), although the effect on hepatic
AGEPC binding is unknown. The diminished glycogenolytic response to AGEPC at
reduced perfusate calcium concentrations can be overcome partly by increasing
the concentration of infused AGEPC. In Fig. 6, the effects of a maximal
glycogenolytic concentration of AGEPC on the kinetics of $^{45}Ca^{2+}$ efflux and net
calcium efflux from livers "loaded" with $^{45}Ca^{2+}$ at two different perfusate
calcium concentrations are described. At both concentrations of perfusate
calcium, i.e. 0.05 and 0.5 mM, 20 nM AGEPC elicits a transient efflux of $^{45}Ca^{2+}$
which is temporally related to the release of glucose but is not associated with
net efflux of calcium from the liver. The efflux of $^{45}Ca^{2+}$ from these livers in
response to AGEPC is approximately 10% of that released by phenylephrine
treatment of livers under similar experimental conditions. This efflux of
calcium in response to AGEPC presumably represents mobilization of calcium from
within the liver, however, at present, the source of the mobilized calcium in
terms of cell type or organelle within a particular cell remains unknown. Efflux
of calcium from the liver in response to calcium-mobilizing agonists can be
demonstrated also in hepatocytes and is thought to be a consequence of these
agonist's effects on increasing hepatocyte cytosolic calcium levels (36-38). In

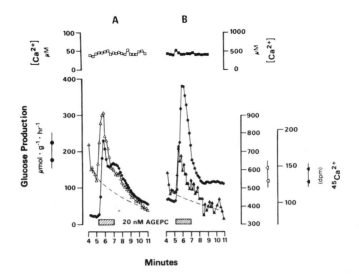

Fig. 6. AGEPC stimulation of ^{45}Ca^{2+} release from perfused rat livers preloaded with ^{45}Ca^{2+}. Livers were loaded with ^{45}Ca^{2+} for 50 min and washout of label begun at time 0. Loading and washout of ^{45}Ca^{2+} was performed in livers perfused with buffer containing 0.05 mM calcium (Panel A) and 0.5 mM calcium (Panel B). David S. Lapointe, personal communication.

contrast, AGEPC does not lead to measurable ^{40}Ca^{2+} efflux from the liver and does not increase cytosolic calcium in isolated hepatocytes (30). Thus, it is possible that AGEPC stimulates calcium release from non-parenchymal cell types within the liver. In endothelial cells preloaded with ^{45}Ca^{2+}, Bussolino et al (39) found that AGEPC stimulated cellular ^{45}Ca^{2+} efflux in a time- and dose-dependent manner. The possibility that cAMP was involved in the activation of glycogen phosphorylase in the liver by AGEPC was assessed by measuring this nucleotide in livers which were freeze-clamped following AGEPC infusion. No increases in cAMP occurred in response to either 0.2 nM or 20 nM AGEPC infusion into the liver (22). Together these data indicate that AGEPC shares neither the characteristic of increasing hepatocyte calcium levels leading to net calcium efflux from the liver nor of elevating hepatic cAMP levels as found with calcium-mobilizing agonists and hormones such as glucagon or beta-adrenergic agonists, respectively.

AGEPC has been reported to possess vasoactive properties. Contraction of various types of smooth muscle (16-18), vasoconstriction in hamster cheek pouches (21), and decreases in coronary flow in perfused hearts (19,20) are caused by AGEPC. AGEPC injection into rats and dogs results in reduced blood flow to the liver and increases in portal pressure, respectively (40,41). Further, Maegraith et al (42) observed constriction of the hepatic vasculature during anaphylactic shock in rats and postulated that the resulting anoxia may have important metabolic consequences. Blood flow through the hepatic vasculature appears to be regulated at the level of the portal venules and sinusoids (43,44). By constriction of either the portal venules or the sphincters controlling flow through the sinusoids, flow may be redistributed resulting in local hypoxia within the liver. Hepatic glycogenolysis is accelerated in anoxic liver (45). Although the precise mechanism of stimulated glycogenolysis has not been proven, it has been suggested that increases in inorganic phosphate (i.e. a substrate for phosphorolysis) and AMP mediate this response. AMP is both an allosteric activator of glycogen phosphorylase and an inhibitor of glycogen phosphorylase phosphatase (45,46). Although several glycogenolytic agents exert a constrictor action on the portal vasculature (e.g.

angiotensin II and epinephrine), the glycogenolytic action of these agonists is not dependent upon hepatic vasoconstriction since they promote glycogenolysis in isolated hepatocytes where there is no question of an ischemic origin for the response. In view of the reported vasoactive properties of AGEPC and the potential for stimulated glycogenolysis as a consequence of hypoxia within the liver, the effect of AGEPC on hepatic portal pressure (i.e. a measure of hepatic vasoconstriction) was examined. Fig. 7 illustrates the dose-dependent stimulation of hepatic portal pressure upon infusion of AGEPC into perfused livers. As the AGEPC concentration was increased, both the rate of pressure

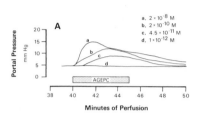 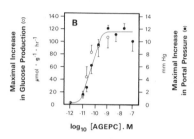

Fig. 7. Effect of AGEPC on hepatic portal vein pressure and glucose output in the perfused rat liver. A, representative pressure recordings obtained at different AGEPC concentrations; B, dose-response for AGEPC stimulation of hepatic portal pressure and glucose output (for details see reference below). Reprinted by permission from: Buxton, D.B., Fisher, R.A., Hanahan, D.J., and Olson, M.S. The Journal of Biological Chemistry 261: 644-649 (1986).

increase and the maximum extent of pressure increase were enhanced. Over a wide range of AGEPC concentrations, a close correlation was observed between AGEPC stimulation of glycogenolysis and increases in portal pressure (Fig. 7B). Likewise, the dose-dependent reduction in AGEPC-stimulated hepatic glycogenolysis observed upon reduction of perfusate calcium concentrations (Fig 8) or coinfusion of verapamil (22) was accompanied by a similar dose-dependent reduction in AGEPC-stimulated portal pressure. Further, tachyphylaxis (i.e. homologous desensitization) of the glycogenolytic response of the liver to AGEPC was accompanied by tachyphylaxis of portal pressure increases (22). Thus, under a variety of experimental conditions, a close association between increases in hepatic portal pressure and glycogenolysis in response to AGEPC infusion into the perfused liver were apparent.

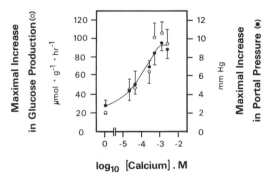

Fig. 8. Effect of perfusate calcium concentrations on the portal pressure and glucose output response of the perfused liver to 0.2 nM AGEPC (for details see reference in Fig. 7). Reproduced as described in Fig. 7.

Ischaemia in the liver leads to rapid increases in tissue ADP, AMP, P$_i$, lactate, and the lactate/pyruvate ratio (47,48). Measurement of adenine nucleotides in freeze-clamped livers did not show large changes in response to AGEPC; the only values which differed significantly from control values were increases in ADP in response to 20 nM AGEPC infusion (22). However, AMP and ADP values tended to be elevated in AGEPC-treated livers and it is possible that significant local changes in these nucleotides occurred yet were obscured in the overall tissue measurement. Increases in the production of lactate and in the lactate/pyruvate ratio in the effluent perfusate did occur in response to AGEPC infusion (49). Oxygen consumption by the liver in response to AGEPC was increased at low concentrations (e.g. 10^{-11} M) and converted to a transient respiratory burst followed by decreased consumption at higher doses (22). The maximal inhibition of oxygen consumption at higher doses of AGEPC coincided temporally with the peak of increased portal pressure. These results are consistent with the concept that the respiratory response to AGEPC may represent a balance between stimulated oxygen consumption as a consequence of an increase in flux in the Krebs cycle (i.e. glycogenolytic provision of substrate) and a decrease in the consumption of oxygen as a consequence of vasoconstriction-induced shutting down of regions of the liver.

In microvasculature studies of the liver using the transillumination technique, beta-adrenergic agonists cause significant relaxation of the portal venules and sinusoids (50,51). The beta agonist terbutaline reverses the dramatic constriction of hepatic sinusoids which occurs following the induction of cardiogenic shock in rats (52), and spontaneous electrical and mechanical activity of the isolated isometrically contracting portal vein is completely inhibited by beta agonists (53). If AGEPC exerts its glycogenolytic effect in the perfused liver via an indirect mechanism involving vasoconstriction, it seemed important to examine whether beta-adrenergic stimulation of the liver modified these hepatic responses. Fig. 9 illustrates the effect of infusion of isoproterenol into the liver on hepatic responses to AGEPC. Clearly, prior infusion of isoproterenol into the liver inhibited significantly both vasoconstriction and glycogenolysis in response to AGEPC. The lack of an effect of isoproterenol on basal portal pressure is likely due to the low portal vascular resistance of the liver. The inhibitory effect of isoproterenol toward AGEPC-stimulated glycogenolysis was mediated via beta-adrenergic receptors and was not the result of hepatic glycogen depletion (54). Glucagon, which increases parenchymal cell cAMP levels but does not possess portal vasodilative properties, had no effect toward AGEPC-stimulated glucose output and portal pressure (54). Also, the inhibitory action of isoproterenol toward these hepatic responses to AGEPC occurred in perfused livers from mature rats (54). In livers from such rats, hepatocytes lack functional beta-adrenergic receptors (55,56) and consequently there is no beta-receptor-mediated stimulation of

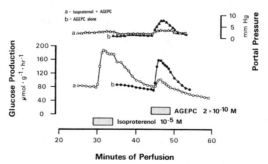

Fig. 9. The effect of isoproterenol on AGEPC-stimulated glucose output and portal pressure in the perfused rat liver (for details see reference below). Reprinted by permission from: Fisher, R.A., Kumar, R., Hanahan, D.J., and Olson, M.S. The Journal of Biological Chemistry 261: 8817-8823 (1986).

glycogenolysis by isoproterenol in these livers. Together, these data demonstrate that isoproterenol inhibits glycogenolysis and vasoconstriction in perfused livers by a mechanism involving interaction of isoproterenol with non-parenchymal cells within the liver.

In summary, AGEPC represents a novel lipid chemical mediator of glycogenolysis in the liver. The observation that this lipid agonist exerts its metabolic effects in the liver at concentrations which are encountered *in vivo*, e.g. during anaphylaxis and acute serum sickness (57,58), suggests that AGEPC may be an important regulator of hepatic glycogenolysis and hence blood glucose during pathophysiological conditions. Recent studies in our laboratory have demonstrated that the liver itself produces significant amounts of AGEPC in response to stimulation with immune aggregates and zymosan (59,60). Thus, it is likely that AGEPC possesses, in addition, an autocoid role in the liver. Finally, the observations noted in this communication demonstrate that AGEPC stimulates hepatic glycogenolysis by a mechanism different from that of calcium-mobilizing and cAMP-dependent hormones. Although clearly a calcium-dependent glycogenolytic agonist in the liver, AGEPC appears to mediate its effect by an indirect mechanism via hemodynamic effects on the hepatic microcirculation.

REFERENCES

1) Sirganian, R.P., and Osler, A.G. (1971) J. Immunol. 106, 1244-1251.
2) Benveniste, J., Henson, P.M., and Cochrane, C.G. (1972) J. Exp. Med. 136, 1356-1377.
3) Lotner, G.Z., Lynch, J.M., and Henson, P.M. (1980) J. Immunol. 124, 676-684.
4) Clark, P.O., Hanahan, D.J., and Pinckard, R.N. (1980) Biochim. Biophys. Acta 628, 69-75.
5) Camussi, G., Mencia-Huerta, J.M., and Benveniste, J. (1977) Immunology 33, 523-534.
6) Pinckard, R.N., Farr, R.S., and Hanahan, D.J. (1979) J. Immunol. 123, 1847-1857.
7) Lynch, J.M., Lotner, G.Z., Betz, S.J., and Henson, P.M. (1979) J. Immunol. 123, 1219-1226.
8) Demopoulos, C.A., Pinckard, R.N., and Hanahan, D.J. (1979) J. Biol. Chem. 254, 9355-9358.
9) O'Flaherty, J.T., Wykle, R.L., Miller, C.H., Lewis, J.C., Waite, M., Bass, D.A., McCall, C.E., and DeChatelet, L.R. (1981) Am. J. Pathol. 103, 70-79.
10) Valone, F.H., Coles, E., Reinhold, V.R., and Goetzl, E.J. (1982) J. Immunol. 129, 1637-1641.
11) Hwang, S.-B., Lee, C.-S.C., Cheah, M.J., and Shen, T.Y. (1983) Biochemistry 22, 4756-4763.
12) Tokumura, A., Homma, H., and Hanahan, D.J. (1985) J. Biol. Chem. 260, 12710-12714.
13) Sugatani, J., and Hanahan, D.J. (1986) Arch. Biochem. Biophys. 246, 855-864.
14) Lapetina, E.G., and Siegel, F.L. (1983) J. Biol. Chem. 258, 7241-7244.
15) Shukla, S.D., and Hanahan, D.J. (1982) Biochem. Biophys. Res. Commun. 106, 697-703.
16) Findlay, S.R., Lichtenstein, L.M., Hanahan, D.J., and Pinckard, R.N. (1981) Am. J. Physiol. 241, 130-134.
17) Tokumura, A., Fukuzawa, K., and Tsukatani, H. (1984) J. Pharm. Pharmacol. 36, 210-212.
18) Kester, M., Ledvora, R.F., and Barany, M. (1984) Eur. J. Physiol. Pflugers Arch. 400, 200-202.
19) Levi, R., Burke, J.A., Guo, Z.-G., Hattori, Y., Hoppens, C.M., McManus, L.M., Hanahan, D.J., and Pinckard, R.N. (1984) Circ. Res. 54, 117-124.
20) Benveniste, J., Boullet, C., Brink, C., and Labat, C. (1983) Br. J.

Pharmacol. 80, 81-83.

21) Bjork, J., and Smedegard, G. (1983) Eur. J. Pharmacol. 96, 87-94.

22) Buxton, D.B., Fisher, R.A., Hanahan, D.J., and Olson, M.S. (1986) J. Biol. Chem. 261, 644-649.

23) Soling, H.-D., Eibl, H., and Fest, W. (1984) Eur. J. Biochem. 144, 65-72.

24) Lapetina, E.G. (1982) J. Biol. Chem. 257, 7314-7317.

25) Michell, R.H., Kirk, C.J., Jones, L.M., Downes, C.P., and Creba, J.A. (1981) Phil. Trans. R. Soc. B296, 123-137.

26) Creba, J.A., Downes, C.P., Hawkins, P.T., Brewster, G., Michell, R.H., and Kirk, C.J. (1983) Biochem. J. 212, 733-747.

27) Thomas, A.P., Alexander, J., and Williamson, J.R. (1984) J. Biol. Chem. 259, 5574-5584.

28) Joseph, S.K., Thomas, A.P., Williams, R.J., Irvine, R.F., and Williamson, J.R. (1984) 259, 3077-3081.

29) Burgess, G.M., Godfrey, P.P., McKinney, J.S., Berridge, M.J., Irvine, R.F., and Putney, J.W. (1984) Nature 309, 63-66.

30) Charest, R., Prpic, V., Exton, J.H., and Blackmore, P.F. (1985) Biochem. J. 227, 79-90.

31) Shaw, J.O., Klusick, S.J., and Hanahan, D.J. (1981) Biochim. Biophys. Acta 663, 222-229.

32) Hill, C.E., Olson, M.S., Sheridan, P.J., and Hanahan, D.J. (1985) Fed. Proc. 44, 480.

33) Blackmore, P.F., Dehaye, J.-P., and Exton, J.H. (1979) J. Biol. Chem. 254, 6945-6950.

34) Althaus-Salzman, M., Carafoli, E., and Jakob, A. (1980) Eur. J. Biochem. 106, 241-248.

35) Chesney, C.M., Pifer, D.D., and Huch, K.M. (1983) INSERM Symp. 23, 177-184.

36) Blackmore, P.F., Brumley, F.T., Marks, J.L., and Exton, J.H. (1978) J. Biol. Chem. 253, 4851-4858.

37) Chen, J.-L.J., Babcock, D.F., and Lardy, H.A. (1978) Proc. Natl. Acad. Sci. 75, 2234-2238.

38) Exton, J.H. (1983) in "Calcium and Cell Function" (Cheung, W.Y., ed.) Vol IV, pp 63-97, Academic Press, New York.

39) Bussolino, F., Aglietta, M., Sanavio, F., Stacchini, A., Lauri, D., and Camussi, G. (1985) J. Immunol. 135, 2748-2753.

40) Bessin, P., Bonnet, J., Apffel, D., Soulard, C., Desgroux, L., Pelas, I., and Benveniste, J. (1983) Eur. J. Pharmacol. 86, 403-413.

41) Goldstein, B.M., Gabel, R.A., Huggins, F.J., Cervoni, P., and Crandall, D.L. (1984) Life Sci. 35, 1373-1378.

42) Maegraith, B.G., Andrews, W.H.H., and Wenyon, C.E.M. (1949) Lancet 2, 56-57.

43) McCuskey, R.S. (1966) Am. J. Anat. 119, 455-477.

44) Rappaport, A.M. (1973) Microvas. Res. 5, 212-228.

45) Hems, D.A., and Whitton, P.D. (1980) Physiol. Rev. 60, 1-50.

46) Hers, H.G. (1976) Ann. Rev. Biochem. 45, 167-189.

47) Hems, D.A., and Brosnan, J.T. (1970) Biochem. J. 120, 105-111.

48) Faupel, R.P., Seitz, H.J., and Tarnowski, W. (1972) Arch. Biochem. Biophys. 148, 509-522.

49) Buxton, D.B., Shukla, S.D., Hanahan, D.J., and Olson, M.S. (1984) 259, 1468-1471.

50) Koo, A., Liang, I.Y.S., and Cheng, K.K. (1976) Clin. Exp. Pharmacol. Physiol. 3, 391-395.

51) Reilly, F.D., McCuskey, R.S., and Cilento, E.V. (1981) Microvas. Res. 21, 103-116.

52) Koo, A., Tse, T.-F., and Yu, D.Y.C. (1979) Clin. Exp. Pharmacol. 6, 495-506.

53) Ljung, B., Isaksson, O., and Johansson, B. (1975) Acta Physiol. Scand. 94, 154-166.

54) Fisher, R.A., Kumar, R., Hanahan, D.J., and Olson, M.S. (1986) J. Biol. Chem. 261, 8817-8823.

55) Blair, J.B., James, M.E., and Foster, J.L. (1979) J. Biol. Chem. 254, 7579-7584.

56) Morgan, N.G., Blackmore, P.F., and Exton, J.H. (1983) J. Biol. Chem. 258, 5103-5109.

57) Pinckard, R.N., Farr, R.S., and Hanahan, D.J. (1979) J. Immunol. 123, 1847-1857.

58) Camussi, G., Tetta, C., Deregibus, M.C., Bussolino, F., Segoloni, G., and Vercellone, A. (1982) J. Immunol. 128, 86-94.

59) Buxton, D.B., Hanahan, D.J., and Olson, M.S. (1984) J. Biol. Chem. 259, 13758-13761.

60) Fisher, R.A., Kumar, R., Hanahan, D.J., and Olson, M.S. (1986) Fed. Proc. 45, 1838.

ROLE OF LOCAL [Ca+2] IN THE CONTROL OF CELL FUNCTION

Fredric S. Fay, David A. Williams, Gary Kargacin,
Robert W. Tucker* and Mary Scanlon

Dept. of Physiology
University of Massachusetts Medical School
55 Lake Avenue North
Worcester, MA 01655

*Oncology Center
Johns Hopkins University
School of Medicine
Baltimore, MD 21205

Ca^{+2} is believed to play an essential role in the regulation of cell function. While this has been suspected for many years, the inability to directly measure $[Ca^{+2}]$ in small cells of physiological interest precluded obtaining definitive insights into many aspects of this process. We have been interested in the mechanisms underlying the generation and regulation of force in smooth muscle and thus for many years, have been interested in the role of Ca^{+2} in this process.

We have pursued these questions directly at the cellular level by utilizing a system of enzymatically disaggregated smooth muscle cells (1). These cells appear to be unaltered by the isolation procedure; they respond to a wide range of natural stimuli by changes in contraction (2, 3) and, in general, represent a superb model system for addressing questions about the cellular and subcellular events underlying smooth muscle contraction.

The first indication that the contractile changes seen in these cells in response to application of a stimulus was due to calcium, came from observations during insertion of a micropipet into these single cells (4). During insertion of the pipet, there is a momentary leakage of ions from the medium into the cell, and the cell contracts. If this pipet is filled with an agent like EGTA or EDTA that binds very strongly to calcium and one pumps fluid into the cell containing these calcium chelators, the cell can be induced to re-extend. If one applies a second excitatory stimulus, one can induce the cells to contract again. Re-injection of more calcium chelator causes them to re-extend. So, one can, in fact, control the contractile state of the cell apparently just by varying calcium in this manner.

More direct evidence for the change in calcium underlying the contractile response to these cells was obtained from measurements of $[Ca^{+2}]$, in populations of these cells, with the fluorescent Ca^{+2} indicator, QUIN-2 (5). We found that stimulation of these cells by potassium depolarization or with carbachol, results in a rapid increase in $[Ca^{+2}]$. The $[Ca^{+2}]$ change is biphasic, exhibiting an initial brief, but large, transient increase followed by a secondary more prolonged small increase.

The time course and magnitude of these changes can be compared to the changes in contraction in cells loaded with this indicator. We find that the bulk of the calcium changes as well as the contractile changes observed in these cell suspensions exhibit generally similar time courses. The change in $[Ca^{+2}]$ clearly proceeds the change in contraction, which is what one would expect if calcium is, in fact, the mediator of the changes in contraction.

Further evidence for a role of calcium in controlling contraction comes from studies where we have studied the effect of exposing cells to inhibitory substances such as isoproterenol (ISO). In response to ISO, we find that the contractile response of these cells to excitatory stimuli is diminished. Associated with that, we find that the elevation in calcium induced by these stimuli is also suppressed (5). For example, there is a large depression of the rise in calcium associated with the action of the excitatory stimulus carbachol if cells are pre-incubated with isoproterenol. Associated with that, we find that the cells do not contract in response to this supramaximal concentration of carbachol. By contrast, in response to high potassium, we find there is no attenuation of the calcium transient, nor is there at these concentrations any effect on the contractile response. So, once again, calcium and contraction seem to be tightly associated.

The decrease in calcium that takes place within the cells in response to beta adrenergic stimulation comes about by activation of a wide range of processes within the cell. Binding of agents like isoproterenol (ISO) to its receptor activates an enzyme adenyl cyclase, leading to the production of cyclic AMP, the second messenger, which, in turn, activates a protein kinase, which in turn, we believe, leads to activation of a number of cellular processes (3). For one, we believe that ISO induces activation of the sodium/potassium pump, which steepens the sodium gradient, accelerates Na/Ca exchange which would have the effect of pumping calcium out of the cell (3). The activation of the sodium/potassium pump also would tend to hyperpolarize the membrane which would tend to close voltage-sensitive calcium channels within the membrane, again, diminishing calcium availability (6). There is also an activation of a potassium conductance mechanism which, again, decreases the membrane potential and further shuts down Ca^{+2} gates. We also have some evidence of a more indirect nature that indicates that there is an increase in the rate of pumping of calcium into storage sites within these cells (8).

The general finding is that a number of processes are activated by B-adrenergic activation of smooth muscle, all of which tend to drive calcium down within the cell. Similarly, in response to excitatory stimuli, we find that again a wide range of cellular processes are activated, all of which tend to drive calcium up within the cell, bringing about the observed physiological change (9, 10).

While the magnitude and timecourse of the rise in $[Ca^{+2}]$ in response to K^+ depolarization and carbachol stimulation are quite similar in magnitude and timecourse, they come about by different actions within the cell. In response to agents like carbachol we see that the increase in calcium appears to be independent of the presence or absence of high levels of calcium outside the cell whereas, the response to potassium depolarization is highly dependent on the presence of extracellular Ca^{+2}. Thus, some agents derive their Ca^{+2} from extracellular stores whereas others seem to be highly dependent upon calcium stored within the cell (5).

In order to directly visualize such stores and to get more direct insights into the cellular mechanisms involved in the control of cell function by calcium, we have developed methods to directly visualize calcium in living cells. The approach has been made possible by: 1) the development of new dyes such as Fura 2 that are calcium-sensitive and highly fluorescent (11), and; 2) the development of the digital imaging microscope, a tool for measuring fluorescence with sub-micron resolution at a number of wavelengths (12). With knowledge of some constants for the dye in the system we can calculate free calcium point by point within a cell. If we do that at high resolution in a resting smooth muscle, a map of free Ca^{+2} such as that shown in Figure 1 may be obtained (13).

The map reveals that there is a ring of high calcium around the periphery of the cell which we believe reflects calcium stored in the sarcoplasmic reticulum of these cells. It has the same distribution as sarcoplasmic reticulum as revealed in electron micrographs. The signal from this region responds to agents that specifically permeabilize that particular store (13). Beyond this region, where calcium is stored at high concentration along the cell periphery, we see lower values of $[Ca^{+2}]$ which we believe reflect calcium within the cytoplasm. This is the same space in which the contractile material is present presumably controlled by changes in calcium. The calcium concentration within that space is much lower than that in the sarcoplasmic reticulum. It is about 140 nanomolar. Very similar values are obtained by a variety of different techniques (13).

What happens when a signal is applied that causes the cell to contract? What we find is that there is a rapid rise in $[Ca^{+2}]$ within this compartment of the cell to around 750 nM, and several seconds thereafter the cell begins to contract and does so as long as the $[Ca^{+2}]$ is above resting levels. As the calcium again is restored back to its original level following cessation of the stimulus, the cell begins to re-extend again (14). There is a considerable lag between the rise in calcium and the increase in force, again, exactly as one would predict for a cause and effect relationship between the rise in calcium and the activation of the contractile machinery. When measuring calcium and force in the same single cell simultaneously, we find that there is about a 200 millisecond delay which probably reflects the kinetics of the reactions linking calcium arrival at the contractile machinery and activation of the contractile process. We believe that this lag is most probably imposed by the reactions causing phosphorylation of the myosin light chains involved in this process.

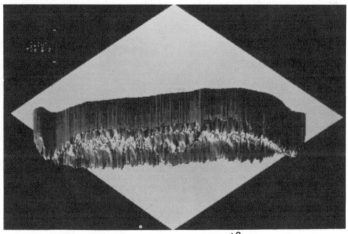

Figure 1. Map of spatial variation in $[Ca^{+2}]$ in resting smooth muscle cell obtained with Fura 2 using the digital imaging microscope (13). Vertical height proportional to the pCa at that location within the cell. The areas of highest Ca^{+2} are associated with sub-sarcolemmal sites, most probably sarcoplasmic reticulum, and over the nucleus.

The increase in calcium that we see in these cells in response to potassium stimulation or acetylcholine stimulation seems to plateau or reach a maximal level of around 750 to 1000 nM. We believe that this plateau or ceiling on the maximum increase in calcium is most probably set by a negative feedback of calcium on calcium entry into the cell. Certainly processes which transport Ca^{+2} out of the cytoplasm would also be an important determinant of the level at which the $[Ca^{+2}]$ ceiling is observed but the principal mechanism for setting this limit, we believe, reflects a negative feedback of calcium on calcium permeability. The existence of such a mechanism in these cells has already been reported (5).

How does the change in calcium from about 150 nM at rest to about 800 nM in response to maximal physiological stimuli correspond to the Ca^{+2} sensitivity of the contractile machinery. Is it sufficient to fully activate the contractile machinery? The answer is, quite probably, yes. Looking at the calcium sensitivity of the contractile process in saponin skinned single cells maximum activation is observed around 2000 nM $[Ca^{+2}]$ but almost complete activation is already seen at 1000 nanomolar $[Ca^{+2}]$. No contraction is observed at 100 nM $[Ca^{+2}]$ So, it seems that the strategies that the cell uses for controlling resting calcium and the ceiling set on maximum calcium in the cell corresponds well to the calcium sensitivity of the contractile machinery (15).

While $[Ca^{+2}]$ changes in the cytoplasm appear to control contraction, $[Ca^{+2}]$ changes in other cellular regions may also be expected to effect changes in those compartments. It is for this reason that we have also examined to what extent $[Ca^{+2}]$ within the nucleus reflects that in the cytoplasm. In resting smooth muscle cells, calculated $[Ca^{+2}]$ over the nuclear region appears to be higher than that in the cytoplasm (13). We have examined if the properties of the dye inside the nucleus are significantly altered in a way which might possibly explain this observation. We find that there is, in fact, no alteration in dye properties in the nucleus compared to that of the cytoplasm and are thus forced to look for a biological rather than a methodological basis for this observation. The difference in nuclear/cytoplasmic $[Ca^{+2}]$ suggests that calcium within the nucleus is independently regulated from that of the cytoplasm. In order to explore this regulatory mechanism, the $[Ca^{+2}]$ outside the cell was varied so as to induce changes in the $[Ca^{+2}]$ within the cytoplasm. We then determined how changes in cytoplasmic $[Ca^{+2}]$ affect calcium within the nucleus. We found that increases in cytoplasmic $[Ca^{+2}]$ above that at rest, led to very small increases in intranuclear $[Ca^{+2}]$, whereas a decrease in cytoplasmic $[Ca^{+2}]$ below that at rest led to significant decreases in intranuclear $[Ca^{+2}]$. This behavior is inconsistent with the notion that intranuclear $[Ca^{+2}]$ passively follows cytoplasmic $[Ca^{+2}]$ and suggests that there is a mechanism present within the nucleus for independently regulating its $[Ca^{+2}]$. It suggests that this mechanism would act to prevent changes in cytoplasmic $[Ca^{+2}]$ above rest from greatly affecting the intranuclear environment, perhaps screening the nucleus from fluctuations in $[Ca^{+2}]$ that take place within the cytoplasm of these cells as they contract in response to excitatory stimuli. We find just that. Movements of intranuclear $[Ca^{+2}]$, when $[Ca^{+2}]$ within the cytoplasm rises to greater than 1000 nM in response to K^+ or electrical stimulation, reveal that nuclear $[Ca^{+2}]$ seems to be maintained quite constant. It increases by, at most 50 nM, but goes no higher than about 300 nM. This suggests that the nucleus is screened from the fluctuations in cytoplasmic $[Ca^{+2}]$ that are associated with activation of these cells (14). Why might the nucleus be screened from fluctuations in cytoplasmic calcium? While we have no further information from these cells to answer this question, it may be that Ca^{+2} controls reactions within the nucleus that the cell might not wish to trigger on a contraction by contraction basis. The screening mechanism would thus tend to isolate the nucleus and intranuclear reactions from fluctuations in cytoplasmic $[Ca^{+2}]$ that take place during each contraction of these cells. Recent work in other cells (16) reveals the existence of enzymes within the nucleus that are calcium-sensitive, some of which control the structure of DNA, and it might be disadvantageous for the cell, for such reactions to be accelerated each time the smooth muscle cell contracted.

There are, however, situations where the calcium signal appears to be propagated into the nucleus. One example of that is the response of 3T-3 cells to mitogenic stimulation by PDGF (17). We find that in response to stimulation by growth factors, $[Ca^{+2}]$ within both nucleus and cytoplasm rises in response to this stimulus which leads eventually to mitotic activity in these cells. In such circumstances propagation of the calcium signal into the nucleus may have some important signaling effect. The rise in $[Ca^{+2}]$ induced by PDGF appears to be necessary for its mitogenic actin as loading these cells with calcium chelators at levels expected to blunt the calcium transient, strongly inhibits the mitogenic effect of such growth factors.

The studies which have been discussed to this point have focused on changes in $[Ca^{+2}]$ in the nucleus and cytoplasm. The calcium changes that take place within the cytoplasm within the resolution of our measurements appear to be entirely uniform. That is not true, however, for all cells which respond to stimulatory agents by a rise in $[Ca^{+2}]$ within the cytoplasm. One example of this is the human neutrophil which responds to agents like formyl-methionyl-leucyl-phenylalanine (FMLP), a peptide of bacterial origin, by changing from a stationary, basically round cell to a highly polarized cell. The cell will migrate in the direction of increasing concentrations of this chemo-attractant, which eventually triggers reactions in the cells that fight infection. We find that in response to this agent, the calcium within the cytoplasm of these cells increases, and this is associated with an increased polarization of the population of cells, which can also be observed at the single cell level (18). We can blunt the polarization response, as well as the calcium transient by acutely removing calcium from the extracellular medium suggesting that calcium plays a role in the development of the polarized phenotype. We cannot, however, mimic the response by adding a calcium ionophore like ionomycin, to these cells. Although calcium rises, we find no polarization response. The inability of ionomycin to produce a polarized cellular response is not due to the absence of some cellular co-factor required for Ca^{+2} action produced in the presence of FMLP as similar results are obtained with ionomycin in the presence of FMLP. These results suggest either that calcium is not involved in creating the polarized morphology and steering the cell towards the site of infection or alternatively that it is not a global increase in calcium that is required but rather a highly localized change in $[Ca^{+2}]$.

In order to investigate this we have measured the distribution of $[Ca^{+2}]$ in both resting and polarized neutrophils. Images of calcium distribution in these cells reveal that in a non-polarized resting cell there are bright spots along the edge which may represent calcium stored within regions of these cells along the periphery. The cytoplasm contains uniform $[Ca^{+2}]$. By comparison, when the cell is moving towards a chemo-attractant, we see a band of high calcium behind the leading edge. The tail has less calcium. We believe that these gradients of calcium within the cytoplasm, perhaps brought about by localized entry or pumping of Ca^{+2} may play a very important role in setting up and maintaining the polarized morphology of these cells and steering the cell up gradients of increasing levels of chemo-attractant, eventually to the site of infection.

In summary then, we find that changes in cytoplasmic $[Ca^{+2}]$ appear to mediate the action of many agents on cellular function. The changes in calcium often result from changes in several systems, all of which tend to drive calcium in the same direction. The magnitude of the change in $[Ca^{+2}]$

is limited by mechanisms which set a ceiling on the extent of the change in $[Ca^{+2}]$. The range of changes in $[Ca^{+2}]$ within the cytoplasm are well-matched to the calcium-sensitivity of contractile function, at least in the smooth muscle. Finally, changes in $[Ca^{+2}]$ are often localized to specific compartments of the cell resulting in very specific and localized control of the cell function, often resulting in a highly stereotypic response pattern from the cell as a whole.

Acknowledgements – We gratefully acknowledge the skilled technical assistance of Ms. Lisa Harris and Ms. Shirley Borsuk in these studies. Thanks also to Ms. Rita Hutchinson for expert secretarial help. This work was supported in part by grants from the NIH (HL 14523 and CA 34472) and the Muscular Dystrophy Association of America.

References

1. F.S. Fay and C.M. Delise, Contraction of isolated smooth muscle cells – structural changes, Proc. Natl. Acad. Sci. (USA) 70:641–645 (1973).
2. J.J. Singer and F.S. Fay, Detection of contraction of isolated smooth muscle cells, Am. J. Physiol. 232:C138–C143 (1977).
3. C.R. Scheid, T.W. Honeyman and F.S. Fay, Mechanism of B-adrenergic induced relaxation of smooth muscle, Nature 277:32–36 (1979).
4. F.S. Fay and S.R. Taylor, Relaxation of isolated smooth muscle cells induced by microinjection of cyclic nucleotides, Biophys. J. 21:184a (1978).
5. D.A. Williams and F.S. Fay, Calcium transients and resting levels in isolated smooth muscle cells as monitored with quin2, Am. J. Physiol. 250 (Cell Physiol. 19): C779–791 (1986).
6. J.V. Walsh Jr. and J.J. Singer, Identification and characterization of major ionic currents in isolated smooth muscle cells using the voltage-clamp technique, Pflugers Arch. 408:83–97 (1987).
7. H. Yamaguchi, T.W. Honeyman and F.S. Fay, Mechanisms of beta-adrenergic membrane hyperpolarization in single isolated smooth muscles, Amer. J. Physiol., Cell, submitted for publication.
8. C.R. Scheid and F.S. Fay, Effect of the B-adrenergic agent isoproterenol on the ^{42}K fluxes in isolated smooth muscle cells, Am. J. Physiol., Cell 246:C415–C421 (1984).
9. S.M. Sims, J.J. Singer and J.V. Walsh, Jr., Cholinergic agonists suppress a potassium current in freshly dissociated smooth muscle cells of the toad, J. Physiol. (London) 367:503–529 (1985).
10. L.H. Clapp, M.B. Vivaudou, J.V. Walsh, Jr. and J.J. Singer, Acetylcholine increases voltage-activated Ca^{2+} current in freshly dissociated smooth muscle cells, Proc. Natl. Acad. Sci. USA 84:2092–2096 (1987).
11. G. Grynkiewicz, M. Poenie and R.Y. Tsien, A new generation of Ca^{2+} indicators with greatly improved fluorescence properties, J. Biol. Chem. 260:3440–3450 (1985).
12. F.S. Fay, K.E. Fogarty and J.M. Coggins, Analysis of molecular distribution in single cells using a digital imaging microscope. in: "Optical Methods in Cell Physiology," P. De Weer and B. Salzberg, eds., John Wiley & Sons, (1986).
13. D.A. Williams, K.E. Fogarty, R. Y. Tsien and F.S. Fay, Calcium gradients in single smooth muscle cells revealed by the digital imaging microscope, Nature 318:558–561 (1985).
14. D.A. Williams, P.L. Becker and F.S. Fay, Regional changes in Ca^{++} underlying contraction of single smooth muscle cells, Science 235:1644–1648 (1987).
15. G.J. Kargacin and F.S. Fay, Physiological and structural properties of saponin skinned single smooth muscle cells, J. Gen. Physiol. 90 (1987).
16. N. Sahyoun, H. Levine and P. Cuatrecasas, Ca^{2+}/calmodulin-dependent protein kinases from the neuronal nuclear matrix and post-synaptic density are structurally related, Proc. Natl. Acad. Sci. USA 81:4311–4315 (1984).

17. F.S. Fay and R.W. Tucker, Studies of free cytosolic calcium (Ca_i) in quiescent Balb/c 3T3 cells using quin2 and fura 2, J. Cell Biol. 101:476a (1985).

18. M. Scanlon, Cellular Mechanism of Neutrophil Chemotaxis: The role of Ca^{+2}, as viewed with the fluorescent dye, fura-2, in the polarization of human polymorphonuclear leukocytes following stimulation with the chemoattractant, f-methionyl-leucyl-phenylalanine, Ph.D. Thesis (1987).

CALCIUM AND MAGNESIUM MOVEMENTS THROUGH SARCOPLASMIC RETICULUM, ENDOPLASMIC RETICULUM, AND MITOCHONDRIA

A.V. Somlyo, M. Bond, R. Broderick, and A.P. Somlyo

Pennsylvania Muscle Institute, University of Pennsylvania
Philadelphia, Pennsylvania 19104-6083

INTRODUCTION

Free cytoplasmic [Ca^{2+}] is normally maintained at or below micromolar levels by actively transporting cell membranes and organelles, and by binding to high affinity, Ca-binding proteins. Until recently, the structural identity of the organelles that normally regulate cytoplasmic Ca^{2+} has been the subject of considerable debate (A.P. Somlyo, 1984). The primary role, in skeletal muscles, of the well-organized sarcoplasmic reticulum (SR) is generally accepted (Ebashi and Endo, 1968; Martonosi and Beeler, 1983) but, because of the smaller volume of SR in smooth muscle (A.V. Somlyo, 1980; A.P. Somlyo, 1985a) and in cardiac muscle (Sommer and Johnson, 1979), its dominant role in regulating cytoplasmic Ca^{2+} was not as readily recognized. It had been suggested, erroneously in retrospect, that in these muscles and in nonmuscle cells, mitochondria play a major role in Ca^{2+} regulation. This conclusion was based largely on studies of isolated organelles and on compartmental analysis of [45]Ca fluxes, but the question whether the mitochondria or the endoplasmic reticulum (ER) regulate cytoplasmic Ca^{2+} could be conclusively resolved only by direct measurements of their calcium content in situ. This became possible with electron probe X-ray microanalysis (EPMA) (reviewed in A.P. Somlyo, 1985b) of rapidly frozen tissues. The results of these studies, that we summarize here, have shown that the ER, not mitochondria, are primarily responsible for physiological Ca^{2+} regulation and also revealed unexpected, and possibly physiologically significant, changes in mitochondrial magnesium.

CALCIUM AND MAGNESIUM CONTENT OF SARCOPLASMIC AND ENDOPLASMIC RETICULUM: THE EFFECTS OF ACTIVATION OF MUSCLE AND HORMONAL STIMULATION IN LIVER

Tetanic stimulation of frog skeletal muscle causes the release of approximately 60% of the total calcium stored in the terminal cisternae (TC) of the SR; the resultant rise in total cytoplasmic calcium is sufficient to saturate the Ca^{2+} binding sites on troponin and on the high affinity, soluble calcium binding protein, parvalbumin (A.V. Somlyo et al., 1981; 1985a). Influx of Mg^{2+} and K^+ into the TC accompanies the release of Ca^{2+}, although in amounts insufficient to account for the total charge released as Ca^{2+} (A.V. Somlyo et al., 1981; 1985a; Kitazawa et al., 1984). Therefore, we suggested that H^+ influx into the SR provides the remaining charge compensation. This is also consistent with the reported alkalinization of skeletal muscle during Ca^{2+} release (Baylor et al, 1987) and the very rapid movement of H^+ (or OH^-) across the SR membrane (Nunogaki and Kasai, 1986). The K^+ and Cl^- content of the TC also indicated that there is no large, maintained electrical potential across the SR membrane, either at rest or during a tetanus, although Ca^{2+} release is probably electrogeneic: it is not obligatorily coupled to the movement of any specific co- or counterion.

The time course of the posttetanic return of Ca^{2+} to the TC indicated the presence of two processes: one rapid and accounting for the initial 25% of return and the other slow, accounting for the remaining 75%. The rapid process accompanied relaxation and occurred at the rate of the SR Ca^{2+} pump removing Ca^{2+} from the Ca^{2+}-specific sites on troponin; the slow component accounted for Ca^{2+} redistribution after relaxation, and its rate was similar to the off-rate of Ca^{2+} from parvalbumin (A.V. Somlyo et al., 1985a; Robertson et al., 1981; Kretsinger et al., 1982).

The SR has also been identified in smooth muscle as the intracellular source of activator Ca^{2+} released by neurotransmitters (Bond et al., 1984a; Kowarski et al., 1985; and for review, A.P. Somlyo, 1985a). Even smooth muscles that contain a relatively small volume (about 2.5% of total cell volume) of SR can store sufficient Ca^{2+} for repeated maximal activation in the absence of extracellular Ca^{2+} (Bond et al., 1984a), suggesting that a sparsely developed endoplasmic reticulum could also play a similar role in nonmuscle cells.

The endoplasmic reticulum has been identified as a major Ca^{2+} storage site in nonmuscle cells in numerous studies (reviewed in A.P. Somlyo, 1984), showing accumulation of Ca^{2+} by both ER in situ and by isolated microsomes. This conclusion is in keeping with the phylogenetic relationship between the ER and the SR. The major structural question remaining is whether or not Ca^{2+} storage, uptake, and release, are segregated and occur in specialized regions of the interconnected ER. The continuous lumen between the rough and the smooth (A.P. Somlyo and A.V. Somlyo, 1975) and the central and peripheral (A.V. Somlyo, 1980) SR poses considerable difficulty in establishing whether the loss of Ca^{2+} from a given storage site, such as the central SR in smooth muscle (Kowarski et al., 1984) or the rough endoplasmic reticulum of hepatocytes (see below), reflects release through regulated Ca^{2+} channels at these same sites or diffusion to a distant, subplasmalemmal portion of the ER/SR. EPMA of stacks of rough ER in cryosections if intact liver (Fig. 1) established that in unstimulated liver these organelles store a significant proportion of hepatocellular Ca^{2+} (A.P. Somlyo et al., 1985). Furthermore, a brief (11 sec) injection of vasopressin into the portal anterior mesenteric vein of anesthetized rats prior to freezing the liver in vivo caused a highly significant (P<0.01) reduction of the Ca content of stacks of rough ER from 4.4 $\pm$ 0.2 to 2.6 $\pm$ 0.2 mmol/kg dry wt $\pm$ SEM (Bond et al., 1987). These and other results (Burgess et al., 1983) identify the ER as the major source of hormone-mobilizable Ca^{2+} in hepatocytes, although they clearly do not rule out the possibility that Ca^{2+} from other sources, such as the smooth ER that is not visualized in cryosections, could also be mobilized by hormones.

THE MECHANISMS OF Ca^{2+} RELEASE AND INFLUX

The mechanism of Ca^{2+} release from its intracellular storage site has been and, to a large extent, still remains one of the most interesting aspects of cellular regulation. Electromechanical coupling and pharmacomechanical coupling, originally defined on the basis of studies of smooth muscle (A.V. Somlyo and A.P. Somlyo, 1968), appear to be the two broad categories of mechanism-modulating cytoplasmic Ca^{2+} in most, if not all,

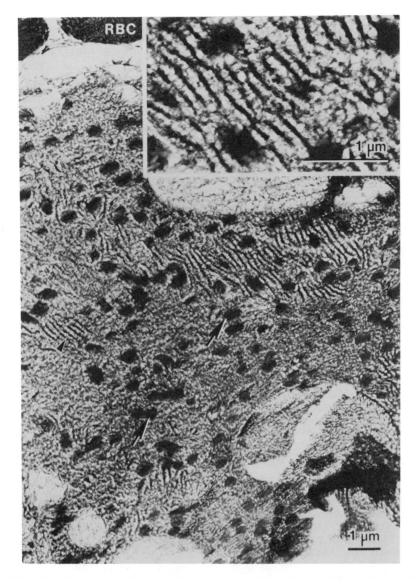

Fig. 1. Electron micrograph of cryosection of rat liver frozen in
situ. Mitochondria (arrows) and stacks of rough endoplasmic reticulum (ER) (arrowhead) are clearly identi-
fiable. The inset shows a region of rough ER at high
magnification. Note the close association of the rough
ER with the mitochondria, which could interfere with
separation of these organelles into isolated cell
fractions. (From A.P. Somlyo et al., 1987.)

cells. Electromechanical coupling, as the name implies, is mediated by
changes in cell membrane potential; it includes depolarization-induced Ca^{2+}
release from the SR (ER), as classically described for frog striated muscle
(Hodgkin and Horowicz, 1960), as well as Ca^{2+} influx through voltage-gated
Ca^{2+} channels (reviewed in Tsien et al., 1987). Pharmacomechanical
coupling, equally broadly defined, includes, but is not limited to, Ca^{2+}
influx through voltage-independent (ligand-gated) channels (A.P. Somlyo and
A.V. Somlyo, 1971; Benham and Tsien, 1987) and Ca^{2+} release from the SR/ER,
by a mechanism independent of the surface membrane potential.

223

Inositol 1,4,5-trisphosphate (InsP$_3$) has been established as the major second messenger-mediating Ca^{2+} release from the ER of nonmuscle cells (for review, Berridge and Irvine, 1984). Agonists can stimulate polyphosphatidylinositol turnover in depolarized smooth muscle (Baron et al., 1984), and InsP$_3$ can release Ca^{2+} (Suematsu et al., 1984; A.V. Somlyo et al., 1985b) and so, contract smooth muscle (A.V. Somlyo et al., 1985b). These observations and the rapid time course of contraction induced by InsP$_3$ released by laser photolysis from a photolyzable (caged) precursor (Walker et al., 1987) indicate its role as a physiological messenger of pharmacomechanical coupling in smooth muscle. The mechanism of electromechanical Ca^{2+} release, in contrast to the mechanism of pharmacomechanical Ca^{2+} release, is not understood (A.P. Somlyo, 1985c).

MITOCHONDRIAL CALCIUM AND MAGNESIUM: PHYSIOLOGY AND PATHOLOGY

The uniformly low (less than 3 nmol/mg mitochondrial protein) Ca^{2+} content of mitochondria in situ, in a variety of muscle and nonmuscle cells, and the absence of any significant change in mitochondrial Ca^{2+} during maximal, sustained contraction in muscle (A.P. Somlyo et al., 1979; Bond et al., 1984b; A.V. Somlyo et al., 1981), are clearly inconsistent with a significant physioloigcal role of mitochondria in regulating cytoplasmic Ca^{2+}. Assuming the ratios of free/bound Ca^{2+} estimated in isolated mitochondria [approximately 10^{-3} (Coll et al., 1983; Hansford and Castro, 1982)] to be valid in situ, mitochondrial matrix free Ca^{2+} is much lower than the K$_m$ of the mitochondrial Ca^{2+} efflux pathway that is required for mitochondria to establish a "set point" of [Ca^{2+}] in the cytoplasm (for review, Hansford, 1985; Nichols and Crompton, 1980). The low affinity (apparent K$_m$ 10-20 µM) of the mitochondrial uniporter for Ca^{2+} (Scarpa and Graziotti, 1973; for review, A.P. Somlyo et al., 1981) prevents mitochondria from regulating Ca^{2+} in intact cells, in which normal cytoplasmic free Ca^{2+} is generally submicromolar; the aforementioned failure of mitochondria to accumulate significant amounts of Ca^{2+}, even in maximally activated smooth muscle, indicates the absence of "cytoplasmic factors" that could sufficiently increase the affinity of mitochondria for Ca^{2+} to physiological levels. Recently, low Ca^{2+} (Kleineke and Soling, 1985), comparable to that measured with EPMA in situ, was found in mitochondria isolated from liver perfused with Ca^{2+}-free solutions. However, we must note that normal, endogenous mitochondrial Ca^{2+} in situ (Bond et al., 1984b) can also be reduced by the incubation of cells in Ca^{2+}-free solutions, indicating that measurements obtained on isolated organelles (and extrapolated to in situ values) must be viewed with caution.

The question of mitochondrial Ca^{2+} in liver has been of particular interest, given the importance of this organ in metabolic regulation. Once EMPA studies established that normal mitochondria contain low concentrations of Ca^{2+} (reviewed in A.P. Somlyo et al., 1987), subsequent work focused on the possibility that micromolar fluctuations in matrix free Ca^{2+} may regulate certain mitochondrial enzymes, such as pyruvate dehydrogenase (Denton et al., 1980). Consequently, having demonstrated that mitochondrial Ca^{2+} in the heptocytes of intact, anesthetized rats constitutes no more than 5% of total hepatocellular Ca^{2+} (A.P. Somlyo et al., 1985), we determined the effects of vasopressin and glucagon on mitochondrial Ca^{2+} in situ (Bond et al., 1987). These studies showed no significant change in mitochondrial Ca^{2+} following either brief (11 sec) injection of vasopressin alone or prolonged (11-1/2 min) injection of a combination of vasopressin and glucagon. The Ca^{2+} content of mitochondria in these experiments ranged between 1.0 and 2.3 mmol/kg mitochondrial dry wt (equivalent to approximately 1.0 and 2.3 nmol Ca^{2+}/mg mitochondrial protein), compared to a value of 1.3 to 1.7 mmol/kg dry mitochondrial wt of control and sham-injected animals. Any difference among these values was no greater than the biological, animal-to-animal, variation. Cytoplasmic Ca^{2+}, assessed by phosphorylase A activity, was increased by the hormones used in these experiments. Thus, these results indicate that mitochondrial matrix free Ca^{2+} either does not increase, or increases by less than the 0.2-0.3 µM detection limit, in rat liver stimulated with effective concentrations of vasopressin with or without glucagon. Thus, changes in mitochondrial Ca^{2+} are probably not obligatorily coupled to physiological fluctuations in cytoplasmic Ca^{2+}. The increased Ca^{2+} content of mitochondria isolated from perfused rat livers following treatment with vasopressin and glucagon (Altin and Bygrave, 1986; Assimacopoulos-Jeannet et al., 1986) may reflect different sensitivity of the perfused organ and/or inclusion of endoplasmic reticulum or a heterogenous mitochondrial population (A.P. Somlyo et al., 1978) in the mitochondrial fraction.

Mitochondrial Mg^{2+} increased by approximately 33%, from 43 to 57 mmol/kg dry wt, following prolonged intrajugular injection of vasopressin plus glucagon (Bond et al., 1987). Lesser, but nevertheless significant, increases in mitochondrial Mg^{2+} occurred following brief (11 sec) injection of vasopressin alone and with the manipulation associated with sham injection into the portal anterior mesenteric vein. These, and earlier observations on physiological fluctuations in mitochondrial Mg^{2+} during illumination of retinal rods (A.P. Somlyo and Walz, 1985) and in contracting smooth muscle (Bond et al., 1984b) suggest a physiological role for the active mitochondrial Mg^{2+} transport system identified in isolated mitochondria (Sloane et al., 1978). Inasmuch as mitochondrial pyruvate dehydrogenase is sensitive to Mg^{2+} as well as to Ca^{2+}, mitochondrial matrix free Mg^{2+} may regulate this, and possibly other, mitochondrial functions.

It is well known that mitochondria exposed to sufficiently high concentrations of free Ca^{2+} can accumulate massive amounts of Ca^{2+} in the presence of substrate (Carafoli, 1982) and may lead to pathological changes, particularly in cardiac muscle (e.g. Jennings et al., 1975; A.V. Somlyo et al., 1975). Abnormal mitochondrial Ca uptake in situ has been easily demonstrated in damaged smooth muscle (A.P. Somlyo et al., 1978, 1979) and in cardiac muscles (Chiesi et al., 1981) that had been permeabilized and exposed to high (approximately 10 µM) free Ca^{2+}. We have recently been able to reproduceably induce pathological mitochondrial Ca^{2+} loading in intact (unpermeabilized) smooth muscle by Na^+ loading these tissues, and removing the accumulated Na^+ through a oubain-resistant pathway, into Li^+ solution (Broderick and Somlyo, 1987). Such pathological Ca loading of mitochondria was reversible: all the accumulated (approximately 300 mmol/kg dry mitochondrial wt) was removed from mitochondria within one to two hours (Fig. 2). The normal maximal contractility, ultrastructure, and monovalent ion composition of these cells suggested that reversible mitochondrial Ca^{2+} loading was compatible with survival of smooth muscle cells.

A massive, approximately 3-fold increase in mitochondrial Mg^{2+} accompanied the pathological accumulation of mitochondrial Ca^{2+} (Broderick and Somlyo, 1987). This increase in mitochondrial Mg^{2+} occurred even when Ca^{2+} accumulation was reduced by reducing extracellular Ca^{2+} to 0.2 mM. However, Ca^{2+}-free (with EGTA) washout solutions abolished the uptake of not only Ca^{2+}, but also that of Mg^{2+} by mitochondria, in spite of the very large increases in cytoplasmic Mg^{2+}. These observations suggest that a certain level of cytoplasmic free Ca^{2+} or matrix Ca^{2+} is required for mitochondrial Mg^{2+} transport, and that the latter can be regulated independently of cytoplasmic Mg^{2+}. The combined accumulation of Ca^{2+} and Mg^{2+} by mitochondria under these conditions is also reminiscent of the increased Ca^{2+} and Mg^{2+} content of mitochondria isolated from vascular smooth muscle of atherosclerotic animals (Sloane et al., 1978; A.P. Somlyo et al., 1978), although the mechanism and significance of these observations remain to be established.

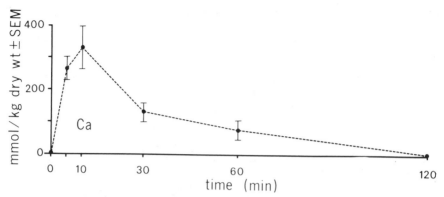

Fig. 2. Time course of mitochondrial Ca^{2+} loading/unloading in
rabbit portal vein. Tissue was Na^+-loaded for 3 h at
$37^\circ C$ (1 mM ouabain) and washed at time 0, with a Na^+-
free, K^+, Li^+ solution (1 mM ouabain) at $37^\circ C$, then flash
frozen. _In situ_ mitochondrial Ca^{2+} concentrations were
determined in cryosections by EPMA. Note that the
massive (>100-fold) increase in mitochondrial Ca^{2+},
induced by washing the Na^+-loaded tissue for 5 or 10 min
in the Na^+-free solution, was fully reversible with
continued incubation. Mitochondrial Ca^{2+} concentrations
are expressed as mean ± SEM; each point represents
analysis of 20-80 mitochondria from at least two animals.
(From Broderick and Somlyo, 1987.)

CONCLUSIONS

1) The sarcoplasmic and the endoplasmic reticulum are the intracellular organelles primarily regulating cytoplasmic free Ca^{2+}, and are the
major targets of Ca^{2+}-releasing hormones and their messengers.

2) Mitochondrial Ca^{2+} in normal cells is low, and mitochondria do not
play a significant role in the physiological regulation of cytoplasmic Ca^{2+}
in either muscle or nonmuscle cells. The available _in situ_ measurements
show no major (≥0.5 nmol/mg protein) change in mitochondrial Ca^{2+} in
hormone-stimulated liver and smooth muscle or in electrically-stimulated
skeletal muscle.

3) Mitochondrial Mg^{2+} _in situ_ shows physiological fluctuations influenced by hormones, raising the possibility that changes in matrix free Mg^{2+}
have metabolic regulatory functions.

4) Pathological accumulation of Ca^{2+} in mitochondria is reversible
and, at least in smooth muscle, can be accompanied by large increases in
mitochondrial Mg^{2+}.

ACKNOWLEDGEMENTS

Supported by NIH Grants HL 15835 and HL 07499 to the Pennsylvania
Muscle Institute; NIH Grant 38820 to M. Bond, Cleveland Clinic; and American Heart Association of Southeastern Pennsylvania Grant to R. Broderick.

REFERENCES

Altin, J.G., and Bygrave, F.L., 1986, Synergistic stimulation of Ca^{2+} uptake by glucagon and Ca^{2+}-mobilizing hormones in the perfused rat liver, Biochem J., 238:653-661.

Assimacopoulos-Jeannet, F., McCormack, M.G., and Jeanrenaud, B., 1986, Vasopressin and/or glucagon rapidly increase mitochondrial calcium and oxidative enzyme activities in the perfused rat liver, J. Biol. Chem., 261:8799-8804.

Baron, C.V., Cunningham, M., Strauss III, J.F., and Coburn, R.F., 1984, Pharmacomechanical coupling in smooth muscle may involve phosphatidylinositol metabolism, Proc. Natl. Acad. Sci. USA, 81:6899-6903.

Baylor, S.M., Hollingsworth, S., and Page, P., 1987, Myoplasmic pH transients monitored with indicator dyes in frog skeletal muscle fibers, Biophys. J., 51:549a.

Benham, C.D., and Tsien, R.W., 1987, A novel receptor-operated Ca^{2+}-permeable channel activated by ATP in smooth muscle, Nature, 328:275-278.

Berridge, M.J., and Irvine, R.F., 1984, Inositol trisphosphate, a novel second messenger in cellular signal transduction, Nature, 312:315-321.

Bond, M., Kitazawa, T., Somlyo, A.P., and Somlyo, A.V., 1984a, Release and recycling of calcium by the sarcoplasmic reticulum in guinea pig portal vein smooth muscle, J. Physiol. (London), 355:277-295.

Bond, M., Shuman, H., Somlyo, A.P., and Somlyo, A.V., 1984b, Total cytoplasmic calcium in relaxed and maximally contracted rabbit portal vein smooth muscle, J. Physiol. (London), 357:185-201.

Bond, M., Vadasz, G., Somlyo, A.V., and Somlyo, A.P., 1987, Subcellular calcium and magnesium mobilization in rat liver stimulated in vivo with vasopressin and glucagon, J. Biol. Chem., in press.

Broderick, R., and Somlyo, A.P., 1987, Calcium and magnesium transport in situ mitochondria: electron probe analysis of vascular smooth muscle, Circ. Res., in press.

Burgess, G.M., McKinney, J.S., Fabiato, A., Leslie, B.A., and Putney, Jr., J.W., 1983, Calcium pools in saponin-permeabilized guinea pig hepatocytes, J. Biol. Chem., 258:15336-15345.

Carafoli, E., 1982, The transport of calcium across the inner membrane of the mitochondria, in: "Membrane Transport of Calcium," E. Carafoli, ed., Academic Press, London.

Chiesi, M., Ho, M.M., Inesi, G., Somlyo, A.V., and Somlyo, A.P., 1981, Primary role of sarcoplasmic reticulum in phasic contractile activation of cardiac myocytes with shunted myolemma, J. Cell Biol., 91:728-742.

Coll, K.E., Joseph, S.K., Corkey, B.E., and Williamson, J.R., 1983, Determination of the matrix free Ca^{2+} concentration and kinetics of Ca^{2+} efflux in liver and heart mitochondria, J. Biol. Chem., 257:8696-8704.

Denton, R.M., McCormack, J.G., and Edgell, N.J., 1980, Role of calcium in the regulation of intramitochondrial metabolism, Biochem. J., 190:107-117.

Ebashi, S., and Endo, M., 1968, Calcium ion and muscle contraction, in: "Progress in Biophysics and Molecular Biology,", J.A.V. Butler and D. Noble, eds., Pergamon Press, Oxford and New York.

Hansford, R.G., 1985, Relation between mitochondrial Ca transport and control of energy metabolism, Rev. Physiol. Biochem. Pharmacol., 102:1-72.

Hansford, R.G., and Castro, F., 1982, Intramitochondrial and extramitochondrial free calcium concentrations of suspensions of heart mitochondria with very low, plausibly physiological, contents of total calcium, J. Bioenerg. Biomembr., 14:361-376.

Hodgkin, A.L., and Horowicz, P., 1960, Potassium contractures in single muscle fibers, J. Physiol., 153:386-403.

Jennings, R.B., Ganoti, C.E., and Reimer, K.A., 1975, Ischemic tissue injury, Am. J. Pathol., 81:179-198.

Kitazawa, T., Somlyo, A.P., and Somlyo, A.V., 1984, The effects of valinomycin on ion movements across the sarcoplasmic reticulum in frog muscle, J. Physiol. (London), 350:253-268.

Kleineke, J., and Soling, H.D., 1985, Mitochondrial and extramitochondrial Ca^{2+} pools in the perfused rat liver, J. Biol. Chem., 260:1040-1045.

Kowarski, D., Shuman, H., Somlyo, A.P., and Somlyo, A.V., 1985, Calcium release by norepinephrine from central sarcoplasmic reticulum in rabbit main pulmonary artery smooth muscle, J. Physiol. (London), 366:153-175.

Kretsinger, R.H., Thomasin, D., Lefevre, J., and Gillis, J.M., 1982, Parvalbumins and muscle relaxation: a computer simulation study, J. Muscle Res. Cell Motil., 3:377-398.

Martonosi, A.N., and Beeler, T.J., Mechanism of Ca^{2+} transport by sarcoplasmic reticulum, 1983, in: "Handbook of Physiology-Section 10. Skeletal Muscle," L.D. Peachey, R.H. Adrian, and S.R. Geiger, eds., American Physiological Society, Washington.

Nicholls, D.G., and Crompton, M., 1980, Mitochondrial calcium transport, FEBS Lett., 111:261-268.

Nunogaki, K., and Kasai, M., 1986, Determination of the rate of rapid pH equilibration across isolated sarcoplasmic reticulum membrane, Biochem. Biophys. Res. Commun., 140:934-940.

Robertson, S.P., Johnson, J.S., and Potter, J.D., 1981, The time course of Ca^{2+} exchange with calmodulin, troponin, parvalbumin and myosin in response to transient increases in Ca^{2+}, Biophys. J., 34:559-569.

Scarpa, A., and Graziotti, P., 1973, Mechanism for intracellular calcium regulation in heart. I. Stopped-flow measurements of Ca^{2+} uptake by cardiac mitochondria, J. Gen. Physiol., 62:756-772.

Sloane, B.F., Scarpa, A., and Somlyo, A.P., 1978, Vascular smooth muscle mitochondria: magnesium content and transport, Arch. Biochem. Biophys., 189:409-416.

Somlyo, A.P., 1984, Cellular site of calcium regulation, Nature, 308:516-517.

Somlyo, A.P., 1985a, Excitation-contraction coupling and the ultrastructure of smooth muscle, Circ. Res., 57:497-507.

Somlyo, A.P., 1985b, Calcium measurement with electron probe and electron energy loss analysis, Cell Calcium, 6:197-212.

Somlyo, A.P., 1985c, Excitation-contraction coupling. The messenger across the gap, Nature, 316:298-299.

Somlyo, A.P., and Somlyo, A.V., 1971, Electrophysiological correlates of the inequality of maximal vascular smooth muscle contraction elicited by drugs, in: "Vascular Neuroeffector Systems," J.A. Bevan, R.F. Furchgott, R.A. Maxwell, and A.P. Somlyo, eds., S. Karger AG, Basel.

Somlyo, A.P., and Somlyo, A.V., 1975, Ultrastructure of smooth muscle, in: "Methods of Pharmacology, Vol. 3," E.E. Daniel and D.M. Paton, eds., Plenum Press, New York.

Somlyo, A.P., and Walz, B., 1985, Elemental distribution in Rana pipiens retinal rods: quantitative electron probe analysis, J. Physiol. (London), 358:183-195.

Somlyo, A.P., Somlyo, A.V., Shuman, H., Sloane, B., and Scarpa, A., 1978, Electron probe analysis of calcium compartments in cryosections of smooth and striated muscles, Ann. N.Y. Acad. Sci., 307:523-544.

Somlyo, A.P., Somlyo, A.V., and Shuman, H., 1979, Electron probe analysis of vascular smooth muscle: composition of mitochondria, nuclei and cytoplasm, J. Cell Biol., 81:316-335.

Somlyo, A.P., Somlyo, A.V., Shuman, H., Scarpa, A., Endo, M., and Inesi, G., 1981, Mitochondria do not accumulate significant Ca concentrations in normal cells, in: "Calcium Phosphate Transport Across Bio-membranes," F. Bronner and M. Peterlik, eds., Academic Press, New York.

Somlyo, A.P., Bond, M., and Somlyo, A.V., 1985, The calcium content of mitochondria and endoplasmic reticulum in liver rapidly frozen in situ, Nature, 314:622-625.

Somlyo, A.P., Somlyo, A.V., Bond, M., Broderick, R., Goldman, Y.E., Shuman, H., Walker, J.W., and Trentham, D.R., 1987, Calcium and magnesium movements in cells and the role of inositol trisphosphate in muscle, in: "Cell Calcium and the Control of Membrane Transport," D.C. Eaton and L.J. Mandel, eds., Rockefeller University Press, New York.

Somlyo, A.V., 1980, Ultrastructure of vascular smooth muscle, in: "The Handbook of Physiology: The Cardiovascular System. Vol. II. Vascular Smooth Muscle," D.F. Bohr, A.P. Somlyo, and H.V. Sparks, eds., American Physiological Society, Washington.

Somlyo, A.V., and Somlyo, A.P., 1968, Electromechanical and pharmacomechanical coupling in vascular smooth muscle, J. Pharmacol. Exp. Ther., 159:129-145.

Somlyo, A.V., Silcox, J., and Somlyo, A.P., 1975, Electron probe analysis and cryoultramicrotomy of cardiac muscle: mitochondrial granules, in: "Proceedings of the Thirty-Third Annual Meeting of the Electron Microscopy Society of America," G.W. Bailey, ed., Electron Microscopy Society of America, Baton Rouge.

Somlyo, A.V., Somlyo, A.P., Gonzalez-Serratos, H., Shuman, H., McClellan, G., and Somlyo, A.P., 1981, Calcium release and ionic changes in sarcoplasmic reticulum of tetanized muscle: an electron probe study, J. Cell Biol., 90:577-594.

Somlyo, A.V., McClellan, G., Gonzalez-Serratos, H., and Somlyo, A.P., 1985a, Electron probe X-ray microanalysis of post tetanic Ca and Mg movements across the sarcoplasmic reticulum in situ, J. Biol. Chem., 260:6801-6807.

Somlyo, A.V., Bond, M., Somlyo, A.P., and Scarpa, A., 1985b, Inositol-trisphosphate ($InsP_3$) induced calcium release and contraction in vascular smooth muscle, Proc. Natl. Acad. Sci. USA, 82:5231-5235.

Sommer, J.R., and Johnson, E.A., 1979, Ultrastructure of cardiac muscle, in: "Handbook of Physiology Section 2: The Cardiovascular. System Vol. I. The Heart," R.M. Berne, N. Sperelakis, and S.R. Geiger, eds., American Physiological Society, Washington.

Suematsu, E., Hirata, M., Hashimoto, T., and Kuriyama, H., 1984, Inositol 1,4,5-trisphosphate releases Ca^{2+} from intracellular store sites in skinned single cells of porcine coronary artery, Biochem. Biophys. Res. Commun., 120:481-485.

Tsien, R.W., Hess, P., McCleskey, E.W., and Rosenberg, R.L., 1987, Calcium channels: mechanism of selectivity, permeation, and block, Ann. Rev. Biophys. Chem., 16:265-290.

Walker, J.W., Somlyo, A.V., Goldman, Y.E., Somlyo, A.P., and Trentham, D.R., 1987, Kinetics of smooth and skeletal muscle activation by laser pulse photolysis of caged inositol 1,4,5-trisphosphate, Nature, 327:249-251.

RELATIONSHIP BETWEEN CYTOSOLIC FREE CALCIUM ION CONCENTRATION AND THE

CONTROL OF PYRUVATE DEHYDROGENASE IN ISOLATED CARDIAC MYOCYTES AND

SYNAPTOSOMES

Richard G. Hansford

Gerontology Research Center
National Institute on Aging
Baltimore, Maryland

INTRODUCTION

It is clear that the Ca^{2+} ion plays a central role in the mechanism
of excitation-contraction coupling in muscle and in excitation-secretion
coupling at the synapse (see, e.g. Katz, 1970; Rasmussen, 1981). What is
perhaps not so well known is that in each case Ca^{2+} may also act as a
signal to cause the activation of mitochondrial substrate oxidation. The
increase in cytosolic free Ca^{2+} ($[Ca^{2+}]_c$) on excitation of muscle cells
activates actomyosin ATPase; the increase in $[Ca^{2+}]_c$ in a presynaptic
nerve terminal upon depolarization triggers transmitter substance
release, and occurs essentially at the same time as a decrease in the
magnitude of Na^+ and K^+-ion gradients, the latter requiring increased
flux through the Na^+-K^+-ATPase for re-establishment. In each case,
tissue activation is accompanied by increased utilization of ATP, with a
consequently increased demand upon oxidative phosphorylation to
re-synthesize ATP. It is the thesis of this article that Ca^{2+} acts as a
signal to enhance mitochondrial substrate oxidation, so that energy
supply and demand can be kept in balance.

METHODS

The procedures for the isolation of synaptosomes, the loading with
Quin-2, and the studies of synaptosomal $[Ca^{2+}]_c$ and pyruvate
dehydrogenase have all been described in detail in Hansford and Castro
(1985).

The procedures for the isolation of Ca^{2+}-tolerant cardiac myocytes from adult rats, the Quin-2 studies of myocytes and the measurement of myocyte pyruvate dehydrogenase have been described by Hansford (1987).

RESULTS AND DISCUSSION

Activation of Pyruvate Dehydrogenase by Ca^{2+} in Isolated Heart and Brain Mitochondria.

Micromolar concentrations of Ca^{2+} ions activate pyruvate dehydrogenase phosphatase (Denton et al., 1972; Petitt et al., 1972) and thereby increase the fraction of pyruvate dehydrogenase which exists in the active, dephospho, form (PDH_A). It is seen from Fig. 1a that such an activation is also seen when intact, coupled and respiring heart mitochondria are exposed to an increase in the free Ca^{2+} concentration of the surrounding medium, over the range 10^{-7} to 10^{-6}M. It is noted that whereas the sensitivity of enzyme interconversion to extra-mitochondrial free Ca^{2+} concentration can be manipulated by changing the Na^+ concentration (Fig. 1 and Denton et al., 1980) or Mg^{2+} concentration (Denton et al., 1980; Hansford, 1981), procedures which change the magnitude of the Ca^{2+} ion gradient across the mitochondrial membrane, 50% activation of pyruvate dehydrogenase occurs at a Ca^{2+} concentration of 0.41 µM when the ionic composition of the medium mimics that of the cytosol. This value is somewhere between resting and stimulated values for $[Ca^{2+}]_c$ in heart cells: see below.

Fig. 1b shows that brain mitochondria show a very similar sensitivity to Ca^{2+}, when exposed to media containing Na^+ and Mg^{2+} at concentrations appropriate for the cytosol (10 mM and 1 mM, respectively).

These results with isolated mitochondria established the plausibility of control of pyruvate dehyrdogenase by Ca^{2+}. But can it be demonstrated to occur in the intact cell? The remainder of the article describes work from this laboratory in which we follow the response of PDH_A content to the elevation of $[Ca^{2+}]_c$, to determine whether this is consistent or not with a cause-and-effect relationship.

Response of PDH_A Content and of $[Ca^{2+}]_c$ of Cardiac Myocytes to Plasma Membrane Depolarization.

Suspensions of cardiac myocytes can be depolarized in a graded fashion by treatment with increasing extracellular K^+ concentration: such a procedure leads to an increase in $[Ca^{2+}]_c$ (Powell et al., 1984; Sheu et al., 1986). It is seen from Table 1 that the elevation of extracellular K^+ concentration from 50 to 80 mM also gives rise to a progressive increase in PDH_A content. Similarly, the treatment of the myocytes with veratridine plus ouabain, a procedure which might be expected to lead to plasma membrane depolarization and cellular Na^+-overload (Escueta and Appel, 1969; Ohta et al., 1973), gives rise to a large increase in PDH_A content.

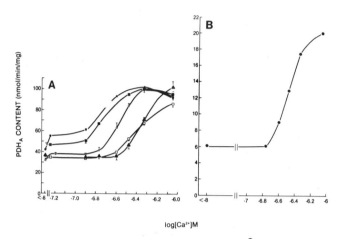

Fig. 1. Effect of varying extramitochondrial Ca^{2+} concentration on the PDH_A content of respiring coupled mitochondria from a. heart and b. brain. Mitochondria were incubated in media containing the indicated $[Ca^{2+}]$, stabilized with EGTA buffers, and sampled for PDH_A content when enzyme interconversion had reached a steady state. a. Mitochondria were from rat heart and were oxidizing glutamate plus malate: full details are given in the original paper. Concentrations of Na^+ in the incubation were: ●, none; ■, 0.1 mM; O, 1 mM; □, 10 mM; ▲, 20 mM. (Redrawn from Hansford, 1981). b. Mitochondria were from rat brain and were oxidizing succinate in a medium containing 10 mM Na^+ and 1 mM Mg^{2+}: full details are given in the original paper. (Redrawn from Hansford and Castro, 1985).

The response of $[Ca^{2+}]_c$ to these interventions is shown in Fig. 2. Raising $[K^+]$ to 40 mM gives a larger increase (a) than does raising $[K^+]$ to 10 mM (b). Ouabain alone, added to inhibit the Na^+-K^+-ATPase (Escueta and Appel, 1969), gives a very modest increase in $[Ca^{2+}]_c$, consistent with the known insensitivity of the rat to cardiac glycosides (c). However, ouabain does potentiate the effect of a non-saturating concentration of veratridine (e), which acts through holding open Na^+-channels (Ohta et al., 1973; Blaustein and Goldring, 1975). Veratridine alone gives a large, rapid increase in $[Ca^{2+}]_c$ (d) when added to the high concentration (25 μM) used for the pyruvate dehydrogenase studies.

TABLE 1

Effect of ruthenium red and ryanodine on the increase in PDH_A content
of cardiac myocytes induced by KCl and veratridine plus ouabain

	Condition	PDH_A (% of Total)
a.	5 mM KCl	31.7 ± 1.4 (32)
	20 mM KCl	39.5 ± 0.6 (4)
	40 mM KCl	49.5 ± 4.6 (6)
	55 mM KCl	49.3 ± 3.6 (8)
	80 mM KCl	60.6 ± 3.9 (11)
b.	5 mM KCl + ruthenium red	31.5 ± 2.7 (3)
	40 mM KCl + ruthenium red	38.7 ± 2.3 (3)
	55 mM KCl + ruthenium red	35.2 ± 3.0 (5) †
	80 mM KCl + ruthenium red	37.8 ± 3.3 (7) *
c.	20 mM KCl + ryanodine	39.8 ± 4.1 (3)
	40 mM KCl + ryanodine	56.0 ± 6.9 (8)
	55 mM KCl + ryanodine	62.3 ± 7.0 (8)
	80 mM KCl + ryanodine	72.7 ± 9.2 (8)
d.	5 µM veratridine	37.6 ± 4.5 (6)
	25 µM veratridine	51.0 ± 1.9 (10)
	25 µM veratridine + 0.2 mM ouabain	57.6 ± 3.9 (8)
	0.2 mM ouabain	45.6 ± 5.0 (5)
	25 µM veratridine + 0.2 mM ouabain + ruthenium red	35.8 ± 2.0 (10) **
e.	25 µM veratridine + 0.2 mM ouabain + ryanodine	52.6 ± 4.1 (3)

†$p < 0.05$
*$p < 0.005$ **$p < 0.001$

Suspensions of rat cardiac myocytes were incubated and sampled for
PDH_A content as described in the original paper. The basal medium
contained 5 mM KCl: higher concentrations of K^+ were achieved by
mixing volumes of an isotonic medium in which K^+ replaced Na^+ ions.
Sampling was 10 min after the addition to the suspension of
K^+-containing medium or of veratridine plus ouabain, as appropriate.
Where indicated, ruthenium red and ryanodine were added 3 min before
the K^+-containing medium or veratridine, to give concentrations of
12 µM, and 1 µM, respectively. Data are presented as the mean $\pm$
SEM, with the number of preparations in parentheses.

Values of PDH_A are significantly lower in the presence of ruthenium
red than in otherwise identical incubations omitting ruthenium red:
†$p < 0.05$; *$p < 0.005$; **$p < 0.001$. From Hansford (1987).

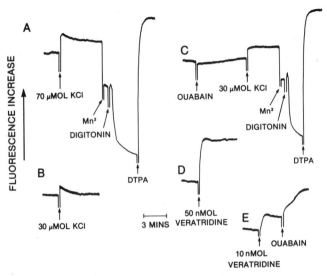

Fig. 2. The effect of plasma membrane depolarization on the
fluorescence of suspensions of cardiac myocytes loaded
with Quin-2. Cells were incubated at 3.5 mg of
protein/ml in medium containing 7.5 μM Quin-2/AM, for
30 min at 37°. This generated cells containing 0.73
nmol of Quin-2/mg protein. After this loading step,
the cells were washed by centrifugation and used for
the fluorescence studies shown. Where indicated, Mn
Cl_2 was added to 0.1 mM to quench the fluorescence of
extracellular Quin-2, digitonin was added to 5 μM to
allow the Mn^{2+} to react with intracellular Quin-2, and
diethylenetriaminepentaacetic anhydride (DTPA) was
added to 1 mM to remove Mn^{2+} from the Quin-2/Mn^{2+}
-chelate, and therefore generate maximal fluorescence.
Full details are given in the original paper. From
Hansford (1987).

It is clear that there is a relation between the degree of increase
in $[Ca^{2+}]_c$ shown in Fig. 2 and the degree of increase in PDH_A content
shown in Table 1. It is not possible, in our opinion, to define the
changes in $[Ca^{2+}]_c$ more quantitatively, as the calibration of the
fluorescence signal from Quin-2 is marred by the apparent presence of
more than one compartment for the dye within the cell (see Hansford, 1987
and Staddon and Hansford, 1986 for more discussion).

Whenever $[Ca^{2+}]_c$ is sufficiently elevated, a muscle will undergo
contraction and the availability of ADP to the mitochondria will increase. Pyruvate dehydrogenase interconversion is sensitive to changes

in the mitochondrial ATP/ADP ratio, as ADP inhibits the pyruvate dehydrogenase kinase (Hucho et al., 1972; see also Hansford, 1976) and so the
question arises as to how important are changes in $[Ca^{2+}]_c$ per se in
signaling metabolic demand to this enzyme system, vis a vis changes in
ATP/ADP ratio which occur consequent to muscle contraction. The
following arguments bear on this point.

     a. The presence of ruthenium red, an inhibitor of the uptake of
Ca^{2+} by the mitochondria (Moore, 1971) largely prevents any increase in
PDH_A content due to high concentrations of K^+ or to treatment with
veratridine + ouabain (Table 1). Yet ruthenium red does not attenuate
the response of $[Ca^{2+}]_c$ to these interventions (results not shown). Nor
does ruthenium red alter the frequency of spontaneous "waving" which
occurs in a significant fraction of these cell populations and which has
been taken to reflect values of $[Ca^{2+}]_c$ (Kort et al., 1985).

     b. Treatment of the cell suspensions with ryanodine, an inhibitor
of sarcoplasmic reticulum Ca^{2+} transport (Sutko and Kenyon, 1983) renders
the cells totally quiescent when viewed under the microscope, but has no
effect on the elevation of PDH_A content in response to the interventions
shown in Table I.

     c. Loading of the cells with the Ca^{2+}-chelating agent Quin-2, to an
intracellular content of 0.5 to 0.7 nmol per mg of protein, makes the
cells totally quiescent, but does not diminish the response of PDH_A
content to procedures which elevate $[Ca^{2+}]_c$. These data are presented in
Table 2.

TABLE 2

Effect of addition of KCl and of veratridine plus ouabain on the
PDH_A content of Quin 2-loaded cardiac myocytes

Condition	PDH_A (% of Total)
5 mM KCl	34.2 + 4.6 (6)
20 mM KCl	41.5 (2)
40 mM KCl	45.3 + 3.1 (4)
55 mM KCl	44.7 + 5.1 (5)
80 mM KCl	57.3 + 5.5 (3)
25 μM veratridine + 0.2 mM ouabain	62.5 + 2.8 (4)

The experiment was conducted as described for Table 1, with the
exception that the myocytes were loaded with Quin 2 by a prior 30
min incubation with 7.5 μM Quin 2/AM. The data are derived from the
number of experiments indicated but only three preparations of cells
were used. From Hansford (1987).

From these results, it seems quite clear that increased mechanical work is not a pre-requisite for the activation of pyruvate dehydrogenase and that the enzyme system is capable of responding to changes in $[Ca^{2+}]_c$ alone. However, that does not rule out a supplementary effect of a decreased mitochondrial ATP/ADP ratio in actively-contracting heart muscle and it is noted that the degree of mechanical work performed by the "waving" cells in this study is likely to be very small compared to their work-load in the animal. Nevertheless, the efficacy of the Ca^{2+}-signal is established.

Response of PDH_A Content and of $[Ca^{2+}]_c$ of Synaptosomes to Plasma Membrane Depolarization. Pinched-off presynaptic nerve-terminals formed on homogenization of brain cortical tissue (synaptosomes) provided a convenient vehicle in which to study pyruvate dehydrogenase interconversion. We adopted a very similar approach to that described above, in an attempt to dissect apart the respective contributions of Ca^{2+} and of the ATP/ADP ratio to dehydrogenase regulation.

Depolarization of synaptosomes by increasing medium K^+ ion concentration from 4 to 33 mM resulted in a modest increase in PDH_A ($60.2 \pm 2.7\%$ of total activity rose to $69.2 \pm 2\%$, in work with 9 preparations of synaptosomes. Treatment with veratridine, which is considered to depolarize neuronal preparations by holding open Na^+ channels (Ohta et al., 1973; Blaustein and Goldring, 1975) gave a larger increase in enzyme activity (Table 3), and therefore was used for subsequent studies.

It is seen from Table 3 that the increase in PDH_A content due to veratridine is only partly diminished if EGTA is added just prior to the alkaloid, such that transplasmalemmal influx of Ca^{2+} is interdicted.

When $[Ca^{2+}]_c$ is monitored in suspension of synaptosomes by the use of Quin-2 (Fig. 3) it is seen that the addition of 10 μM veratridine causes a large increase in $[Ca^{2+}]_c$, with 1 μM being less effective. The addition of EGTA just prior to veratridine, to decrease extracellular Ca^{2+} concentration to approximately 0.15 μM, entirely prevents any rise in $[Ca^{2+}]$ - Fig. 4b. Thus, only a portion of the rise in PDH_A content caused by depolarization of the synaptosomes by veratridine can be attributed to a mechanism based on Ca^{2+}.

The same conclusion emerges from a study of the effect of Ruthenium Red. It is seen that this inhibitor leads to a profound lowering of

236

resting values of PDH_A, but does not completely abolish the increase due to veratridine (Table 3). Ruthenium Red does not at all diminish the rise in $[Ca^{2+}]_c$ due to veratridine (Fig. 4a), indicating that it does not inhibit transplasmalemmal influx of Ca^{2+} in synaptosomes. Thus, the results are consistent with Ruthenium Red acting by preventing uptake of Ca^{2+} into the mitochondria in response to a rise in $[Ca^{2+}]_c$, as it does in the cardiac myocytes; however, Ca^{2+} is not the only signal to pyruvate dehydrogenase interconversion generated by exposure to veratridine.

TABLE 3

Response of pyruvate dehydrogenase to depolarization of synaptosomes
with veratridine

	Preincubation Conditions	Addition	PDH_A (% of Total PDH	
1	-	-	68+1 (13)	
2	-	Veratridine (30 μM)	81+1 (19)	p<0.001 vs 1
3	EGTA (0.67 mM)		69+1 (6)	
4	EGTA (0.67 mM)	Veratridine (30 μM)	80+3 (6)	p<0.001 vs 1
5	-	Veratridine (30 μM) + Ouabain (0.45 mM)	74+1 (13)	p<0.005 vs 2; N.S. vs 6
6	-	Ouabain (0.45 mM	71+1 (9)	p<0.05 vs 1
7	-	Veratridine (30 μM) + EGTA (1.3 mM)	73+1 (18)	p<0.005 vs 1; P<0.001 vs 2
8	-	EGTA (1.3 mM)	69+1 (4)	
9	Ruthenium Red (20 μM)		42+2 (7)	p<0.001 vs 1
10	Ruthenium Red (20 μM)	Veratridine (30 μM)	53+1 (9)	p<0.001 vs 9

Synaptosomes were incubated at 37° in a medium comprising 0.13 M NaCl, 4 mM KCl, 1 mM $CaCl_2$, 1 mM $MgSO_4$, 20 mM Na Hepes, 1.2 mM Na phosphate and 10 mM D-glucose, of pH 7.4. As indicated, further components were also present in some experiments ("preincubation"). At 20 min, veratridine was added, except in the control incubation (1), in which no further addition was made. Where indicated, ouabain and EGTA were added 5 sec before veratridine, to give the concentrations indicated. Portions of the incubation were removed at 25 min and assayed for PDH_A as described in the original paper. Results are mean values $\pm$ SEM with the number of experiments in parentheses. The maximal activity of pyruvate dehydrogenase was 7.04 $\pm$ 0.14 nmol/min/mg of protein at 25°, in 24 preparations of synaptosomes. (From Hansford and Castro, 1985).

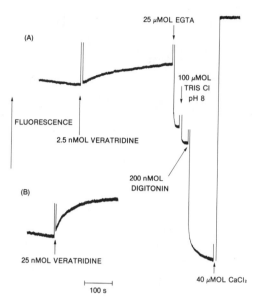

Fig. 3. The effect of plasma membrane depolarization on the fluorescence of suspensions of synaptosomes loaded with Quin 2. Synaptosomes were loaded by exposure to 100 μM Quin-2/AM at 37° for 60 min. Fluorescence was recorded as described in the original paper. The effects of adding veratridine to 1 μM (a) and to 10 μM (b) are contrasted. (From Hansford and Castro, 1985).

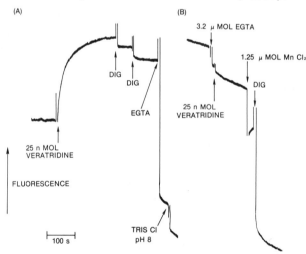

Fig. 4. The response of synaptosomal $[Ca^{2+}]_c$ to depolarization with veratridine (a) in the absence of extracellular Ca^{2+} and (b) in the presence of Ruthenium Red. In (a) EGTA was added 15 sec before the veratridine, to give an extracellular free Ca^{2+} concentration of approximately 0.15 μM. In (b) the synaptosomes were incubated with 4 μM Ruthenium Red from the beginning of the experiment. (From Hansford and Castro, 1985).

The same conclusion emerges from the effect of the cardiac glycoside ouabain, which inhibits the Na^+-K^+-ATPase (Esueta and Appel, 1969). This is seen in Table 3 to diminish partially the increase in PDH_A content due to veratridine. This suggests that a portion of the response of PDH_A content to the addition of veratridine reflects the effect of a decreased ATP/ADP ratio, caused by enhanced activity of the Na^+-K^+-ATPase, or of a consequent decrease in the mitochondrial NADH/NAD^+ ratio.

General Discussion: Consequences for Bioenergetics. In both cardiac myocytes and synaptosomes the depolarization of the plasma membrane leads to an increase in $[Ca^{2+}]_c$ and an increased content of PDH_A. It is clear that in the myocyte experiments the increase in $[Ca^{2+}]_c$ is an important part of the mechanism of enzyme regulation. In view of the localization of the pyruvate dehydrogenase complex within the mitochondrion, it is highly likely that a net influx of Ca^{2+} into the mitochondrion is necessary for the activation of pyruvate dehydrogenase to occur, and that this transport process is the locus for the inhibition by Ruthenium Red. This would support the findings and conclusions of McCormack and England (1983), based on experiments with the intact heart.

The experiments with synaptosomes yielded quantitatively different results. It was possible to establish a role for Ca^{2+} in the activation of pyruvate dehydrogenase, but this was not the only mechanism involved. It seems possible to infer that decreases in the cell ATP/ADP ratio were probably also involved, and this is not surprising in view of the very active Na^+-K^+-ATPase in neuronal preparations.

In addition, it should be pointed out that these experiments were designed to show whether changes in $[Ca^{2+}]_c$ could lead to changes in PDH_A content. In both preparations, the answer was affirmative. There is no intent to deny a role for control by ATP/ADP and NADH/NAD^+ ratios, acting at the level of enzyme interconversion. It is thought likely that increased $[Ca^{2+}]$ in the mitochondrial matrix, and a decreased ATP/ADP ratio, serve to activate not only pyruvate dehydrogenase but also NAD-linked isocitrate dehydrogenase (Denton et al., 1978) and 2-oxoglutarate dehydrogenase (McCormack and Denton, 1979). The experimental design of the present studies does not closely relate to the functioning of heart and nerve, in that depolarization of the plasma membrane was maintained. In the case of heart, this prohibits the generation of normal action potentials and, therefore, contractions. Hence, quantitative conclusions on relative importance of Ca^{2+} and adenine nucleotide signals to enzyme activation would not be of clear relevance to the physiology of the organ.

In general terms, it is apparent that activation of dehydrogenases increases the potential activity of oxidative phosphorylation by either increasing mitochondrial NADH/NAD$^+$ ratios, or at least minimizing the decline in this parameter, when the tissue is exposed to a higher work load. The relevant parameters are presented in Fig. 5, which is schematic in nature.

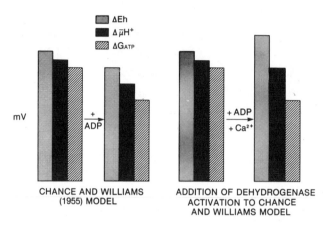

Fig. 5. Energetics of oxidative phosphorylation; the effect of superimposing the activation of dehydrogenases by Ca^{2+} and ADP on the classical model. The height of each bar represents one of the thermodynamic quantities involved in oxidative phosphorylation. ΔEh is the difference in observed reduction potentials between the redox couple acting as an electron donor and the couple acting as an acceptor for a given redox loop, or loops, of the respiratory chain. In the experiments of Johnson and Hansford (1977) and Hansford and Castro (1981), two spans were considered, from NADH/NAD$^+$ to cytochrome C Fe^{++}/Fe^{+++}. $\Delta\bar{\mu}$H$^+$ is the proton electrochemical gradient, or protonmotive force of Mitchell (1966,1979). The parameter measured is multiplied by an assumed stoichiometry of protons-per-site to allow the comparison with the other thermodynamic parameters. ΔG$_{ATP}$ is the free energy of synthesis of ATP, under prevailing conditions of concentration of reactants and products and Mg^{2+}. The purpose of this plot is didactic, and it is accordingly stylized. For real results, the reader is referred to Johnson and Hansford (1977).

On the basis of the chemiosmotic theory of energy transduction (Mitchell, 1966, 1979) the rate of hydrogen flow down the respiratory chain is driven by the drop in free energy between the ΔEh of the span of the respiratory chain being considered and the proton electrochemical gradient $\Delta\bar{\mu}H^+$. Equally, the rate of phosphoryl group transfer to ADP is driven by the free energy drop between the $\Delta\bar{\mu}H^+$ and the free energy of ATP synthesis, under prevailing cellular conditions (ΔG_{ATP}). An increase in NADH/NAD$^+$ due to dehydrogenase activation necessarily increases the ΔEh component for the respiratory chain as a whole, as the terminal acceptor couple $1/2\ O_2/H_2O$ is unchanged. Given near-equilibrium at sites 1 and 2, and non-equilibrium at site 3 (see Hansford, 1980, for a review), the increase in NADH/NAD$^+$ ratio would be expected to raise the cytochrome c Fe^{++}/Fe^{+++} ratio, and thus the flux through site 3. The enhanced rate of respiration would be expected to lead to elevated values of $\Delta\bar{\mu}H^+$. The latter change in turn will make possible higher rates of phosphorylation of ADP and the generation of elevated values of the ATP/ADPxPi ratio in the steady-state.

Unlike the situation in liver where the response to Ca^{2+}-mobilizing hormones involves an increase in ATP/ADP and NADH/NAD$^+$ ratios (Siess et al., 1977; Bryla et al., 1977; Staddon and Hansford, 1987) activated states in excitable tissues are normally associated with increased availability to the mitochondrion of both Ca^{2+} and ADP. Increased availability of ADP per se leads to a drop in $\Delta\bar{\mu}H^+$, because it acts as a substrate for the proton-transporting ATP-synthase (Mitchell 1966, 1979). In turn respiration is activated and the steady-state mitochondrial NADH/NAD$^+$ ratio tends to fall. This is a re-statement in chemiosmotic terms of the classic Chance and Williams (1956) mechanism of respiratory control. Superimposed on this, we believe, is activation of dehydrogenases by Ca^{2+} and, indeed, by ADP (Denton et al., 1972; Pettit et al., 1972; Hansford, 1972; Hucho et al., 1972; Denton et al., 1978; McCormack and Denton, 1979). The net effect of activation of both ATP-synthase (by ADP) and of pyruvate, NAD-isocitrate and 2-oxoglutarate dehydrogenases (by Ca^{2+} and by ADP) is that mitochondrial NADH/NAD$^+$ ratios decreases little, if at all, on activation: certainly they decrease less than they would on the Chance and Williams (1956) model. In heart mitochondria oxidizing 2-oxoglutarate, the NADH/NAD$^+$ ratio does not change on adding both ADP and Ca^{2+}, to 0.5-1 μM (Hansford and Castro, 1981), in an experiment simulating the imposition of a heavier work load: with suspensions of cardiac myocytes the mitochondrial NADH/NAD$^+$ ratio changes very little on depolarization of the cells with elevated concentrations of KCl (not shown). In mitochondria from fly flight muscle, a tissue which is exquisitely well adapted to energy transduction and which shows dehydro-genase-level control to a very pronounced degree, the addition of ADP plus Ca^{2+} (0.5-1 μM) results in an increase in $NADH/NAD^+$ ratio, when the substrate is pyruvate plus glycerol 3-phosphate (Hansford and Sacktor, 1971). At the same time, rates of O_2-uptake are increased by 30 fold.

The consequence of this preservation, or enhancement, of $NADH/NAD^+$ ratio in the face of increased energy demand upon the mitochondria is that the free energy drop between ΔEh and $\Delta \bar{\mu} H^+$ and between $\Delta \bar{\mu} H^+$ and ΔG_{ATP} can be increased, allowing higher rates of oxidative phosphorylation, without ΔG_{ATP} being allowed to fall to the point where the $ATP/ADPxPi$ ratio could no longer support the ATP-driven reactions of the rest of the cell.

REFERENCES

Blaustein, M. P., and Goldring, J. M., 1975, Membrane potentials in pinched-off presynaptic nerve terminals monitored with a fluorescent probe: evidence that synaptosomes have potassium diffusion poten-tials, J. Physiol. (Lond.), 247:589.

Bryla, J., Harris, E. J., and Plumb, J. A., 1977, The stimulatory effect of glucagon and dibutyryl cyclic AMP on ureogenesis and gluconeogen-esis in relation to the mitochondrial ATP content, FEBS Lett., 80:443.

Chance, B., and Williams, G. R., 1956, The respiratory chain and oxidative phosphorylation, Adv. Enzymology, 17:65.

Denton, R. M., McCormack, J. G., and Edgell, N. J., 1980, Role of calcium ions in the regulation of intramitochondrial metabolism. Effects of Na^+, Mg^{2+} and ruthenium red on the Ca^{2+}-stimulated oxidation of oxoglutarate and on pryruvate dehydrogenase activity in intact rat heart mitochondria, Biochem. J., 190:107.

Denton, R. M., Randle, P. J., and Martin, B. R., 1972, Stimulation by Ca^{2+} of pyruvate dehydrogenase phosphate phosphatase, Biochem. J., 128:161.

Denton, R. M., Richards, D. A., and Chin, J. G., 1978, Calcium ions and the regulation of NAD^+-linked isocitrate dehydrogenase from the mito-chondria of rat heart and other tissues, Biochem. J., 176:899.

Escueta, A. V., and Appel, S. H., 1969, Biochemical studies of synapses in vitro. II. Potassium transport, Biochemistry, 8:725.

Hansford, R. G., 1972, The effect of adenine nucleotides upon the 2-oxo-glutarate dehydrogenase of blowfly flight muscle, FEBS Lett., 21:139.

Hansford, R. G., 1976, Studies on the effects of coenzyme A-SH: acetyl coenzyme A, nicotinamide adenine dinucleotide: reduced nicotinamide adenine dinucleotide and adenosine diphosphate: adenosine triphos-phate ratios on the interconversion of active and inactive pyruvate dehydrogenase in isolated rat heart mitochondria, J. Biol. Chem., 251:5483.

Hansford, R. G., 1980, Control of mitochondrial substrate oxidation, Curr. Top. Bioenergetics, 10:217.

Hansford, R. G., 1981, Effect of micromolar concentrations of free Ca^{2+} ions on pyruvate dehydrogenase interconversion in intact rat heart mitochondria, Biochem. J., 194:721.

Hansford, R. G., 1987, Relation between cytosolic free Ca^{2+} and the con-trol of pyruvate dehydrogenase in isolated cardiac myocytes, Biochem. J., (in press).

Hansford, R. G., and Castro, F., 1981, Effect of micromolar concentrations of free calcium ions on the reduction of heart mitochondrial NAD (P) by 2-oxoglutarate, Biochem. J., 198:525.

Hansford, R. G., and Castro, F., 1985, Role of Ca^{2+} in pyruvate dehydrogenase interconversion in brain mitochondria and synaptosomes, Biochem. J., 227:129.

Hansford, R. G., and Sacktor, B., 1971, Oxidative metabolism of Insecta, in: "Chemical Zoology," Vol. 6, Part B. M. Florkin and B. T. Scheer, eds., Academic Press, New York and London, p. 213.

Hucho, F., Randall, D. D., Roche, T. E., Burgett, M. W., Pelley, J. W., and Reed, L. J., 1972, α-Keto acid dehydrogenase complexes. XVII Kinetic and regulatory properties of pyruvate dehydrogenase kinase and pyruvate dehydrogenase phosphatase from bovine kidney and heart, Arch. Biochem. Biophys., 151:328.

Johnson, R. N., and Hansford, R. G., 1977, The nature of controlled respiration and its relationship to protonmotive force and proton conductance in blowfly flight-muscle mitochondria, Biochem. J., 164:305.

Katz, A. M., 1970, Contractile proteins of the heart, Physiol. Rev., 50: 63.

Kort, A. A., Capogrossi, M. C., and Lakatta, E. G., 1985, Frequency, amplitude, and propagation velocity of spontaneous Ca^{++}-dependent contractile waves in intact adult rat cardiac muscle and isolated myocytes, Circ. Res., 57:844.

McCormack, J. G., and Denton, R. M., 1979, The effects of calcium ions and adenine nucleotides on the activity of pig heart 2-oxoglutarate dehydrogenase complex, Biochem. J., 180:533.

Mitchell, P., 1966, Chemiosmotic coupling in oxidative and photosynthetic phosphorylation. Glynn Research, Bodmin.

Mitchell, P., 1979, Compartmentation and communication in living systems. Ligand conduction: a general catalytic principle in chemical, osmotic and chemiosmotic reaction systems, Eur. J. Biochem., 95:1.

Moore, C. L., 1971, Specific inhibition of mitochondrial Ca^{2+} transport by ruthenium red, Biochem. Biophys. Res. Commun., 42:298.

Ohta, M., Narahashi, T., and Keeler, R. F., 1973, Effect of veratrum alkaloids on membrane potential and conductance of squid and crayfish giant axons, J. Pharmacol. Exp. Ther., 184:143.

Pettit, F. H., Roche, T. E., and Reed, L. J., 1972, Function of calcium ions in pyruvate dehydrogenase phosphatase activity, Biochem. Biophys. Res. Commun. 49:563.

Powell, T., Tatham, P. E. R., and Twist, V. W., 1984, Cytoplasmic free calcium measured by Quin 2 fluorescence in isolated ventricular myocytes at rest and during potassium-depolarization, Biochem. Biophys. Res. Commun., 122:1012.

Rasmussen, H., 1981, "Calcium and cAMP as synarchic messengers," Wiley and Sons, New York.

Sheu, S.-S., Sharma, V. K., and Uglesity, A., 1986, Na^{+}-Ca^{2+} exchange contributes to increase of cytosolic Ca^{2+} concentration during depolarization in heart muscle, Am. J. Physiol. 250:C651.

Siess, E. A., Brocks, D. G., Lattke, H. K., and Wieland, O. H., 1977, Effect of glucagon on metabolite compartmentation in isolated rat liver cells during gluconeogenesis from lactate, Biochem. J. 166:225.

Staddon, J. M., and Hansford, R. G., 1986, 4-β-Phorbol 12-myristate 13-acetate attenuates the glucagon-induced increase in cytoplasmic free Ca^{2+} concentration in isolated rat hepatocytes, Biochem. J. 238:737.

Staddon, J. M., and Hansford, R. G., 1987, The glucagon-induced activation of pyruvate dehydrogenase in hepatocytes is diminished by 4β-phorbol 12-myristate 13-acetate: a role for cytoplasmic Ca^{2+} in dehydrogenase regulation, Biochem. J. (in press).

Sutko, J. L., and J. L. Kenyon. 1983. Ryanodine modification of cardiac muscle responses to potassium-free solutions. Evidence for inhibition of sarcoplasmic reticulum calcium release. J. Gen. Physiol., 82:385.

THE ACTIVATION OF PYRUVATE DEHYDROGENASE BY GLUCAGON IN HEPATOCYTES IS

DIMINISHED BY PHORBOL MYRISTATE ACETATE: A ROLE FOR CYTOPLASMIC CALCIUM IN

DEHYDROGENASE REGULATION

James M.Staddon and Richard G.Hansford

National Institutes of Health
National Institute on Aging
Gerontology Research Center
4940 Eastern Ave., Baltimore, MD 21224

INTRODUCTION

It is known that glucagon, vasopressin and phenylephrine each cause an increase in the active, non-phosphorylated, form of the intramitochondrial enzyme pyruvate dehydrogenase (PDHa) when added to suspensions of hepatocytes (Assimacoupolos-Jeannet et al.,1983; Oviasu & Whitton,1984). The interconversion is mediated by a specific kinase and phosphatase (see Reed,1981). The observation that the phosphatase can be activated by Ca2+ (Denton et al.,1972) has led to the proposal that the increase in PDHa content occurring in response to the hormones may be due to an increase in the mitochondrial Ca2+ content, [Ca2+]m, occurring as a consequence of an increase in the concentration of cytoplasmic free Ca2+, [Ca2+]c, (Denton & McCormack,1980). Consistent with this hypothesis is the observed increase in [Ca2+]c in hepatocytes in response to glucagon, vasopressin and phenylephrine (Charest et al.,1983; Berthon et al.,1984; Thomas et al.,1984; Sistare et al.,1985; Staddon & Hansford,1986). Further, the PDHa content of liver mitochondria can be regulated by extramitochondrial, physiological, free [Ca2+] (McCormack,1985).

Phorbol myristate acetate, PMA, by antagonizing the increases in [Ca2+]c due to glucagon (Staddon & Hansford,1986) and phenylephrine, but not vasopressin, (Cooper et al.,1985; Lynch et al.,1985) allowed us to investigate whether or not the increase in PDHa in response to the hormones is related to the increase in [Ca2+]c. NAD(P)H content of the cells was also measured to include changes in the activity of the other intramitochondrial Ca2+-sensitive enzymes NAD+-isocitrate dehydrogenase and 2-oxoglutarate dehydrogenase (see Denton & McCormack,1980).

Methodology and the sources of materials have previously been described (see Staddon & Hansford,1986; Staddon & Hansford,1987).

RESULTS AND DISCUSSION

Hormone Effects on PDHa and the Influence of PMA

Glucagon, vasopressin and phenylephrine each caused an increase in PDHa in hepatocytes from fed rats (Fig.1a), confirming the previous reports. The total activity of PDH was 4.67±0.28 (n=8) nmol/min per mg of cell protein. Thus resting PDHa was 22% of the total activity and was increased, respectively, to 49, 36 and 26% in the presence of glucagon, vasopressin and phenylephrine. PMA alone had no effect on PDHa, or on the ability of vasopressin to increase PDHa (Fig.1b). However, the phorbol ester did significantly diminish the activation due to glucagon and completely inhibited that due to phenylephrine. Thus the influence of PMA on the ability of different agonists to increase PDHa is entirely as expected, if indeed $[Ca2+]c$ determines $[Ca2+]m$ and thereby PDHa.

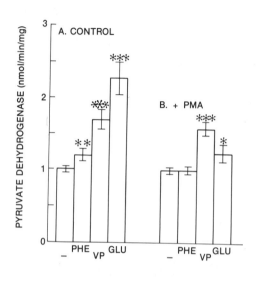

Figure 1. Activation of PDH by phenylephrine, vasopressin and glucagon in hepatocytes and the influence of PMA.

Hepatocytes were incubated at 37°C in physiological saline containing 2.5mM$-CaCl2$ and 0.5% albumin. The cells were pretreated with 500nM$-$PMA for 3min and then the various agonists were added. The PDHa content was assayed at 30°C 5min later. Values shown are means $\pm$ S.E.M. for 6-8 cell preparations. Statistical significance of the difference in values with respect to the control is: $*P{<}0.05$; $**P{<}0.01$; $***P{<}0.001$. The final concentrations of agonists were: 25μM$-$phenylephrine (PHE); 25nM$-$vasopressin (VP); 10nM$-$glucagon (GLU). From Staddon & Hansford (1987).

Hormone Effects on NAD(P)H Fluorescence and the Influence of PMA

Glucagon, phenylephrine and vasopressin each caused an increase in NAD(P)H fluorescence in hepatocytes (Fig.2a,c,e). The interpretation of such an increase is complex. There are, however, several lines of evidence indicating that it may be due to an increase in the rate of mitochondrial NADH formation. Inhibition of the respiratory chain is unlikely as the hormones increased oxygen consumption (Balaban & Blum,1982; Assimacoupolos -Jeannet et al.,1983). Prior treatment of the cells with 5μM$-$rotenone and 20mM$-\beta-$DL$-$hydroxybutyrate, to reduce mitochondrial NAD+, prevented the hormones from causing the increase in fluorescence. Conversely, pretreatment with 0.2mM$-$aminooxyacetate and 20mM$-$ethanol did not block the response to the hormones (results not shown). The latter conditions reduce cytoplasmic NAD+ while blocking the transfer of redox equivalents into the mitochondria.

PMA alone caused small, nonreproducible, changes in NAD(P)H fluorescence. The phorbol ester, however, consistently compromised the increase seen in response to glucagon (Fig.2b) and greatly diminished that due to phenylephrine (Fig.2d): in contrast, PMA was without influence on the increase due to vasopressin (Fig.2f). Thus NAD(P)H fluorescence changes in concert with $[Ca2+]c$, consistent with a causal relationship.

In conclusion, PMA, presumably by a mechanism involving the activation of protein kinase C (Castagna et al.,1982), leads to an attenuation of the ability of glucagon to raise $[Ca2+]c$ in hepatocytes (Staddon & Hansford,1986). The present work establishes a similar attenuation of the glucagon-induced increases in both PDHa and mitochondrial NADH content. The parallel behaviour of these three parameters is in strong support of the thesis that changes in [Ca2+]c due to glucagon do exert meaningful effects on intramitochondrial Ca2+-sensitive dehydrogenase activity via changes in [Ca2+]m.

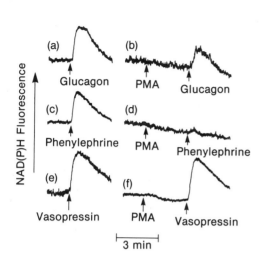

Figure 2. Effects of glucagon, phenylephrine and vasopressin on NAD(P)H fluorescence in hepatocytes and the influence of PMA.

The incubation of the hepatocytes is described in the legend to Fig.1. The cells were excited with light at 365nm; emitted light was measured at wavelengths greater than 460nm. The concentrations of added compounds are given in Fig.1. Fluorescence is in arbitrary units. Increases in fluorescence due to glucagon, phenylephrine and vasopressin, added in the presence of PMA, are respectively 54+5% (n=11; P<0.001), 9+2% (n=3;P<0.001) and 106+6% (n=5) of the changes obtained in the absence of the phorbol ester.

REFERENCES

Assimacoupolos-Jeannet,F., McCormack,J.G. & Jeanrenaud,B.,1983, FEBS Lett.,159:83-88.
Balaban,R.S. & Blum,J.J.,1982, Am.J.Physiol.,242:C172-C177.
Berthon,B., Bent,A., Mauger,J-P. & Claret,M.,1984, FEBS Lett., 167:19-24.
Castagna,M., Takai,Y., Kaibuchi,K., Sano,K., Kikkawa,U. & Nishizuka,Y., 1982, J.Biol.Chem.,257:7847-7851.
Charest,R., Blackmore,P.F., Berthon,B. & Exton,J.H., 1983, J.Biol.Chem., 258:8769-8773.
Cooper,R.H., Coll,K.E. & Williamson,J.R.,1985, J.Biol.Chem.,260:3281-3288.
Denton,R.M. & McCormack,J.G.,1980, FEBS Lett.,119:1-8
Lynch,C.J., Charest,R., Bocckino,S.B., Exton,J.H. & Blackmore,P.F., 1985, J.Biol.Chem.,260:2844-2851.
McCormack,J.G.,1985, Biochem.J.,231:581-595.
Oviasu,O.A. & Whitton,P.D., 1984, Biochem.J.,224:181-186
Reed,L.J.,1981, Curr.Top.Cell.Reg.,18:95-129.
Sistare,F.D., Picking,R.A. & Haynes,R.C., 1985, J.Biol.Chem., 260:12744-12747.
Staddon,J.M. & Hansford,R.G.,1986, Biochem.J.,238:737-743.
Staddon,J.M. & Hansford,R.G.,1987, Biochem.J.,in press.
Thomas,A.P., Alexander,J. & Williamson,J.R.,1984, J.Biol.Chem., 259:5574-5583.

HORMONAL REGULATION OF INTRAMITOCHONDRIAL Ca^{2+} AND OXIDATIVE METABOLISM IN MAMMALIAN TISSUES

James G. McCormack* and Richard M. Denton**

*Department of Biochemistry, University of Leeds,
Leeds LS2 9JT, United Kingdom, and
**Department of Biochemistry, University of Bristol
Medical School, Bristol BS8 1TD, United Kingdom

INTRODUCTION

In mammalian cells, many of the hormones which stimulate energy-requiring processes such as contraction or secretion do so by causing increases in the cytoplasmic concentration of Ca^{2+} (1). The increased supply of ATP which is thus required is achieved by a concomitant stimulation of oxidative metabolism by the hormones (2). However, in many of these instances there appear to be little or no decreases or even increases in the cellular ATP/ADP and NADH/NAD$^+$ concentration ratios, and therefore this raises the question as to how these increases in oxidative metabolism are achieved. This article will review some of the growing evidence which suggests that at least a part of the mechanism may involve an increase in the concentration of Ca^{2+} in the mitochondrial matrix and the resultant activation of three key Ca^{2+}-sensitive intramitochondrial dehydrogenases. All of these enzymes produce NADH and it is argued that this increased NADH production may be an important means whereby cells can increase oxidative metabolism yet maintain high ATP/ADP ratios. Another important consequence arising from such a scheme is that it suggests that the primary function of the Ca^{2+}-transport system of the mitochondrial inner membrane under normal physiological conditions in mammalian cells is to relay changes in cytoplasmic Ca^{2+} concentrations into the mitochondrial matrix and, hence, to control the concentration of Ca^{2+} in this compartment rather than to buffer or set cytoplasmic Ca^{2+} concentrations as suggested by others (see 3,4).

THE Ca^{2+}-SENSITIVE INTRAMITOCHONDRIAL ENZYMES

The Ca^{2+}-activated intramitochondrial enzymes are the pyruvate (PDH), NAD$^+$-isocitrate (NAD-ICDH) and 2-oxoglutarate (OGDH) dehydrogenases. Ca^{2+} activates PDH indirectly by causing increases in the amount of active, non-phosphorylated, PDH (PDH$_a$) through activation of PDH phosphate phosphatase (5), whereas it activates NAD-ICDH (6) and OGDH (7) more directly by causing decreases in their respective K_m values for threo-D$_s$-isocitrate and 2-oxoglutarate. These enzymes are all exclusively intramitochondrial in mammalian tissues. The effective Ca^{2+} concentration range is approximately 0.1-10 M and half-maximal effects are observed at about 1 µM Ca^{2+} in each case, and each enzyme can be activated several-fold by Ca^{2+}. Sr^{2+} can mimic the effects of Ca^{2+} on the enzymes, but at approximately 10-fold higher concentrations. The Ca^{2+}-sensitive properties have been found in extracts of all vertebrate tissues so far studied, but not in invertebrates (8), suggesting that Ca^{2+}-regulation may be a recent evolutionary acquisition.

PDH, NAD-ICDH, and OGDH are generally regarded to be key regulatory sites in mammalian oxidative metabolism, and they can all also be activated by increases in the ADP/ATP and NAD^+/NADH concentration ratios (7). However, this "intrinsic" regulation by local metabolite end-products appears to be distinct and largely independent to that exerted by Ca^{2+} which can thus be viewed as "extrinsic" (9) as it therefore may potentially allow a means whereby extracellular agents such as hormones could override the intrinsic mechanisms. This concept is in agreement with the observations and ideas outlined in the Introduction. Interestingly, the "intrinsic" regulatory properties can also be observed in extracts of non-vertebrate tissues and indeed they are probably the main means of control in these instances (10).

The three mammalian enzymes are known to show similar sensitivity to 0.1–10 μM extramitochondrial Ca^{2+} when they are located in uncoupled mitochondria as they do in mitochondrial extracts. This can be demonstrated under conditions of apparent free-equilibrium of Ca^{2+} across the mitochondrial inner membrane, suggesting that the enzymes retain similar Ca^{2+}-sensitivity in their natural locale, and thus their Ca^{2+}-sensitive properties can be used as probes for the estimation of intramitochondrial Ca^{2+} concentrations (11).

Ca^{2+}-TRANSPORT AND Ca^{2+}-CYCLING BY MAMMALIAN MITOCHONDRIA

Under normal cellular conditions, the concentration of Ca^{2+} to which the enzymes are exposed is determined by the relative rates of Ca^{2+} uptake and egress across the mitochondrial inner membrane, and the extramitochondrial $[Ca^{2+}]$. Ca^{2+}-uptake is by a uniporter mechanism which is driven electrophoretically by the membrane potential set up by proton extrusion by the respiratory chain (see 2–4). It can be inhibited physiologically by Mg^{2+} ions or artificially by ruthenium red. Recently it has been shown that it may be activated by spermine (12). The major pathway for Ca^{2+} egress is by electroneutral exchange with Na^+ ions which themselves are then egressed by the Na^+/H^+ exchanger, i.e., this process is also ultimately driven by respiration. Na^+/Ca^{2+} exchange can be inhibited physiologically by Ca^{2+} ions and artificially by diltiazem and other similar drugs. There is also a less well-characterized Na^+-independent pathway (perhaps $2H^+$/Ca^{2+}), and the relative activity of this with respect to the Na^+-dependent pathway appears to vary in mitochondria prepared from different tissues.

Thus, it is envisaged that Ca^{2+} ions continuously cycle across the mitochondrial inner membrane (13). However, under normal physiological conditions it can be calculated that this would not account for more than 0.5–1% of the maximal respiratory capacity of the mitochondria.

EVIDENCE FOR THE REGULATORY ROLE OF INTRAMITOCHONDRIAL Ca^{2+} USING ISOLATED MITOCHONDRIA

Studies have been carried out using intact, fully coupled mitochondria from a number of mammalian tissues, including rat heart, skeletal muscle, liver, kidney, brain, and adipose tissue (2). These studies demonstrated that the three Ca^{2+}-sensitive matrix enzymes, when located within such mitochondria, can all be activated by increases in the extramitochondrial concentration of Ca^{2+} within the expected physiological range, i.e., approximately 0.05-5 μM. This activation is achieved in the presence of physiological concentrations of Mg^{2+} and Na^+. In the absence of either or both of these effector cations the effective ranges for extramitochondrial $[Ca^{2+}]$ are decreased. This is shown in Table 1 where the effects of Na^+ and Mg^{2+} on the $K_{0.5}$ values for extramitochondrial Ca^{2+} in the activations of PDH and OGDH in rat heart and liver mitochondria are given, together with effects of uncoupler and ruthenium red. It should be noted in this context that Ca^{2+} transport across the mitochondrial inner membrane can be effectively studied in this way by using the enzymes as probes for matrix Ca^{2+}.

Table 1. Summary of Activation Constants ($K_{0.5}$ Values) for the Effects of Extramitochondrial Ca^{2+} in Stimulating PDH and OGDH Activities in (a) Rat Heart and (b) Liver Mitochondria[a]

	$K_{0.5}$ Values for Ca^{2+} (nM) in Rat			
	(a) Heart Mitochondria		(b) Liver Mitochondria	
	For Activation Of:		For Activation Of:	
Additions to Mitochondrial Incubations	PDH	OGDH	PDH	OGDH
None	39	21	109	121
10 mM NaCl	210	82	184	202
1 mM MgCl$_2$	185	96	356	420
NaCl plus MgCl$_2$	480	330	484	560
1 M FCCP	980	940	1059	–
1 M Ruthenium Red	3700	3300	–	–

[a] Data are taken from refs. 11, 14, and 15.

Indeed, this may be the only way presently available for studying the properties of the mitochondrial calcium transport system in the presence of physiological (and buffered) concentrations of extramitochondrial Ca^{2+} and physiological loads of mitochondrial calcium (see below).

These studies had several important implications. First of all they suggest that increases in cytoplasmic $[Ca^{2+}]$, such as those brought about hormones, would result in increases in intramitochondrial $[Ca^{2+}]$ and, hence, enzyme activation leading to enhanced NADH and ATP production. This is in full agreement with the scheme outlined in the Introduction. However, they also suggest that the gradient of Ca^{2+} ions (in:out) across the mitochondrial inner membrane is only about 2-3 under normal physiological conditions (see Table 1). This is in good agreement with the most recent estimates of _in situ_ mitochondrial total calcium content using both X-ray probe microanalysis (16) and rapid cell fractionation under appropriate conditions (see Table 3 later and refs. quoted therein) which show that this parameter is very similar in magnitude to that obtained for the cytoplasm of normal cells, i.e., this means a value of around 1-2 nmol/mg mitochondrial protein. A further implication is that the Ca^{2+}-transport system of the mitochondrial inner membrane exists primarily to relay changes in cytoplasmic $[Ca^{2+}]$ into the matrix for enzyme regulation and not to buffer or set cytoplasmic [Ca^{2+}] by acting as Ca^{2+}-sinks. This latter function has been proposed by many workers (see 3,4). However, a prerequisite for the mitochondria to exhibit buffering behavior is that the egress pathway(s) for Ca^{2+} has to be saturated (2). This is not achieved until the total amount of calcium associated with the mitochondria is of the order of 10-15 nmol/mg protein. Moreover, the set-point value for extra-mitochondrial [Ca^{2+}] in the presence of physiological concentrations of Na^+ and Mg^{2+} appears to be always greater than 1-2 µM, i.e., at a value saturating for the cytoplasmic Ca^{2+}-regulated processes (1,2). It is far more likely that the principal determinants of cytoplasmic Ca^{2+} concentrations will rather be the Ca^{2+}-transporting systems in the plasma membrane and the endoplasmic reticulum (2,17). The large capacity for mitochondria to accumulate Ca^{2+} may therefore be reserved as a protective mechanism which will come into operation when the cytoplasmic [Ca^{2+}] is especially high, as e.g. in damaged cells (2).

EVIDENCE USING INTACT TISSUE PREPARATIONS THAT HORMONES CAN AFFECT THE ACTIVITIES OF THE INTRAMITOCHONDRIAL DEHYDROGENASES THROUGH CHANGES IN MATRIX [Ca^{2+}]

This evidence, has, as yet, only been obtained from studies on the rat heart and liver. In both of these tissues increases in cytoplasmic [Ca^{2+}] are brought about as part of the mechanism of action of various hormones. Thus, for instance, positive inotropic agents such as adrenaline or a raised perfusate [Ca^{2+}] cause increases in cytoplasmic [Ca^{2+}] in the heart, whereas vasopressin, α-adrenergic agonists and glucagon are known to increase liver cytoplasmic [Ca^{2+}] (1,18). All of these treatments also bring about increases in the amount of PDH_a (19,20) in the two tissues (Table 2) together with increases in O_2 uptake.

Table 2. Effects of Various Hormones and Other Treatments on the Amounts of PDH_a in Intact Tissue Preparations of Rat (a) Heart and (b) Liver[a]

Hormone or Other Treatment	PDH_a (as % of Total Activity) In Intact Preparations Of:	
	(a) Rat Heart	(b) Rat Liver
None (Control)	10	13
Adrenaline	41*	22*
Glucagon	33*	21*
Glucagon Plus Adrenaline	-	46*
High Calcium	42*	-
Adrenaline Plus Ruthenium Red	12	-
High Ca Plus Ruthenium Red	13	-

[a]Data are taken from refs. 19-21.
*Indicates significant effect of hormone treatment.

The first direct evidence that increases in intramitochondrial [Ca^{2+}] could be responsible for PDH activation came from studies with the perfused rat heart where it was discovered that perfusion with ruthenium red completely blocked the increases in PDH_a due to adrenaline or raised medium $[Ca^{2+}]$ (Table 2), yet the cytoplasmic Ca^{2+}-dependent stimulations of contraction or phosphorylase were essentially unaffected (21).

However, by far the most convincing evidence for the role of intra-mitochondrial $[Ca^{2+}]$ in these activations of PDH has come from studies with mitochondria rapidly isolated from hormone-treated tissues, where the ability to assay for the Ca^{2+}-sensitive properties of the three matrix dehydrogenases has allowed them to be used as indicators of intramitochondrial $[Ca^{2+}]$. This has been done in studies with both heart and liver (20,22,23), which are now summarized below.

First of all, it was found that these hormone-induced activations of PDH can persist through the preparation (at $0^\circ C$) of mitochondria and then their subsequent incubation (for several minutes) at $30^\circ C$ in Na-free KCl-based media containing respiratory substrates and EGTA. Examples of this are shown in Table 3. Most significantly, however, these persistent activations were rapidly diminished by incubating the mitochondria in the presence of 10 mM Na^+ to stimulate the Ca^{2+}-egress pathway, or else with enough extramitochondrial Ca^{2+} to result in the saturation of the Ca^{2+}-dependent activation of the enzyme (Table 3). Moreover, these effects of Na^+ could be blocked by diltiazem (Table 3). In addition, the results obtained with mitochondria from hormone-treated tissues were essentially similar to those obtained in matched series of experiments where mitochondria from unstimulated tissues were loaded in vitro with Ca^{2+} (20,22) to cause similar increases in PDH_a as the hormones, and then "re-isolated" before being incubated as above. Also, if these experiments were carried out with ^{45}Ca present during the loading phase, it was found that the mitochondria lost very little ^{45}Ca during the preparation of the mitochondria and their incubation in the absence of Na^+, or in the presence of Na^+ together with diltiazem (20,22), whereas addition of Na^+ alone to the incubations caused rapid and near complete losses of ^{45}Ca.

Strong supporting evidence for the role of matrix Ca^{2+} in these hormonal activations of PDH came with the findings that OGDH activities (assayed at non-saturating [oxoglutarate]) within the mitochondria isolated from the variously-treated tissues showed parallel changes to those for PDH (20,22,23) (see Table 3 for examples). In addition, it has now been demonstrated in both of these tissues that these hormones, which increase the cytoplasmic concentration of Ca^{2+} and activate PDH and OGDH, also cause increases in the total amount of Ca^{2+} associated with the subsequently prepared mitochondrial fractions (23,24) (Table 3).

The above experimental approach has also been applied to the study of the role of matrix Ca^{2+} in the increases in PDH_a brought about by insulin acting on both brown and white adipose tissue (see 25). However, in this instance the effects of insulin persist in the mitochondria incubated with Na^+ and there are no effects of insulin on OGDH and NAD-ICDH activities. Therefore it appears that, although the phosphatase appears to be persistently activated in the mitochondria as the result of insulin pretreatment, increases in intramitochondrial $[Ca^{2+}]$ are not involved (25).

CONCLUSIONS AND SOME IMPLICATIONS

The work summarized above illustrates that there is now very substantial evidence, particularly in the two contrasting tissues, heart and liver, that increases in cytoplasmic $[Ca^{2+}]$ brought about by hormones and other external stimuli are relayed into the mitochondrial matrix and result in the activation of the Ca^{2+}-sensitive dehydrogenases. In the case of the heart, the beat-to-beat changes in the concentration of cytoplasmic

Table 3. Effects of Pretreatment of Rat (a) Heart with Adrenaline and (b) Liver with Vasopressin, on the Activities of PDH and OGDH, and the Mitochondrial Ca Content, in Subsequently Prepared Mitochondria Incubated Under Various Conditions[a]

Mitochondrial Incubation Conditions	Effect of Control (C) or Hormone (H) Pretreatment on the Following Parameters in Subsequently Prepared and Incubated (5 min, 30°C, 0.5 mM EGTA) Mitochondria					
	PDH_a (as % Total Activity)		OGDH (as % V_{max} Activity)		Ca Content (nmol/mg protein)	
	C	H	C	H	C	H
(a) Heart						
None	8	20*	23	35*	1.7	4.1*
Plus Na$^+$	8	7*	25	24	–	–
Na$^+$ Plus Diltiazem	8	20*	24	32*	–	–
At Saturating Ca^{2+}	45	47	55	57	–	–
(b) Liver						
None	17	31*	8	13*	1.2	2.1*
Plus Na$^+$	14	16*	8	8*	0.8	1.1
Na$^+$ Plus Diltiazem	18	33*	9	18*	.1.1	2.0*
At Saturating Ca^{2+}	50	51	34	35	–	–

[a]Data are taken from refs. 22-24 or are unpublished observations of J. G. McCormack and F. Assimacopoulos-Jeannet.
*Indicates significant effect of hormone pretreatment.

Ca^{2+} probably greatly exceed the kinetic capacity of the mitochondrial Ca^{2+}-transport system (13) with the result that changes in the intramitochondrial concentration of Ca^{2+} will more likely reflect the "time-averaged" increases in cytoplasmic Ca^{2+}, as indeed presumably the activity ratio of phosphorylase in the cytoplasm itself also does. Interestingly, it has recently been suggested that a somewhat analogous situation may also occur in the liver since it has been discovered that in single liver cells both vasopresin and α-adrenergic agonists may initiate a train of Ca^{2+} pulses (26). Another interesting possiblity is that hormones may alter the activity of components of the Ca^{2+}-transport system and thereby alter the relationship between cytoplasmic and intramitochondrial Ca^{2+}. Indeed, there is already some evidence of such changes being elicited by certain hormones in both heart and liver (24,27,28).

There are many instances where hormones and other external stimuli act on mammalian cells through increasing the cytoplasmic concentration of Ca^{2+} (1). In most, if not all, of these cases demand for ATP is increased under conditions where it is desirable also to maintain ATP levels. It is surely reasonable now to suggest that this increased demand can be achieved at least in part by the activation of these three matrix enzymes by increases in intramitochondrial [Ca^{2+}]. In this way oxidative metabolism may be stimulated while cellular ATP levels are maintained. In the liver, it should be noted that glucagon and the calcium-mobilizing hormones also activate components of the respiratory chain itself by a mechanism which may also follow the increases in matrix [Ca^{2+}] (29).

As a final comment on the work and ideas summarized above, we would like to suggest that the well-known phrase used in respect of Ca^{2+} as a mediator, namely "stimulus-response coupling," should perhaps now be extended to "stimulus-response metabolism coupling" in view of the apparent extension of the 2nd messenger role of Ca^{2+} into the mitochondrial matrix.

ACKNOWLEDGEMENTS

Work in the authors' laboratories has been supported by grants from the Medical Research Council, the British Diabetic Association, and the British Heart Foundation.

REFERENCES

1. H. Rasmussen and P. Q. Barrett, 1984, Physiol. Rev., 64:938.
2. R. M. Denton and J. G. McCormack, 1985, Am. J. Physiol., 249:E543.
3. G. Fiskum and A. L. Lehninger, 1982, in: "Calcium and Cell Function," W. Y. Cheung, ed., Academic Press, New York, Vol. 2, pp. 38-80.
4. K. E. O. Akerman and D. G. Nicholls, 1983, Rev. Phyusiol. Biochem. Pharmacol., 95:149.
5. R. M. Denton, P. J. Randle, and B. R. Martin, 1972, Biochem. J., 128:161.
6. R. M. Denton, D. A. Richards, and J. G. Chin, 1978, Biochem. J., 176:899.
7. J. G. McCormack and R. M. Denton, 1979, Biochem. J., 180:533.
8. J. G. McCormack and R. M. Denton, 1981, Biochem. J., 196:619.
9. R. M. Denton, and J. G. McCormack, 1980, FEBS Lett., 119:1.
10. R. G. Hansford, 1985, Rev. Physiol. Biochem. Pharmacol., 102:1.
11. J. G. McCormack and R. M. Denton, 1980, Biochem. J., 190:95.
12. C. V. Nicchitta and J. R. Williamson, 1984, J. Biol. Chem., 254:12978.
13. M. Crompton and I. Roos, 1985, Biochem. Soc. Trans., 13:667.
14. R. M. Denton, J. G. McCormack, and N. J. Edgell, 1980, Biochem. J., 190:107.

15. J. G. McCormack, 1985, Biochem. J., 231:581.
16. A. P. Somlyo, M. Bond, and A. V. Somlyo, 1985, Nature, 314:622.
17. G. L. Becker, G. Fiskum, and A. L. Lehninger, 1980, J. Biol. Chem., 255:9009.
18. R. Charest, P. F. Blackmore, B. Berthon, and J. H. Exton, 1983, J. Biol. Chem., 258:8769.
19. J. G. McCormack and R. M. Denton, 1981, Biochem. J., 194:639.
20. J. G. McCormack, 1985, Biochem. J., 231:597.
21. J. G. McCormack, and P. J. England, 1983, Biochem. J., 214:581.
22. J. G. McCormack and R. M. Denton, 1984, Biochem. J., 218:235.
23. F. Assimacopoulos-Jeannet, J. G. McCormack, and B. Jeanrenaud, 1986, J. Biol. Chem., 261:8799.
24. M. Crompton, P. Kessar, and I. Al-Nasser, 1983, Biochem. J., 216:333.
25. S. E. Marshall, J. G. McCormack, and R. M. Denton, 1984, Biochem. J., 218:249.
26. N. M. Woods, K. S. R. Cuthbertson, and P. H. Cobbold, 1986, Nature, 319:600.
27. W. M. Taylor, W. Prpic, J. H. Exton, and F. L. Bygrave, 1980, Biochem. J., 188:443.
28. T. P. Goldstone and M. Crompton, 1982, Biochem. J., 204:369.
29. P. T. Quinlan and A. P. Halestrap, 1986, Biochem. J., 236:789.

CONTRIBUTORS

BAILEY, CAROLE A.
Roche Research Center
Nutley, New Jersey 07110

BANERJEE, SRABANI
University of Rochester
School of Medicine and Dentistry
Rochester, New York 14642

BARRY, WILLIAM H.
University of Utah School of
Medicine
Salt Lake City, Utah 84132

BLACKMORE, PETER F.
Vanderbilt University School of
Medicine
Nashville, Tennessee 37232

BOCCKINO, STEPHEN B.
Vanderbilt University School of
Medicine
Nashville, Tennessee 37232

BOND, Meredith
University of Pennsylvania
Philadelphia, Pennsylvania 19104

BORLE, ANDRÉ B.
University of Pittsburgh School
of Medicine
Pittsburgh, Pennsylvania 15261

BRIDGE, JOHN H. B.
University of Utah School of
Medicine
Salt Lake City, Utah 84132

BRIDGES, Michael
University of British Columbia
Vancouver, British Columbia
Canada

BRIERLEY, GERALD P.
The Ohio State University Medical
Center
Columbus, Ohio 43210

BRODERICK, Raymond
University of Pennsylvania
Philadelphia, Pennsylvania 19104

BROEKEMEIER, KIMBERLY M.
University of Minnesota-Hormel
Institute
Austin, Minnesota 55912

BUJA, L. MAXIMILIAN
The University of Texas Health
Science Center at Dallas
Dallas, Texas 75235

BURTON, KAREN P.
The University of Texas Health
Science Center at Dallas
Dallas, Texas 75235

BUXTON, DENIS B.
The University of Texas Health
Science Center
San Antonio, Texas 78284

CHIEN, KENNETH R.
The University of Texas Health
Science Center at Dallas
Dallas Texas 75235

COLL, KATHLEEN E.
University of Pennsylvania
Philadelphia, Pennsylvania 19104

DENTON, RICHARD M.
University of Bristol Medical
School
Bristol BS8 1TD, United Kingdom

EXTON, JOHN H.
Vanderbilt University School of
Medicine
Nashville, Tennessee 37232

FAY, FREDRIC S.
University of Massachusetts
Medical School
Worcester, Massachusetts 01655

FEINBERG, HAROLD
University of Illinois College of
Medicine
Chicago, Illinois 60612

FISHER, RORY A.
The University of Texas Health
Science Center
San Antonio, Texas 78284

FISKUM, GARY
George Washington University
School of Medicine
Washington, D.C. 20037

FITZGERALD, THOMAS
  Vanderbilt University School of
    Medicine
  Nashville, Tennessee 37232
FLESCHNER, C. RICKY
  Kirksville College of Osteopathic
    Medicine
  Kirksville, Missouri 63501

GARLID, KEITH D.
  Medical College of Ohio
  Toledo, Ohio 43699
GUNTER, KARLENE K.
  University of Rochester
  School of Medicine and Dentistry
  Rochester, New York 14642
GUNTER, THOMAS E.
  University of Rochester
  School of Medicine and Dentistry
  Rochester, New York 14642

HAMPONG, Margret
  University of British Columbia
  Vancouver, British Columbia
  Canada
HANAHAN, DONALD J.
  The University of Texas Health
    Science Center
  San Antonio, Texas 78284
HANSEN, CARL A.
  University of Pennsylvania
  Philadelphia, Pennsylvania 19104
HANSFORD, RICHARD G.
  National Institute on Aging
  National Institutes of Health
  Baltimore, Maryland 21224
HARADA, NAOTARO
  Thomas Jefferson University
  Philadelphia, Pennsylvania 19107
HOEK, JAN B.
  Thomas Jefferson University
  Philadelphia, Pennsylvania 19107
HUGHES, HELEN
  Baylor College of Medicine
  Houston, Texas 77030

IGBAVBOA, URULE
  University of Minnesota-Hormel
    Institute
  Austin, Minnesota 55912

JOHANSON, ROY A.
  University of Pennsylvania
  Philadelphia, Pennsylvania 19104
JUNG, DENNIS W.
  The Ohio State University Medical
    Center
  Columbus, Ohio 43210

KARGACIN, GARY
  University of Massachusetts
    Medical School
  Worcester, Massachusetts 01655
KATZ, Sidney
  University of British Columbia
  Vancouver, British Columbia
  Canada
KRAUS-FRIEDMANN, NAOMI
  University of Texas Medical
    School
  Houston, Texas 77225

LAPOINTE, DAVID S.
  The University of Texas Health
    Science Center
  San Antonio, Texas 78284
LAU, William
  University of British Columbia
  Vancouver, British Columbia
  Canada
LOTERSZTAJN, SOPHIE
  Unité INSERM 99
  hôpital Henri Mondor
  94010 Créteil, France
LYNCH, CHRISTOPHER J.
  Vanderbilt University School of
    Medicine
  Nashville, Tennessee 37232

MAHEY, Rajesh
  University of British Columbia
  Vancouver, British Columbia
  Canada
MAITRA, SUBIR R.
  Loyola University Stritch School
    of Medicine
  Maywood, Illinois
MALLAT, ARIANE
  Unité INSERM 99
  hôpital Henri Mondor
  94010 Créteil, France
McCORMACK, JAMES G.
  University of Leeds
  Leeds LS2 9JT, United Kingdom
MITCHELL, JERRY R.
  Baylor College of Medicine
  Houston, Texas 77030
MOEHREN, GISELA
  Thomas Jefferson University
  Philadelphia, Pennsylvania 19107
MOORE, PAMELA
  Rockefeller University
  New York, New York 10021
MURPHY, ANNE N.
  George Washington University
  School of Medicine
  Washington, D.C. 20037

OLSON, MERLE S.
   The University of Texas Health
      Science Center
   San Antonio, Texas 78284

PAVOINE, CATHERINE
   Unité INSERM 99
   hôpital Henri Mondor
   94010 Créteil, France
PECKER, FRANCOISE
   Unité INSERM 99
   hôpital Henri Mondor
   94010 Créteil, France
PFEIFFER, DOUGLAS R.
   University of Minnesota-Hormel
      Institute
   Austin, Minnesota 55912
PORONNIK, PHILIP
   Roche Research Center
   Nutley, New Jersey 07110

REERS, MARTIN
   University of Minnesota-Hormel
      Institute
   Austin, Minnesota 55912
REEVES, JOHN P.
   Roche Research Center
   Nutley, New Jersey 07110
RENGASAMY, APPAVOO
   University of Illinois College of
      Medicine
   Chicago, Illinois 60612
RILEY, WILLIAM W., JR.
   University of Minnesota-Hormel
      Institute
   Austin, Minnesota 55912
ROUFOGALIS, BASIL D.
   University of Sydney
   Sydney, N.S.W. Australia

SAYEED, MOHAMMED M.
   Loyola University Stritch School
      of Medicine
   Maywood, Illinois 60153
SCANLON, MARY
   University of Massachusetts
      Medical School
   Worcester, Massachusetts 01655
SMITH, CHARLES V.
   Baylor College of Medicine
   Houston, Texas 77030
SOMLYO, Andrew P.
   University of Pennsylvania
   Philadelphia, Pennsylvania 19104
SOMLYO, Avril V.
   University of Pennsylvania
   Philadelphia, Pennsylvania 19104
STADDON, JAMES M.
   National Institute on Aging
   National Institutes of Health
   Baltimore, Maryland 21224

STUBBS, CHRIS D.
   Thomas Jefferson University
   Philadelphia, Pennsylvania 19107

THOMAS, ANDREW P.
   Thomas Jefferson University
   Philadelphia, Pennsylvania 19107
TOMSHO, MICHELLE
   Thomas Jefferson University
   Philadelphia, Pennsylvania 19107
TSOKOS-KUHN, JANICE O.
   Baylor College of Medicine
   Houston, Texas 77030
TUCKER, ROBERT W.
   Johns Hopkins University
   School of Medicine
   Baltimore, Maryland 21205

UHING, RONALD J.
   Vanderbilt University School of
      Medicine
   Nashville, Tennessee 37232

VIRJI, ANAR
   University of British Columbia
   Vancouver, British Columbia
   Canada

WILLERSON, JAMES T.
   The University of Texas Health
      Science Center at Dallas
   Dallas, Texas 75235
WILLIAMS, DAVID A.
   University of Massachusetts
      Medical School
   Worcester, Massachusetts 01655
WILLIAMSON, JOHN R.
   University of Pennsylvania
   Philadelphia, Pennsylvania 19104
WILLIAMSON, MICHAEL
   University of Pennsylvania
   Philadelphia, Pennsylvania 19104
WINGROVE, DOUGLAS E.
   University of Rochester
   School of Medicine and Dentistry
   Rochester, New York 14642
WOLKOWICZ, PAUL
   University of Alabama School of
      Medicine at Birmingham
   Birmingham, Alabama 35294
ZIMNIAK, PIOTR
   University of Texas Medical
      School
   Houston, Texas 77225

INDEX